ECONOMIC
SYSTEMS

A COMPARATIVE ANALYSIS

third edition

ECONOMIC

SYSTEMS

A COMPARATIVE ANALYSIS

GEORGE N. HALM

The Fletcher School of Law and Diplomacy
Tufts University

HOLT, RINEHART AND WINSTON, INC.

NEW YORK   CHICAGO   SAN FRANCISCO   ATLANTA   DALLAS

MONTREAL   TORONTO   LONDON

Preface

As in previous editions, emphasis is placed on theoretical analysis rather than on a description of the economies of various countries. Only Parts I, III, and IV, however, are purely theoretical in content. Parts II, V, and VI deal with existing systems though in an analytical rather than a descriptive way. The United States can serve as country of reference for the discussion of the private enterprise system, while the Soviet economy supplies the problems for the treatment of authoritarian socialism. In Part VI, which deals with questions that arise where market pricing, central planning, and government controls meet and intermingle, the experiences of many countries are used: the attempted symbiosis of plan and market in Yugoslavia, the economy of central administration of Hitler Germany, the social market economy of the Federal Republic of Germany, Great Britain's post-World War II experiences with quantitative controls, French indicative planning, planning in India, and Western and Soviet-bloc experiences in international trade.

In the abstract sections, a very generalized picture of the problems faced by all social economies is given in Part I, while a brief explanation and criticism of Marxist doctrine is offered in Part III. Part IV on "Liberal Socialism" deals with mere blueprints because we are still waiting for the emergence of a truly liberal economic order with collective ownership of the material means of production.

While the theoretical discussions of the present volume are imbued with as much realism as possible, it should be understood that the chapters and paragraphs devoted to specific countries serve exclusively as illustrations of theoretical points and are not intended as sufficient description of institutional and historical detail. The number of institutional patterns is infinite—the very reason why a purely descriptive approach would be bewildering, in spite of its more practical appeal. The theoretical approach, illustrated by selected examples from practical experience, is more rewarding. It establishes principles that guide us through the maze of everchanging institution and, explaining what fits the logic of a given system, helps in the formulation of consistent policies.

October 1967   *George N. Halm*

v

From the Preface
to the First Edition

I believe strongly that it is not the task of the economist to pass value judgments, but admit at the same time that it is next to impossible for a book on economic systems to achieve complete objectivity. Such a book will always be exposed to criticism from right and left, it will be censored as "socialist" by conservatives and as "bourgeois" by socialist writers. This cannot be helped; but I hope that a reasonably broadminded reader, though differing in many points from my views, will consider the book a fair introduction to the discussion of capitalism and socialism.

I did not undertake the task of writing a book on economic systems without years of preparation. I have been teaching the course, both in Germany and in the United States, since 1928, interrupted only by three years during which I was forbidden to teach it because I was not considered trustworthy under the Nazi regime. Since my student days in Munich I have been interested in the problems of socialism, stimulated by the contradictory theories of Gustav Cassel and Ludwig von Mises. The revolutionary conditions of the times added zest to the theoretical study of socialism, particularly for students in Munich, where socialist, communist, and national socialist revolts followed each other in the short space of five years (1918 to 1923).

The conclusion which I reached at the time was that a liberal socialist economy would face problems in the allocation of resources which it could not solve. I expressed these ideas in a small book, *Ist der Sozialismus wirtschaftlich möglich?*, published in 1929, which later formed part of the volume *Collectivist Economic Planning*, edited by F. A. Hayek in 1935. The formulations in this early tract were somewhat extreme and I no longer maintain all of them. It must be remembered, however, that these statements preceded the interesting arguments of such writers as Dickinson, Dobb, Lange, and Lerner. The reader of the present volume will see that I am still of the opinion that the arguments which Mises, Hayek, and I had advanced in *Collectivist Economic Planning* are by no means completely refuted.

January 1951   *George N. Halm*

Contents

PART I

The

Social

Economy

CHAPTER 1

Comparative
Economic Analysis

INTRODUCTION

Comparative economics is relatively young. Fifty years ago there existed only one economic system in industrial countries: the private enterprise system, generally referred to as capitalism, particularly by its socialist critics. Books were published that compared capitalism with socialism where capitalism was attacked by socialists or defended against socialist criticism by "bourgeois" economists. Socialist thinking had not advanced to the blueprint stage; it was entirely critical and negative. This statement is particularly true of Marxism, which is not a theory of socialism but a theory of capitalism that predicts the coming of socialism. Apart from a few scattered remarks of little weight, Marx left us completely in the dark regarding the working principles of the socialist economy.

This situation has changed fundamentally for today the private enterprise system is just one among several economic systems. Russia has shown that central planning is technically possible. Therefore any analysis must deal with at least two diametrically opposed systems: the essentially unplanned private enterprise economy and the centrally directed command economy of authoritarian socialism.

Differences exist within these extreme systems that make them more reconcilable than they at first appear. In some centrally planned economies, for instance, a degree of decentralization has taken place, and even in Soviet Russia the trend seems to be toward a growing use of price-and-profit calculations. At the same time, the private enterprise economies are increasingly subject to controls designed to maintain high levels of employment. A comparison of market economies, run by conservative and socialist governments respectively, shows a difference in degree rather than in basic structure.

To some extent we deal here with questions of terminology. If we define as socialist a system in which all material means of production are owned by the state, many so-called socialist countries are not socialist at all because they have market economies based on a predominant private enterprise sector, and a description of even the most capitalist country would have to be rejected as completely unrealistic if it failed to stress the important economic role of the government.

Obviously, the different systems intermingle and overlap. There are no clear-cut dividing lines. This fact makes comparative economic analysis difficult. At first it is tempting to simplify matters by cramming the available material into a few boxes with labels like capitalism, liberal socialism, totalitarian socialism (communism), totalitarian capitalism (fascism). Compartmentalization, however, can be dangerous. It assigns names which can stir up prejudice; it tends to overstress whatever fits readily into boxes and discriminates against more complicated systems that refuse to submit to Procrustean methods.

METHODS OF COMPARISON

But how can we compare economic systems that cannot be separated cleanly from one another? In the beginning we need not know more than the basic working principles of the different types of economic systems. These principles presuppose certain aims and institutional arrangements that can be studied to find out if they are consistent and whether they remain consistent when they are being changed. This approach sheds light on all potential systems, whether they are inherently logical in their construction or composed of incompatible parts and therefore utopian.

Another method of comparing different economic systems is to study countries whose economies are considered typical of each system. The economy of the United States or of West Germany would serve as an example of a democratic private enterprise system; Germany under Hitler would constitute private enterprise under totalitarian control; England under a Labor Government would represent democratic socialism (even though not all the material means of production are owned by the state);

Soviet Russia would exemplify the centrally planned command system of authoritarian socialism; and a country like Sweden might serve to illustrate a mixed or middle-way system. This method would have the advantage of being a realistic approach, but its disadvantages would be considerable. It would set a task of such formidable magnitude that it could hardly be undertaken in one volume, and it would probably fail to achieve the desired result of bringing into focus the decisive differences. These can be understood only if we have criteria by which to select what is important for our purpose. A mere enumeration of policies and institutions would not materially aid our understanding unless a theoretical analysis could tell us what to look for. Supported by the knowledge of what socialism means economically, we may doubt, for instance, that the present British economy is socialist in anything but the more distant goals of the Labor party. Discussions of Russia would bog down in the kaleidoscopic change of institutions and policies during the last fifty years unless we knew the essential problems facing the centrally planned economy. And in all cases it would be very difficult to disentangle the essential features of the economy from transition difficulties or differences in wealth, which may be accidental.

Another approach could be a study of the typical economic problems that arise in the private enterprise system to see whether each problem is found in other economic systems and how it would be handled in these systems. Problems such as the allocation of productive factors to different industries, consumers' demand, capital and interest, money and credit, saving and investment, the distribution of income, competition and monopoly, incentives, management of production, and many other important questions would be examined. This "horizontal" approach can be quite useful, but only after we have become acquainted with the essential framework of the different systems. If we do not know precisely on what assumptions the liberal socialist economy rests, how can we determine whether it has to have a pricing process for the purpose of economic calculation? If we do not know how central planning works, how can we understand the role which money plays in totalitarian socialism or what the function of the State Bank is?

Obviously we must know first what the different systems seek to accomplish and which institutions are considered necessary for this purpose. Ideal types must be selected, models that are reasonably simple and that correspond roughly to existing classifications (such as private enterprise system or centrally planned authoritarian socialism). More complicated systems, or systems that fall between our classifications, can be considered later. After this "vertical" classification has been accomplished, and after a description of the essential features of each system has been given, it is then possible to use the horizontal method of studying the variations of a problem as it appears in the different surroundings of competing economic systems. If a vertical classification has preceded the horizontal cross sections, this method of comparing the place and importance of individual problems within different systems can be used to much better advantage. Likewise a study of the economies of different countries can then be fruitful because we know the aims and the proposed means for reaching these aims and can judge whether means and aims are compatible and whether the economy in question is internally consistent.

We shall not follow slavishly any one of the methods discussed above but shall feel free to make use of them all. It seems obvious, however, that, vertical analysis must precede horizontal and geographical methods of comparison. To apply all three methods successively would involve too much repetition.

VALUE JUDGMENT

Comparative economic analysis should be as free as possible from value judgments. The aims of economic systems lie outside the province of economics. If someone says that he cannot see why consumers should be left free to choose, economists may not be able to convince him to the contrary. Nevertheless, it can be demonstrated that persons left free to choose will better be able to maximize the satisfaction of their wants. On moral, aesthetic, or medical grounds we may object to their choice and strongly favor some kind of interference. But the economist, *as economist*, is no judge in these matters. Still, he may prefer a high to a low employment level, freedom of consumers' choice to dictatorial distribution, and a more equitable income distribution to excessive inequality. High employment helps to maximize the national product available for distribution, free consumers' choice enables the consumer to reach the greatest satisfaction within given means, and a more equal income distribution tends to equalize the importance of the dollars spent by different persons.

Thus it may be possible for the economist to speak with a measure of authority on certain aims as such (although his counsel may be overruled by decisions which are based on entirely different considerations, such as military necessity or the plans of a dictator). Yet even between aims which are desirable from the economic point of view a conflict may arise. Free consumers' choice, for instance, can make it more difficult to reach a sustained high level of employment because an economy which has to adjust production to ever-changing demand conditions tends to be more unstable than an economy in which the product is forced upon the consumer.[1] Or, to use another example, full employment policies may cause

---

[1] In other words, an economy becomes more complicated as the preferences of the consumers are permitted to influence production. According to Jan Drenowski, the

dangerous inflationary pressures. Then the question will arise which aim we should stress—high employment levels, free choice of consumption, or monetary stability—and this political decision cannot be made on scientific grounds alone. The economist will be able to show, however, that price inflation is dangerous or that repressed inflation leads to restrictions in the freedom of the consumers and to misguided allocation of the means of production.

When the economist studies different economic systems he does not try to prove that the ends of one system are better than those of another. He wants to find out whether the means are likely to accomplish the aims, whether different aims or means are mutually incompatible, whether they compete for the same resources or tend to support each other harmoniously.

The economist may show that the desire to achieve one end cuts down the possibility of achieving the competing end. An example is the desire for both protection and tariff revenue: the more protective a tariff is, the less revenue the government receives. Another is the policy to protect bondholders against falling security prices. If we force the central bank to buy all government securities at fixed prices, we force it to create money whenever securities are offered for sale. The result may be price inflation which hurts the creditor. Thus the policy may have achieved stable bond prices at the cost of general price inflation.

Many theorists and practitioners today are convinced that we can have an international payments system that combines fixed rates of exchange with currency convertibility and full employment. This combination is not possible, however, as long as the domestic monetary and fiscal policies of the different participating countries diverge and international liquidity reserves are limited. At fixed rates of exchange, an inflation in country A combined with a deflation in country B must lead to deficits and surpluses in international reserves which will grow until the situation is corrected by a change in domestic policies. But the change in domestic policies may easily conflict with such domestic aims as price stability or high employment. L. Albert Hahn [2] correctly refers to this combination of aims as a "magic triangle" since it would require the powers of a magician to reach them all simultaneously.

An example of an incompatibility of aims would be a social system

---

simplest case would be the economy in which consumers' preferences have no significance and a full rationing system exists; next would follow a system in which a predetermined set of consumer goods is produced and distributed by the market, but without changing future production; the third case would be an economy in which production of consumer goods and finally even of investment goods would be guided by the changing prices of consumer goods. Compare Jan Drenowski, "The Economic Theory of Socialism: A Suggestion for Reconsideration," *Journal of Political Economy*, vol. 69, no. 4 (August 1961).

[2] L. Albert Hahn, "Monetäre Integration—Illusion oder Realität?" *Internationale Währungs—und Finanzpolitik* (Berlin: Duncker & Humblot, 1961), p. 101.

that rests on three basic principles: everybody is free to choose his occupation; wages are completely uniform; and consumers' choices determine the direction of production. Clearly, there can be a combination of two, but not of all three of these principles. Consumers' sovereignty will necessitate constant shifts of labor from industry to industry. With free choice of occupation such a change can be accomplished only through wage differentials: different industries must be able to compete for labor by offering higher wages. A uniform wage scale, therefore, implies allocation of labor by command. Free choice of occupation must then be relinquished. If free choice of occupation is allowed together with the guarantee that the same wage is paid irrespective of the kind of work performed, the variety of consumers' goods produced would be strange indeed, corresponding to what workers want to produce rather than what consumers want to buy.

Perhaps this example seems rather childish, but these inconsistent combinations of aims can be found in socialist literature and not only in that part *known* as utopian.

We see that the economist can perform a useful service within the strict confines of his discipline, without having to indulge in value judgments regarding the ultimate ends of economic life. The economist should be cognizant of this so that he can work objectively no matter how strong his private predilections may be. Ideally speaking, he should devote himself to the calm study of facts and laws in the fields where his scientific methods can be employed. "Of the desirability of keeping one's study and analysis as uninfluenced by personal desires, as objective as possible, there can be no doubt." [3] As Arthur Schopenhauer once said, we have to try to approach our problem with unharnessed will (*mit abgeschirrtem Willen*). This should mean at least that we do not enter a discussion of the relative economic merits of different economic systems with an unshakable conviction that everything belonging to one system is better than anything that belongs to another.

Small indeed is the danger that this attempt toward objectivity will let us remain forever in a wavering state of indecision. As human beings, we prefer one system or another, particularly when we feel that not all systems are equally compatible with our political ideals.

As a rule the reader of a book on economic systems does not have difficulty in ascertaining the social-economic philosophy of the author. In this respect the reader is fortunate because he can then make the necessary

[3] F. St. L. Daly, "The Scope and Method of Economics," *Canadian Journal of Economics*, vol. 11, no. 2 (May 1945), p. 169. See also Barbara Wootton, *Lament for Economics* (New York: Holt, Rinehart and Winston, Inc., 1938, pp. 135–136): "However extensive or limited a view any particular economist may take of his normative functions, all would agree that failure to distinguish between normative and positive propositions is wholly unpardonable. An 'ought' must be plainly labelled as such, and in no circumstances slipped in under cover of an 'is' or a 'might be.'"

critical adjustments. Since perfect objectivity is hardly achievable in comparative economics, the writer should make his basic preferences clear. The author of the present volume believes in the philosophy expressed by J. M. Keynes in the last chapter of his *General Theory*.[4]

IMPORTANCE OF COMPARATIVE
ECONOMIC ANALYSIS

Once acquainted with comparative economic analysis, it is not difficult to list reasons for studying different economic systems.

1. Through comparative economic analysis we gain a better knowledge of our own economic system. By comparing it with other systems we see it as a whole and become aware of its framework, working mechanism, distinctive features. Some economic policies are conducive to the system, spring naturally from its basic assumptions, and are compatible with its aims. Other policies prove to be alien to the system, do more harm than good, and lead, by chain reaction, to further interferences that eventually endanger the functioning of the economy.

2. Comparative economic analysis can warn us not "to take our economic system for granted and to assume that another would begin with all the advantages which exist already."[5] The change from one system to another may destroy the delicate adjustments that have been worked out by the forces of the market. If the market is destroyed and nothing is put in its place, the result will be chaos. Yet this very mistake was frequently made in socialist literature. Instead of trying to show how the market forces could be replaced (for example, by an artificial price-setting process or by a central plan), some authors simply assumed that the destruction of capitalism would somehow abolish most economic problems. The breakdown of the Russian monetary system immediately after the revolution was hailed by some communist writers as the transition to real communism, but it soon became obvious that the new system needed a stable monetary unit as badly as did the old. Russia's experiences have destroyed the naïveté that characterized some of the older socialist literature. We know now that the planning of the production and distribution processes of a whole country is an immensely complicated task. Comparative economic analysis can therefore help those who want to create a new economic system; by showing them how to draw up consistent blueprints, it may cut down considerably the cost of experimentation.

[4] John Maynard Keynes, *The General Theory of Employment, Interest, and Money* (New York: Harcourt, Brace & World, Inc., 1965). See also the discussion of Keynes's philosophy in the last chapter of the present volume.

[5] R. L. Hall, *The Economic System in a Socialist State* (New York: St. Martin's Press, Inc., 1937), p. 105.

3. Comparative economic analysis will lead to a better appreciation of certain theoretical and institutional questions. Some economists consider the institutional setup of the present system in the United States to be the only logical framework for the study of economics; others try to transcend the institutions of the private enterprise system to prove the general applicability of the principles of the market economy; still others emphasize the importance of growth over the equilibrium concepts of the market economy and want to replace the forces of the market through the central planning of development. Only comparative analysis permits us to see these important issues in their proper perspective.

4. Comparative economic analysis acquaints us with systems which are basically different from our own. The East-West conflict makes it imperative that we be able to judge with reasonable accuracy the productive capacity and the rate of growth of the economies of totalitarian countries. To those who want the private enterprise system to continue, the successes of total planning should be more interesting than its shortcomings. If it is true that planned economies can maintain full employment, then the private enterprise system cannot permit the spreading of the disease of mass unemployment, because mass unemployment will not be tolerated any longer; when Russian planning succeeds admirably in the exploration of space, we must discard the myth that bureaucratic regimes are always technologically backward.

5. Comparative economic analysis should even try to find out what the totalitarian socialists of Russia think about our American system, since their theorizing may determine their actions. Because official Russian analysis of capitalism professes to follow strictly Marxian lines, the interpretation of Russian thinking must rest partly on a knowledge of Marx's ideas about the eventual breakdown of capitalism.

6. Comparative economic analysis can be helpful in international economic relations. We must learn that the reactions of others to American foreign trade policies may be the result of an economic philosophy that differs from ours. For instance, our trading partners may not be interested in nondiscriminatory trade, because the monopolistic advantage of their state trading implies discrimination. In our relations with developing countries we must realize that many want to develop their economies in a hurry and that at least some are greatly impressed by the fast growth of Russian heavy industry. What do we have to offer in this competition of basic economic philosophies? If there is a convincing answer to Russia's challenge it will in part have to be furnished by comparative economic analysis.

CHAPTER 2

The Social
Economy

ROBINSON CRUSOE

In all economic systems the basic problem is the allocation of
scarce means among competing ends for the achievement of maximum
results. Even a person living in complete isolation would have to solve this
problem. Robinson Crusoe has to allocate the very limited resources at
his disposal (including his own labor) among the many different tasks
which he plans and performs to satisfy his wants. A detailed study of his
decisions could fill a volume which would acquaint us with such fundamental economic concepts as marginal utility and disutility, saving, capital
goods, consumer goods, and so on. Robinson Crusoe has to decide which
commodities he is going to produce with his limited resources, and he will
obviously try to achieve the combination of goods that will provide the
highest satisfaction of his wants. His considerations will include not only
present but also future wants, and he must realize that he may increase
his future consumption substantially if he first produces instruments that
will improve the productivity of his labor. But while the making of instruments (capital goods) increases his *future* productivity, it leaves him at
present with fewer commodities for immediate consumption because he

has diverted part of his energies from consumer goods to capital goods production. We take it for granted that Robinson Crusoe uses all the resources at his disposal which he cares to use and that he will continue to work until the disutility of working an extra quarter of an hour outweighs the marginal utility of the additional product.

Robinson Crusoe's economic decisions are relatively easy to make because his brain is able to register all the data upon which his decisions depend. His economy is relatively simple because it depends on two sets of data only: those given by his natural surroundings and possessions (which influence his wants and provide the material resources with which to satisfy them), and those given by his personality (his wants, ability, industriousness, foresight, and so forth). His decisions do not require the support of price-and-cost calculations. He is able to allocate his labor and his material resources to the best advantage because he knows what the different satisfactions, present and future, mean to him and because he knows implicitly the discomfort caused by more work or a lengthened period of waiting for future consumption. He balances, without difficulties and often unconsciously, psychic quantities that, if they were to concern different people, could never be compared in the same matter-of-course way.

Robinson Crusoe does not use money, he cannot buy or sell, he cannot go bankrupt or become unemployed. The concepts "capitalism" and "socialism" have no meaning for him. His economy is perfectly isolated and, therefore, no part of a social economy.

THE SOCIAL ECONOMY

Production in a social economy is a process in which millions of people cooperate. These persons have specialized their functions in order to increase the efficiency of production; in the process they become mutually interdependent. Together they create a social product that, owing to the advantages of specialization and cooperation, is many times greater than the aggregate result of isolated individual efforts. But the interdependence of millions of individuals in one gigantic process of cooperation raises many difficult questions. Robinson Crusoe knew all the relevant data and allocated his labor and resources in one comprehensive decision. This comprehensive decision is no longer possible in the social economy. No single person knows all the data: the available resources, the techniques of production, and the wants of the people. In order to organize production and distribute the total product among the members of the social economy, many problems have to be solved, consciously or unconsciously, with or without a general plan.

Production in a modern industrial society is a very intricate process whose ramifications and interrelations elude detailed description. Think of the millions of persons who contribute to the production of consumer goods such as bread, razor blades, and newspapers, to say nothing of automobiles and houses; of the materials and machines used in manufacturing these articles; of the machine tools which helped make the machines; of the steel which went into the tools; of the huge productive apparatus of a steel mill; and so forth ad infinitum. How does this collective effort, whose different branches and stages are interdependent to the point of utter complexity, result in the production of just the right kinds and numbers of commodities? How do the millions of individual activities gear into each other with not too much waste and friction? And how is the total product to be distributed among those who participated in this cooperative effort?

Before trying to answer these questions it is advisable to formulate precisely the problems which must be solved in a social economy. We state these problems on purpose without reference to the economic organization of the social economy, that is, independently of the social-economic system that might be chosen.

1. Somehow it must be decided *what* is going to be produced. In addition we must know *how much* of each product is needed. Since the productive resources can be combined in unending variations, our choice is great, at least in the long run. Total production, however, is limited. Increased production of one commodity means (at least under conditions of full employment) decreased production of another.

2. We must know *how* to produce the commodities on whose production we have decided. As a rule, different techniques can be employed. A bridge can be made of wood, stone, or steel, and similarly most other products can be made by a variety of methods and by the use of different materials. With given technical know-how the economic decision will depend on the relative scarcity of the factors used. If wood is relatively abundant and steel is scarce, it may be advisable to settle for a less durable wooden bridge and to save steel for other production processes in which steel is either more essential or irreplaceable.

3. In a growing economy, part of the productive resources must be set aside for capital goods production. Capital or investment goods help create more consumer goods in the long run. Somehow ·it must be decided how far to restrict *present* consumption in favor of investment goods production and *future* consumption. Although listed separately, this problem is only the most important subdivision of our first problem (of *what* to produce). It is connected to the second problem (of *how* to produce) by the fact that production methods often differ in the amount of investment goods that are being employed in combination with labor.

4. Problems (1), (2) and (3) have to be solved in such a way that all the interdependent production processes are properly balanced. The complexity of this problem is rather staggering. Let one integral part of this cooperative process of social production lag behind, and potentially

all the other parts will suffer. This applies to the supply of raw materials, of intermediary goods, of trained labor, and even of consumer goods, since without adequate supply of consumer goods labor may be less efficient than desired.

5. It should be taken for granted that the social economy makes full use of the available resources and particularly of the labor supply. Experience has shown, however, that some societies have been plagued by open or disguised unemployment. Thus it seems justified to list "full use of available resources" as one of the problems of the social economy. What exactly is meant by this phrase will have to be discussed later.

6. The total product of the social economy, the result of the cooperative effort of millions, has to be distributed. Each member of society must get his share. With this problem we return to our first problem, since in order to know *what* to produce we must know *for whom* we produce.

7. Whatever the social system, human beings must make the necessary economic decisions and must carry them out. Since human beings do not react by means of biological instincts, they must somehow be induced to do the right things at the right time if the production process of the social economy is to function. The degree of self-interest necessary is a most important practical question. The problem of motivation can be expressed as the question *why* the members of the social economy act as they do.

In listing the problems of the social economy, it is better not to refer to any special type of social economy. In trying to suggest solutions to such problems, however, assumptions concerning the nature of the social economic system must be made.

THE BASIC ALTERNATIVES

It may seem natural to assume that the process of cooperation in a social economy should be predetermined in detail in one comprehensive master plan, so that each stage and branch of production will fit the other stages and branches, and the most economical techniques will be employed. In other words, we may be inclined to compare the social economy with a huge factory whose input is the total productive effort of the nation and whose output is the social product.

But the modern industrial economies of the West do not correspond to this picture of a huge, centrally directed factory. Nobody plans the whole economic life of these nations in detail; their citizens are, to a large degree, free to act as they please, and the stages and branches of production gear into one another without conscious management. (Of course, all social economies have a public or state sector which takes care of the satisfaction of collective wants such as education or defense.)

It is important to see how basically different economic systems solve the seven problems of the social economy. However, the philosophies on which the choice of one system over the other is based should be considered first.

To avoid a study of older forms of economic society (which is now becoming important again in the study of poor economies and the reasons for their underdeveloped state), we begin with Adam Smith's often quoted passage on the "invisible hand." In discussing "restraints on particular imports," Smith tries to show that, in almost all cases, it is either a useless or a hurtful regulation "to direct private people in what manner they ought to employ their capitals." He also argues against restraints on imports. In this context he suddenly makes the celebrated remark which highlights his economic philosophy and that of his followers down to the present day.

> . . . every individual necessarily labors to render the annual revenue of the society as great as he can. He generally, indeed, neither intends to promote the public interest, nor knows how much he is promoting it. By preferring the support of domestic to that of foreign industry, he intends only his own security; and by directing that industry in such a manner as its produce may be of the greatest value, he intends only his own gain, and he is in this, as in many other cases, led by an invisible hand to promote an end which was no part of his intention. Nor is it always the worse for the society that it was no part of it. By pursuing his own interest he frequently promotes that of the society more effectually than when he really intends to promote it. I have never known much good done by those who affected to trade for the public good. . . . The statesman, who should attempt to direct private people in what manner they ought to employ their capitals, would not only load himself with a most unnecessary attention, but assume an authority which could safely be trusted, not only to no single person, but to no council or senate whatever, and which would no-where be so dangerous as in the hands of a man who had folly and presumption enough to fancy himself fit to exercise it.[1]

Adam Smith obviously referred only to economic policies such as those practiced by mercantilist statesmen; he could not have visualized a case of total central planning in a modern society.

[1] Adam Smith, An Inquiry into the Nature and Causes of the Wealth of Nations, ed. Edwin Cannan (London: Methuen & Co. Ltd., 1925), vol. 1, p. 421. Adam Smith's reference to the invisible hand must not be interpreted as an expression of "the naive belief that unguided self-interest is necessarily conducive to public benefit. . . . It is . . . a grotesque libel to suggest that men such as Hume, Adam Smith or Bentham regarded government as superfluous. . . . But it may be true that, in their preoccupation with the discovery of the laws of the market, they were apt sometimes to take the market itself for granted. It may be true too that, in their zeal to expose the results of interference with the disposal of property, they may have laid insufficient emphasis upon the framework of law and order which made the institution of property possible." See Lionel Robbins, Economic Planning and International Order (New York: St. Martin's Press, Inc., 1937), pp. 225–226.

In contrast to Smith's statement, the modern economist Joan Robinson,[2] in her popularization of John Maynard Keynes's *General Theory*, makes the following remarks:

> Under a system of private enterprise, it is, in a simple and obvious sense, the decisions of employers—in the main, industrial entrepreneurs—which determine the amount of employment offered to the working population, but the entrepreneurs themselves are subject to general influences which cause them to decide one way or another, and the decisions of each influence the decisions of the rest. There is no central control, no plan of action, and whatever actually occurs in economic life is the result of innumerable independent individual decisions. The course which it is best for each individual to pursue in his own interests is rarely the same as the course best calculated to promote the interests of society as a whole, and if our economic system appears sometimes fantastic or even insane—as when foodstuffs are destroyed while men go hungry—we must remember that it is not surprising that the interaction of free individual decisions should lead so often to irrational, clumsy and bewildering results.

Lest Joan Robinson's statement be taken as an expression of Lord Keynes's own philosophy, it is only fair to add the following passage from the latter's posthumous article "The Balance of Payments of the United States," [3] which expresses the following qualified endorsement of Adam Smith:

> In the long run more fundamental forces may be at work, if all goes well, tending towards equilibrium, the significance of which may ultimately transcend ephemeral statistics. I find myself moved, not for the first time, to remind contemporary economists that the classical teaching embodied some permanent truths of great significance, which we are liable today to overlook because we associate them with other doctrines which we cannot now accept without much qualification. There are in these matters deep undercurrents at work, natural forces, one can call them, or even the invisible hand, which are operating towards equilibrium. If it were not so, we could not have got on even so well as we have for many decades past.

An unbiased reader of *The Wealth of Nations* will find that Adam Smith did not believe in complete laissez faire. He did believe, however, that the forces of the market lead to full-employment equilibrium. Lord Keynes showed that they may not always do so and warns us to watch that part of the productive resources are not left idle, that the equilibrium we achieve is not an underemployment equilibrium.

Joan Robinson's criticism goes much further. She suggests that the course which it is best for the individual to take is *rarely* the course best

---

[2] Joan Robinson, *Introduction to the Theory of Employment* (New York: St. Martin's Press, Inc., 1960), p. 2.

[3] John Maynard Keynes, "The Balance of Payments of the United States," *Economic Journal*, vol. 51 (June 1946), p. 186.

calculated to promote the interests of society as a whole, and she implies that the activities of individuals ought to be coordinated by central planning.

Central planners, of course, will side with Mrs. Robinson. They do not marvel at the wonder of automatic and unconscious cooperation; they emphasize the negative features of the market economy: possible discrepancies between saving and investment, disequilibrium, unemployment, monopoly, and the fact that the distribution of income may be so unequal that the wants of many are not properly satisfied.

This last argument is so basic that it can be used against the market economy even when the latter performs to perfection in every other respect. The planners, furthermore, may argue that static economic equilibrium (even full-employment equilibrium) is less important than economic growth and that growth ought to be planned and not left to private decisions concerning saving and investment.

Once central planning is chosen in preference to the market economy, the whole system is fundamentally changed. For the time being the question is left open whether the planned or the unplanned system is more productive or more amenable to economic growth. It is clear from the outset, however, that central planning must reduce the scope of private decisions. The planned economy abolishes private investment and may affect the free choice of consumption and of occupation.

Depending on our basic philosophies, we may see more merit in one system than in the other. We may also feel that both systems have their good and their weak points and that, accordingly, we should try to combine the best features of both. To what extent such an undertaking could be successful, comparative economic analysis has to find out. Complicated interrelations are to be considered. They will emerge as soon as we ask how the two diametrically opposed systems, the free market economy of the private enterprise system and the master plan of totalitarian socialism, propose to answer the seven questions outlined above.

THE MARKET ECONOMY

The market economy which we have in mind as one of the two basic alternatives rests on the following assumptions: First, the means of production (labor, land, capital) are owned privately and individually by the members of society. Second, production is carried out at the initiative of private enterprise and is not planned in advance by the government. The latter will take care of the satisfaction of communal wants, see to it that the market processes remain orderly, and make sure that aggregate demand is sufficient to avoid involuntary unemployment.

The solution of the basic problems is as follows: The question of *what* commodities (and *how much* of each) are to be produced is decided on the basis of price-and-cost calculations of privately owned, independent business firms. Assuming that the demand for a product is given (once problem 6 concerning the distribution of income has been solved) and assuming, too, that the available techniques of production are known, the private firms decide not only *what* and *how much* but also *how* to produce. Marginal revenue is compared with marginal cost. Costs are known because the services of productive factors are sold by their owners on factor markets for the highest prices these markets will bear. Similarly, product prices and marginal revenues will be determined. Competition leads to prices which equalize supply and demand on both commodity and factor markets. Where marginal revenue exceeds marginal cost, profits appear and encourage further production; where marginal cost exceeds marginal revenue, production will be reduced until equilibrium is achieved at prices which do not lead to further adjustments.

Of course, it is not to be assumed that these decisions and adjustments are always correct, merely that through trial and error the questions of what, how much, and how to produce will be solved by private actions on the basis of the profit motive.

It may seem strange that the private sector of the modern market economy can solve the fourth problem regarding the integration of mutually *interdependent* production processes, in view of the fact that these production processes are undertaken by *independent* private firms. But these firms are connected through the market, and changing prices of both inputs and outputs lead to continuous adjustments and adaptations. The result is indeed astonishing: the complicated process of interrelating thousands of production processes is accomplished without central direction. The result is remarkable even when we admit that the integration is achieved with friction and waste by a trial-and-error process.

Now we have to turn to the problem of distribution, the question *for whom* we produce *what*. In the market economy the distribution problem is solved by the same market mechanism which supplies the data for cost calculations. Since the productive resources are found in private ownership, the distribution of such ownership and the market prices paid for the productive contributions determine, between them, the personal income of the members of the free enterprise economy. Needless to say, personal incomes differ greatly, and the system can be criticized for its inequality of income distribution. It is important to note, however, that the recipients of money incomes are free to buy what they fancy, within the limits of their income, *and that the production process adjusts itself to changes that occur in the wishes of the buyers.* Some of the difficulties and frictions in the market economy are caused by the marked degree of freedom which the consumers enjoy.

This freedom extends to the choice between present and future consumption. Members of the market economy are free to save part of their income. Saving permits the production of capital goods which contribute to the growth of the economy. For the important adjustment of investment to saving, the free market economy relies on changes in interest rates. In his cautious endorsement of Adam Smith, Lord Keynes spoke of "doctrines which we cannot now accept without much qualification." This qualification concerns difficulties which arise in the market economy when intended savings exceed intended investments. It can be shown that reductions of interest rates do *not always* lead to the desired result of equalizing saving and investment. When left to itself the market economy therefore cannot be relied upon to solve our fifth problem (concerning the full use of resources). It needs monetary and fiscal controls which influence the free decisions of its members indirectly, without direct interference through a central plan.

The seventh problem (concerning motivations) is easily answered by the profit motive or, more generally, the desire of the members of the market economy to improve their position, to charge for their contributions to the production process the highest price the market will bear. This tendency has monopolistic dangers, but if competition can be maintained the motive power of self-interest is constantly recharged, because nobody is secure enough to relax his efforts.

THE CENTRALLY PLANNED ECONOMY

Before discussing the operation of a centrally planned economy, some assumptions concerning the system must be made. To distinguish it from a market economy, it might have: a dictator who determines the aims of the plan, government ownership of the material means of production, allocation of labor by command, and management of production by government officials who fulfill predetermined production quotas.

In this system (which does *not* correspond to the Soviet economy), the seven problems would be handled in the following manner:

The aims of the plan (for example, quickest industrialization, modernization of agriculture production, relocation of industry, armament production) would have to be translated into technical details, such as new steel mills or transportation facilities. Since capital goods compete with consumer goods for the limited supply of the factors of production, the plan would have to be all inclusive. *What* is to be produced and *how much* would have to be worked out according to the aims of the plan, the available resources, the technical know-how, and the need for proper balance and integration of the interdependent production processes. The consumers must abide by the dictator's decision regarding the quantity and quality of the consumer goods; labor must carry out its job wherever needed; and the managers must meet their production quotas. If one industry does not fulfill its quota, other industries will not have the necessary materials or machines to complete their assigned tasks. We must assume that the centrally planned economy has to insist that its commands are strictly obeyed.

It is perhaps possible to envisage such a command economy without the use of money. Most likely, however, the planned economy will use money to compare heterogeneous input and output, to check on plan fulfillment when deliveries are paid by money transfers in the State Bank, to balance total wages against the total value of available consumers' goods, and to facilitate the distribution of consumer goods.

The plan determines the amount of capital accumulation. A turnover tax, for instance, may raise the prices of consumers' goods far enough above their costs to cut the consumers' demands down to the size of the available supply.

The intricacies of industrial integration are solved by input-output equations and, in practice, through approximation by trial and error. It is difficult to see how the question of the choice of the most economical techniques of production is to be answered in a system which does not rest on market prices. The prices that may be set by the plan have no guiding function and are not necessarily a true expression of the value of the product or the factor. If the problem of *how* to produce cannot properly be solved in the planned economy, this would constitute a serious weakness. On the other hand, it may be taken for granted that the planned economy makes full (though not necessarily the most economical) use of its resources and that it can push development or growth farther, since it can enforce a reduction in consumption which the consumers would not permit if they had any voice in the matter.

The planned economy envisaged above would do away with most of the freedoms which characterize the market economy of private enterprise. The consumers would perhaps be permitted to choose among the items which the government had decided to produce. But the government would not endanger the consistency of its difficult planning procedure by trying to follow the changing whims of the consumers. The freedom of the individual to invest in plant and equipment would be abolished.

If labor is allocated by command, the question *why* people work is already answered. It may be, however, that command is a rather poor way of inducing labor to the greatest effort, particularly in agriculture.

The planned system may compromise, therefore, and try to induce greater effort through wage differentials. Wage differentials can also be used to guide the labor supply into the right industries. Such a method would introduce free choice of occupation into the centrally planned economy but deprive the planned system of the possibility of fulfilling the ideal (if this should be the ideal) of equal income distribution.

The fact that the dictator sets the aims of the totalitarian economy simplifies the task, inasmuch as one person's decisions replace the varying decisions of millions. But a dictatorship economy is not as simple as Robinson Crusoe's economy. Robinson knew all the data required for his decision. The dictator, on the other hand, is not superman enough to know even the smallest fraction of the data required for a successful coordination of production in a centrally planned economy. Although the ends are set by the dictator, the allocation of the material resources and of labor in a social economy is a most complicated task, which, in the absence of a comprehensive pricing process, will need for its accomplishment an immense bureaucratic apparatus.

MIXED SYSTEMS

Not only are mixed systems possible, but in practice all economic systems are mixed in the sense that market systems contain elements of control and planning, and planned systems make use of markets and monetary accounting procedures. Free market economies and totally planned economies are theoretical extremes. No market economy has ever existed without a public sector which takes care of collective wants. In addition, the governments of market economies see to it that the private sector operates in an orderly fashion, reasonably stable prices and adequate aggregate demand being assured through monetary and fiscal policies. The public sector even has the tendency to grow. There is no fixed boundary line between the public and private sectors.

Starting at the other end of the spectrum, we must emphasize that every centrally planned economy will contain elements akin to market processes. Even though the material means of production are the property of the state, labor may well be privately owned and free choice of occupation may prevail with all the implications of labor markets, wage differentials, and labor movements from industry to industry. Another interference with the fully planned character of the economy is given when consumer goods production is no longer subject to one-sided government decisions as part of the general production plan, but is guided by the wishes of the consumers via price changes in consumer goods markets. In other words, the planning procedures may be relaxed and softened by degrees. The system could move, for instance, from a dictatorial allocation of predetermined "bundles" of consumer goods to a distribution via markets but without responses of production to price changes; later, price changes may be permitted to correct the output of consumer goods within the framework of *given* production facilities; and, finally, the preferences of the consumers may even be considered in the determination of the supply of the investment goods which help turn out the consumer goods.

CHAPTER 3

The Free
Market Economy

A MODEL OF THE PRIVATE
ENTERPRISE ECONOMY

The free market economy is not a system of *laissez faire*. It differs from a laissez-faire economy in the following respects: (1) it is an abstract system rather than a real one; (2) it is an ideally competitive economy; and (3) the factors of production are moved without friction from one industry to another. The free market economy, in other words, represents a *model* of an unplanned economy, which is characterized by the following assumptions:

1. The factors of production (labor, land, capital) are privately owned, and production takes place at the initiative of private enterprise.

2. Income is received in monetary form through the sale of services of the factors of production and from profits of private enterprise.

3. The members of the free market economy have freedom of choice with respect to consumption, occupation, saving, and investment.

4. The free market economy is not planned, controlled, or regulated by the government. The government satisfies collective wants, but it does not compete with private firms, nor does it tell the people where to work

or what to produce. It need not be concerned with monopoly or unemployment, since these shortcomings of the private enterprise economies are excluded by our assumptions.

A study of the free market economy can prove useful, but will not help evaluate today's market economies because the assumptions are too abstract. The private enterprise system will be the subject of a more detailed investigation later. The abstract picture of a free market economy can show, however, how the private enterprise system would perform if the basic assumptions upon which it rests could be found in their pure condition.

This may seem to be the wrong approach. Why should we try to idealize a system whose weaknesses are well known? One answer is that the present-day private enterprise economy is not a pure system. It has been adulterated, and its bad features may be the result of impurities rather than inherent characteristics. A study of the free market economy will reveal what a market system would be if it performed perfectly, on its own terms, without admixtures of alien elements. Another answer is that this approach is permissible because modern socialist theory treats socialism in this abstract and idealistic fashion. Sometimes the *abstract* or *ideal* socialistic economy, which we see in modern blueprints of socialism, is compared with the *real* private enterprise economy of today—a comparison which is inaccurate. If socialism is treated as an economic system in the abstract, the same method should apply to the study of the essential organizing principles of market economies that are based on private property and private enterprise.

FAMILIES, FIRMS, AND DOLLAR BALLOTS

The free market economy is not regulated by a central planning board. The members of such an economy are not told where to work or what to produce, nor does the government control their consumption. They are free to choose their jobs (within the limits of training and ability) and free to spend their income on whichever commodities they prefer to buy. If they decide not to spend their income but to save it, they are free to do so.

Where there is no central plan, the direction of production depends upon private economies, which are the points of crystallization of the market economy. The first type of private economy is *the consuming unit, the family*. It receives a money income through the sale of the services of the factors of production (labor, land, and capital), which are in its private possession. To these sources of income (wages, rents, and interest payments) profits (dividends) are added which the consuming unit may derive from its share of ownership in the producing units.

The second type of private economy is *the producing unit, the firm*. The firms are owned by, and operated for, private individuals, but they have, nevertheless, a life quite their own. Whether small grocery stores, farms, or giant steel corporations, the business units have this in common: they combine the services of the factors of production (which they buy from their owners) in technical processes in order to turn out commodities or services that they sell on the market. These commodities and services are bought either by other firms or by the consuming units. The families receive their money income (which they save or use to buy consumer goods) through the sale of productive services to the business units.

The business units translate the consumers' demand for commodities into a demand for labor, natural resources, and capital goods, that is, into a demand for the services of the factors of production that are privately owned. These factors can be used for the production of a great variety of commodities, and it has to be decided in which fields of industry they shall be employed. This decision depends on what is called the consumer's ballot. As the demand for a commodity increases, its price will rise, other things remaining equal. The producer of the commodity, who wants to expand production because he anticipates higher profits, will be able to offer higher prices for the services of the factors of production. He is able to outbid less fortunate producers. As the consumers shift from coal to oil, the producers of oil burners will hire the men who used to produce coal furnaces. Of course, it does not always happen that the factors needed for the expansion of one industry are the same as those set free by the contraction of the other. In the long run, however, the necessary adjustments will take place in spite of temporary frictions.

The consumer is free to spend his money on whichever commodities or services he decides to buy. Since his total purchases are limited by his personal income, each purchase is made at the expense of foregoing other purchases. The consumer's final choice will depend on (a) his individual circumstances and tastes (age, sex, education, cultural background, size of family); (b) his personal income; (c) the part of his income that he wants to spend on consumer goods (his personal income minus his savings); (d) the prices of the commodities and services which he is actually buying; and (e) the prices of other commodities and services whose purchase he is considering.

In making his choice, our consumer casts his dollar ballots. Though his decisions may seem insignificant for the economy as a whole, the similar decisions of millions of others, to buy or not to buy at given prices, determine whether more or fewer of these commodities and services will be produced. An increasing demand for an article, the willingness on the part of the consumers to spend more money on it, will increase the seller's profit. And since the seller wants to maximize his profit, he will expand his production. A seller, however, whose product has not won the approval of the buyers, faces decreased demand, may have to sell at a loss, and will either have to curtail his production or stop it altogether.

Therefore, by their willingness to pay higher or lower prices for different commodities and services, the consumers actually direct production in such a way that the factors of production are employed in producing the commodities that give the consumers the highest satisfaction.

Here a basic weakness of the free market economy becomes apparent. Since the market counts the dollar of the poor and the rich alike, a free market economy is very far from the ideal (if this should be the ideal) of a uniform restriction of the satisfaction of wants. While individual consuming units within the market economy try, as best they can, to maximize satisfaction within the limits of their incomes, no maximization is attempted (let alone achieved) for the economy as a whole.

In order to achieve maximum satisfaction of wants for the entire economy, the following difficulties would have to be overcome:

First, wants of different persons would have to be made comparable in relation to their respective urgency. This condition cannot be fulfilled. The nearest possible approach to a solution is the use of money. The willingness to spend an equal amount of money on the part of two individuals could be said to indicate wants of equal importance.

Second, it has to be understood that this approximation to an interpersonal comparison of the intensity of wants requires that different persons have the same amount of money to spend. But perfect equality of per capita income is not found and cannot be found in the free market economy.[1]

Third, it might be argued that most individuals do not even know what is best for them and that a staff of experts under a benevolent dictator would be better able to maximize people's satisfactions. It is obvious, however, that this solution could be attempted only in a centrally planned and not in a free market economy.

To say that the consumer directs production in a free market economy may seem to ignore the fact that the consumer does not, as a rule, contract for his goods in advance; he buys what is already on the market. The solution to this problem has been given by Frank H. Knight. The consumer, he argues,

[1] That equality of per capita income cannot be reached is the result of the specific form of income distribution in an economy that is characterized by private ownership of the factors of production. Personal incomes are determined by the market prices of productive services and the distribution of factor ownership. It is particularly important to notice that the free choice of occupation alone would render equality of per capita income impossible. The allocation of labor in a free market economy rests on the determination of wages on labor markets. Supply-and-demand conditions lead to wage differentials which determine the allocation of labor. High wages, for instance, increase the supply of certain kinds of labor in industries that are able to pay these wages and discourage demand for labor by making the substitution of capital for labor profitable.

. . . does not know what he will want, and how much, and how badly; consequently he leaves it to producers to create goods and hold them ready for his decision when the time comes. The clue to the apparent paradox is, of course, the "law of large numbers," the consolidation of risks (or uncertainties). The consumer is, to himself, only one; to the producer he is a mere multitude in which individuality is lost. It turns out that an outsider can foresee the wants of a multitude with more ease and accuracy than an individual can attain with respect to his own. This phenomenon gives us the most fundamental feature of the economic system, *production for a market*.[2]

While the consumer does not contract for his goods in advance, he has at least a veto power in the form of not-buying, which, in the long run, helps to guide production according to his wishes.

SAVING AND INVESTMENT

We have seen that the producing units translate the demand of the consumers into a demand for the services of the factors of production. They buy these services in order to produce consumer goods. The consumer goods are bought by the families, who in turn receive their income through sales of services to business firms. While money is constantly paid out by business units to consuming units (flowing from firms to families), it is spent by the families on commodities and services produced by the firms, thus flowing right back to the firms, only to be paid out again for new services needed for continued production processes.

In this way money remains in the market and flows incessantly from firm to family and from family to firm in a never-ending circle. The services and commodities, on the other hand, flow through the market, disappear in consumption, and are replaced by the output of a continuing productive effort.

If the consuming units save part of their income, this simplified picture of the money flow has to change.

Suppose that these savings are instantly invested, that they are used to finance the production of new capital goods by business firms in the capital goods industries. Capital or investment goods (such as tools, machines, raw materials, and factory buildings) are goods which serve production rather than consumption purposes. With their help the *future* output of consumer goods can increase, but at full employment, capital goods can be produced only at the expense of a reduction of *present* consumption below an otherwise possible maximum.

Savings, when invested, do not interrupt the money flow from family

---

[2] Frank H. Knight, *Risk, Uncertainty, and Profit* (Boston: Houghton Mifflin Company, 1921), p. 241.

to firm. The saved portion of the earned income is being spent on capital goods by the firm which has sold securities (stocks or bonds) in the credit market. In the production of these capital goods, income is earned just as in the production of consumer goods. The model of the circular flow of money remains, therefore, basically correct. The saved part of the earned income of families flows via the credit market to firms in both consumer goods and capital goods industries. Then it is spent by the firms on the products of other firms (in the capital goods industries); these firms in turn make income payments to families and sell securities since they, too, need capital goods.

If families did not save part of their income, the total expenditure on consumer goods would tend to be greater than the supply of consumer goods at cost prices, because the families' income is now earned in producing both consumer and capital goods and therefore is larger than the value of the consumer goods. We see that the process of saving has made it possible to increase the productivity of the economy through the creation of more and better productive equipment. Productive resources, which would have been devoted to consumer goods production had the families insisted on spending their whole income on consumption, are freed through the process of saving, thus permitting the production of additional investment goods which will turn out more and better consumer goods in the future.

Figure 1 illustrates the flow of money through the free market economy.[3]

The assumption that savings will promptly be invested rests, in our model of the free market economy, on the fact that an increased supply of savings will, other things remaining equal, lower the price of loanable funds, that is, the rate of interest. At a lower rate of interest the business units are supposed to borrow more funds than before because their investment activities depend on the relations between the rate of interest and the anticipated rates of profit.

In the real world, these assumptions cannot always be maintained. For certain reasons the demand for loanable funds may fall short of the supply of savings. Money that was saved (and, therefore, by definition, not spent on consumer goods) will then not be spent on capital goods. Total demand will fall, which leads to shrinking production and decreasing factor demand (unemployment). These complications are excluded in our model as well as the difficulties which are caused when total demand is artificially increased by the creation of money that, at full employment, can lead to price inflation.

---

[3] A fuller discussion of the circular flow of money can be found in George N. Halm, *Economics of Money and Banking*, rev. ed. (Homewood, Ill.: Richard D. Irwin, Inc., 1961), chap. 2.

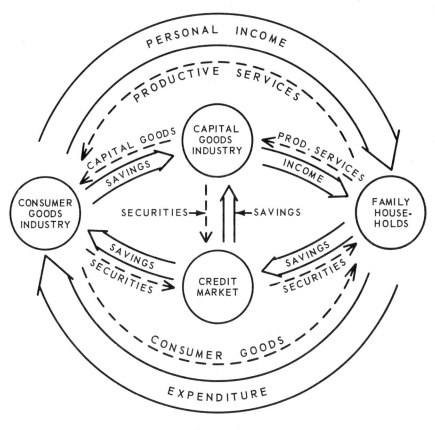

Figure 1

ACQUISITIVENESS AND COMPETITION

In the free market economy, all sellers of goods and services (including labor) try to obtain the highest price possible. At the same time all buyers of goods and services seek to pay the lowest price possible. Although private economies are dependent on exchange, they are also concerned with getting as much as they can out of these exchanges. There are usually several would-be sellers and several would-be buyers available so that the acquisitive tendency, which aims at the payment of low prices and the receipt of high prices, is counteracted by the fear of competition, which produces a readiness to accept, if necessary, lower prices and to pay, if necessary, higher prices. Acquisitiveness and competition together are responsible for the establishment of prices where demand and supply are exactly equal. Each unit of the free market economy trades on two markets. The family is a buyer of consumer goods and a seller of productive services; the firm is a buyer of productive services and a seller of consumer goods. And on each market buyers as well as sellers fight on two fronts: against the person with whom they are bargaining and against their competitors.

Acquisitiveness and competition are the driving forces in the free market economy, which is therefore sometimes referred to as a profit economy or a competitive economy. We assume at present that competition is not hampered by monopolistic tendencies. Competition is assumed to be free, perfect, and pure.

THE TREND TOWARD EQUILIBRIUM

The pricing process of the free market economy is a series of reciprocal price relations that tend to bring the economy to a state of equilibrium. This state is reached when every factor of production is employed where it is paid the highest possible price, where it satisfies the most powerful demand in terms of dollars. In this state of equilibrium prices can no longer change of themselves without a preceding change in the price determinants which lie outside the pricing process.

Demand is determined not only by prices and incomes but also by the primary scale of values of individual human beings (the so-called individual preference function). Supply likewise has ultimate determinants that are largely independent of prices: (1) the supply of the factors of production (size and composition of population, natural resources and capital goods) and (2) the technical know-how that exists at any given time.

The ultimate causes of disequilibrium in the free market economy are therefore changes in human desires (which, however, are measured only according to the purchasing power with which they are endowed), changes in the supply of factors of production, and changes in technical know-how. These changes offer new scope for acquisitive and competitive activities, and there is, again, a tendency for a state to be reached which represents the new optimum position for all private economies (the consuming and the producing units) under the new conditions.

The working of the price mechanism can best be shown if we assume, first, that there was a state of equilibrium; next, that this equilibrium position was disturbed; and finally that we can watch the price adjustments that will lead back again to equilibrium.

Suppose that a new technique permits a lowering of the unit cost of production through a substitution of capital for labor. The equilibrium position which existed is now disturbed because (1) the demand for the factors of production has changed (increased demand for loanable funds and decreased demand for labor), with the consequence of a change in factor prices and further changes in the demand for factors, (2) the incomes of the owners of the factors are affected, (3) the change in incomes alters the demand for consumer goods, (4) the price of the product has to be lowered through cost reduction and competitive pressure, (5) a change in the price of one commodity tends to affect the demand for other commodities, (6) this change in demand for commodities again affects the demand for factors and the incomes of the owners of the factors— and so on ad infinitum.

The demand for loanable funds increases, since the new technique uses more elaborate machinery. The rate of interest tends to rise. The total demand for labor will momentarily fall off because of the substitution of capital for labor. But lower wages and higher rates of interest may, in time, induce other firms, whose production techniques have not changed, to substitute labor for capital. Competition will lower the price of the product, since one unit can be produced more cheaply than before. Whether total expenditure for this product will increase, fall, or stay the same will depend on the elasticity of demand. A high demand elasticity will increase the total amount spent on buying the article in question; production accordingly must increase, leading to a growing demand for the factors needed in its manufacture. If the demand elasticity is low, the reduced price may mean that the total amount spent on purchasing the article decreases. But in this case the consumers will be left with purchasing power in their hands, which may be used for other goods so that the demand for other goods will increase and lead to an increasing demand for different factors of production. Whichever way the demand for the cheapened product changes, there will also be a change in the demand for other products, owing to the absorption or release of purchasing power.

Production and factor allocation will have to adjust themselves to all these changes; as production follows the consumers' demand, as it expands and contracts, the original price changes will reverse themselves because of these adjustments. This is true for the commodity markets as well as for the factor markets. The price changes will not cease as long as there is room for the private economies to improve their positions through further changes. For the consumer, equilibrium is reached when the marginal utility of the products bought corresponds to their price; for the seller of productive services, when he cannot sell at a better price all he wants to sell; and for the businessman, when his return is just enough to keep him in business with no tendency to expand or contract production.

Theoretically, the free market economy performs very well indeed. This fact is not surprising, since we have assumed away all complications and frictions. It is a full employment economy because we endowed it with the power to shift the factors of production with ease from industry to industry and because we assumed instantaneous investment of all forthcoming savings. To praise results which were implied in our very assumptions would be foolish.

And yet it is worth while to consider that we have before us a model of a social economy which solves its problems without conscious leadership, without a central plan of action. Each person in this economic society sees only a tiny section of the whole and acts as though all prices were given. But all persons taken together, driven by their desire to gain and their fear of losing, solve problems even though unaware of their complexity.

SHORTCOMINGS OF THE MARKET ECONOMY

The consistent relations which are maintained between all prices in a free market economy are more than a convenient assumption for the benefit of a simplified model. The whole logic of the market economy depends upon them. Far from belittling this aspect of the market economy, liberal socialist writers are eager to show that the socialist economy could be based on the same consistent pricing which is found in the free market economy. The socialists, however, cannot claim and do not want to claim that the working of the price system would be automatic in socialism. We note that in a free market economy nobody "sets" the prices. In a socialist economy the prices of the material means of production would have to be set and frequently adjusted by the government, because the market forces would not be able to work automatically where the state owns the material means of production. Of this more later.

The driving power of the free market economy is not the command of the government, which would be incompatible with its unplanned character. By the very logic of the system, the private economies can be relied upon to act precisely as required. The model of the free market economy includes the driving power of the profit motive and the checking power of competition. While abstract, the model will work on its own terms without requiring conscious guidance.

That this type of economy offers a degree of freedom of action which the members of a planned economy could not enjoy is quite obvious. It is important, however, to recognize the qualified nature of that freedom. Free choice of consumption, as well as of occupation, is not significant for the person who has a very limited amount to spend on consumption and education. Furthermore, the choice is limited to the alternatives offered on the market. We can sell our services on the market only for the prevailing market price and not for what we would like to get, and we cannot sell at all where no demand exists.

Even in the ideal free market economy income is unequally distributed. Since the government has been left entirely out of the picture, we cannot introduce it now to bring about a more equal income distribution. It is therefore essential that we do not fall into the error of claiming more for the free market economy than is implied in its assumptions.

Individual freedom in this economy has its negative aspects since no one is responsible for the welfare of his neighbor. If anyone is unemployed or bankrupt he will have to bear the consequences. But as long as the model assumes perfect functioning of the free market economy, unemployment will rarely occur and only for short periods.

Finally, it must be stated that the relations between the members of the free market economy are antagonistic rather than harmonious. The private economies meet as buyers and sellers, as employers and employees, and as competitors. The free market economy solves the problems of the social economy without demanding any social integration other than through the "invisible hand," which works via competition rather than through conscious cooperation.[4]

It is legitimate to leave the public sector of the free market economy out of the discussion because this sector is relatively unimportant. Some of the most difficult problems that the governments of real market economies must try to solve do not exist in ideal, theoretical economies. That these ideal assumptions are not realistic is obvious, and the importance of the public sector, accordingly, grows as we approach real conditions.

But even in a free market economy that conforms to the model there would be a state preference function for those goods and services that are beyond the range of individual preference functions. Certain wants, by their very nature, can only be satisfied collectively, because the individual could not be asked to pay a price in connection with the act of satisfying them. Flood control, for instance, would have to be arranged by the government and paid for, indirectly, by taxation.

However, the public sector of the free market economy is relatively so unimportant that it could be ignored without impairing of the usefulness of the model.[5]

---

[4] Some passages of this chapter followed the formulations used in the author's contribution "Further Considerations on the Possibility of Adequate Calculation in a Socialist Community," to Collectivist Economic Planning, ed. F. A. Hayek (London: Routledge & Kegan Paul, Ltd., 1935), pp. 131–200.

[5] The Appendix to Chap. 3 explores the question of whether the pricing process of the free market economy can be applied to other economic systems. The degree of abstraction of this discussion and, accordingly, its difficulty are greater than that of the rest of the book. But if the Appendix can be mastered, it will repay the effort by an increased insight into the problems of factor allocation which must be solved in all social systems. It will, for example, be very useful for a fuller understanding of the basic problems of central planning.

APPENDIX TO CHAPTER 3

The Abstract Pricing Process

CASSEL'S ABSTRACT MODEL

The free market economy discussed in Chapter 3 is a model of the private enterprise economy. Would the pricing process be partially applicable to other economic systems? Could the most basic assumption on which the free market economy rests (private ownership of the material means of production) be changed while still maintaining the consistency of its price relations?

The answer to these questions is of great importance to comparative economic analysis. If the pricing process of the free market economy can be made to work in a different institutional framework, for instance, in an economy with government ownership of the material means of production, the socialist economy can be designed as a market economy rather than a centrally planned economy. In this case it may be possible to maintain a degree of freedom in the socialist state which would be incompatible with totalitarian planning.

But even in the totalitarian planned economy the pricing problem will arise. We have seen in Chapter 2 that even the centrally planned dictatorship economy would have to solve the problem of integrating successfully the productive efforts of millions of persons. Mere reference to a central plan does not solve this problem. No man, no board is wise enough to coordinate the thousands of production processes in which millions cooperate. How can this coordination and integration be achieved? Will not even the centrally planned economy have to use some methods of consistent calculation? Will not the government managers need the guidance of prices?

The answers to these questions are diffcult and will not be attempted at this stage of our analysis.[1] Whether the pricing process can be applied to other social economies should, however, be briefly discussed at this point.

An answer to the question has been attempted by Gustav Cassel, who

[1] See Part 5.

believes that he has succeeded in providing a model of the pricing process which in abstract will fit any kind of social economy, whether capitalist or socialist (132).[2]

Cassel takes "the exchange economy in the widest sense, stipulating only that it shall allow the individual freedom of occupation and freedom of consumption within the limits imposed by his means" (132). The principles of pricing, therefore, "hold good for every exchange economy, and are independent of the particular organization of production within the economy. . . . These principles would remain unchanged in an exchange economy in which the State had assumed control of production and reserved for itself the ownership of the material factors of production" (132).

In this socialist economy "the demand of consumers is indirectly a demand for factors of production, which . . . can be adequately restricted only by placing suitable prices on the factors of production. The principle of scarcity thus has exactly the same application to the socialist economy as to the present economic system . . ." (135).

However, the institutions of Cassel's socialist economy differ considerably from those found in the private enterprise economy. To select only a few points: The producing units are publicly owned, but we are not told how the necessary decisions are made. Competition does not seem to play a major part in the pricing process because Cassel wants to show "how untrue it is that free competition is a theoretically necessary condition for giving effect to the principle of cost . . ." (132–133). Prices are not always determined by the market; rather they are "set," but we are not told how or by whom. We shall see that Cassel replaces the driving forces of the market (acquisitiveness and competition) through the commands of abstract principles.

Such a system is possible in the abstract. Whether its "teleological" relations (relations requested to exist in furtherance of a stated purpose) can be translated into practical working principles, without reproducing at the same time the essential features of the private enterprise economy, is a difficult question. But it must be solved before it would be possible to construct an economy that avoids both private enterprise and an all-inclusive central plan.

CASSEL'S EQUATIONS

Cassel considers first the simple case where "the quantities of goods available to consumers in a particular period are given" (138). This case resembles a dictatorship economy where the decision of what to pro-

[2] Page numbers in parentheses refer to Gustav Cassel, *The Theory of Social Economy* (New York: Harcourt, Brace & World, Inc., 1932).

duce is made independently of the wishes of the consumers, but where the consumers are free to buy commodities if they are willing to pay the price, which equalizes demand and supply. In other words, Cassel assumes at first free choice of consumption but not consumers' sovereignty.

Cassel also assumes that the sum of money which each consumer spends during the relevant period for the satisfaction of his wants is fixed in advance. The demand of each consumer for the various commodities during the period is thus settled as soon as the prices of these articles are known. As we add the demands of the individuals, we get the total demand for each commodity. The demand for a commodity does not depend solely on its own price; it is influenced also by the prices of all other commodities. If the price of shoes goes down, we may be inclined to buy another pair of socks; if the price of cigarettes increases, we may cut down on buying magazines.

Demand is a table that sets forth the amounts of a commodity that are purchased at different prices and indicates, therefore, the relation between two variables: amounts purchased and prices. This relation we call "demand function." We have seen, however, that the demand for a commodity is influenced, in addition, by changes of prices of other goods, since these changes either set free or absorb purchasing power, depending on the elasticities of demand for these goods. No price can change without potentially influencing the demand for all other commodities.

The . . . total demand of consumers in the aggregate for any particular commodity is thus determined by the prices of the n commodities. If we represent the total demand for the n commodities in the given period by $D_1, D_2 \cdots D_n$, we can then express these magnitudes as functions of the n prices:

$$D_1 = F_1 (p_1 \cdots p_n)$$
$$D_2 = F_2 (p_1 \cdots p_n)$$
$$\cdots\cdots\cdots\cdots\cdots \quad (1)$$
$$D_n = F_n (p_1 \cdots p_n)$$

where $p_1 \cdots p_n$ are the prices of the n commodities.

Now, the demand for any particular commodity, given a state of equilibrium, must coincide with the supply, since the fixing of prices, in accordance with the principle of scarcity, must be such as to restrict demand so as to satisfy it with the available supply of commodities. It follows therefore that:

$$D_1 = S_1, \ D_2 = S_2 \cdots D_n = S_n$$

and hence, according to (1):

$$F_1 (p_1 \cdots p_n) = S_1$$
$$F_2 (p_1 \cdots p_n) = S_2$$
$$\cdots\cdots\cdots\cdots\cdots \quad (2)$$
$$F_n (p_1 \cdots p_n) = S_n \ (139\text{-}140)$$

It is obvious that these equations have no precision. They do *not* enable us to calculate the prospective demand for shoes or typewriters, once we know the purchasing power of the consumers, the prices of shoes and typewriters, and the prices of all the other products which the consumers may also want to buy. The demand function depends on such elusive elements as individual tastes, which cannot be expressed with sufficient precision.[3]

Equilibrium exists according to Cassel when the demand for each article is equal to the "given" supply. He simply assumes that demand and supply "must" be equal. *We note that he has not explained how equality between demand and supply has been reached.* The previous discussion of the market economy makes it easy to substitute the competitive solution. In the future, this substitution cannot be used because Cassel's institutional assumptions do not permit its further application.

According to Cassel, the "principle of scarcity" requires that the demand for all commodities be restricted until it can be met with the available supply. Since Cassel assumes as given both the supply of the commodities and the sum of money which each consumer can spend during a given period, he "solves" the pricing problem by setting on each commodity a price which equilibrates demand and supply.

To introduce the process of production, Cassel drops the assumption of a given supply of consumer goods and takes, instead, the factor supply as given. The number of the different kinds of factors is r, and $R_1 R_2 \cdots R_r$ are the available quantities of these factors (or their services) during a given unit period. The prices of the factors of production (or their services) are $q_1 \cdots q_r$.

Cassel's scheme no longer resembles a dictatorship economy, since it is now assumed that production follows the wishes of the consumers as expressed by the demand functions.

With the factors of production we produce commodities of n different kinds. The quantities of different factors needed to produce one unit of commodity 1 is the technical coefficient (a_1). We need a certain quantity of factor 1, another quantity of factor 2, perhaps nothing of factor 3, and so on until we reach factor r. Thus we can say that in order to produce a unit of commodity 1 we need $(a_1)1 + (a_1)2 + \cdots (a_1)r$. To produce a pair of shoes we need, for example, 5 minutes of one kind of labor, 2 minutes of another kind, a given amount of leather, and so forth. Similarly, we can express the technical coefficient in the production of commodity 2 as (a_2). To produce a unit of commodity 2 requires $(a_2)1 + (a_2)2 + \cdots (a_2)r$; and to produce a unit of commodity n: $(a_n)1 + (a_n)2 + \cdots (a_n)r$.

[3] See also T. J. B. Hoff, *Economic Calculation in the Socialist Society* (London: William Hodge & Company, Ltd., 1949), p. 132: "The author of this treatise can confirm that Halm is right and that Professor Cassel never regarded his equations as a basis for an arithmetical or a mathematical computation of prices, but merely as an expression of principles that are generally applicable to an exchange economy."

In equilibrium the commodity prices must be equal to the cost of production of the commodities. Costs of production are known when we multiply the quantities of the different factors (used according to the technical coefficients) by the prices of the factors. These factor prices are $q_1 \cdots q_r$.

According to equations

$$
\begin{aligned}
(a_1)1q_1 + (a_1)2q_2 + \cdots (a_1)rq_r &= p_1 \\
(a_2)1q_1 + (a_2)2q_2 + \cdots (a_2)rq_r &= p_2 \\
&\cdots\cdots\cdots\cdots\cdots\cdots\cdots\cdots\cdots \\
(a_n)1q_1 + (a_n)2q_2 + \cdots (a_n)rq_r &= p_n
\end{aligned}
\tag{3}
$$
(143)

the prices of the n commodities are known.

Once the prices of the finished goods are known, however, then . . . the aggregate demand for each commodity in each unit period is known and can be calculated by means of the following series of equations:

$$
\begin{aligned}
D_1 &= F_1 (p_1 \cdots p_n) \\
D_2 &= F_2 (p_1 \cdots p_n) \\
&\cdots\cdots\cdots\cdots\cdots \\
D_n &= F_n (p_1 \cdots p_n)
\end{aligned}
\tag{4}
$$

In accordance with the principle of scarcity, when prices are in equilibrium every demand must be satisfied by the supply, and we thus get

$$
D_1 = S_1, \; D_2 = S_2 \cdots D_n = S_n
\tag{5}
$$

where S_1, S_2, S_n are the quantities of each of the different commodities produced within a unit period.

Thus we know the quantities of the particular commodities which are to be produced in each unit period. From this we can calculate the demands which are made upon the factors of production of a particular unit period, let us say the present, as follows. In order constantly to produce in each unit period a unit of commodity 1, we require quantities $(a_1)1 \cdots (a_1)r$ of these factors of production. For the quantity S_1 we therefore require the quantities $(a_1)1S_1 \cdots (a_1)rS_1$. The same thing holds in the case of the remaining products. In all, therefore, for the continuous production of quantities $S_1 \cdots S_n$, we require

the quantity $(a_1)1S_1 + (a_2)1S_2 + \cdots (a_n)1S_n$ of factor of
                     production 1

the quantity $(a_1)2S_1 + (a_2)2S_2 + \cdots (a_n)2S_n$ of factor of
                     production 2   (6)

$\cdots\cdots\cdots\cdots\cdots\cdots\cdots\cdots\cdots\cdots\cdots\cdots\cdots\cdots\cdots$

the quantity $(a_1)rS_1 + (a_2)rS_2 + \cdots (a_n)rS_n$ of factor of
                     production r.

These quantities thus represent the indirect demand of consumers for the factors of production needed in each unit period in the continuous stationary society. In accordance with the principle of scarcity, this demand for each factor of production must be equal to the quantity of that factor available within the particular unit period, since it is the task of pricing to limit demand as far as it necessary for this purpose. Therefore

$$R_1 = (a_1)\,1S_1 + (a_2)\,1S_2 + \cdots (a_n)\,1S_n$$
$$R_2 = (a_1)\,2S_1 + (a_2)\,2S_2 + \cdots (a_n)\,2S_n$$
$$\cdots\cdots\cdots\cdots\cdots\cdots\cdots\cdots\cdots \quad (7)$$
$$R_r = (a_1)\,rS_1 + (a_2)\,rS_2 + \cdots (a_n)\,rS_n$$

The S, in conformity with the series of equations (5) and (4), are here functions of the p, and therefore, from equations (3), functions of the q. The series of equations (7) thus contains as unknowns the r prices of the factors of production. It also contains r equations, and the series is thus in general sufficient for determining the unknowns. Once the prices of the factors of production are known, the prices of the products can be calculated in accordance with the series of equations (3). Similarly, the demand for each of the finished commodities in each unit period is obtained from the series of equations (4). Consequently, we can calculate the demands which are made on production. Equations (5) show how much of each particular commodity must be produced in each unit period which determines the distribution of the factors of production among the various branches of production. The requirements which the continuous demand, regulated by these prices, makes of the different factors of production available in a particular unit period are to be calculated according to formulae (6). The coincidence of these requirements with the available quantity of factors of production is guaranteed by equations (7). The pricing problem is thus completely solved for the case considered here (143–145).

Finally Cassel drops the assumption that the quantity of money every consumer spends is fixed in advance. Incomes are now determined by the pricing process itself. "The problem of distribution is, therefore, not an independent problem . . . , but is to be regarded essentially as a special aspect of the general problem of prices" (151).

CRITICAL REMARKS

There are three exogenous factors which may disturb the equilibrium position of a social economy: changes in tastes, in factor supply, and in technical know-how. Cassel's scheme can be used to illustrate how any one of these disturbances will affect the whole system. Take a change in tastes which will affect the demand function. With a change in demand, supply must change. A change in production affects the demand for the factors of production, factor prices, and incomes. A change in factor prices and incomes influences the prices of finished goods, and these price changes, in turn, affect demand and supply, and so on ad infinitum until the surface of the pool into which we throw the stone regains its previous unruffled surface.

A change in production techniques will change the technical coefficients, the demand for factors, the prices of the finished products, the spending power of the consumers, demand, supply, again the demand for factors, and so on.

An interesting example of the re-establishment of a disturbed equilibrium is the essence of Bertil Ohlin's book *Interregional and International Trade*.[4] Two isolated countries have found their individual equilibrium positions. This equilibrium is destroyed through the beginning of international trade. Factor prices are dissimilar in the two regions, owing to different endowment of the countries with the various factors of production. Product prices must be dissimilar, too, and these price differences invite international trade. When the price systems of the two countries are linked together by a rate of exchange between their currency units, the differences in product prices must lead to exports and imports and to adjustments of prices, costs, and production, until a new equilibrium is achieved at a rate of exchange which balances exports and imports.

Cassel succeeds in giving a lucid picture of the interdependence of all prices. We have to remember, however, that Cassel does not want to depict the basic structure of the private enterprise system but rather the fundamental relationships in any exchange economy. This he can do only on so high a level of abstraction that the indicated relationships are of a purely teleological nature. However, for a working model of the social economy it is not enough to show what *must* be done. The model of our free market economy made it clear *why* under the pressure of acquisitive and competitive propensities the members of the economy acted in such a way that the system tended toward equilibrium. In Cassel's scheme the equilibrium position is stated as an aim, but we are not told which forces can be relied upon to accomplish the task that real exchanges on real, competitive markets accomplish in the free market economy.

Cassel does not introduce the businessman who controls the business unit, nor is his place taken by a public manager. The whole scheme consists of abstract requests addressed to abstract units of production and consumption. The scheme shows what the inner structure of an abstract system of equilibrium would have to be. However, it gives no inkling how in the real world this state of equilibrium is to be achieved. The reader may not notice this because Cassel starts, realistically enough, with consumer income and consumer buying on the market. But since he suggests that the government will take over production, it is difficult to see how the process of pricing is to be carried out in markets (if they can be called

[4] Bertil Ohlin, *Interregional and International Trade* (Cambridge, Mass.: Harvard University Press, 1933), chaps. 1, 2, and Ap. I.

markets at all) where sellers as well as buyers are government agencies.

Before continuing this criticism, it must be pointed out that Cassel's scheme does not answer the important question of *how* the most economical choice among different techniques of production is decided. Cassel assumes that there is only one technique to be considered in the production of a given commodity. This simplification is legitimate in the beginning (just as, for example, his initial assumption that the available quantities of commodities are given) but must be removed immediately if the scheme is to illustrate the complexity of the tasks faced by any social economy. Since, as a rule, many substitutions of capital for labor (or vice versa) are possible, the choice of production techniques becomes a major problem when the most economical allocation of the factors of production is to be found. The proper choice must rest on the relative scarcity of the factors as expressed by uniform prices.

Cassel is not consistent in his tendency to generalize. He does not do full justice to the completely abstract character of his model. His teleological system does not have to rest on free consumers' and occupational choices. This assumption enables Cassel to begin with a real consumer goods market. But he soon gives up the pretense of discussing real markets and replaces markets by certain principles which "must" be fulfilled. Now, if we can dispense with the market for the government-owned material means of production, we can as well dispense with the rest of the markets and replace their function by requests that the scarcity and cost principles have to be fulfilled throughout the economy. This means that Cassel's scheme can cover not only the "exchange" economies but equally any social economy based on the command principle. The important difference emerges not on this abstract level but only when we try to make the model work in real life under the various institutions of different social-economic systems.

The totalitarian socialist economy substitutes the state's preference function for the consumers' ballots. However, it should face the same basic economic problems that any social economy has to meet: the factors of production ought to be allocated to different industries in such a way that the state's aims are achieved in the most economical manner. Cassel's scheme can be used to show what the totalitarian economy ought to do, though, again, it does not show how it could do it.

That Cassel's assumptions are not abstract enough can be seen when he discusses problems of income distribution. The way in which he derives the determination of personal incomes from the prices of the factors is too narrow and does not take account of the fact that the government owns the material means of production. In such an abstract scheme we can divorce "functional" distribution completely from "personal" distribution.

Applied to the present Russian economy, Cassel's abstract pricing process suggests the following important points. As far as consumer goods are concerned, the Russian economy still corresponds in the main to Cassel's "simple" case in which the supply of consumer goods is assumed to be given. Free choice of consumption exists and the prices of consumer goods are set just high enough to equate demand and supply. But consumers' sovereignty does not exist since production does not follow changes in consumer demand and in consumer goods prices. The consumers' preference functions have been replaced by the preference function of the state. Consumer goods prices are not the result of demand and supply. Where costs of production are lower than prices, the difference is made up by a turnover tax, which (together with other taxes and planned and unplanned profits) finances the capital goods production of the Soviet economy.

While the consumer cannot guide production, the state can change the production pattern whenever the state's preference function is modified. According to Cassel, the state preference function would presumably guide production so that the factors of production would be allocated in the most economical manner on the basis of uniform factor prices. In present-day Russia this is not the case. Outside of labor, real factor markets do not exist and the needed equalization of factor demand and supply is not achieved through equilibrium prices but through physical allocations. The planners try to make sure that each production process can count on the physical input that is required to reach a given output quota under prescribed production norms. In turn, the output of each enterprise and industry must be high enough to allow for other industries (and consumer goods outlets) the promised allocations.

This arrangement seems to correspond to Cassel's request that the factors of production be allocated economically according to technical coefficients and output quotas in such a way that full employment of all factors is achieved. This impression would be wrong, however.

If we assume, realistically, that most commodities can be produced in different ways (labor intensive, capital intensive) the Casselian scheme is incomplete. Given the production targets of the plan (which themselves should be chosen under consideration of opportunity costs) each branch of production should use that input mix which would be the most economical on the basis of uniform factor prices. Lacking the needed price-and-cost data, or basing calculations on incorrectly chosen or outdated prices, an economic answer to the question of *how* to produce is not possible. However, input allocations and production norms may see to it that production techniques are applied according to command. In high priority industries they may approach the best solution from the engineering standpoint; at the lower end of the priority scale they may be entirely outmoded.

Where price-and-cost data are lacking, the equalization of demand and supply and the integration of production are the result of material and financial balances. The planners have to make sure that each production process can count on the allocation of the means of production which are required because of the production norms which must be applied and the output quotas which must be reached. In turn, the output of each individual industry must be high enough to supply all other industries (or the consumers) with the needed allocations. Material balances alone are not sufficient, because different physical things are incomparable. We gain, both in Russia and in Cassel's scheme, financial balances when we multiply the factor units with factor prices. In this way costs find a common denominator and can be compared with product prices.

In Cassel's scheme the consumer is the final judge whose demand functions are decisive. In Russia these demand functions are replaced by the decisions of the planners. But if the planners want to act rationally, they have to see to it that the internal relations of the planned economy resemble the consistent logic of the Casselian scheme: the factors must be fully employed; they must be uniformly priced and employed where the value of the product corresponds to the costs; and all individual production processes must be able to count on a sufficient allocation of factors if they are to reach their respective quotas. That they reach their quotas is imperative since they, in turn, are counted upon to supply other parts of the economy with the necessary intermediate or final products.

We see that the elimination of consumers' sovereignty does not alter the fact that the social economy must establish consistent interrelations between all its production processes.

PART 2

The

Private

Enterprise

Economy

CHAPTER 4

The Private
Enterprise Economy

TERMINOLOGY

The market economies that are based on private property were formerly referred to as *capitalist*, but this usage has become less popular today, probably because the term "capitalism" has the weakness of calling forth Marxist impressions of exploitation, is in no way descriptive of the modern market economy, and fits fewer and fewer countries where the public sector constantly grows and the government increasingly regulates the private sector of the economy.

Today, all social economies try to use as much capital as possible, and socialist criticism is not directed at the use of investment goods but rather at the private ownership of these goods. Reference to a private enterprise economy, furthermore, points to the most essential feature of a genuine market economy, namely, the fact that its organization rests on the reactions of private economic units to changing market prices. These units own and operate the factors of production and are not subject to the command of a central plan. Central planning excludes private property and private enterprise and does not permit the emergence of genuine markets.

For these reasons, the term "private enterprise economy" is preferable to the term "capitalism." [1] Where an alternative expression is desired, the terms "market economy" or "genuine market economy" can be used. True, the socialist economies, too, may resort to markets and market prices in their distribution and allocation processes. But state ownership of the material means of production will lead to a mere imitation of real markets and to price-setting arrangements clearly distinct from the genuine markets and pricing processes in economies based on private property and private enterprise.

The present chapter attempts to describe the essential features of the private enterprise economy as it really is and not as it appears in the model of Chapter 3. Even this picture cannot be fully realistic, however. It draws, as it were, only a map of reality.[2] It must be remembered that the private enterprise economies of the West differ in many respects: in historical development, factor endowment, and, most important in the context of a comparison of economic systems, the economic activities of their respective governments. Some governments have gone much farther than others in the regulation of the private sector of the economy or the expansion of the public sector. These deviations from the model of the free market economy can become so important that the economy in question may gradually lose the most distinctive feature of a private enterprise system —the absence of a central plan. Later, a private enterprise system will be discussed, which was, in effect, a totalitarian command economy. At the other extreme, what has been referred to as laissez-faire capitalism will be omitted. None of the existing private enterprise economies corresponds to this somewhat vague concept; indeed, it is doubtful that *laissez faire* ever was a good description of an existing economic state, even in the past.[3]

ABSENCE OF A CENTRAL PLAN

The economies of the developed countries of the West rest, in the main, on the independent (but interdependent) actions of millions of private economies. These actions are not coordinated by a central plan.

[1] We also could use the terms "free enterprise economy" or "individual enterprise economy." Both expressions would be preferable to "capitalism." But the term "free enterprise economy" tends, perhaps, to overstate the uncontrolled character of the private sector of the market economies of the West since "free" is less neutral than "private." The adjective *individual*, on the other hand, may create the picture of an economic system that antedates the era of the big private corporation.

[2] Kenneth E. Boulding, *Economic Analysis*, vol. 1, *Microeconomics*, 4th ed. (New York: Harper & Row, Publishers, 1966), p. 15.

[3] See T. S. Ashton, "The Treatment of Capitalism by Historians," *Capitalism and the Historians*, ed. F. A. Hayek (Chicago: The University of Chicago Press, 1954), pp. 33–63.

Market prices, on which the decisions and calculations of consuming and producing units are based, are, as a rule, not set by the government; under competitive conditions they are the result of market forces. However, prices may be set by private firms and labor organizations in instances of monopolistic market control. Since this is a very important deviation from the principles of our competitive model, close attention should be paid to these phenomena.

Absence of a central plan does not constitute a case of *laissez faire*. The government has important tasks to fulfill. These tasks can be divided into two major functions: (1) The government has to see to it that communal wants are properly satisfied. These are the wants for the satisfaction of which a market price either could not be charged to the individual (as for national defense or flood control) or ought not be charged (as for ordinary education). (2) The government has to see to it that the actions of the private economies are properly regulated. The government ought to establish healthy monetary and credit conditions, maintain an aggregate demand which is neither too large nor too small, and see to it that monopolistic powers are kept in check. Later these regulatory activities of the government will be considered. Here it is only important to emphasize that they do not constitute a central plan and need not interfere with the price mechanism or the economic freedom of the private economies. On the contrary, the market economy can function satisfactorily only when sound monetary conditions are maintained, recessions are prevented from developing into depressions, and a sufficient degree of competition is upheld.

Needless to say, the governments in private enterprise economies do not always limit themselves to these indirect controls that support the working of the price mechanism; often they interfere clumsily and haphazardly with market pricing, without a sufficient understanding of the working principles of the economy. From these misdirected government activities we need not draw the conclusion that the government sector of the market economy ought to be as small as possible. It is essential, however, that the price system be supported by *indirect* controls and not replaced by *direct* ones.

CONSUMERS' SOVEREIGNTY

It should be clearly understood that free choice of consumption in the private enterprise economy has the full meaning of consumers' sovereignty. Even in a centrally planned totalitarian economy the citizens may be given a money income and permitted to buy freely (without ration cards) whatever they may be able to procure at set prices. This freedom of consumers' choice, however, does not constitute consumers' sovereignty, unless the effects of these purchases on consumer goods prices are used as a guide for future production.

Whether the principle of consumers' sovereignty should be adhered to is a basic question whose implications transcend the field of economics. Indeed, one may well ask whether the consumer is a wise or stupid sovereign.[4] Nevertheless, John Maynard Keynes was probably right when he said that the greatest loss of the homogeneous or totalitarian state was the loss of personal choice.[5] As economists we cannot answer these questions with authority. But should we decide for consumers' sovereignty, we argue strongly for the private enterprise economy, because our freedom of personal choice is more securely embedded in a private enterprise system than in an economy where the government owns the material means of production. The very existence of centralized power endangers consumers' sovereignty, because those who have the duty and the power to plan are invariably tempted to substitute their (supposedly superior) decisions for the wishes of the consumers. Barbara Wootton [6] reminds us that

> the temptation to exact unnecessary cultural uniformity is always likely to be strong among those men and women who are personally responsible for making the decisions which constitute economic planning. It will be strong because it is, generally speaking, easier to plan for uniformity than for diversity. It will be strong because people who arrive at positions of power are, inevitably, people who enjoy the exercise of power. This is, of course, as true of the powerful whose intentions are good as of those whose designs are evil.

Socialists claim that consumers' sovereignty has little meaning in a system with unequal income distribution. Thus, if dollar ballots guide production, the socialist will claim that because of the much larger number of votes the rich can cast, the private enterprise system cannot be con-

---

[4] See Alfred R. Oxenfeldt & Vsevolod Holubnychy, *Economic Systems In Action*, 3d ed. (New York: Holt, Rinehart and Winston, Inc., 1965), p. 27. See also John Stuart Mill, *Principles of Political Economy* (New York: The Colonial Press, 1899), vol. 2, p. 454: "Now, the proposition that the consumer is a competent judge of the commodity, can be admitted only with numerous abatments and exceptions . . . The uncultivated cannot be competent judges of cultivation. Those who most need to be made wiser and better, usually desire it least, and if they desire it, would be incapable of finding the way to it by their own lights. It will continually happen, on the voluntary system, that, the end not being desired, the means will not be provided at all, or that, the persons requiring improvements having an imperfect or altogether erroneous conception of what they want, the supply called forth by the demand of the market will be anything but what is really required."

[5] John Maynard Keynes, *The General Theory of Employment, Interest, and Money* (New York: Harcourt, Brace & World, Inc., 1965), p. 380.

[6] Barbara Wootton, *Freedom under Planning* (Chapel Hill, N.C.: The University of North Carolina Press, 1945), p. 31.

sidered a true consumers' democracy. "Wants which cannot clothe themselves in money are left undetected and unsatisfied and the luxurious fancies of the rich exert a stronger pull on the productive resources of the community than the stark needs of the poor." [7]

FREE CHOICE OF OCCUPATION

In the private enterprise economy the individual is free to choose his job, but is limited by ability, training, and the existing market conditions. Free choice of occupation implies that, in order to attract a sufficient supply of a special kind of labor to an industry, where this labor is more urgently needed than elsewhere, wages must be high enough to provide the needed pull. Free choice of occupation, therefore, is incompatible with equal income distribution. When attempts are made to make the income distribution within a market economy somewhat more equal, care must be taken lest the allocation process be disturbed.

It must be emphasized that free choice of occupation does not imply a "right to work." Free occupational choice may mean little in an economy suffering from prolonged mass unemployment. Then jobs might not be available for those who are qualified and are willing to work at prevailing market wages.[8] It has sometimes been argued that, at sufficiently low wages, employment could always be found for all who are willing to work. That such an oversimplified application of demand-and-supply analysis is not justified will be shown later. Situations can arise when wage cuts will not increase employment but will actually make matters worse.

Unemployment means that the wage earner is potentially insecure. If millions are exposed to protracted unemployment, they may be tempted to choose a centrally planned in preference to private enterprise system, even though the security of the totalitarian system may be that of the barracks. Adolf Hitler's rise to power during the mass unemployment of the early 1930s should always be remembered.

Karl Marx suggested that the laborer in the capitalist system is "free in the double sense, that as a free man he can dispose of his labor-power as his own commodity and that, on the other hand, he has no other commodity for sale, is short of everything necessary for the realization of his labor-power." [9] Marx wanted to show that, lacking the modern instruments

[7] D. H. Robertson, *The Control of Industry* (London: Cambridge University Press, 1923), p. 87.

[8] We must add that unemployment can be of the "voluntary" type, where those offering their services are not willing "to accept a reward corresponding to the value of the product" attributable to the marginal product of a unit of labor. See Keynes, p. 6.

[9] Karl Marx, *Capital: A Critique of Political Economy* (Chicago: Charles H. Kerr & Company, 1906), vol. 1, pp. 187–188.

of production, the laborer, though a free agent, has to sell his services to the owner of these instruments, the capitalist, at the lowest possible wage, the wage that just permits the laborer's subsistence and reproduction. Marx's argument was one-sided. Capital, in turn, depends on labor. But it is true that labor must first establish its proper bargaining power through association—a point which was clearly seen by Adam Smith.

Marx was the first to emphasize another point which is of importance for a realistic appraisal of the private enterprise economy. He pointed out that, once the worker had sold his labor power, he was no longer free during the labor day but under the command of his capitalist employer. However, a changeover from a market economy to a centrally planned economy would not alter the dependent status of most workers and it may still be preferable to work for a private firm (whose domination one may escape), than for the all-powerful state.

Socialist writers followed Marx in pointing out that freedom in capitalism suffers from the fact that "the bulk of workers find themselves divorced from the ownership of the instruments of production in such a way as to pass into the position of wage earners, whose subsistence, security and personal freedom seem dependent on the will of a relatively small proportion of the nation." [10] William H. Beveridge,[11] for the same reason, excludes from his list of essential liberties in a free society the "liberty of a private citizen to own means of production and to employ other citizens in operating them at a wage." This liberty, he says, "is not and never has been enjoyed by more than a very small proportion of the British people," and he is willing to abolish private property if this should be necessary for the achievement of full employment. Beveridge is conscious of the fact that, together with private property, he would abolish private enterprise. However, he does not tell his readers how freedom in his society could then be maintained under state ownership of the material means of production.

PRIVATE ENTERPRISE

Free choice of consumption and occupation imply private ownership of consumer goods and labor. The freedom of private enterprise necessitates private ownership of the material means of production. Without these property rights it would be next to impossible to have an unplanned economy, just as a central plan cannot be in operation where private property *in its full meaning* exists. If private property is to mean more than the right to income from ownership of land and capital, if it is

[10] Sidney Webb and and Beatrice Webb, *The Decay of Capitalist Civilization* (New York: Harcourt, Brace & World, Inc., 1923), p. 2.

[11] William H. Beveridge, *Full Employment in a Free Society* (New York: W. W. Norton & Company, Inc., 1945), p. 23.

to mean the right to control, to dispose, to invest—then private property and the unplanned economy are inseparable.

The unplanned character of the private enterprise economy, furthermore, implies freedom of individual initiative. Where the government does not co-ordinate the productive efforts of the citizens, such co-ordination must be the result of the activities of private enterprise.

Where the business unit is small (in the farm, the store, the small manufacturing plant, even in the small corporation) the owner controls the productive process, develops entrepreneurial initiative, makes profits and incurs losses, as the case may be. This is no longer true, however, for the big corporation where management may easily be divorced from ownership, where shareholders are entitled to income when profit is made, but where management and entrepreneurial initiative are delegated to hired functionaries. The "owners" are, in this case, not very different from those who merely lend their savings at fixed rates of interest. It has been said that the development of the modern corporation has resulted in "the dissolution of the old atom of ownership into its component parts, control and beneficial ownership" and that "this explosion of the atom of property destroys the basis of the old assumption that the quest for profits will spur the owner of industrial property to its effective use." [12]

These conclusions weaken the argument that profits are always made and allocated so as to produce a maximum of individual initiative. We cannot be sure that individual initiative will be directed toward increased efficiency and not toward devices by which management may enrich itself at the expense of the owners.[13]

Berle and Means [14] believe that

> . . . for the tens and even hundreds of thousands of workers and of owners in a single enterprise, individual initiative no longer exists. Their activity is group activity on a scale so large that the individual, except he be in a position of control, has dropped into relative insignificance. . . . Group activity, the coordinating of the different steps in production, the extreme

[12] Adolf A. Berle, Jr., and Gardiner C. Means, *The Modern Corporation and Private Property* (New York: Crowell-Collier & Macmillan, Inc., 1933), pp. 8, 9.

[13] That the theory of Berle and Means is not altogether new is shown in the two following quotations. Alfred Marshall refers to the fact that "the great body of the shareholders of a joint-stock company are . . . almost powerless" and adds, "It is a strong proof of the marvelous growth in recent times of a spirit of honesty and uprightness in commercial matters, that the leading officers of great public companies yield as little as they do to the vast temptations to fraud which lie in their way."—*Principles of Economics*, 8th ed. (New York: St. Martin's Press, Inc., 1925), p. 303. John Stuart Mill wrote half a century earlier, "The administration of a joint stock association is, in the main, administration by hired servants, . . . the business being the principal concern of no one except those who are hired to carry it on. But experience shows, . . . how inferior is the quality of hired servants, compared with the ministration of those personally interested in the work . . ."—Mill, vol. 1, p. 136.

[14] Berle and Means, pp. 125, 349.

division of labor in large scale enterprise necessarily imply not individualism but coöperation and the acceptance of authority almost to the point of autocracy. . . . At the very pinnacle of the hierarchy of organization in a great corporation, there alone, can individual initiative have a measure of free play.

These statements are important for a realistic interpretation of the private enterprise system. But we cannot agree with writers who claim that this situation (the "managerial revolution") obliterates the essential differences between the various economic systems and argue that in all systems the managers are the ruling class.[15]

The big private corporation and a nationalized industry are similar in the internal functional division of labor. But it is a mistake to confuse this *internal* division of functions with the problems of *external* relations. The private manager makes free investment decisions which are based on cost-price relations; the public manager in a centrally planned economy fulfills prescribed production quotas as the plan commands. In this respect there is a world of difference between the private and the public manager.

Having stressed the importance of the big corporation, it is necessary to add that there exist hundreds of thousands of private enterprises in which ownership and control are still in the same hands. Perhaps it is even more important that the freedom of the market system leads to a great diversity of industrial units. This diversity makes it more likely "in every unexpected contingency, that somewhere there will be found a type of institution best fitted to master the new conditions. Industrial diversity offers a better chance that somewhere and somehow the ideas of innovators will at least be given a trial and provided with the facilities for development."[16]

This fact could be listed separately in an enumeration of economic freedoms: that the forms and sizes of private enterprise are adjustable to their tasks and provide a flexibility unparalleled in bureaucratic systems.

THE FREEDOM TO SAVE AND INVEST

The freedom to save is already included in the free choice of consumption, since it simply amounts to the freedom to choose between consumption now or in the future. Saving can be defined as not-consuming. The abstention from present consumption is a sacrifice made for the

[15] See James Burnham, *The Managerial Revolution* (New York: The John Day Company, Inc., 1941), and recently, from the communist side, Milovan Djilas, *The New Class: An Analysis of the Communist System* (New York: Frederick A. Praeger, Inc., 1957).

[16] See John Jewkes' contribution to *Problems of United States Economic Development* (New York: Committee for Economic Development, 1958), vol. 1, p. 263.

enjoyment of future consumption. The right to save is supported and enhanced by the right to bequeath wealth, so that the choice between present and future consumption is not limited to the adult life of one person. The right to bequeath (or to inherit) cannot be granted too readily in economic systems which aim at government ownership of the material means of production. The accumulation of savings means the accumulation of wealth which will have to consist, directly or indirectly, in claims on income from the ownership of the material resources of the nation. The freedom to save, inherit, and accumulate wealth is therefore a right which is perhaps more typical for the private enterprise system than is the free choice of consumption and of occupation.

The freedom to invest is implied in the unplanned character of the economy. By investment we mean the purchase or production of new capital goods. Private firms are under no obligation to invest. We cannot be sure, therefore, that the production of investment goods will always correspond to intended savings during any given period. In our model of the free market economy we assumed that rates of interest would be just high or low enough to bring about equality between saving and investment. In this case unemployment and deflation will be avoided. But if money has been earned as income and is spent neither on consumer nor on capital goods, the result will be a decline in employment and national income. Such discrepancy is possible in an unplanned economy because of the freedom to consume, save, and invest and because of the fact that those who save are, as a rule, a different group from those who invest. True, the market is supposed to bring saving and investment into balance, but under certain circumstances it may fail to do so. Then it is the task of the government to see to it that aggregate spending is adequate.

In its attempt to maintain a sufficient amount of spending, the government may overshoot its aim and let inflationary pressures develop. But centrally planned systems, too, can be exposed to inflation.

COMPETITION AND MONOPOLY

Our model of the free market economy is a competitive model; it has to be, because a sufficient amount of competition is indispensable if the whole production and distribution process is to be regulated by market forces. This same thought made John Stuart Mill [17] say more than 100 years ago that "only through the principle of competition has political economy any pretension to the character of a science."

Competition is necessary in a private enterprise economy to keep initiative constantly on the alert, protect the consumer, and maintain a

[17] Mill, vol. 1, p. 235.

sufficiently flexible price system. Nevertheless, monopolistic tendencies are an intrinsic feature of the system. They are the outgrowth of the consistent and unrelenting application of the profit motive by private interests; it is indeed just because competition keeps the acquisitive tendencies in check that it is eliminated wherever feasible.

Where the producing units are small and numerous, a monopolistic position cannot be achieved; but where the average size of the firms has grown very large and only a few constitute the whole industry, competition has become more limited. In this situation monopolistic policies have been defended as a legitimate reduction of the risk implied in the investment of the enormous amounts of capital that form the technical apparatus of modern large-scale production. We shall examine these claims later. Monopolistic tendencies are inherent in modern industry but are a negation of the basic philosophy and justification of the private enterprise system, according to which no private agent should be strong enough to rig the market. Some of the most ardent defenders of the private enterprise system, therefore, have emphasized that it may be necessary for the state to "plan for competition." [18]

Earlier it was mentioned that each member of the economy trades on two markets (as consumer and producer) and that on each market buyers as well as sellers fight on two fronts: against the person with whom they are bargaining and against their competitors. If much competition exists on one side of the market (for example, among employees) but not on the other side (among employers), the chances are that the side with the lesser competition gains the advantage in bargaining. This fact, which was already clearly stated by Adam Smith,[19] has recently been emphasized in John Kenneth Galbraith's theory of countervailing power.[20] Galbraith suggests that our system can work reasonably well, in spite of its monopolistic tendencies, since new restraints have, in part, taken the place of the restraints imposed by competition. These restraints do not appear on the same side of the market but on the opposite side. Thus the employers who, according to Adam Smith, can so easily band together, are faced with "a contrary defensive combination of workmen." [21] Similarly, the suppliers of consumer goods may meet a consumers' cooperative on the other side or a food chain or mail-order house. Galbraith does not claim that countervailing power is always effective, and he states expressly that it fails to

---

[18] See F. A. Hayek, *The Road to Serfdom* (Chicago: The University of Chicago Press, 1944); Henry C. Simons, *Economic Policy for a Free Society* (Chicago: The University of Chicago Press, 1948).

[19] Adam Smith, *The Wealth of Nations* (London: Methuen & Company, Ltd., 1925), vol. 1, book 1, chap. 8.

[20] John Kenneth Galbraith, *American Capitalism: The Concept of Countervailing Power* (Boston: Houghton Mifflin Company, 1952), chaps. 9, 10.

[21] Adam Smith, vol. 1, p. 69.

work in times of inflation. But his theory suggests that the government can maintain a reasonable balance in the market place not only by breaking up monopolies but also by strengthening "countervailing" against "original" power.

If we want to express these thoughts in terms of economic freedom, competition can be described as the right to, or the possibility of, free entry into a market, and countervailing power as the freedom of association.

PRIVATE ENTERPRISE AND PRODUCTIVITY

To compare the productivity of different economic systems is an important task of comparative economics, but the difficulty is that a country's economic system is only one of many factors which determine the size of the country's per capita income, growth rate, and other measures of productivity. We can compare either the economies of different countries during the same period or the economy of one country at different periods; but we cannot carry through a controlled experiment, changing the economic system but keeping all the other data constant. Thus, even if we are able to show that the private enterprise system has performed rather well in the United States during the last 100 years, we may not be able to impress others with our figures, because they will argue that their chosen system would have performed even better under such favorable circumstances.

Karl Marx was fully aware of the tremendous productive power of capitalism. In *The Communist Manifesto* [22] we read:

> The bourgeoisie during its rule of scarce 100 years, has created more massive and more colossal productive forces than all preceding generations together. Subjection of Nature's forces to man, machinery, application of chemistry to industry and agriculture, steam-navigation, railways, electric telegraphs, clearing of whole continents for cultivation, canalization of rivers, whole populations conjured out of the ground—what earlier century had even a presentiment that such productive forces slumbered in the lap of social labor?

Yet we know that Marx was convinced that a socialist society would be *infinitely more* productive because it would remove capitalism's "antagonistic conditions of distribution," which create an increasing discrepancy between consumption and production.

The enormous impact which the news of Russia's launching of the first satellite had on the western world indicates that the event exploded

[22] Karl Marx, *Capital, The Communist Manifesto, and Other Writings* (New York: The Modern Library, Inc., 1932), p. 326.

a cherished myth about the inefficiency of Soviet bureaucracy. The question is no longer whether a bureaucracy can technically do what we can do; it is only one of cost, both in resources and in freedom. There is little doubt that free countries can match totalitarian nations in such exploits if they are willing to pay the price. The price may even be much lower in terms of the necessary reduction of consumer goods production owing to better resource allocation. But the *political* question is whether even this lower sacrifice can be extracted in a free system under conditions of peace.

The astonishing thing about the private enterprise economy's performance is its seemingly haphazard nature, the fact that nobody planned it, that the system simply grew and that it achieved its results under conditions of unparalleled freedom. It is not surprising, then, that the system's productivity was ascribed precisely to its unplanned nature and to the twin forces of profit motive and competition. Without suggesting that this explanation is wrong, it can be pointed out, however, that technical progress is not always the strongest where competition is found in its purest form. On the contrary, some have come to the conclusion "that there must be some element of monopoly in an industry if it is to be progressive." [23] This need arises from the high cost of developing new products and the fact that a firm which is not sufficiently protected (through an element of monopoly) has no incentive to undertake large research and development expenditures if the results can be copied at much less cost by its competitors. If, therefore, technological development is to a large extent concentrated in the big corporations, we approach again the territory where, to some observers, the differences between the various economic systems seem to disappear.

FOUR CHARGES

Perhaps objective standards. for the evaluation of a social-economic system are impossible to find. Nevertheless, a discussion of the most serious charges that have been made against the private enterprise system is worth pursuing. The following four chapters, which undertake this task, however, are not meant to indicate that the private enterprise economy is mainly characterized by defects and that nothing much can be said in its favor. They will serve equally to defend the market economy where the attacks seem to have gone too far.

Four charges stand out: (1) The oldest criticism aims at the unequal distribution of wealth and income. (2) The private enterprise system is often considered less productive than systems which consciously and centrally plan for development. In particular, it is argued that profitability

[23] Galbraith, p. 93.

is not identical with productivity and that competition is often excessive. (3) At the same time, the private enterprise economy is, in the opinion of many observers, not competitive enough. The profit motive and the competitive struggle, together with modern technology, lead to monopolistic tendencies which seem to violate the very philosophy of the private enterprise system. In this criticism, therefore, socialists and the proponents of free private enterprise join their forces, though they disagree on the proper remedies. (4) The private enterprise economy does not always maintain high levels of employment. In a depression, productive resources are wasted and the national income may be kept far below a potential maximum. Apart from this loss in productivity, prolonged mass unemployment is one of the most dangerous social diseases to which an economic system can be exposed.

In discussing these criticisms it must be remembered that no economic system can accomplish everything, that every economic system must be a compromise. But it is worthwhile to disentangle aims, demands, claims, and counterclaims and to show what the private enterprise system can be expected to achieve on the basis of its inherent logic.

After the charges against the private enterprise system have been presented, a discussion of government policies that try to answer these charges follows. Only when a study of the government sector has been added to a survey of the private sector has the foundation been laid for a fair comparison between the private enterprise system and systems with state ownership of the material means of production.

CHAPTER 5

Private Property
and Income Distribution

FUNCTIONAL AND PERSONAL DISTRIBUTION

The pricing process of a free market economy takes care of the problem of distribution. The prices that are paid for the services of the factors of production become the income of the owners of the factors; and since the factors are privately owned, the national income is automatically distributed.

This identity of the pricing- and income-distribution processes has been the cause of some misconceptions. The two distribution concepts, personal and functional distribution, must be disentangled.

Many classical economists failed to see how the personal distribution of income could possibly differ from the functional distribution. To them the factor prices which created equilibrium between demand and supply were the "natural" prices, and incomes derived from these prices were considered "just." Moreover, these prices performed the function of allocating the factors, of guiding them into the right industries. The factor owners' self-interest could be relied upon; command or general plan was unnecessary. Indeed, within the framework of the private enterprise economy there was no point in trying to disentangle what was practically one and the same thing: the functional and the personal distribution. Any attempt to divorce the two would have changed the basic structure of the system.

But there was one flaw in this arrangement. The resulting income distribution was very unequal—so unequal, indeed, that what classical writers had called just seemed to socialist critics most unjust. The socialists accordingly aimed at a system with a far more equal personal distribution, but they failed to see all the implications of their aim. They often assumed, for instance, that once the state had acquired ownership of the material factors of production, payment of interest and rent would no longer be necessary. Interest and rent could be abolished and the social product distributed among the working class, though certain deductions for purposes of accumulation (that is, capital formation) would have to be made.

Their preoccupation with the problem of personal distribution prevented the socialist writers from seeing the so-called allocation problem. Scarce factors of production like capital and land must have prices which reflect the exact degree of their scarcity if there is to be a rational distribution of available factors among different users. This allocation is the essence of the functional distribution process. It is *theoretically* independent of the question of personal distribution.

Had it been clear to the socialist critics that this functional distribution or allocation process is essential, they would also have seen that changes in personal distribution can have far-reaching consequences. For instance, a bureaucratic system of accounting would have to replace the pricing processes of all markets; all scarce factors (and not only human labor) would have to be accounted for, and equal wage rates would not properly distribute labor among different industries.

Failure to distinguish between personal and functional distribution explains the *raison d'être* of Marx's labor theory of value which was designed to prove that the value of commodities is exclusively determined by the social labor needed to produce these commodities. Marx's effort was unnecessary. He could have accepted the idea that all scarce factors (and not only labor) must be included in the accounting process without having to accept the particular personal income distribution which is characteristic of the private enterprise economy.

The concept of personal income distribution, which is readily understood, concerns the shares of the national income which go to the individual members of the economy. The concept of functional distribution is more difficult to grasp. By functional distribution we mean the shares of the national income which are imputed to the factors of production according to their relative scarcities. These shares may or may not be paid to individual human beings. They may go to the state if the material factors of production have been nationalized. It is important to see that this accounting in terms of factor values is indispensable in an economic system that wants to make the most economical use of its productive resources in the achievement of its aims.[1]

Personal and functional distribution are very closely related in a system where the factors of production are privately owned (government ownership being the exception from the rule). The individual members of the economy receive, as their private income, whatever the market pays for the use of the factors that they happen to own. The resulting personal income distribution thus depends on (1) the factor prices, which are determined on factor markets according to the relative scarcity of each factor, and (2) the distribution of factor ownership among members of the economy.

Even if private property in the material factors of production were abolished, differences in personal income distribution would remain, owing to the greater scarcity of one kind of labor than another. It can also be seen that personal income in a market economy must be exposed to constant variations as changing demand and supply make the various factors relatively more or less scarce and their services more or less expensive.

Suppose that we wanted to equalize the income from labor. Wage differentials would then be eliminated, at least in the process of personal distribution. It would then still be possible for the government to maintain wage differentials in its accounting procedures.[2] But this separation of personal and functional distribution would mean that labor would no longer be automatically pulled in the right direction, because the elimination of wage differentials has simultaneously eliminated the inducement on which the allocation of labor rests in a market economy. Labor must now be moved by command, that is, the free choice of occupation must be ended. This allocation by command may not be practical. But it will be observed that the maintenance of wage differentials in the government's accounting processes would, at least, tell those in command where a given kind of labor should be used.

Let us assume that the functional distribution is also the personal distribution in the case of labor, that various kinds of labor are paid according to their scarcity. Nevertheless, would it be possible to achieve a much more equal income distribution through nationalization of the material factors? Again, we could maintain the functional distribution process intact; we could establish prices for the material factors according to their relative

---

[1] The share of the national income which can be considered the contribution of a given factor of production (in the functional distribution process) is determined by the equilibrium price of one service unit (an hour of labor) times the total supply of these services during the income period. In terms of the Casselian equations, discussed in the Appendix to Chap. 3, these shares are $R_1q_1, R_2q_2, \cdots R_rq_r$.

[2] See H. D. Dickinson, *Economics of Socialism* (New York: Oxford University Press, 1939), p. 119.

scarcity, and the resulting interest, rent (and profit) would be paid to their new owner, the state. The government might decide to distribute as a "social dividend" all or part of the state's share in the national income. In such an event the government must be extremely careful not to upset the allocation of labor through the labor market. If the government seeks to compensate those receiving low incomes by giving them a relatively large social dividend, the allocation process of the labor market will be destroyed just as certainly as it would have been by directly equalizing income from labor.

It is difficult to disentangle the personal and functional distribution processes. A social economy with state ownership of the material means of production, but with free choice of occupation, would be rather limited in its attempts to equalize personal income. A dictator could possibly allocate labor by command alone and bring about whatever personal distribution of income he desires. But even he is likely not to dispense with the inducements which are implied in a partial connection of personal and functional distribution on the labor market. A consistent functional distribution of income is a "must" in every social economy that wants to act rationally, including the dictator's.

THE CRITIQUE OF INEQUALITY

The economist can criticize the inequality of income distribution on the grounds that it eliminates the possibility of satisfying wants of different persons in the order of their importance.

Abba P. Lerner [3] argues that "total satisfaction is maximized by that division of income which equalizes the marginal utilities of the incomes of all individuals in the society." This follows from the principle of diminishing marginal utility, which asserts that "the amount of satisfaction that every individual obtains from his income depends upon the size of his income in such a manner that he always gets more satisfaction from a larger income, *and that the extra satisfaction he gets from a given increase in his income* (the marginal utility of income) *is less if his original income is greater.*"

It is true, of course, that we cannot compare the marginal utilities of the incomes of two individuals, even if incomes are identical. Nevertheless, unequal income distribution means unequal chances for the satisfaction of individual wants. No one would argue that the rich are, by and large, more cultured than the poor and that their higher incomes correspond,

[3] Abba P. Lerner, *The Economics of Control* (New York: Crowell-Collier & Macmillan, Inc., 1946), pp. 26, 28. Copyright 1944 by Crowell-Collier & Macmillan, Inc., and used with their permission.

therefore, to more refined and diversified wants. A positive correlation of income and power of enjoyment may exist in individual cases. If it is used to defend an unequal income distribution, however, we can argue (1) that "a man with a high income gets used to the luxuries he can afford so that he consumes them almost automatically, hardly noticing that he does so and so getting practically no enjoyment out of what would give a great thrill to the poor man unused to these expenditures"; (2) that the lower incomes are, the more urgent are the wants which are satisfied by spending the marginal dollar; and (3) that "in the long run . . . different individuals' capacities for *acquiring* the power of enjoying income can be put in the place of the *actual* capacity for satisfaction." [4]

These same ideas have often been expressed through examples that showed that luxuries were produced when large parts of the population lack the necessities of life. George Bernard Shaw, for instance, calls a nation "that spends money on champagne before it has provided enough milk for its babies . . . a badly managed, silly, vain, stupid, ignorant nation" and, he adds, "the only way in which a nation can make itself wealthy and prosperous is by good housekeeping: that is, by providing for its wants in the order of their importance, and allowing no money to be wasted on whims and luxuries until necessities have been thoroughly served." [5] Many similar passages could be quoted both from socialist and "bourgeois" writers. It seems to be common opinion that the market economy does not maximize total satisfaction. This opinion is not just another value judgment since it rests on the application, to the economy as a whole, of principles which are considered sound economics for every individual economy.

That most people share, at least unconsciously, this criticism of income distribution is obvious because the principles that govern the satisfaction of individual wants in the private sector of the economy are not allowed to be applied to the public sector. Because the individual economies have to pay indirectly, through taxation, for the satisfaction of collective wants, they have to curtail the satisfaction of private wants. But how are we to fit the satisfaction of collective wants into private household plans that differ as widely as do the individual incomes on which they are based?

The solution of this problem is basically quite obvious. The satisfaction of collective wants concerns all individual households, whereas each of these individual households reaches a different degree of satisfaction of private wants. It is necessary, therefore, to adjust compulsory tax contributions so that the poor pay little or nothing and the rich not only a proportionally but a progressively larger share of their incomes as taxes. Certainly, it would be absurd for each person to contribute exactly the

[4] Lerner, pp. 34, 35.
[5] G. Bernard Shaw, *The Intelligent Woman's Guide to Socialism and Capitalism* (New York: Brentano's, 1928), pp. 50–55.

same amount, the poor family of five members five times as much as the rich bachelor. However, this very principle is applied to the satisfaction of private wants. In the private sector of the economy, the poor pay, indeed, just as much for the necessities of life as do the rich.

To emphasize these considerations, we reiterate the following points:

1. Only *within* the individual consuming unit is an attempt made to fulfill the "economic principle" of allocating the available means to the satisfaction of wants in the order of the latter's importance.

2. The unequal distribution of income and the market price system prevent such a maximization from being aimed at, let alone achieved, for the private sector of the economy *as a whole*.

3. The distribution problem must be faced in the public sector of the economy, where the satisfaction of collective wants requires an indirect method of financing.

4. This method of financing the satisfaction of collective wants is radically different from the way in which consumption is paid for in the private sector of the economy.

5. To tax the rich more than the poor is considered necessary in order to fit the satisfaction of collective wants into the household budget of people of different means.

6. General acceptance of modern tax systems implies a criticism of the way in which the national product is distributed in the private sector of the economy.

The same criticism is even more obviously implied in the fact that, in times of war, price controls and rationing have become generally accepted practice. As soon as a sudden and unusual scarcity of important consumer goods leads to sharp increases in price, it is considered necessary to replace commodity distribution via market prices with an allocation which is based on entirely different principles. The sudden accentuation of a shortage points out that the method of distribution is not at all equalitarian. Then, and because of a generally different attitude to such problems in times of war, the government is willing to introduce controls that are alien to the basic principles of the private enterprise system. That they are alien is shown not only by the partial abolition of free choice of consumption through rationing, but also by the fact that these controls, first introduced in relatively few markets, tend to multiply as if by chain reaction. Selective rationing will have to include more and more articles because the purchasing power released through price control and rationing shifts to unrationed markets, which, in turn, through higher prices, attract the factors of production. Producers are tempted to leave the fields under price control and rationing, thus increasing the very scarcities which brought about the controls. Consequently, an ever-increasing number of industries must be brought under price and production controls.

Rationing and price controls teach two interesting lessons. They bring to light a widespread disapproval of the present system of distribution; and they demonstrate, in their effect upon the economy, how any change in the distribution process can fundamentally affect the whole economy.

INCOME DISTRIBUTION AND SAVING

The more unequal the distribution of income, the higher will be the rate of saving, other things remaining equal. "The fundamental psychological law, upon which we are entitled to depend with great confidence both a priori from our knowledge of human nature and from the detailed facts of experience, is that men are disposed, as a rule and on the average, to increase their consumption as their income increases, but not by as much as the increase in their income." [6] In other words, men are apt to save a larger proportion of their income as they grow richer and a smaller proportion of their income as they become poorer.

Here we come to an argument that is often used in the defense of the inequality of income distribution. Receivers of large incomes spend only a small fraction of these incomes on consumption. The rest is saved and invested. Investment, the production of capital goods, increases the productivity of the economy and therefore the national product that can be distributed. If the rich would not save, the function of capital accumulation would have to be fulfilled by the government through taxation. Unequal income distribution therefore leads, in the long run, to higher incomes all around; while equal income distribution would only insignificantly increase the incomes in the lower brackets.[7] The distribution, finally, of what the rich actually consume would allow only a negligible expansion of the consumption of the lower-income classes.

There should be general agreement that a substantial and continued increase in real incomes cannot be brought about by redistribution alone. The decisive factor is the increase in productivity, which depends on capital formation. Questions of distribution (which remain important, if only for psychological reasons) must therefore be discussed from the point of view of the effect that measures aimed at redistribution have on the size of the national income.

Since capital formation is absolutely essential for the growth of an

---

[6] John Maynard Keynes, *The General Theory of Employment, Interest, and Money* (New York: Harcourt, Brace & World, Inc., 1965), p. 96.

[7] Carl Snyder estimated that the net annual savings for reproductive capital in the United States during the period of the 1920s (of not more than $3 to $4 billion per annum), if diverted to augment the incomes of the 50 million gainfully employed, would have amounted to only $60 per person per year, $5 per person per month.—Carl Snyder, *Capitalism the Creator* (New York: Crowell-Collier & Macmillan, Inc., 1940), p. 143.

economy, it is obvious that consumption must be restricted, either through private or public saving. The economic growth of the Soviet economy at the expense of a very low consumption level illustrates the case in point. Where private saving is responsible for capital formation, greater inequality of income distribution tends to lead to greater savings, while greater equality could dangerously decrease the supply of loanable funds. But the savings argument, as stated above, does not contain all we need to know. Saving is not in itself virtuous, nor is its effect upon the economy always favorable.

N. W. Senior claimed in his famous theory of "abstinence" that interest payments are "earned" much in the same way as wages and Carl Snyder [8] answered the question of "who created the gigantic industrial apparatus of modern capitalism" to the effect that "in a sense, 'labor' contributed almost nothing," and that it was capital savings alone "which has alike created this wondrous industry, and all the modern world of comfort, convenience, and luxury besides." These statements are hardly correct or fair. Interest is not paid according to the amount of "abstinence" implied in a given amount of saving since in this case the poor would receive higher interest rates than the rich.

Capital accumulation in the private enterprise economy is a matter of chance. Nobody can be praised or blamed for it, because saving is an act that is completely devoid of any intentions concerning the economy as a whole. Whether the amount of savings at a given level of the national income is too much or too little cannot be decided on a priori grounds. Until recently it was assumed that oversaving was impossible because of the regulating effect of the rate of interest and the permanent availability of untapped investment opportunities. These assumptions are not always safe. If profitable investment opportunities are lacking, the tendency to save more than can be readily invested will lead only to contraction and unemployment. In this case a more equal income distribution, with the consequence of more consumption and less saving, could help maintain a higher income level. However, this does not mean that saving is bad and that a more equal income distribution (which decreases saving) is always advisable. Generalizing statements of this sort are not permissible. Whether the effect of a more equalitarian distribution upon the size of the national income is favorable or unfavorable depends entirely on the circumstances. [9]

[8] N. W. Senior, *Outline of the Science of Political Economy* (London: George Allen & Unwin, Ltd., 1938); Snyder, p. 4.
[9] "If in the long run it appears that we face a problem of 'oversaving,' the cure is an onslaught, not against savings, but against the institutional obstacles to investment. As long as the material welfare of the lower income groups leaves much to be desired, as long as vast quantities of capital can be used for slum clearance, hospitals, schools, etc., for the benefit of the broad masses of people, it is a cruel myth that we have 'too much saving.' To remedy unemployment arising from uninvested savings by at-

Chapter 9 will discuss the policies by which the government can try to reduce the inequality of income distribution in a private enterprise economy.

---

tacking saving is analogous to reducing mortality from diabetes through lowering the birth rate."—Howard S. Ellis, "Economic Expansion through Competitive Markets," in *Financing American Prosperity*, P. T. Homan and F. Machlup, eds. (New York: The Twentieth Century Fund, 1945), p. 133.

CHAPTER 6

Private Enterprise
and Productivity

INTRODUCTION

The preceding chapter came to the conclusion that the distribution of the national income cannot be radically changed if we want to maintain a private enterprise system. This conclusion shifts the argument to the question of how large a product can be distributed, how productive the system is. Assuming a given distribution pattern, the absolute size of the personal shares will depend on how large a social product the economy is able to produce.

The two main criticisms of the private enterprise system on the grounds of insufficient productivity concern monopolistic practices and the recurrence, at least in the past, of periods of mass unemployment. These problems will be discussed in the two following chapters. First, however, we shall examine several socialist claims that the private enterprise system would not be as productive as a planned system even if it were sufficiently competitive and free from cyclical fluctuations of economic activity. Socialists would still maintain that the inequality of income distribution checks the inherent productive powers of the system because of deficiencies in demand, that profitability does not guarantee productivity, and that socialism could produce a larger national product than the private enterprise economy even at full employment.

INADEQUACY OF DEMAND?

The theory of underconsumption is an old stand-by of the critics of the private enterprise system, though few modern socialists would support this theory in its naïve formulations. Modern economists admit that increasing purchasing power as such is not a panacea that opens the doors to a fool's paradise where, after the removal of all scarcities, economic problems cease to exist. Innumerable proposals have been made for reaching the land of plenty through the creation of money. Usually the proposals have rested on fantastic assumptions about what modern industry could produce, provided the products could be marketed.

The underconsumption theory assumes either that the exploitation of wage earners creates a chronic deficiency in demand or that saving increases production and reduces consumption simultaneously.

The simple underconsumption theory, according to which "the working class receive too small a portion of their own product," which could "be remedied by giving them a larger share of it, or raising their wages," was rejected by Karl Marx, who pointed out that "crises are precisely always preceded by a period in which wages rise generally." [1] The trouble is that if wages are increased in order to raise the purchasing power of the masses "this rise in demand merely offsets the rise in cost of production due to higher wages. A larger expenditure of money is now needed to buy the same goods, and the increase in money income is not an increase in real purchasing power." [2] The result is price inflation.

The theory that saving is dangerous because it increases the supply of consumer goods at the very time it decreases consumers' demand is easily refuted. When savings are actually invested, that is, when capital goods are produced, the productivity of the economy increases and more consumer goods are eventually supplied. But there is no inherent necessity for consumers' demand to be deficient at any time. The decrease in consumption, owing to saving, and the increase in consumer goods output, as a result of increased investment, are not simultaneous. It takes time to produce machinery and, with the machinery, consumer goods. The decreased consumption will at first be counterbalanced by an increased demand for investment goods; and when higher productive efficiency lowers

[1] Karl Marx, *Capital: A Critique of Political Economy* (Chicago: Charles H. Kerr & Company, 1933), vol. 2, p. 476.
[2] Joan Robinson, *Introduction to the Theory of Employment* (New York: St. Martin's Press, Inc., 1938), p. 50.

the unit cost of production and the price of the products, purchasing power is released for the absorption of additional consumer goods.[3]

With this criticism we do not mean to deny that the economy can be exposed to a dangerous inadequacy of aggregate demand because of insufficient profitable investment opportunities or faulty monetary policies. We shall return to these problems later.

TECHNOCRATIC UTOPIA

Even a full employment economy of the private enterprise type would, in the opinion of many socialists, remain far below the level of productivity which a socialist economy could achieve.

> In the capitalist economy, production is carried on not for the purpose of increasing commodity supply but for the purpose of increasing entrepreneurial wealth. Not the highest productivity for the social economy but the highest profitability for the individual economy is the final aim of production. The mightiest machine which can be created in the capitalist era is, therefore, the machine which satisfies existing demand but never the infinitely more powerful machinery which satisfies *absolute* demand.[4]

This quotation is characteristic of a group of writers who tended to overestimate the productive power of the modern industrial system to a fantastic degree. The group included such men as Bebel, Ballod, Hertzka, Tugan-Baranovsky, and the members of the technocratic movement in the United States. These socialists and technocrats asserted that our technical knowledge would enable us to produce a much higher national product with a much smaller effort (2½ hours daily labor, according to Bebel; 20 percent of the available labor, if we can believe Hertzka; a patriotic obligation to work 5 to 6 hours, if we follow Ballod, whose estimates were considered too modest by Tugan-Baranovsky).[5] Oppenheimer believed that "it is entirely within our power to grant to each member of society an average income as it is at present enjoyed by the millionaire." [6] That Karl Marx, the critic of the naïve underconsumption theory, held similar views will be shown in Part 3.

[3] For the most famous modern version of the underconsumption theory, see W. T. Foster and W. Catchings, *Profits* (Boston: Houghton Mifflin Company, 1925). For a critique of Foster and Catchings, see A. H. Hansen, *Business Cycle Theory* (Boston: Ginn & Company, 1927), and F. A. Hayek, *Profits, Interest, and Investment* (London: Routledge & Company, 1939).

[4] Franz Oppenheimer, *Die soziale Frage und der Sozialismus* (Jena: Gustav Fischer, 1925), pp. 183–184.

[5] See Ludwig Pohle, *Kapitalismus und Sozialismus*, 4th ed., ed. Georg Halm (Berlin: Julius Springer, 1931), pp. 125–126.

[6] Oppenheimer, p. 187.

What mistakes led to these fantastic assertions? Part of the answer is to be found in the exclusively technological preoccupation of the above-mentioned writers, when they discuss problems of productivity. They compare the result of modern labor with the result of labor not aided by modern machinery and find that the labor time necessary to produce a given article has often been reduced by an astonishing degree. Then they speculate how large the total national product could be if all labor were supported by the most modern machinery. In addition, they emphasize the advantages of mass production and seem to believe that costs can be lowered ad infinitum as the volume of production increases. Carried away by their enthusiasm, they forget to count the labor needed to produce capital goods; they neglect the labor needed to distribute the output of mass production through transportation and commerce; they overlook the fact that many improvements in production techniques concern products which are of only minor importance to the consumer (pins, buttons, pencils, envelopes), while the main items in the consumers' budgets (shelter, food, clothing) are still relatively expensive to produce; they overestimate the possibilities of mass production because they forget that, as production grows, diseconomies develop which lead to increasing unit costs; and, above all, they fail to see that we cannot produce all the machinery which we should like to employ, because present consumption cannot be reduced ad libitum.

The effort of the Soviet Union to accumulate capital at a rapid rate, and at the cost of a low standard of living for the masses, shows that scarcity of capital is not a special feature of the private enterprise economy. Those who blame the latter for its unequal income distribution and correspondingly high rate of saving should not blame it in the same breath for an inadequate supply of modern machinery.

Though the problem of capital accumulation is essentially the same in any social economy, socialists could still try to base their claim to greater productivity on the assertion that technical knowledge would develop faster in a society with government ownership of the material means of production. This claim will be discussed later. Defenders of the private enterprise system, on the other hand, point to the high degree of inventiveness and technological progress which they consider characteristic for their system compared with the bureaucratic impediments to progress in a centrally planned economy.

Some confusion exists concerning inventiveness and initiative. We must distinguish between scientific research on the one side and the practical application of newly invented techniques on the other. Research as such seems to be rather independent of the economic order in which we live. It is only when we come to the actual introduction of new methods, to innovation—a process which is disturbing and distasteful to the bureaucrat—that the private enterprise system may have the edge over collec-tivist systems. The totalitarian system, on the other hand, may have the advantage where extremely expensive research and production processes have to be financed at the expense of consumption.

PRODUCTIVITY AND PROFITABILITY

Socialist writers often maintain that what is profitable is not necessarily productive and that, accordingly, the private enterprise system must not be trusted to achieve a high degree of productivity. To discuss this well-known criticism, the meaning of the terms "profitability" and "productivity" must first be determined.

Profitability is easily understood. An economic activity is profitable if it leads to an excess of total revenue over total cost. Profitability can be expressed with precision in monetary terms where product prices and factor prices are given. But for this very reason government activities are often not profitable. Many government services cannot be sold, however costly and productive they may be. The government can sell postage stamps but not flood control or preparedness in case of war.

Productive is what improves permanently the possibility of satisfying our wants. The term "productivity" is not limited to the private enterprise economy as is the term "profitability." However, it is too elusive to lend itself to quantitative measurements. Furthermore, the quantity of the social product is not alone significant; its quality and composition are equally important. The larger physical output of a dictatorship economy could be inferior to the smaller output of a system in which production is directed by the consumer. Similarly, the product of a system with more equal in-come distribution may mean more, in terms of want satisfaction, than the equally large product of a country with a more pronounced income stratification.

To get a firmer grasp of the problems involved in this conflict between productivity and profitability, we have to go back to the most fundamental concept in economics—value. Anything that has value must be useful and scarce. If it is abundant, a good cannot have value in spite of its utility. In economics we are exclusively concerned with goods that are scarce in relation to our wants. With these goods we have to be careful so as to maximize the satisfaction of our wants.

If value is the product of utility and scarcity, we can increase value either by increasing the utility of a commodity or by increasing its scarcity.

Now we can see when productivity and profitability coincide and when they are conflicting. Anything that increases the profitability of a firm by increasing the usefulness of its products tends, at the same time, to be productive; activities, on the other hand, which increase profit by increasing the scarcity of the product, or by wasting productive resources, tend to reduce the productivity of the economy.

Since, under competitive conditions, businessmen are not free to raise commodity prices or lower factor prices, they must take pains to use the most economical methods of production and try to serve the consumer as best they can. Producers will reduce costs by substituting factors of production for one another, so that scarce factors are replaced wherever possible by more abundant factors. In addition, producers will try to "rationalize" production through improved techniques to lower the unit cost of production. By these activities they increase the profitability of their firms and set factors free for other productive employment.

Under reasonably competitive conditions the producer will be eager to introduce newer and better techniques and to disturb an existing equilibrium. Equilibrium means that he can merely cover his cost of production, that competition has succeeded in eliminating that difference between cost and revenue for which he is striving. In his endeavor to re-create the profit margin, the capitalist entrepreneur is the driving force behind technological change.

Private enterprise follows the command of the consumer; but as far as new products are concerned, the initiative of introducing them lies with the entrepreneur. In his attempt to introduce new products, the entrepreneur fulfills an important function and assumes a substantial risk. Some writers have criticized the considerable amount of waste caused by the incessant attempt to create new consumers' demand for new products. At this point the discussion sometimes tends to go off on a tangent or, rather, to return to the problem of unequal income distribution. If the private enterprise economy is condemned because it produces unnecessary things while essential products are, relatively speaking, in short supply, the basic trouble is to be found in a faulty income distribution and not in the attempt of the entrepreneur to satisfy a demand of his own creation. Whether this demand will materialize and remain effective is for the consumer to decide. If the consumers do not want the new article, resources have been wasted. This is the price that is paid in this system for the incessant attempt to advance into unexplored territory. Whether this price is too high cannot be decided in objective terms.

Profitability and productivity have a tendency to coincide when, under reasonably competitive conditions, businessmen (1) endeavor to reduce costs through factor substitution, (2) introduce better production techniques, and (3) anticipate correctly consumers' demand. In all these situations the activities of entrepreneurs are utility-creating and not scarcity-creating. This argument rests on the assumption, however, that the producer has the function of satisfying existing or potential demand and that questions of income distribution are eliminated from the profitability-productivity controversy.

Profitability and productivity do not coincide where profits are increased by methods which increase the scarcity of commodities, either through monopolistic practices or through the waste of productive resources.

The profit motive cannot be trusted in this respect. It is selfish and unmoved by social obligations. Only when checked by competition will those who aim for higher profits be induced to undertake the laborious tasks which increase the productivity of the economy. To remove the safeguard of competition means to open the door to monopolistic practices by which profits can be obtained through the creation of artificial scarcities. The next chapter will deal with these monopolistic problems.

Unfortunately, the elimination of monopoly is not always sufficient to create an ideally competitive situation. There can be too much as well as too little competition. Too much competition may lead to a waste of resources when efforts are unnecessarily duplicated or too much is spent on advertising. The high mortality rate of small business, competition of four gas stations at an intersection, milk distribution compared with mail distribution, excesses of radio and television advertising, cutthroat competition between giant firms, and other similar examples have been used to show that often we pay a high price for competition. These charges cannot be dismissed with the argument that competition is necessary and worth a high price. Where there is waste, it should be eliminated. Much can be done without creating monopolistic controls. Where the regulation of competition implies monopolistic organizations or government controls, we must proceed with caution, balancing the diseconomies of excessive competition against those of bureaucratic or monopolistic arrangements.

Competitive waste is sometimes not as great as it seems. Take as an example the high mortality rate of small business. The fact that nearly a third of those entering business may discontinue within a year has been considered proof of wastefulness, but no particular waste need be involved. "Entries and exits of individuals with negligible capital, which build up the heavy count of births and deaths, may be compared with labor turnover; they consist largely of the self-employed who hire no help and who move in and out according to the shifts in opportunities for self-employment as against employment for others." [7]

American history shows that an unregulated private enterprise system tends to exploit natural resources (forests, soil, natural gas, oil, and so forth) in a way that is eminently profitable for private enterprise in the short run but extremely wasteful for the economy as a whole in the long

[7] A. D. H. Kaplan, *Small Business: Its Place and Problems* (New York: McGraw-Hill, Inc., 1948), p. 234.

run. A well-known example is the cutting of virgin timber by private firms at a prohibitive cost for necessary reforestation. Another famous example concerns the exploitation of oil. Because underground pools of oil are independent of property boundaries at the surface, the discovery of oil leads to a wild outbreak of drilling completely neglectful of efficient methods of exploitation, which would require treatment of the oil pool as a unit.

Government action clearly becomes imperative whenever the circumstances demonstrate that profit motive and competition are lacking in conscious social purpose. Care must be taken, however, that government regulation accomplishes its purpose and is not merely misused to establish monopolistic controls.[8]

In other situations, the profit system is criticized with less reason. Suppose that a crop is not fully harvested because the price of the additional supply would not pay for the extra amount of labor and capital. To have harvested the whole crop would not have been profitable. Would it have been productive? Hardly, since the loss caused by the additional application of labor shows that the labor could be more effectively applied in other fields of production. The impression of waste is created by the virtual destruction of a product which could have been enjoyed by many people, at home or abroad, had only its harvesting not depended on profitability. But income distribution (domestic and international) and the whims of nature rather than the profit motive are to be blamed.

Stock exchange speculation has been criticized as the prototype of a profitable but unproductive activity. In reality, stock speculation performs a useful function in maintaining a permanent market for securities and does not, as is often believed, divert capital from potentially productive employment. Loanable funds, used by a speculator to buy securities, are passed on to the seller of the security and are not tied up. Even an increase in security prices does not absorb capital, because the purchasing power spent by the speculator is always to be found in the hands of the seller.[9]

The private enterprise economy has been criticized (1) for wasting its resources in outmoded productive processes where modern methods are already available; and (2) for introducing new machinery at a rate which eliminates old equipment before it has been fully used. These two criticisms cannot both be right. New production techniques are not introduced unconditionally; they are introduced when they lower the costs of pro-

---

[8] See Fritz Machlup, *The Political Economy of Monopoly* (Baltimore: The Johns Hopkins Press, 1952), pp. 299–304.

[9] It must be admitted, however, that the stock market does not necessarily establish correct security prices, for those who buy and sell on the stock market are not interested in long-run production trends. Either they are ignorant or they are professionals who use their skills, not in correcting the mistakes of the ignorant, but rather in trying "to beat the gun" or "to outwit the crowd." See John Maynard Keynes, *The General Theory of Employment, Interest, and Money* (New York: Harcourt, Brace & World, Inc., 1965), pp. 151–156.

duction. The decision will depend on considerations such as: what is the cost of the machine; what rate of interest has to be paid for loanable funds; how much in terms of wages will be saved through the substitution of capital for labor; how will the efficiency of production increase; and what will be the unit costs of production.

Price-and-cost calculations will supply the correct answers. Often the new machine will be introduced and the old machine will continue to be employed, while the price of the product will adjust itself to the lower unit costs of production connected with the new technique. The producer who uses the old machine cannot expect to earn the going rate of interest on his invested capital. However, as long as he can earn some return on his old investment, he will use the old machine rather than throw it on the junk heap. In scientific language, he will produce as long as his total revenue exceeds the total of his variable costs. A more precise and satisfactory method of weighing old against new methods of production could hardly be found. The new method, if it does lower the cost of production, will be introduced; and the old method will be discontinued only if it cannot compete even after complete depreciation of the old equipment. We note that the entrepreneurs who introduce the new techniques are those who will not suffer from depreciation more than they gain through the change, and that those who suffer more than they gain are powerless to stop progress unless they are protected by a monopolistic market position. Thus the private enterprise system steers a rational middle course, not demanding that old investments be protected until fully amortized, nor insisting on the exclusive use of the newest techniques. Later we shall see that totalitarian systems are in danger of choosing the best *technical* solutions because they do not have a comprehensive pricing process which would permit them to make the best *economic* decision.

We do not include in our list of possible deficiencies of the private enterprise economy cases in which the productivity of the system is being impaired by wrong government policies, particularly those that interfere directly and clumsily with the pricing process. These policies are often the result of a desire to help individual groups whose market position is deteriorating. In some instances government action may be justified, for instance, when the nature of demand and supply in special markets leads to excessive price fluctuations. But basically wrong are policies which try to perpetuate the economic position of given groups in the face of a permanent decline in the demand for their services or products. The artificial maintenance of prices under such conditions leads to misallocations of the factors of production and reduces the productivity of the economy in terms of the products which consumers want.

Since policies which fall under this category contradict the very principle on which the functioning of the private enterprise economy is based, it would be wrong to blame the system for these violations of its code.

CHAPTER 7

Monopoly
and Competition

THE PROBLEM OF MONOPOLY

The private enterprise economy is supposed to be competitive, but those fighting the competitive struggle and driven by the profit motive strive, whenever possible, to eliminate competition because it tends to destroy their profits. Since monopoly is the outgrowth of the competitive struggle—the monopolist being the final victor—it is correct when Eduard Heimann says that "monopoly is the annulment of competition and at the same time its logical conclusion." [1]

The substitution of monopoly for competition changes the very nature of the private enterprise economy, because as monopoly eliminates the major driving force of competition, it leaves self-interest and the profit motive unchecked. Monopoly violates the philosophy of individual freedom. A philosophy based on the idea of *free* private enterprise cannot accept a monopolistic concentration of economic power without giving up its very foundation.

There is no denying, on the other hand, that modern technology often

[1] Eduard Heimann, *Soziale Theorie des Kapitalismus* (Tübingen: J. C. B. Mohr, 1929), p. 38.

78

requires huge production units. To some observers monopoly is simply an outgrowth of mass production. If monopoly is the precondition of modern production techniques, monopolistic practices can be defended on technological grounds. In addition, even the biggest producers are still subject to substantial competitive pressure. Monopolistic practices, furthermore, seem to be a method of avoiding the wastes of cutthroat competition, which may easily develop when the competing firms are few in number and large in size. The classical ideal of competition rested on the assumption of a large number of small producing units. Perhaps orderly production and supply under monopolistic conditions are superior to the chaotic conditions of cutthroat competition.

In this controversy a clear-cut answer is not possible. Economic theory has worked out a series of models from pure monopoly to pure competition. General conclusions about the social-economic consequences have not been derived from these models, since they merely tried to show how profit is maximized under varying conditions—a problem of micro- rather than macroeconomics.

Regarding the possible social-economic consequences of monopolistic concentration of economic power, some tentative statements can be made.

THE CASE AGAINST MONOPOLY

One of the most dangerous consequences of monopolistic power for the social economy is *the removal of the automatic protection of consumers and producers, through competition, against excesses of self-interest.* As J. M. Clark [2] puts it:

> The public will not tolerate the mere fact of being dependent upon the good will of a private monopolist to use his power humanely. Such power amounts to "taxation without representation" and is regarded as tyranny, quite apart from the weight of the taxes the ruler may impose. Competition, then, is the option the public has of dealing with anyone who may wish to deal with it, and this option frees it from servitude. But it also frees the producers and dealers from the obligation to serve which could be laid upon them if the public did not have this option.

As long as competition is sufficiently strong, exploitation of buyers (and, in the case of monopsony, of sellers) is impossible; the prices charged cannot long remain above the cost level. *The monopolist has the power to restrict output* and to increase his profit by artifically increasing the scarcity of his product. In the case of monopoly, profitability does not always

[2] Reprinted from *Social Control of Business*, 2d ed., by J. M. Clark, p. 126. Copyright 1939. Courtesy of McGraw-Hill, Inc.

coincide with productivity. The profit motive, when controlled by competition, leads to constant effort, higher efficiency, and an increased social product. The producer under conditions of pure competition [3] has no reason to decrease his output. He can sell at the market price whatever he produces because his individual supply can be considered as an infinitesimally small part of the total supply. Only if the market price should fall below his average cost of production will he, in the long run, reduce output or stop producing altogether. The monopolist may reduce his output and increase his selling price. His decision will depend on the elasticity of demand for his product and on his production costs. If restriction of output and a higher price will lead to higher profits, the monopolist will restrict output. The profit motive may lead in this case to contraction rather than expansion of production. This is the very negation of everything the classical philosophy stood for.

The existence of *monopoly removes the self-generating character of private initiative.* The monopolist does not have constantly to re-create his profit through actions that, under the fresh breeze of competition, would be likely to benefit society. A monopolistic position creates an atmosphere of privilege, the very atmosphere the classical philosophy set out to destroy. It should not be forgotten that society, as Adam Smith and Benjamin Franklin saw it, was predominantly a society of small businessmen. In their time everybody had a fair chance to own the tools of his trade. "But the tools of trade which are protected by the unanimous voice of the lawmakers of America are not the tools by which modern workers maintain their lives." [4] Competition has ceased to be what it used to be when wise men believed they could safely rely on it.

The pricing process of the market economy rests on the assumption of sufficient price flexibility. Prices should adjust themselves to changes in demand, in production techniques, and in the supply of the factors of production. Changes in prices would cause the necessary adjustments in production, factor demand, and individual incomes. If we assume that *monopolistic price control is identical with price rigidity,* we come to the conclusion that the price mechanism will lead to results which are deviations from the optimum which could have been achieved under competitive conditions. Under the assumption of a stable supply of money and a stable general price level, monopolistic policies will tend to reduce the prices of products which are produced under competitive conditions; and if the

---

[3] "Pure competition exists if the seller thinks that at the market price he could sell as much as he wanted while at a higher price he could sell nothing at all."—Fritz Machlup, *The Political Economy of Monopoly* (Baltimore: The Johns Hopkins Press, 1952), p. 14.

[4] *Final Report and Recommendations of the Temporary National Economic Committee* (Washington, D.C.: Government Printing Office, 1941), p. 6.

competitive industries cannot lower their cost of production, the result may be increasing unemployment.

If we remove the condition of a stable supply of money, we may be able to avoid unemployment, but only at the price of creeping inflation. When monopolistic price rigidity makes it impossible for many prices to be *lowered*, the necessary changes in the price signals that guide production must be achieved with relative price *increases*—a situation which implies inflation. Furthermore, where monopolistic prices and wages are raised autonomously, that is, without the pull of increased demand, the central bank may be forced to support these monopolistic policies to avoid a contraction of the trade volume through falling demand in the competitive sector. *The resulting inflation is then monopoly-induced* even though the purchasing power was created by the banking system.

The monopolist not only restricts output if restriction promises to increase his profit; he also secures a *larger* share of a *reduced* national income, thus cutting doubly into competitive incomes. *The monopolist's increased share is not derived from any social-economic function.* While it is possible to impute wages, interest payments, and competitive profits to "functional" contributors to the social product, no such imputation is possible in the case of monopolistic profits. "Now for the first time there arises the fundamental possibility within the system to earn more through worse than through good and abundant performance, and monopoly is, therefore, the quasi incarnate refutation of the system of private economy." [5]

Monopolistic profits lead to increased savings, and these savings are not completely reinvested in the monopolized field of production. Additional investment might increase output, reduce prices, and lower profits.[6] Thus it would undermine the very source from which monopolistic profits flow. The monopolist, therefore, will search for investment outlets in competitive fields of industry, where entry is free. "Thus the immediate effect of accumulation is simply to intensify the distortions in the pattern of profit rates which monopoly originally brings with it." This distortion may become particularly dangerous if it leads to, or intensifies, a situation in which savings tend to exceed investments. If anticipated rates of profit in competitive fields are too low, investment falls short of intended saving, with the consequence of unemployment. It must not be forgotten, however, that an increased supply of savings may press down the rates of interest, thus inducing more investment.

[5] Heimann, p. 46.

[6] "The decisive factor is that the very maintenance of monopoly necessitates the blocking off of investment from the monopolized, and hence most profitable, fields of industry." From *The Theory of Capitalist Development* by Paul M. Sweezy, pp. 275, 277. Copyright 1942 by Oxford University Press, Inc.

Lack of competitive pressure may prevent the introduction of new techniques as long as existing capital goods are not amortized. It has been suggested that "the monopolist tends to finance his technological progress from depreciation accruals instead of from net saving." [7] Joseph A. Schumpeter, on the other hand, asserts that private management "will always adopt a new method of production which it believes will yield a larger stream of future income per unit of the corresponding stream of future outlay, both discounted to the present, than does the method actually in use." [8] Schumpeter's statement is correct, but it cannot be denied that, on the basis of a given technology, the monopolist may find it profitable to produce less efficiently than he could. Emphasis on dynamic changes in technology tends to confuse the issue unless the argument is directed against those who maintain that monopolies bar all technological progress.

Summing up these indictments, the monopolistic tendencies seem to be the very negation of everything the classical philosophy stood for. That production may be restricted instead of being increased is, indeed, a fatal blow to the dogma of the close correlation of profitability and productivity. Not only may it be permissible to conclude that all individual cases of restriction add up to a substantial decrease of the national product, but it is also likely that the total effect is worse than the mere addition of single instances. The functioning of the price mechanism suffers when the savings from monopolistic profits are forced into competitive fields. Not only are the competitive industries exposed to extra pressure, they are simultaneously faced with inelastic prices for intermediate products, which they must buy from monopolies. If the economy happens to be sensitive to oversaving, because of inadequate investment opportunities, conditions would be made worse by monopolistic practices. Finally, autonomous price and wage increases may force the monetary authorities into inflationist policies to avoid mass unemployment.

THE APOLOGY FOR MONOPOLY: COMPETITIVE ADMIXTURES

Some observers believe that the case against monopoly has been overstated and that monopoly, far from being the negation of the classical philosophy, is much more likely the latter's logical and consistent adjustment to the era of mass production.

Perhaps the strongest argument in defense of monopoly is the re-

---

[7] Sweezy, p. 277.

[8] Joseph A. Schumpeter, *Capitalism, Socialism, and Democracy* (New York: Harper & Row, Publishers, 1942), p. 97.

minder that *monopoly in pure form is rarely found.* Since the arguments against monopoly center around the alleged absence of competition, the defenders of monopoly can attempt to prove that competition is maintained in forms that, though less clear-cut than the cases of pure and perfect competition,[9] are still sufficient. These forms of competition are the following:

(1) *The Competition of All Products for the Buyer's Dollar.* This competition is not very useful in controlling monopoly. The monopolist has to face a demand situation which is determined not only by the effect on sales of the respective monopolistic prices chosen, but also by the prices of all other products which the consumers' dollars may buy. This can serve as a reminder that even the monopolist's power is not unlimited. He has to consider the elasticity of demand for his product and also the cross elasticities, the effect on the quantity demanded of changes in the prices of *other* products.

(2) *The Competition of Substitutes of Different Ranges of Proximity.* Meant as a defense of monopoly capitalism, the argument for this type of competition says that even the monopolist will have to consider the price policy of the makers of products which are close substitutes for his own product and therefore liable to make the demand for the monopolist's product more elastic. But even in the case of a close substitute, the dissimilarity may be great enough to offer substantial possibilities for monopolistic profits.

(3) *Potential Competition.* According to J. M. Clark,[10] a considerable part of the power of competition is the fear of competition that is not yet actively in existence. In other words, the expectation of stirring up active competition is enough to restrain businessmen from following extortionate policies, especially if it is fortified by recollections of painful experiences in the past. This takes many forms, including (a) the expectation that new plants will be built or new enterprises launched, (b) the possibility that producers serving other markets will reach out and invade this one, if prices go high enough to make such an invasion profitable, or (c) the possibility of stirring up cutthroat competition among existing producers in a trade where rivalry is now on a tolerant live-and-let-live basis.

All this, of course, is a question of the degree of monopolistic power and monopolistic profits. The more attractive the monopolistic profit, the stronger must be the armor of the monopolist. Consideration of the case of potential competition is important because the *invisibility* of this form of competition may cause monopolistic power to seem stronger than it is.

---

[9] See footnote 3. "Perfect competition requires that everybody is free to move unlimited amounts of productive resources into any field that looks promising to him. . . ." Machlup, p. 19.

[10] Clark, p. 136.

When monopoly rests on a temporary arrangement—as in a cartel—competition remains a potential menace, a fact which limits monopolistic practices. If the restrictions imposed upon the members of the group seem greater than justified by the gain derived from control of the market, members will leave the cartel. This type of monopoly is an armistice between competitive forces and is therefore constantly under the shadow of a potential outbreak of hostilities.

(4) Monopolistic Competition. This is the competition in differentiated products by many sellers.[11] It is not a case of competition of substitutes unless we define substitutes to include the "same" goods when sold by rival makers.[12] But the two cases shade into each other. The differentiation in the case of monopolistic competition is not of such an appreciable degree that each field would constitute an "industry" of its own. "Differentiation may be based upon certain characteristics of the product itself. . . . It may also exist with respect to the conditions surrounding its sale."[13] These cases are a blending of monopolistic and competitive elements. In its differentiated field or location, the firm is a monopolist. The differentiation acts as a deterrent to the entry of competitors into the "field." But other firms may offer a product only slightly different in quality or conditions surrounding the sale. In scientific language: competition is neither pure nor perfect. In pure competition an identical article is offered for sale by many firms. It makes no difference from whom the buyer buys, and the seller can sell at the market price whatever he produces. The demand for branded articles, on the other hand, is not perfectly elastic. At a lower price the producer will sell more than at a higher price. However, since there are other sellers selling similar products, such as different makes of automobiles or different brands of cigarettes, the demand for a particular brand will decrease as other firms enter the industry. Advertising is characteristic of this type of competition. We do not find much advertising in cases of pure monopoly and none at all in cases of pure competition.

We have listed this hybrid of monopoly and competition in order to emphasize the strong mixture of competition and monopoly in the private enterprise system. The ubiquity of this form of monopoly (or competition) suggests, however, that the monopolistic element is stronger, though more diffused, than the rare appearance of pure monopoly may lead us to believe. Monopolistic competition may not be exposed to the severe criticism that is directed against monopoly in general. But it has this in common with the negative features of monopolistic practice: the firm that

[11] See Fritz Machlup, "Monopoly and Competition: A Classification," American Economic Review, vol. 27 (September 1937), p. 447.

[12] Clark, p. 129.

[13] Edward Chamberlin, The Theory of Monopolistic Competition, 5th ed. (Cambridge, Mass.: Harvard University Press, 1946), p. 56.

supplies a differentiated product has the choice between different prices and may be induced to restrict output in order to increase profits.

(5) Competition from the New Commodity. Joseph A. Schumpeter [14] refers to *"the competition from the new commodity, the new technology, the new source of supply, the new type of organization* (the largest-scale unit of control for instance)—competition which commands a decisive cost or quality advantage and which strikes not at the margins of the profits and the outputs of the existing firms but at their foundations and their very lives." This kind of competition is, according to Schumpeter, so much more important than competition in the ordinary textbook meaning of the word "that it becomes a matter of comparative indifference whether competition in the ordinary sense functions more or less promptly; the powerful lever that in the long run expands output and brings down prices is in any case made of other stuff." This argument is an important reminder that long-run problems of economic growth should not be forgotten. The argument is not so strong for the short-run analysis, which may include whole business cycles.

THE APOLOGY FOR MONOPOLY: FURTHER ARGUMENTS

The theory of countervailing power [15] suggests that the search for restraints of monopolistic power should not be confined to one side of the market, that is, the various kinds of competition just outlined. *Restraints may appear also on the opposite side of the market, where monopolists meet monopsonists* and vice versa. Thus the monopsony of employers' associations is met and counterbalanced by labor unions. These considerations are important for a realistic appraisal of the private enterprise system, but they cannot prove that all market parties can unite with the same ease or success. Furthermore, the power of these groups may be additive rather than countervailing, as when strong labor unions and industrial monopolies join forces in the exploitation of the consumer.

If *monopoly* really leads to a curtailment of production, it *releases factors of production* which can be used in other fields. Monopolistic policies, therefore, lead to restrictions in individual plants, firms, and industries but need not decrease total production. If full employment can be maintained, the net effect of monopoly is not a reduction of the national product but a change in its product mix. Lower wages may help absorb into competitive fields those who cannot find employment in the monopolistic industries, and saved-up monopolistic profits may lower interest

---

[14] Schumpeter, pp. 84, 85 (italics are mine).

[15] See John Kenneth Galbraith, *American Capitalism: The Concept of Countervailing Power* (Boston: Houghton Mifflin Company, 1952), chaps. 9, 10.

rates and lead to increased investments in competitive firms. Even then, however, it is clear that consumers do not get the selection of goods that they would have under competitive conditions. We can argue, on the other hand, that this diversion is relatively unimportant when compared with the influence of unequal income distribution on the product mix.

Perhaps the most frequently heard argument in defense of monopolistic practices consists of references to the unhealthy conditions of cutthroat competition, which may make its appearance where there are only a few large firms in a field and the entrance of just one more competitor precludes fair rates of return for all concerned. The same argument can be formulated as follows. The ideal competitive economy is based on small but numerous business units. Modern industrial economy with its big mass-production units no longer conforms to this picture. Since mass production is here to stay, new forms of market behavior must be found. The way back to pure and perfect competition is closed. *If we disapprove of cutthroat competition we must be willing to admit some sort of market control.*

The tendency toward mass production does not, as a rule, lead to the survival of only one producing unit. The advantages of mass production are limited. After an optimum point is reached, a further increase in the size of the producing unit would lead to decreasing returns. On technological grounds the optimum size will often be reached before one production unit comprises the whole industry. Several firms will supply the market. Monopoly is therefore rarely the direct outgrowth of the advantages of mass production. But wherever the market is supplied by only a few firms, the normal adjustment of supply to changes in demand may be impeded. The addition of one more production unit may make competition too severe, while a reduction of output is difficult to achieve under these conditions. Marginal firms may eventually be forced to shut down, but even the marginal firms have made large investments in fixed capital which they will write off before they stop producing. Thus entry into an industry will be easier than withdrawal from it.

Fritz Machlup [16] points out that the extent to which concentration has proceeded is entirely out of proportion to so-called technological necessities or economies:

> Most of the growth of corporate empires during the last fifty or sixty years was not a matter of technological integration but rather financial integration of control. And this integration and concentration of control in larger and larger corporate units was, of course, directly related to the building up of monopoly positions both in the sense of reducing the number of actual competitors in the field and in the sense of reducing the ease with which potential competitors could enter the field.

[16] Machlup, *The Political Economy of Monopoly*, p. 239.

We must make sure that industrial efficiency is not used as an excuse for industrial empire building. The optimum size for producing units can be reached, as a rule, without interlocking financial controls. "If prices are to be managed and administered, if the Nation's business is to be allocated by plan and not by competition, that power should not be vested in any private group or cartel, however benevolent its professions profess to be." [17]

Schumpeter [18] suggests that *monopolistic practices* can often be considered *a necessary protection against the uncertainties that insurance is unable to cover.* He argues that monopolistic restrictions, which seem synonymous with loss of opportunities to produce, are often unavoidable incidents of a long-run process of expansion which they protect rather than impede. "There is no more of paradox in this than there is in saying that motorcars are traveling faster than they otherwise would *because* they are provided with brakes." This argument cannot easily be refuted, though we may well ask whether the necessary controls should be vested in a private monopoly and "whether investment on balance will not be more restricted than encouraged . . . if we foster investment by 'leaders' through restricting investment by 'followers.' " [19] Schumpeter admits that his argument "does not amount to a case against state regulation. It does show that there is no general case for indiscriminate 'trust-busting' or for the prosecution of everything that qualifies as a restraint of trade." [20]

The argument that monopolistic policies lead to a less flexible price system is difficult to refute, but it *is* equally *difficult to prove.* Edward S. Mason [21] has pointed out that "it is frequently inferred, because many prices are now rigid, that the degree of monopoly control must now be greater in the economy than it was at some time in the past. All of these deductions seem to be highly dubious to say the least." The fact that prices of agricultural products fall during a depression without much decline in output does not justify the conclusion that if industrial prices had declined output would have been maintained. This conclusion would be correct only if the price-determining factors were the same in both cases. The problem of the economic relevance of price rigidities cannot be solved

---

[17] TNEC, *Final Report*, p. 15. John Stuart Mill had already reached this conclusion; a hundred years ago. He wrote, "When . . . a business of real public importance can only be carried on advantageously upon so large a scale as to render the liberty of competition almost illusory, it is an unthrifty dispensation of the public resources that several costly sets of arrangements be kept up for the purpose of rendering to the community this one service. It is much better to treat it at once as a public function." —*Principles of Political Economy* (New York: The Colonial Press, 1899), vol. 1, p. 141.

[18] Schumpeter, p. 88.

[19] Machlup, *Political Economy of Monopoly*, p. 68.

[20] Schumpeter, p. 91.

[21] Edward S. Mason, "Price Inflexibility," *Review of Economic Statistics*, vol. 20 (May 1938), 55.

without an analysis of many variables. Since the derived demand for capital goods resulting from changes in the demand for consumer goods is an extremely sensitive variable, it is quite impossible to conclude that industrial prices and output would behave like agricultural prices and output were it not for monopolistic practices in industry. Under demand conditions as they prevail on the market for capital goods during a depression, it is likely "that in the most conspicuous cases price rigidity is motivated precisely by the low sensitiveness of demand to short-run price changes within the practicable range." [22] This argument can hardly be used in defense of monopolistic practices, however. If the chances for a revival rest on profit expectations, and profit expectations depend in turn on cost-price relations, it is quite possible that price rigidities postpone the upswing. Schumpeter argues that the refusal to lower prices strengthens the position of industries that adopt such a policy, but it is doubtful that this argument can afford similar comfort to industries that are buyers of monopoly products.

Adolf Weber [23] suggests a simple psychological reason for the public's negative attitude toward concentration of economic power. The public, he says, is always dissatisfied with some features of the economy. Since the private enterprise system is atomistic and unplanned, responsibility cannot be fixed upon individual firms as long as these firms are relatively small and numerous. Responsibility can be fixed, however, either upon the government which "interferes" with private business or upon monopolies which "exploit" competitive business and the consumer. Quite obviously, Weber concludes, government and monopolies are blamed for almost all the shortcomings of the economy.

Summing up these points in defense of monopoly, it is true that pure monopoly is only infrequently found and that competition remains effective in many forms; that original bargaining power leads to countervailing power; that monopoly does not reduce total production as much as it changes the product mix; that modern production units have grown too big for a normal competitive process and that monopolistic market control is sometimes preferable to cutthroat competition; that monopoly protects against uncertainties, which, if no protection were possible, would prevent large-scale investment in new fields; and that price rigidities are, perhaps, not as strong an argument against monopoly as it may seem.

Whether the arguments *for* or the arguments *against* monopoly are stronger cannot be decided on purely theoretical grounds. The problem has a normative character. However, the norm on which monopolistic policies can be evaluated is difficult to establish. If we acknowledge the principle

[22] Schumpeter, p. 95.
[23] Adolf Weber, *Allgemeine Volkswirtschaftslehre*, 4th ed. (München und Leipzig: Duncker und Humblot, 1932), vol. 2, p. 175.

of competition, why stop those who emerge victorious? If we acquiesce in glaring inequalities of income distribution, why get excited about monopolistic profits? If we eulogize the profit motive, why not idolize men who have driven it to the extreme? No wonder antimonopolistic policies are often half-hearted, incomplete, and inefficient. They dare not be consistent lest they plunge the economy from the frying pan of monopoly into the fire of government control and government ownership.[24] Without competition, the market economy cannot work; but it can work under conditions of less than pure and perfect competition. It must be our aim to keep competition as strong as feasible; to see to it that inherently weak bargainers are strengthened; to eliminate monopolies which are not technologically justified and control, perhaps even through government ownership, those that are needed. And we must abstain, of course, from policies that indirectly foster the growth of private monopoly.

Policies designed to achieve these ends will be discussed in Chapter 9.

LABOR UNIONS

A discussion of the monopolistic character of the private enterprise economy would be incomplete without a consideration of the bargaining power of labor. Is "labor" being exploited or are, on the contrary, labor unions themselves monopolistic organizations?

Most economists agree that unorganized labor cannot hope to bargain successfully on the labor market. Unorganized labor does not have the necessary monetary reserves that would permit it to withdraw its services temporarily from the market; it lacks mobility (both geographical and occupational), which would permit ready movement to more highly paid jobs; it is menaced by unemployment, which creates pressure to accept any offer rather than to have to risk idleness; and it faces employers who are comparatively few, can come to secret agreements, and have a much better knowledge of the market situation.

Labor can improve its position through organization. The original monopsonistic bargaining power of the employers is now being met by the countervailing monopolistic power of the employees. Ideally speaking,

---

[24] "Perhaps the basic difficulty had its origin not in the vastness and complexity of business but in the confusion of the American mind. Americans feared big business, but they admired it, too. They wished to protect themselves against the dangers of monopoly, but also to enjoy the benefits of mass production and the elimination of costly duplication. They believed in government regulation of business, but believed with equal fervor in the virtues of private enterprise and 'rugged individualism.' What they really wanted to do was to purify the trusts, not to smash them."—Allan Nevins and Henry Steele Commager, *The Pocket History of the United States* (New York: Pocket Books, Inc., 1942), p. 304.

labor can now appropriate that extra profit which employers could pocket before labor was organized.

Labor unions undoubtedly are monopolies in the economic sense of the word. Whether their monopolistic position leads to wages that are higher than they would be under ideally competitive conditions depends on many circumstances. The following conditions are important: the strength of the monopoly, that is, the degree of control over a given kind of labor supply; the economic position of the other contracting party (even a union cannot cut into profits where no profits are made); the general economic situation (unemployment, full employment); and the framework of economic policy within which labor and management bargain.

To approach the same question from a different angle, who ultimately pays when a labor union succeeds in raising the wages of its members? Several answers are possible.

1. Already mentioned was the case where labor simply appropriated the share of the employers' profits that was withheld from labor as long as the latter's bargaining position was weak.

2. Labor unions may be able to get a share in the monopolistic profits of certain industries—at the expense of consumers and of other labor groups. A strong union can actually help a monopolistic industry to fortify its position, as when nation-wide bargaining raises labor costs to potential intruders.

3. A monopolistic labor group can raise its wages at the expense of labor by restricting entry into the organized field and by increasing the competitive pressure on other labor markets.

4. Unions can try to get a share of the competitive profits of industry, but at the danger that marginal producers will have to quit, with the consequence that unemployment increases.

5. The danger of unemployment can be reduced when a liberal monetary policy permits general price inflation. In this case the increase in real wages will not be as great as the increase in money wages, but organized labor will still gain at the expense of parts of the population which cannot increase their money income.

6. Wage rates can be increased, without inflationary consequences, if the increasing purchasing power of wage earners is met by a sufficiently increased supply of commodities. However, it cannot be assumed that wages should be more or less automatically raised in firms or industries whose efficiency has been increased. The logic of the price mechanism requires an upward adjustment in wage rates only if the demand for the particular kind of labor involved has increased in relation to supply. For the same kind of labor the same wage rates should everywhere prevail—not different rates depending on the varying profitability of the firms in-

volved; or, to be exact, the differences ought to be limited to the amounts needed to bring about the proper allocation of labor.

How to deal with the labor problem is one of the most crucial and difficult issues faced by modern economic policy. Assuming that we know how to deal with industrial monopolies, a pact between industrial and labor monopolies is no longer feasible. Furthermore, assuming conditions of high employment, then labor has a very strong bargaining position. "Labor," of course, is a term that oversimplifies matters. The labor factor is not homogeneous; it is subdivided into numerous "noncompeting" groups among which occupational mobility does not exist, at least not in the short run. Each organized group tries to obtain for itself the highest possible wage rates, without consideration of the general economic consequences of its policy. Indeed, no other attitude can be expected of labor (or any other group) in times of peace. Nobody, therefore, sees to it that the total wage bill, which is the result of all bargaining processes on the labor market, is correct in terms of aggregate demand. In the full employment situation, which is assumed to exist, it is likely that aggregate demand will exceed the amount at which price stability can be maintained. The explanation is that employers will be willing to concede wage increases, provided they in turn can count on raising their prices.

The monetary authority, to which the problem of price stability is entrusted, could see to it that the total amount of spending is sufficiently curtailed. The monetary authority would simply have to regulate the supply of money. This was the conservative concept of monetary policy. In this case,

> wage negotiations were conducted, as it were, within a steel framework not absolutely rigid indeed, but known not to be indefinitely extensible. . . . If the framework is scrapped, if monetary authorities are always prepared to create without question whatever *flow of money* is needed to discharge whatever *wage-bill* is needed to reconcile full employment with whatever *wage-rate* is demanded by the Trade Unions, they have indeed abdicated from exercising that sovereignty over the standard of value which we thought we had committed to their charge.[25]

As yet nobody has found a solution for this dilemma which seems to make it impossible to achieve simultaneously the three aims of (1) collective wage bargaining, (2) full employment, and (3) monetary stability. Two of the problems could always be solved if the third were neglected: powerful unions could bargain within the mentioned steel framework— at the price of unemployment; unions could bargain successfully in a high

[25] D. H. Robertson, *Utility and All That* (New York: Crowell-Collier and Macmillan, Inc., 1952), p. 91.

employment economy—at the price of creeping inflation; or both full employment and monetary stability could be maintained—if controls would take from labor (and other groups), as in totalitarian systems, the power to bargain collectively.

Liberal socialist system would face similar difficulties. Only totalitarian systems might have simple solutions to offer—at the price of freedom.

CHAPTER 8

Employment
in the Private
Enterprise Economy

FRICTIONAL AND TECHNOLOGICAL UNEMPLOYMENT

In a model of a free market economy, unemployment is, by definition, excluded. In a real market economy, a moderate amount of frictional unemployment is unavoidable. Adjustments to changing conditions imply factor movements and, since labor does not enjoy perfect occupational or geographical mobility, some idleness results, because of changes in demand and in production techniques.

This type of unemployment is not the concern here. It would exist in any economic system (even a totalitarian) that attempted to adjust production to changing conditions. A realistic interpretation of such "frictional" unemployment

> . . . legitimately allows for various inexactnesses of adjustment which stand in the way of continuous full employment: for example, unemployment due to a temporary want of balance between the relative quantities of specialised resources as a result of miscalculation or intermittent demand; or time-lags consequent on unforeseen changes; or to the fact that change-over from one employment to another cannot be effected without

a certain delay, so that there will always exist in a non-static society a proportion of resources unemployed "between jobs." [1]

Some of these instances of frictional unemployment are probably more serious in a market economy than in a centrally planned economy. The private enterprise economy is characterized by consumers' sovereignty and free occupational choice. Adjustments to changes in demand and supply, therefore, will be more frequent and difficult than in a command economy.

The dangerous cases of unemployment, however, are of a different nature. Consider first a special case of frictional unemployment, which has played an important part in the socialist critique—technological unemployment.

Many writers believed that a constantly growing use of capital goods would lead to ever-increasing unemployment. Machines would be substituted for labor, unemployment would press wages down, and the increased social product could not be sold, owing to the insufficiency of purchasing power in the hands of the people. This argument was presented before when the system was criticized for its inability to reach high levels of productivity. Now it is time to find out whether the private enterprise economy must suffer from permanently increasing technological unemployment.

Classical economics rejected the above argument. Jean-Baptiste Say [2] pointed out "that a product is no sooner produced, than it, from that instant, affords a market for other products to the full extent of its own value," and John Stuart Mill [3] explained that,

> could we suddenly double the productive powers of the country, we should double the supply of commodities in every market; but we should, by the same stroke, double the purchasing power. Everybody would bring a double demand as well as supply: everybody would be able to buy twice as much, because every one would have twice as much to offer in exchange.

This theory took for granted that increased efficiency of labor would lower the unit cost of production and that, at lower prices, purchasing power would be set free to purchase additional commodities. To produce these commodities, more labor would be needed and the technologically unemployed would be absorbed by an ever-expanding production. That the process need not be deflationary was already suggested by Say, who pointed

---

[1] John Maynard Keynes, *The General Theory of Employment, Interest, and Money* (New York: Harcourt, Brace & World, Inc., 1965), p. 6.

[2] Jean-Baptiste Say, *A Treatise on Political Economy* (Philadelphia: John Grigg, 1830), p. 78.

[3] John Stuart Mill, *Principles of Political Economy* (New York: The Colonial Press, 1899), vol. 2, p. 77.

out that in such cases of increased "traffic" merchants would well know how to find substitutes for the product serving as a medium of exchange.

The Say-Mill argument was merely a consistent (though highly simplified) application of the principles of the free market economy to problems of technological change. The history of the nineteenth century, with its remarkable record of creating employment for a rapidly rising population, shows that the theory of the automatic long-run absorption of the technologically unemployed came much nearer to the truth than did the gloomy predictions of the pessimists who expected, as the result of rapid industrial progress, ever-increasing unemployment, even for a stationary population.

While Say and Mill were right in rejecting the theory of a general overproduction, they overestimated the ease with which the market economy adjusts itself to technological and other changes. Experience teaches that our economy does not expand evenly and steadily, that it is subject to cycles of prosperity and depression. These wavelike, self-aggravating movements are the manner in which the unregulated market economy reacts to outside shocks. These economic fluctuations must be considered because the causes of the disease of mass unemployment must be discovered before the proper remedies can be prescribed.

ECONOMIC FLUCTUATIONS

How the private enterprise economy tends to swing in cycles of increasing and decreasing employment, of prosperity and depression, can be indicated by the following sketchy remarks.

Assume that a period of depression changes into revival. This change may be caused by an accumulated replacement demand, by innovations, by an improved cost-price relation, or by government action.

Unemployment, excess capacity of industrial plant, and stocks of materials in different stages of production permit a substantial expansion of output under the impulse of improved profit expectations. The rate of interest is low and will be kept low through credit expansion. Because production can be increased, the expansion of credit need not raise the general price level.

As the revival is financed by credit expansion and new money flows into circulation, the national income increases. Newly employed men will spend part of their newly earned income on consumer goods. New consumer goods will be ordered and produced, and the money spent will become income of an ever-widening circle for those who participate, directly and indirectly, in the production and marketing of consumer goods. This is the so-called multiplier-effect.

Part of the newly created income will be saved. These savings will be invested (that is, spent on capital goods), because an increased demand for consumer goods will cause an increased demand for capital goods. This derived demand may easily be accelerated or magnified, owing to circumstances which a simple example can explain.

Assume that the production of consumer goods, such as shoes or electric fixtures, has been carried on at full capacity when, upon a rise in income, the demand for these articles increases by 10 percent. Assume, furthermore, that in order to produce these consumer goods a considerable amount of capital goods is needed. Let us say that the production of 1000 units of a given kind of consumer goods per year requires 500 units of capital goods. These units, constituting plant and equipment, have to be replaced at a rate which depends on the average durability of the capital goods. Assuming an average durability of 10 years, we must replace 50 units each year. The capital goods industry has to produce these 50 units per year to maintain the flow of 1000 units of consumer goods per year. Because we assumed that the plant was fully used, a 10 percent increase in the demand for consumer goods (from 1000 to 1100 units) will require 550 units of capital equipment instead of only 500. The new demand for investment goods, added to the normal replacement demand of 50 units, raises the production of capital goods from 50 to 100 units, or by 100 percent. Since the assumed increase in consumption was only 10 percent, we see that the derived demand for capital goods has been greatly magnified.

If we assume the existence of unused plant capacity, this principle of magnification will not work immediately and its effect will be weakened. However, the principle remains a powerful tool of analysis in the explanation of economic fluctuations.

Increasing investment causes employment, income, and consumption to grow; and increased consumption, in turn, increases investment still further. How an upswing, once under way, gathers momentum is easy to understand. Revival propels itself into prosperity while continuous credit expansion finances the absorption of unemployed factors of production.

But the upswing must come to an end when full employment is reached and when the expansion of credit has to be stopped to avoid a dangerous price inflation. The private enterprise economy reaches a state of high employment only to be forced into recession and depression by disproportionalities which have developed in the economy during its upswing.

As consumer goods production and capital goods production increase side by side, they stimulate their mutual growth. But as unemployed resources are gradually absorbed it becomes increasingly difficult to expand both consumer goods and capital goods production. At full employment, investment can be increased only at the expense of consumption, and consumption, only at the expense of investment. This constitutes a situation of great instability.

Both consumer and capital goods production are geared to a mutual rate of growth which it is now impossible to maintain. Investment cannot continue to increase when consumption decreases; it cannot even increase when the *rate* of growth of consumption falls or when consumption is only maintained at a given level. Using this latter case as an example, we remember that an increase in consumption from 1000 to 1100 units (an increase of 10 percent) caused an increase in capital goods production from 50 to 100 units (an increase of 100 percent). Assuming that consumption is maintained at 1100 units, the capital goods industry would have to maintain a replacement demand of 55 (10 percent of 550 units of capital). This would mean a fall in investment expenditure from 100 to 55. The mere maintenance of a given level of consumption is, therefore, not enough to maintain investment. On the other hand, if investment is not continued at the former level, it will not be possible to maintain consumption, owing to unemployment in the investment goods industry.

We see that the principle of acceleration of derived demand helps to explain the downswing of the business cycle. Another cause of the rise and fall of investment is cyclical change in the interest rate.

Owing to credit creation, the rate of interest is low during the earlier part of the upswing, lower than it would be if the supply of loanable funds were limited to savings. The comparison of low rates of interest with high rates of profit leads to a rising investment activity, for the value of capital goods is high when high returns are capitalized by low interest rates. Suppose that a capital good costs $1 million to produce and that its expected yearly net return is $50,000. If the rate of interest should fall from 5 to 4 percent, the value of the capital good would tend to rise from $1 million to $1,250,000 (because $50,000 would be a 4 percent return on $1,250,000).

But assuming that, as the economy approaches full employment, further credit creation must be discontinued to avoid a dangerous price inflation. Credit creation was permissible as long as a substantial growth of the social product prevented price inflation. Once full employment is reached, however, credit creation must be stopped and the interest rate be raised. Production processes which were considered profitable at a lower rate may no longer be profitable: At the same expected return of $50,000 a capital good could be considered to be worth only $833,333 if the rate of interest had risen from 4 to 6 percent.

Another important factor to explain the overdevelopment of the capital goods industry during the prosperity period is the time-consuming character of investment goods production. If it takes time for the products or services produced with the new capital goods to emerge, it also takes time for the increased supply of these products and services to have an effect on prices. Profits therefore remain high for a considerable period, and during this time many new investment projects may get started. But when they are ready and begin to increase the supply of goods and services, the rate of profit may fall precipitously. In our example the real return would then be substantially lower than the anticipated $50,000.

These considerations reveal the probability that during a prosperity period expansion projects will be undertaken in the investment goods industries which cannot be finished under the same favorable price-cost relations that prevailed when the projects were started. This difficulty could be overcome only by a reduction of the rate of interest or by a further growth in consumption. Obviously, these two conditions are mutually exclusive if we are determined to avoid further credit creation. Interest rates could be decreased only by a rise in savings. Savings, however, can be increased only by a reduction of consumption, and it is on consumption that the demand for investment goods depends.[4]

Once the decline in investment goods production is accounted for, it is easy to show that unemployment and a decline in consumer spending will cause the economy to contract still further. The impact of a declining demand upon a supply that had recently been greatly expanded leads to a general fall in prices. Many individuals and firms are then reluctant to purchase because they expect prices to fall still further. The interest rate, however, does not fall readily. When goods are hard to sell and when credits remain frozen (in the form of unsold goods) the striving for monetary liquidity becomes general and tends to keep interest rates high. Furthermore, the so-called real rate of interest, that is, the rate which is corrected for changes in the general price level, rises as prices fall.

Downward adjustments of some commodity and factor prices would be necessary for the correction of the existing state of overinvestment (or underconsumption) through a regrouping of the factors of production. Changes in the price structure, however, get lost in a general deflationary spiral. Thus the equilibrating tendencies "may not be strong enough to restore equilibrium, since the disturbance of the latter will have still further increased in the meantime." [5]

KEYNES'S GENERAL EQUILIBRIUM THEORY

These considerations concerning the disequilibrating forces of contraction are likely to weaken confidence in the pricing system of the market economy. Where will this deflationary process end?

[4] Of course, not all private investment depends directly on consumption. This is only true for what we can call "induced" investment. "Initial" or "autonomous" investment arises from innovation and the hope that future consumption will finally justify the outlay. But even initial investment will be determined by anticipated profits and rates of interest, and will be subject to exaggerations owing to delayed price effects.

[5] Gottfried von Haberler, *Prosperity and Depression* (Geneva: League of Nations, 1939), p. 355.

To this question modern theory offers a clear answer. According to Lord Keynes,[6] a new equilibrium will be found and the downward process arrested when the national income has declined to the point where the net savings forthcoming at this level can be absorbed by net investments. Once all the income earned is again spent on either consumer goods or producers' goods, there is no reason why the deflationary process should continue.

When profitable investment opportunities are lacking even at low rates of interest, the level of the national income will fall to the point where the public wishes to spend its whole income on consumer goods (that is, where savings are exactly offset by dissavings or consumers' credit). When savings are zero, no investment is required to compensate for savings. The income level at which the whole income is spent on consumer goods may be called the "basic" level of the national income.[7] At this level a given volume of consumption is self-perpetuating because there is no danger of further "leaks" in total spending. This point is a point of equilibrium, but a point which may be far below full employment. For purposes of theoretical analysis this is the true rock bottom of depression in the private enterprise economy.

The Keynesian theory explodes the argument that the price mechanism tends constantly toward a full employment equilibrium; it shows that the price system does not always work satisfactorily in real life. It also shows that the disequilibrating forces may finally come to rest at an equilibrium position which is not brought about by full employment of productive resources but rather by such poverty that no saving occurs.

The classical theory assumed an accumulation of uninvested savings during depression, that is, an increasing supply of loanable funds, which would put the rate of interest under pressure; and it expected that, at low interest rates, enough investment outlets could be found. In Keynes's theory, savings do not accumulate but are destroyed by a fall in the national income which itself becomes the main equilibrating factor. When investments fall short of what savings would be at a given income level, the national income shrinks. As the national income decreases, consumption as well as saving will decrease; and it is to be expected that, as the nation becomes poorer, saving will fall proportionately more than consumption. Changes in national income thus tend to maintain equilibrium between investment and saving. The national income is lowered or raised until equality of investment and saving is established. Instead of one full employment equilibrium, this analysis suggests the possible existence of any number of equilibrium positions. All of them but one, however, are underemployment equilibria.

[6] Keynes, chap. 18.
[7] See Alvin H. Hansen, *Fiscal Policy and Business Cycles* (New York: W. W. Norton & Company, Inc., 1941), pp. 184–185.

The contribution of this general equilibrium theory lies not only in the analysis of the self-deflationary process of contraction but also in the suggestion that the unregulated market economy may, at times, lack reliable automatic powers to extricate itself from stagnation. The economy may hit the rock bottom of the depression and may stay there for an indefinite period if no profitable investment opportunities are found and if we are not willing to substitute government action for the automatic forces which are lacking.

Keynes's theory grew out of the stagnation of the 1930s. During these difficult years of seemingly permanent mass unemployment it was argued that the mature industrial economy lacked sufficient investment opportunities as a result of "the combined effect of the decline in population growth, together with the failure of any really important innovations of a magnitude sufficient to absorb large capital outlays." [8] Today this attitude seems overly pessimistic.

The pessimism of the 1930s probably rested also on a misconception of the so-called consumption function. True, it can be assumed that the rich save proportionately more than the poor; but this does not mean that the saved portion of the national income will increase in percentage terms with an absolute increase of the national income. On the contrary, a relatively strong increase in consumption may occur if the increase in income is, in part, inflationary rather than real, if income distribution is gradually altered in favor of the lower-income brackets, or if the appearance of new consumer goods and the tendency to "keep up with the Joneses" reduce thrift in favor of consumption.

The danger that our investment outlets will fall short of the amount needed to absorb all the savings which would be forthcoming at a high income level was decidedly exaggerated during the Great Depression. Nevertheless, because investment depends on profit expectations, it is to be expected that investment will sometimes be insufficient to sustain a high income level. The economy may then lack the power to lift itself from a depression it would not have had in the first place if the deflationary spiral could have been halted.

Once we admit that the national income may shrink, that expenditures for consumer goods may decline, and that savings, instead of pressing upon the credit market, may disappear through hoarding and debt cancellation, we have to admit, too, that anticipated rates of profit may be very low. When overinvestment leaves an aftermath of unused capital goods and discourages temporarily even normal replacement demand, and when the anticipated profits of yesterday turn out to be the losses of today —then it is not at all surprising that investment opportunities seem to disappear even in the atomic age.

[8] Hansen, pp. 184–185.

Depression may therefore develop into stagnation, and nobody can predict when such stagnation will be overcome. Only when the inducement to invest is strong enough to necessitate credit expansion will the situation improve. Investment will then be greater than saving, and the national income will increase, just as it had to shrink as long as investment tended to fall short of intended savings.

The strength of the impulses needed to overcome stagnation depends on the severity of the antecedent downward process, the depth it reaches, and the duration of the stagnation at this level.

Only very few economists would suggest that we wait until the necessary stimuli appear of their own accord; the consensus prescribes artificial inducements. However, regarding their nature and the timing of their application, substantial disagreement exists.

Government policies aiming at the maintenance of a sustained high level of employment will be discussed in Chapter 9.

CHAPTER 9

The Role
of Government
in the Private
Enterprise Economy

THE PUBLIC SECTOR

A private enterprise economy is inconceivable without a public sector in which the state satisfies so-called collective wants which cannot be taken care of in the private sector of the economy because no price can be charged for the services rendered. The consumers enjoy military security or stable monetary conditions passively and sometimes unconsciously. Since private enterprise cannot operate where prices cannot be charged or profits made, the government must step in, make the necessary arrangements, pay for them and distribute the costs among the citizens through taxation.

Where wants cannot be satisfied by private enterprise we deal with collective wants in an absolute sense. In addition there are collective wants which could *technically* be satisfied in the private sector because a price can be charged. Nevertheless, we may decide to shift their satisfaction to the public sector, for instance, where the nature of the production process favors government ownership. This situation exists in the so-called octopoid industries, which like transport, gas, electricity, telephone, and telegraph "are those involving the use of large and widely ramifying plant, which it would clearly be wasteful and inconvenient to duplicate, and whose installation, since it involves interference with public and private property, calls in any case for some intervention on the part of the State." [1] That public ownership might be preferable to mere public control (public utilities) can be due to the fact that nationalization would "obviate expense, overlapping and, above all, frictions, if, instead of there being a controlling authority *plus* a controlled one, control and operation were united in one and the same hand." [2] The argument may be extended to other cases of private monopoly, but it should be remembered that the government can try to eliminate cases of private market control possibly without having to take the ultimate step of nationalization.

Another reason for the collective satisfaction of wants, which could conceivably be taken care of in the private sector, can be found in the fact that private demand often tends to remain inadequate as long as it has to be satisfied at regular market prices. Outstanding are the cases of education and social security. The demand for education may be far too low either because incomes are so limited that there is no room left for education expenses in the individual demand schedules or else because "the persons requiring improvement have an imperfect or altogether erroneous conception of what they want." [3] The state, interested in a high level of education and making primary education compulsory, is forced to take education, at least in part, out of the individual preference function and the private sector of the economy. Very similar arguments apply in the case of social security.

Absolute collective wants are, as a rule, not very controversial, although there are differences of opinion concerning the length to which the state should go in satisfying these wants at the price of reduced individual want satisfaction. Where the state takes over areas in which the principles of the market economy *could* apply, the controversy multiplies. A clear dividing line cannot be drawn, but democratic processes have gradually pushed in the direction of a relatively growing public sector.

Since government activity must be paid for by taxation, the citizens of a democracy will instinctively oppose the growth of the public sector. Its size will be determined in part by the marginal utility of the voters' dollars in the private sector of the economy. However, this barrier can be pushed back by progressive taxation though, once more, it is impossible to come to precise results. Opinions will always differ as to the relative

[1] D. H. Robertson, *The Control of Industry* (London: Cambridge University Press, 1923), p. 87.

[2] A. C. Pigou, *Socialism Versus Capitalism* (New York: St. Martin's Press, Inc., 1939), pp. 45–46.

[3] John Stuart Mill, *Principles of Political Economy* (New York: The Colonial Press, 1899), vol. 2, p. 454.

merits of government expenditures or the relative marginal utilities of money spent in the private and public sectors.

The introduction of progressive taxation into our argument has nothing to do with the desire to use the tax system to achieve a more equal income distribution. Progressive taxation is needed to make room for increased government expenditures in individual households, particularly when we consider that mere proportional taxation could easily become regressive in percentage terms. The connection between tax system and personal income distribution will be taken up presently.

The very concept "collective want" implies that the satisfaction of collective wants should be in the interest of all citizens. This rule would eliminate special treatment of selected groups, were it not for the fact that some of these groups succeed in procuring favors by arguing that they are so important for the economy as a whole that anything that benefits them benefits the nation. This trend of the private enterprise system toward growth of the public sector via the demand of pressure groups is not always beneficial. Sometimes special interests argue against an extension of the activities of the state where this extension is desirable. A recent case was the opposition of the American Medical Association to Medicare.

Resistance to the growth of the public sector rests often on the mistaken assumption that such expansion implies the operation of state enterprise in the private sector of the economy and in unfair competition with private enterprise. In reality, there are only a few cases where state ownership and operation of producing units are called for. Indeed, there is no reason whatever why the state should enter the private sector where it operates reasonably well. Competition with private enterprise on the basis of the unfair advantage of financing losses with the taxpayers' money must be excluded.

Normally, the activities of the government should support private enterprise. Where the state needs the products of private industry, tax money, spent in procuring the needed material, flows right back into the private sector. Where aggregate private demand falls short of the amount that would secure a high employment level, government deficit spending may maintain or increase a level of *private* economic activity that otherwise would fall. These most important fiscal policies will be discussed later in this chapter.

A summary of this introductory discussion of the public sector in the private enterprise economy can claim that state regulation of private economic activity should, wherever possible, be *indirect* rather than *direct* and should *support* the forces of the market rather than *interfere* with them.

One type of policy can be exposed as clearly contradicting the basic principles of the market system; this is the policy designed to secure for different groups a *fixed* portion of the national income. The distribution of income is part and parcel of the whole pricing process, and to guarantee stable returns under changing conditions (to freeze a given pattern of distribution) means to destroy the allocation process on which the private enterprise economy rests. When one group is guaranteed absolute income security, it enjoys this advantage at the cost of security for the rest. When all groups are given complete and proportionate income security, the scheme becomes absurd, at least in a market economy.

THE CORRECTION OF INCOME DISTRIBUTION

The most important attack on excessive inequality of income distribution in the private enterprise system is found in the tendency of the public sector to grow relative to the private sector. This tendency works as a two-pronged drive. (1) The indirect way of financing public expenditures requires and permits preferential treatment of lower income groups and the imposition of heavier burdens on the higher income brackets through death duties, steeply progressive income taxes, different treatment of earned and unearned income, and the like. (2) In the satisfaction of collective wants, the poor and the rich share alike. In the public sector, therefore, the system of want satisfaction differs radically from the demand and supply situation in the private sector.

We have already seen that these principles would apply even if we had no specific intention of toning down the inequalities of income distribution. If such intentions are added, there is further inducement to permit a relative growth of the public sector. However, we have also seen that the logic of the private enterprise system sets limits to the trend toward progressive taxation. When the receiver of a high income in the United States has to earn (as far as the Federal income tax alone is concerned) at the margin $100 to be permitted to retain $30, the incentive to try to increase his income may be weakened, with negative effects for the productivity of the economy. A high marginal tax rate makes leisure cheap, discourages risk taking, and may even impair the division of labor, as James E. Meade has convincingly shown.[4] He argues that if a man has to earn £200 to be able to spend £5 to have a certain piece of work done, he may well decide to do the work himself, because only if he is 40 times more productive in his special job will it be profitable for him to hire help!

There are other means by which the state can attempt to reduce the inequality of income distribution, some even more objectionable than

[4] James E. Meade, *Planning and the Price Mechanism* (London: George Allen & Unwin Ltd., 1948), p. 40.

excessively progressive taxation. An example is the reduction of the prices of certain staple foods, a policy of direct interference with the market mechanism, which ought to be avoided. If generally applied, the measure leads to an artificial distortion of prices with undesirable consequences for the supply of the commodities in question and unavoidable violation of the basic principle of consumers' sovereignty. If applied to special groups, the measure will be degrading. Similarly, rent control, one of the most frequently found instances of interference with the price system, may eventually lead to a situation in which (owing to the reduction in new housing and removal of the inducement to economize with respect to the available space) the deterioration of the demand-supply relation becomes so great that further government activities are called for, such as the provision of public housing and minute rationing.

Perhaps the most promising long-run approach to more equal income distribution is the provision of adequate educational opportunities. As inequalities in income distribution mean inequalities in educational opportunities, they tend to perpetuate themselves to some extent. High income, invested in the development of special skills through higher education, creates more earning power, which in turn leads to higher income, out of which expensive training for the children in higher income groups can be paid. Poverty, on the other hand, deprives the children of the poor of proper educational opportunities, weakens their earning power, and so tends to perpetuate itself.

According to A. C. Pigou,[5] these considerations constitute a powerful argument for *some sort* of change aimed at increased equality. They also show how we can get at the very root of the problem and still maintain a free market economy. A determined effort can be made to free educational opportunity as far as possible from limitations imposed by uneven distribution of income.[6] But free education alone does not solve the problem, as long as those who are eager to enjoy the advantages of higher learning cannot be maintained out of private means during the training period.

Educational reforms (through their long-run effect on the national product) are proof that the government's efforts toward greater equality need not always take from the rich what they give to the poor. If this were so, if the public sector were as parasitic as some writers want us to believe, production would cease altogether once the public sector had

[5] Pigou, p. 22.

[6] "There is no extravagance more prejudicial to the growth of national wealth than that wasteful negligence which allows genius that happens to be born of lowly parentage to expend itself in lowly work. No change would conduce so much to a rapid increase of material wealth as an improvement in our schools, and especially those of the middle grades, provided it is combined with an extensive system of scholarships, which will enable the clever son of a working man to rise gradually from school to school till he has the best theoretical and practical education which the age can give."—Alfred Marshall, *Principles of Economics*, 8th ed. (New York: St. Martin's Press, Inc., 1925), p. 212.

devoured the private sector, as in Soviet Russia today. Actually, government policies can help maintain and even increase the income stream, and some of these policies may, in rare cases, operate through the maintenance of a high consumption level via a more equal income distribution. It is not always necessary for the government to take in order to give, just as higher wages need not always be taken out of profits, or as one country's gains in international trade are possible without a corresponding loss by other countries.

RESTRICTION OF MONOPOLISTIC PRACTICES

Minimum requirement for an antimonopolistic government policy should be the abstention from measures which indirectly tend to strengthen monopolistic tendencies in the private sector of the economy. Competition rests on the free movement of commodities, labor, and capital. Whenever the government restricts mobility, it tends to strengthen the monopolistic forces in the economy. A case in point is the protection of domestic producers against foreign competition through tariffs, quotas, exchange controls, and the like. Once foreign competition has been excluded, it seems only natural that domestic producers should try to regulate competition in the sheltered domestic market. The chances that they may achieve a monopolistic position are strengthened. But the government's inconsistency is not restricted to its anticompetitive policies in international trade. In the domestic sphere, too, the government will often be subject to pressure by interested groups to introduce policies which stifle competition. Regulatory policies may be defensible, however, where the government tries to strengthen the countervailing power of previously weak bargainers.

We have seen that the concentration of economic power was to a large extent achieved with the aid of corporation laws which permitted monopolistic controls that exceeded the needs of modern technology. These laws (which were often very lucrative for the states that passed them) were not designed to minimize the dangers of monopoly. To deal decisively with the monopoly problem these laws would have to be rewritten. Corporations, for instance, would be denied the right to own stocks in other corporations or the possibility of effecting interlocking officeholding.[7]

Patent laws are a special case of well-meant government policy which may support monopolistic tendencies. Patents are supposed to promote the progress of science and useful arts. Experience often shows, however, that patents can be used for a system of industrial control (even on an interna-

[7] Fritz Machlup, *The Political Economy of Monopoly* (Baltimore: The Johns Hopkins Press, 1952), pp. 236–249.

tional basis) which stifles new enterprise, divides markets, limits productive capacity, and shields against charges of conspiracy.[8] An important part of the government's antimonopolistic policy is, therefore, a patent law which achieves its ends with a minimum of danger that the patent may become "an invitation to predatory litigation."[9]

The government can try to support competitive enterprise through a tax system which encourages competitive small business against monopolistic large enterprise. Such a policy, however, may easily become arbitrary and discriminate against the economies of mass production. Monopolistic profits are, unfortunately, much too elusive to be made the subject of special taxation, and yet it is monopoly rather than mere bigness or efficiency against which such a policy should be aimed. More successful may be a credit policy which sees to it that small business has access to credit at reasonable rates of interest. These credits could come from public credit institutions, or they could be given by private institutions under public guarantee.

Competitive pressure may be exerted by public corporations. Care must be taken, however, that this competitive pressure is not unfair, as when the cost of government agencies is artificially reduced or losses are covered through public revenues.

The government may control prices charged by public utilities. These public utilities, though monopolistic for technological reasons, are still embedded in a competitive economy, and thus the task of cost determination and price regulation is not unmanageably difficult. The socialist economy faces a far more difficult task; where production is completely in the hands of the government it is very difficult to correct monopolistic pricing through a comparison with competitive pricing.

The state may acquire the ownership of monopolistic industries. Although this action is often referred to as "nationalization" or "socialization," it does not imply the introduction of socialism if state ownership remains the exception to the rule of private enterprise and if such nationalization is based upon clear evidence of monopolistic power. In this case, the difference between government ownership and government control is not decisive. A modicum of public ownership can be tolerated by private enterprise economy, but only prevailing circumstances dictate whether

[8] See Wendell Berge, *Cartels: Challenge to a Free World* (Washington, D.C.: Public Affairs Press, 1944), pp. 38–39.

[9] "In order to curb monopolistic abuse, consideration should be given to proposals for compulsory licensing of patents, and for licensing without restriction upon licensee or buyer of the patented article. Since much of the control exercised by monopolies proceeds not so much directly from the patent as from aggressive use of infringement suits and the costs they impose upon small competitors, appropriate protection of the defendant in such cases should be provided."—Howard S. Ellis, "Monopoly and Unemployment," in *Postwar Economic Studies No. 4, Prices, Wages, and Employment* (Washington, D.C.: Board of Governors of the Federal Reserve System, May 1946), pp. 85–86.

state ownership or state control of private management is preferable. The issue of monopoly is not limited to the private enterprise system. Not all monopoly problems are solved when the state owns and operates all material means of production.

THE EMPLOYMENT BUDGET

In discussing "full" employment policies it is impossible to give a reasonably precise definition of full employment. Abba P. Lerner [10] suggested that full employment is reached when inflation begins. But price inflation begins very gradually and may even continue when employment falls. Similarly vague is William H. Beveridge's [11] definition that full employment means "having always more vacant jobs than unemployed men." This definition points out that labor enjoys a sellers' market under full employment, a situation that tends to be inflationary. Bertil Ohlin [12] explains that such a situation is not necessarily a blessing. It leads to bottlenecks and an excessive labor turnover, and because of its inflationary impact the government may turn to price controls and rationing. In the field of international trade balance of payments difficulties would follow, with the probable result of foreign exchange controls.

These considerations suggest that it may be better to aim for something less than "full" employment. A high employment level, though one of the most important aims of economic policy, is not the only goal. We should not try to reach it at all cost. A reasonable degree of monetary stability and the maintenance of economic freedom may be at variance with the desire to reach or to maintain full employment.

That economic freedom may conflict with a full employment policy is already implied in the relatively greater ease with which a totalitarian regime may handle the employment problem. But even a nontotalitarian system may be forced into direct controls (and a corresponding loss of freedom) if it overemphasizes the employment aspects of its policies. Clearly, then, it is necessary to find a compromise between employment policies on one side and monetary stability and economic freedom on the other.

When employment policies are being formulated in a private enterprise system in peace, it is unwise to make major concessions concerning

[10] Abba P. Lerner, *Economics of Employment* (New York: McGraw-Hill, Inc., 1951).
[11] William H. Beveridge, *Full Employment in a Free Society* (New York: W. W. Norton & Company, Inc., 1945), p. 18.
[12] Bertil Ohlin, *The Problem of Employment Stabilization* (New York: Columbia University Press, 1949), chap. 1.

economic freedoms. In the following discussion it is taken for granted, therefore, that free collective bargaining is maintained, that the price system remains free of controls (with the exception of monetary and fiscal controls), and that currency convertibility is maintained. Furthermore, since most of the direct controls are the outgrowth of monetary instability, the goal is to achieve a high level of economic activity with a minimum of price inflation.

It has been shown that mass unemployment may develop in the private enterprise economy when savings exceed investments and investment and consumption spending both decline in a vicious circle. A modern government has the task of stopping this downward spiral at the earliest possible moment. How is this to be accomplished?

Where automatic safeguards are not operating, monetary and fiscal policies must be used. These policies concern aggregate spending and should be designed to protect the economy against the evils of both deflation and inflation. To avoid inflation, modern governments have always tried (though not always successfully, by any means) to keep the money supply sufficiently limited. Monetary policy has also been intended to guard the economy against harmful price deflations. More recently, however, it has been proved that monetary policy does not work equally well in both directions. Inflation can always be avoided through credit restriction if the people are prepared to face the possible consequences of price deflation and unemployment. But monetary policy alone may not be able to reverse a deflationary trend and create full employment. The monetary authority can make more money available, but it cannot make people borrow. If private enterprise does not anticipate profits, firms will not be willing to invest even at the lowest practicable interest rates. Monetary policy has then reached the end of its rope, and it will be necessary to turn to fiscal policy.

For its policy to maintain employment through an adequate amount of aggregate spending, a modern government needs a new type of budget, "which will be concerned with income and expenditure of the community as a whole, not only with public finance, ... will take the manpower of the country as a datum and plan outlay to that datum rather than by consideration of financial resources." [13] This budget need not always in-

[13] Beveridge, p. 30. In the United States the Employment Act of 1946 declares "that it is the continuing policy and responsibility of the Federal Government to use all practicable means consistent with its needs and obligations and other essential considerations of national policy, with the assistance and cooperation of industry, agriculture, labor, and State and local governments, to coordinate and utilize all its plans, functions, and resources for the purpose of creating and maintaining, in a manner calculated to foster and promote free competitive enterprise and the general welfare, conditions under which there will be afforded useful employment opportunities, including self-employment, for those able, willing, and seeking to work, and to promote maximum employment, production, and purchasing power."

volve deficit spending and may be subscribed to by persons of otherwise widely diverging viewpoints, since it is not more than a survey that estimates forthcoming expenditures in the private and public sector of the economy.

Differences of opinion exist, of course, regarding the policy conclusions which should be drawn from the results of such a survey. Policies could be proposed that are incompatible with the institutions of a private enterprise economy. But a variety of powerful measures can be employed, which do in no way interfere with the pricing process or the economic actions of the members of a market economy. On the contrary, the maintenance of adequate aggregate demand will create a healthy climate for the operations of private enterprise.

The acceptance of this new attitude toward government employment policies is astonishingly unanimous in the western world today. Only concerning the details of the policy and its aggressiveness and timing do the experts disagree. The nature of the policies chosen will depend in part on how high the sights are set—whether, for instance, 5 percent or only 3 percent of unemployment is considered bearable—and how much importance is attached to monetary stability, international equilibrium, and economic freedom.

In analyzing the elements that constitute the total flow of a nation's expenditures, the following categories are discernible:

1. Private consumption expenditures (C)
2. Private investment expenditures (I)
3. Public expenditures financed by regular revenue (R), that is, without increasing the public debt
4. Public expenditures financed by loans (L) which increase the public debt
5. The balance of international trade (B) which may be either positive (excess of exports over imports) or negative (excess of imports over exports)

It is desirable that aggregate expenditure $(C + I + R + L) \pm B$ be equal to F, which stands for the output capacity of the economy at or near full employment. If F is larger than E, which stands for aggregate expenditure, the difference would be U, or unemployment. If E is larger than F, the result would be price inflation.

Government policies can try to influence one or more of these items. As a matter of fact, the elements of aggregate expenditure are so closely interrelated that policies that influence one cannot help having some effect upon one or more of the others. For example, if the government tries to finance increased expenditures by raising tax rates, it must be assumed that we pay for the increase in R by a decrease in C or I or both. Increased government expenditures out of loans L, on the other hand, will increase C and I if the money borrowed was newly created money. As C and I increase, R will automatically increase unless the government decides to use its increased revenue to reduce its debt. If the debt was held by the banks, the effect may be deflationary; if it was held outside banks, C and I may increase.

Suppose that government analysts have found that during the next year aggregate expenditure E will fall short of F, the output capacity of the economy and that the government is charged with the responsibility of proposing ways and means by which total outlay can be increased. Three different roads are open:

1. Whatever the government does, it desires neither to change its expenditures and revenues nor to increase the public debt.

2. The government is willing to increase its expenditures but unwilling to raise the public debt.

3. The government permits the public debt to increase.

When public expenditures and the public debt remain unchanged, the possibilities to increase aggregate expenditure are limited to measures which might induce private economies to spend more on consumption and investment. Monetary policy can do relatively little if private investment refuses to be induced by low rates of interest; and a change in the tax structure (which leaves tax revenues unchanged) can, at the best, have only a modest influence on $C + I$. There are many other policies to consider (agricultural and commercial policies, for instance), but, again, these policies can decisively affect the magnitude of aggregate demand only if the government is willing to spend more than before (for example, for farm support or foreign loans and grants).

When government expenditures are increased but the public debt is not permitted to rise, the effect on aggregate spending is not much greater. This might seem to be a conservative road to high employment because it avoids "deficit spending." Actually, however, it could turn out to be, in practice, less conservative than deficit spending. If R is to be increased without an increase in L, money has to be collected through additional taxation, and the increase in R is therefore compensated by a decreased C and I:

> In a serious depression, elimination of the bulk of unemployment by this method would probably require exorbitant increases in expenditures and of tax rates, implying a drastic redistribution of income, and the system would soon become incompatible with a free-enterprise economy. . . . This may sound paradoxical to many, for what most conservatives are afraid of is a deficit and a growing public debt. Their obsession with the public debt may thus lead them into a much more dangerous alley.[14]

[14] Gottfried Haberler in "Five Views on the Murray Full Employment Bill," *Review of Economic Statistics*, vol. 27 (August 1945), pp. 108–109.

Therefore, the only effective means by which government can increase expenditure is a policy that raises the public debt at least temporarily.

To understand the economic implications of a rising public debt we have to distinguish two kinds of government borrowing:

1. If the money is borrowed from savings, the effect is similar to the effect of increased taxation; that is, total expenditure will increase only under special circumstances. The savings of the private sector of the economy, instead of being cut into by taxation, are borrowed by the government, with the result that there will be an increase in total expenditure only if the borrowed sums would have run to waste for lack of profitable investment opportunities. The government, not limited to profitable investments, can spend these funds and maintain a given income level. Whether the method of borrowing uninvested savings is superior to the method of taxing them away depends partly on psychological circumstances. The effect of government borrowing upon private investment may conceivably be less unfavorable than the effect of taxation, unless the increase in the public debt is considered very dangerous by the business community.

2. The government can borrow newly created funds. If newly created money is spent by the government, private expenditures C and I need not decrease, and total spending is likely to grow with favorable effects on C, I, and R. Here, then, is the most powerful instrument at the disposal of the government in the latter's effort to raise aggregate spending.

Cases (1) and (2) have entirely different monetary implications. If the government spends borrowed savings, it will affect the income level only if these savings would have remained uninvested. If the government disburses newly created funds, total spending is sure to increase and to stop the deflationary spiral. The government may incur a deficit in two ways. It can spend more than it earns from taxation, that is, it can raise expenditures without raising taxes. But it can also spend more than it receives by maintaining its expenditures while simultaneously cutting taxes.

1. By reducing taxes while maintaining public expenditures at a given level, the government may stimulate either private consumption or private investment. This tax-remission program designed to increase total expenditure is favored by those who want to keep direct government spending as low as possible and to achieve the desired effects, in the main, through the private sector of the economy. This policy seems to be better adapted to the basic structure of the private enterprise economy than is increased government spending. The difficulty is that, given a certain amount of government deficit created through tax remission, the effect on total expenditure is much less certain than it would be if an equal amount had been spent by the government. C and I may not increase by the full amount of the tax reduction. To achieve an increase of this amount in

total aggregate expenditure, a larger budget deficit will probably be needed in the case of tax remission than in the case of government spending. Once more, therefore, the seemingly more conservative approach may lead to the bigger deficit.

2. Direct government deficit spending is the most powerful and reliable way to increase or to maintain employment through an adequate total outlay. In making sure that newly created money will actually be spent (and not only used to increase liquid balances), deficit spending "is the logical sequel of central bank policy." [15] If the monetary authority is willing but not able to maintain enough money in active circulation, deficit spending can be used as a device to increase expenditure, because government investment is independent of profit anticipations. Deficit spending, of course, is not independent of monetary policy. But in this relation between monetary and fiscal policy the monetary authority is only *permitting* the expansion, whereas deficit spending supplies the driving force.

Before we discuss different kinds of deficit spending we must understand clearly that the government does not as a rule carry out the production activities which are implied in these spending programs. The government employs the help of private firms, stimulates the demand for the products of private firms, and avoids the mistake of competing with private firms—unless such competition is meant as antimonopolistic policy. Increasing government spending, therefore, is less likely to bring about fundamental changes in our economic system than is often taken for granted.

Deficit spending can be carried through in different ways and with different intentions. It is advisable to distinguish: (1) pump priming, (2) countercyclical spending, and (3) permanent deficit spending.

1. The implication of pump priming is that government deficit spending is a limited and temporary injection of money and that the mechanism (the pump, the market economy), once successfully primed, will be able to continue to operate without further help. Pump priming is a stimulus that pulls the economy out of a depression, the igniting spark that starts a stalled economic machine. It rests on the belief that the private sector of the economy has not lost all its vitality, though it may need help in overcoming the effects of a preceding process of self-deflation. Pump priming does not aim at more than the initiation of a period of revival.

A policy of pump priming is difficult to administer. The principle of acceleration of derived demand shows how hard it is to taper off government spending in such a way that total investment, employment, and national income continue to increase. Pump priming can succeed only when, with increased optimism, private investments are undertaken that

[15] John H. Williams, "Deficit Spending," *American Economic Review*, vol. 30 (February 1941), p. 55.

do not depend exclusively, as do induced investments, on the government's initial expenditures.

2. A policy of countercyclical spending is more ambitious. In its milder forms it proposes stable tax rates, which lead to fluctuating tax revenues during the business cycle, combined with a shifting of government expenditures (as far as they can be shifted at all) into periods of recession or depression. A more forceful application of the same principle would lower tax rates during the downswing and simultaneously step up government expenditures through public works. In both cases the budget would be overbalanced during prosperity.

The logic of these proposals is obvious. The peaks of the cycle would be chopped off and the troughs filled in. While economic fluctuations would not disappear, they would be dampened. Theoretically, at least, it would be possible to carry through this countercyclical taxing and spending policy without a permanent increase in the public debt, because the budget could be balanced if one period were averaged with another and a yearly balancing of the budget were not required. It is doubtful, though, that democratic processes enable the government to muster the fortitude to apply the principle of compensatory spending with equal zeal to prosperity and depression. During prosperity they must refrain from spending when government revenues increase, in order to be able to pay off the debt which was incurred during the depression.

While countercyclical spending is sound economics it is not necessarily appealing to the layman. The layman often fails to see that it is sound to spend in bad times and to be thrifty in good times. He wants the government's budget to balance every year; the government is to spend in good times but to cut expenditures to the bone when times are bad. This was, indeed, the basic mistake of traditional budget policy. The government raised taxes and cut expenditures during the downswing, thus accentuating economic fluctuations which originated in the private sector of the economy. During periods of prosperity, on the other hand, government investment was superimposed on private investment as increased tax revenues seemed to invite such additional spending. An anticyclical fiscal policy means that we give up these understandable misconceptions and consider deficit budgeting during depressions a virtue rather than a sin.[16]

A countercyclical policy is easy to apply with the so-called built-in stabilizer which automatically uses the taxing and spending processes of the government as a counterweight to fluctuations in the private sector of the economy. The Committee for Economic Development [17] states the principles of such a policy as follows:

[16] Gunnar Myrdal, "Fiscal Policy in the Business Cycle," *American Economic Review*, vol. 29 (March 1939), p. 184.

[17] Committee for Economic Development, *The Stabilizing Budget Policy* (New York: CED, 1950), p. 8.

Set tax rates to balance the budget and provide a surplus for debt retirement at an agreed high level of employment and national income. Having set these rates, leave them alone unless there is some major change in national policy or condition of national life.

The advantages of this policy are obvious. When national income falls, government revenues decline in relation to government expenditures, and vice versa. Furthermore, certain government expenditures increase automatically as private economic activity declines. Unemployment compensation, farm income supports, and similar relief payments add to the discrepancy between government receipts and disbursements. Far from being dangerous, this deficit is the crucial feature of the stabilizer.

The more ambitious compensatory policies want to operate with tax cuts and public works programs. They lose, therefore, the advantage of automaticity and require a careful diagnosis of the cyclical position in which we find ourselves at a given point of time. "To make such a diagnosis presents a problem soluble for the past, with hindsight, but hardly for the present, without the gift of foresight." [18] Obviously, it is very difficult to determine just when the government should stop deficit spending and when it should try to overbalance the budget. The record of forecasting is poor.[19] Governments lack simple criteria. The danger is great that they will be tempted to use deficit spending whenever a substantial amount of unemployment is present. But if unemployment alone is made the criterion of government spending, the spending might continue through most of the upswing. Too little leeway would then be left for private investment. Another danger is that people are too eager to fight pockets of unemployment, which are caused by a normal shift in demand, with the heavy guns of increasing total expenditure.

To the difficulties of forecasting is added the delay encountered before countercyclical measures take effect. For "the appropriateness of the action will depend upon how well it fits the situation when it takes

[18] Fritz Machlup, in *Financing American Prosperity*, ed. Paul T. Homan and Fritz Machlup (New York: Twentieth Century Fund, Inc., 1945), p. 455.

[19] "The poor record of forecasters in the past warns us to the dangers of this course. Thus in the fall of 1945 virtually all of the economic forecasters predicted that there would be a tremendous postwar slump which would create from 8 to 12 million unemployed by the spring of 1946. This did not occur; and, instead, we had rising production and even more rapidly rising prices with substantially full employment. For us to have embarked on a tremendous program of public works at this time, as the forecasters had urged, would not only have been unnecessary but it would have intensified and heightened the inflation. In fact, the accumulation of a surplus and the retiring of a portion of the public debt beginning in the latter part of 1946 helped to dampen down inflation and prevented matters from becoming still worse. Again in the winter of 1949 the official economic forecasters stated that the real problem was inflation, to prevent which they wanted further restrictive controls. Since it then developed that we were in a recession which continued for some time, the putting into effect of these recommendations could only have deepened the recession."—*Monetary, Credit, and Fiscal Policies* (Douglas Committee Report), 81st Cong., 2d Sess., Sen. Doc. 129, 1950), pp. 14–15.

effect, not how well it fits the situation when the decision is made. But when the decision is made no one knows what the situation will be when the action takes effect." [20]

But while these difficulties are great, they are not insuperable. We can increase the flexibility of fiscal policy to some extent. As far as tax reduction is concerned, "it might be possible to short-cut this process by legislation providing for a tax cut to go into effect automatically under certain conditions, or by giving the President authority to reduce certain taxes under specified conditions." [21] Public works can be authorized and blueprinted in advance to be started with a minimum of delay. This planning is not easy. Apart from political and technical difficulties in the budgeting process, it is hard to find projects that are useful, noncompetitive with private industry, and that can be discontinued without loss as soon as general economic conditions demand that government spending be reduced. However, through long-term planning, necessary work in the public sector, such as road construction, social housing, or flood control, should preferably be scheduled for periods of low private investment.

The proper application of countercyclical policy requires considerable moral fortitude. The conservative mistake of trying to balance the budget every year must be avoided, as well as the opposite extreme. The Committee for Economic Development envisages "the really frightening possibility . . . that we shall oscillate between adherence to the annual balance principle in prosperity and belief in compensatory spending in depression." [22] A tendency in this direction certainly exists, since politically it is the way of least resistance. Deficit spending would only be interrupted but never reversed, and the public debt would continue to increase even in peacetime. Apart from the possible dangers of a growing public debt, such a course could not claim the counterbalancing advantages of compensatory spending, would tend to exaggerate the boom, lead to inflation, and permanently enlarge the public sector of the economy.

THE DANGER OF INFLATION

Since modern employment policies are creating inflationary tendencies, the dangers implied for the private enterprise economy must be studied.

[20] Committee for Economic Development, *Defense against Recession: Policy for Greater Economic Stability* (New York: CED, 1954), pp. 31–32.
[21] Committee for Economic Development, *Defense against Recession: Policy for Greater Economic Stability*, p. 33. See also "The Problem of Economic Instability," a report prepared under the auspices of the American Economic Association, *American Economic Review*, vol. 40 (September 1950), p. 524.
[22] Committee for Economic Development, *The Stabilizing Budget Policy*, p. 7.

Consider first the different concepts of inflation: *Credit inflation* means creation of money through a process of credit expansion in the banking system. The term is neutral. Whether credit inflation is good or bad depends on the circumstances and particularly on the state of employment. It need not lead to price inflation if increasing employment and output offset the increase in aggregate demand. This situation is called *hidden inflation*. *Price inflation* is characterized by an increase in the general price level. If increased demand is the main cause of the rise in prices, it is *pull-type inflation;* if rising costs are the cause, it is called *push-type inflation*. The causes of the latter are often monopolistic price-and-wage policies rather than monetary policies, though monetary policies are in this case at least "permissive." It is important to keep in mind that changes in the general price level are always connected with changes in the relative price structure. This fact is extremely important in a market economy. *Creeping inflation* is a continuous or intermittent price inflation of relatively modest amount per annum. The concept is vague because opinions differ regarding what degree of price inflation is tolerable. To clarify this matter Alvin H. Hansen [23] suggests the concept of *pure inflation:* "a condition in which prices rise without any appreciable increase in output." He contends that "at no time in our history, nor indeed in that of any other country, can it be shown that price increases have injured the economy and the general welfare if in the period in question the increase in aggregate output has exceeded percentagewise the increase in prices. *Runaway inflation* is a price inflation over which the monetary authority has lost control. It occurs when the public expects prices to rise so fast and so continuously that to save becomes foolish, and people tend to spend their money with increasing rapidity. The result is *hyperinflation,* sometimes of astronomical proportions, in which voluntary savings are zero, the velocity of circulation of money is extremely high, the government is forced into continuous money creation (since tax revenues lose most of their purchasing power during the process of tax collection), and output falls as a result of enormous distortions which develop in the production process. An alternative to excessive price inflation, finally, is *repressed inflation* which occurs when the government tries to cure the symptoms of price inflation through a freezing of prices and wages, an attempt which implies rationing and production controls.

Credit inflation is necessary to increase aggregate outlay; it supports the most promising attempts to raise the employment level and check a process of self-deflation. Suppose that the government can create or maintain a desired employment level and can also maintain stable prices. This seemingly ideal state of affairs has been called *hidden inflation* to point out

[23] Alvin H. Hansen, *The American Economy* (New York: McGraw-Hill, Inc., 1957), p. 43.

(1) that a credit inflation has taken place, (2) that the creation of new money has lowered the interest rate, and (3) that investment has been artificially stimulated. The theory of neutral money holds that in the case of increasing productive efficiency it would be better to let prices decline to the lower cost level and that the maintenance of a stable *general* price level leads to a disruptive effect in the structure of *relative* prices.[24] The difference between lower costs and higher prices leads to artificial profits. These profits, together with the lowering of the rate of interest (implied in credit creation!) cause the very condition that promotes overinvestment.

Some economists, therefore, do not even consider a stable price level good enough. However, we cannot be perfectionists at a time when simple price stability seems preferable to creeping inflation, yet politically out of reach. Rather, we have to ask the practical question: can we live with creeping inflation if this should be the price for a sustained high level of employment?

Nobody knows the answer, but if it can be given at all it must depend on such factors as the degree of price inflation, the experience of the people with inflation, the rise in output, and the distortions in the structure of production, which may result from a cheap money policy. Since a case of hidden inflation is potentially dangerous, the case of creeping inflation is even more critical.

More important than the rise in prices is the comparison of the percentage increase in prices with the percentage increase in output. Suppose that output increases more than prices. Is creeping inflation within this margin safe? Again, no definitive answer is possible. A politically feasible compromise between employment and monetary stability must be found. The possible destabilizing effects of credit inflation will be less dangerous in a system in which the government has assumed responsibility for the maintenance of aggregate demand. Also, the maintenance of a satisfactory state of employment is so important that we must sacrifice for it the considerations of social justice that come to mind when we discuss inflation problems. Price inflation has rightly been called the most unjust of all taxes. But from a general social point of view, widespread unemployment would be even worse than creeping inflation.

It is most essential that a creeping inflation be kept from developing into a runaway inflation. The psychological nature of the problem makes it impossible to know precisely when this is likely to occur. However, there is safety as long as the inducement to save remains unimpaired.

It would be dangerous to argue that runaway inflation is a thing of the past since the government can instantly repress price developments. It is true that repressed inflation may take the place of price inflation,

[24] See F. A. Hayek, *Prices and Production* (New York: Crowell-Collier and Macmillan, Inc., 1932).

but it may be even more objectionable for those who want to maintain the market economy in good working order.

Chapter 5 showed what price fixing implies. Prices are kept below the level determined by demand and supply; and since, at the official price, supply falls short of demand, demand must be restricted by rationing. Price control and rationing of selected commodities, however, have the effect of directing excess purchasing power into the markets of other goods whose prices are still free to rise. The production of these commodities becomes more profitable, and the whole production process is given a wrong twist until practically all goods are included in the control scheme.

When price control has reached its logical conclusion, when all prices are frozen, the market ceases to function and central planning must take over. The market economy has become a planned economy. These developments are practically unavoidable in times of total war, when a single aim predominates and freedoms that characterize the private enterprise economy are voluntarily and temporarily suspended. The problem takes on a different complexion when these same direct controls are the peacetime result of ambitious full-employment policies of a welfare state. Those who want to maintain a private enterprise economy will not be willing to pay this price in terms of economic freedoms for a policy that, after all, cures only the symptoms of the disease. Once the function of relative price movements is understood, it is obvious that a system that freezes all prices either will not work or will work only when the direct controls have become integrated in a central plan. If production is not centrally guided, repressed inflation will lead to distortions in the production process that can be even more dangerous than those which accompany an open price inflation.

Since in repressed inflation the newly created money is not permitted to find a vent in price inflation, the pressure mounts. The "inflationary gap" between commodities that are for sale at low prices in restricted quantities, and the money income that would like to buy more of these commodities, increases. An ever-growing amount of purchasing power remains idle. If this pressure is permitted to rise too high, and if the controlling powers of the government are not strong enough, the repressed inflation will erupt in open inflation (via black markets).

After a period of repressed inflation it may be necessary to burn up the excess purchasing power that has been accumulating and to close the inflationary gap through price inflation. Another method, used by several countries after World War II, consists of removing excess purchasing power by blocking existing money reserves and converting old money into new money at a chosen ratio. After such drastic methods are employed, market forces must be permitted to create a totally new price pattern.

THE PUBLIC DEBT

One more problem—the growth of the public debt—remains to be discussed in connection with deficit spending. Is a growing national debt a danger for the economy? Does it lead to inflation or stifle private enterprise?

The dangers of a growing public debt have generally been overstated. The major fear seems to be that the debt will, at some future date, have to be repaid and that this will put a heavy burden on our future. Taxes will weigh more and more on the private sector of the economy. Finally, when the limit of taxation is reached, the government will have to revert to inflationary means in financing the debt service.

There are several points that this pessimistic attitude fails to see. The amount of debt should always be considered in comparison with the size of the national income. If the policy of deficit spending lifts the national income to a higher level than would otherwise prevail, if it helps to employ factors of production which would otherwise remain idle, the debt is really no burden at all. Nor is an increasing debt in itself inflationary. Whether it is or not depends on the methods of financing and on the general economic conditions prevailing at the time. Taxes that are used to pay interest on the debt go right back to the taxpayers as a group. The transfer of income from taxpayer to bondholder may influence the economy favorably or unfavorably, depending on the circumstances; but a domestic debt cannot burden the people as a whole. Also, while the public debt may be reduced (as in the case of countercyclical spending), it does not have to be paid in full. As a matter of fact, its repayment could prove to be inconvenient for security holders and dangerous for the economy as a whole, since it could cause either inflation or deflation, depending on the circumstances.

From the end of World War II until March 1951, the public debt exerted a strong inflationary pressure in the United States, but only because of a dangerous policy of price-fixing which violated the basic principles of the private enterprise economy. It was thought that security prices had to be pegged and the given pattern of interest rates maintained to keep the cost of the debt service low, protect patriotic security holders against a fall in security prices, and stimulate private investment. The Federal Reserve Banks stood ready to absorb with newly created money the securities which could not be sold in the market at the fixed price. This meant that the monetary authority had abdicated the right to regulate the money supply according to any other criteria. The result was price inflation.

Were these aims worth the price of the complete abandonment of monetary policy? Certainly not. Price inflation meant that the government had to pay more for all its purchases; security holders, too, suffered from price inflation (which always particularly hurts creditors); and the stimulation of private investment should not have been entrusted to interest rates which had been frozen years before. Correct, not "low" rates of interest were needed. The pegging of security prices from 1946 to 1951 is a classic example of a price-fixing policy that is incompatible with the principles of a private enterprise economy. It is not even able to achieve the narrower aims it sets out to accomplish.

The fixing of security prices at the cost of losing control over the monetary system is only one example of unwise government control over the private enterprise economy. Other instances are agriculture policies, quantitative controls of international trade and payments, and even the maintenance of rigid exchange rates. The latter policy is a particularly interesting case that violates the principles of the market economy, because it still enjoys the support of many who believe that they are following the philosophy of private enterprise.

These mistakes emphasize the importance of the basic rule that government policies used in a given economic system must conform to its logic. However, other economic systems can be guilty of the same inconsistency. Furthermore, there is no reason why we should not, in time, learn how to practice consistency by conforming to the basic principles of our chosen economic order.

PART 3

Marxian

Economics

CHAPTER 10

An Outline
of Marxian Economics

THE IMPORTANCE OF MARXIAN ECONOMICS

Marxism is not a theory of socialism, which we study to inform ourselves about the socialist economy. Marx says surprisingly little about the economic system that is to follow capitalism. His theory deals mainly with capitalism; more precisely, Marx wanted to study the specific historical character of capitalism as a social system that follows feudalism and precedes socialism. Marx was interested in the process of social change. He tried to show how capitalism, having fulfilled its historic mission to accumulate capital and to develop new productive techniques, turns into a fetter of production. Then follows a social revolution out of which socialism emerges by necessity.

Unfortunately, this historical approach to the problems of capitalism and socialism discouraged "any inquiry into the actual organization and working of the socialist society of the future. If the change was to be brought about by the inexorable logic of history, if it was the inevitable result of evolution, there was little need for knowing in detail what exactly the new society would be like." [1] Thus, if we find the economic theory of

[1] F. A. Hayek, *Collectivist Economic Planning* (London: Routledge & Kegan Paul Ltd., 1935), p. 13.

socialism completely undeveloped even as late as 1917–1918, Marx must be blamed more than anyone else for this serious state of affairs.

Marx's economic theories should be studied, at least in broad outlines, for the following reasons:

1. Marx was by far the most powerful of all critics of capitalism. It is advisable, therefore, to follow a discussion of the private enterprise system by a discussion of Marx's impassionate challenge.

2. Millions have accepted Marxism as gospel truth and have embraced it as a religion "which promises paradise on this side of the grave." [2] This fact alone makes it imperative that the student of economic systems know what Marx believed.

3. Often socialist writings cannot be interpreted without a knowledge of Marxian theory. Soviet Russian statements, for instance, are frequently clad in Marxian terminology and cannot be understood by those who are ignorant of Marx's economic interpretation of history.

4. Marx's critique of capitalism, though inaccurate and contradictory, is an absorbingly interesting attempt to see capitalism as a passing phase of economic development and not merely as a given state of affairs which is not likely to change.

5. Marx's theory, when accepted, makes it impossible to believe in any long-run improvement of the private enterprise system. Orthodox Marxists therefore are basically hostile to it. Only revolution, not evolution, can be successful. This belief is incompatible with peaceful reforms and perhaps also with peaceful coexistence. Their faith may, however, induce Marxists to wait for the end of capitalism rather than try to bring about its fall by force of arms.

6. Marxism was an understandable reaction against the way in which orthodox classical economics had drained off all specific social content from economic theory.[3] Against a conceptual apparatus constructed "to transcend any particular set of social relations" Marx's theory of class struggle seemed realistic, even though it is incorrect in its assumptions and conclusions.

7. Marx's description of capitalism as a process of industrial change throws light on certain features of the private enterprise system, which tended to be neglected in the classical picture. The concentration of economic power, the deficiency of total demand, unemployment, the periodic crises—all these phenomena were considered earlier by Marx than in orthodox classical literature, and they were better integrated by Marx than in the writings of his socialist contemporaries.

---

[2] Joseph A. Schumpeter, *Capitalism, Socialism, and Democracy* (New York: Harper & Row, Publishers, 1950), p. 5.

[3] See Paul M. Sweezy, *The Theory of Capitalist Development* (New York: Oxford University Press, 1942), p. 5. Copyright 1942 by Oxford University Press.

8. Joan Robinson [4] points out that, while orthodox economists argued in terms of harmony of interests, Marx "conceives of economic life in terms of a conflict of interests between owners of property who do not work and workers who own no property." Even if we grant that there was more logic in the old harmonistic viewpoint than in Marx's theory of the class struggle, Marx may nevertheless be read with some advantage by those who were brought up on too heavy a diet of the classical idea of a general harmony of interests.

While in Part 2 the concept "private enterprise economy" was used, in Part 3 the term "capitalism" will underline the difference between the real private enterprise system and Marx's fascinating picture of it. Indeed:

9. A study of Marxian economics is needed to explain why certain critics of the private enterprise system see it the way they do.

10. While Marxian economics contributes little to the understanding of the private enterprise system and its potential development, the student of comparative economics must have some knowledge of the economic ideas of Marx or he may feel that he missed some essential point, either in the criticism of the private enterprise system or in the understanding of socialism.

The term *"Marxian"* instead of *"Marxist"* is used to refer to the theories of Karl Marx. The term "Marxist" is less precise and can be applied to schools of thought that differ widely in their interpretation of Marxian economics.

THE ECONOMIC INTERPRETATION OF HISTORY

In his preface to *The Critique of Political Economy* Marx [5] briefly describes his general conclusion, which "once reached, continued to serve as the leading thread" in his future studies:

> In the social production which men carry on they enter into definite relations that are independent of their will; these relations of production correspond to a definite stage of development of their material powers of production. The sum total of these relations of production constitutes the economic structure of society—the real foundation on which rise legal and political superstructures and to which correspond definite forms of social consciousness. The mode of production in material life determines the general character of the social, political, and spiritual processes of life. It is not the consciousness of men that determines their existence, but, on the contrary, their social existence determines their consciousness. At a

[4] Joan Robinson, *An Essay on Marxian Economics* (New York: St. Martin's Press, Inc., 1947), p. 1.

[5] Karl Marx, *A Contribution to the Critique of Political Economy* (Chicago: Charles H. Kerr & Company, 1911), Preface.

certain stage of their development, the material forces of production in society come in conflict with the existing relations of production, or— what is but a legal expression for the same thing—with the property relations within which they had been at work before. From forms of development of the forces of production these relations turn into their fetters. Then comes the period of social revolution. With the changes of the economic foundation the entire immense superstructure is more or less rapidly transformed.

This economic interpretation of history must not be too narrowly interpreted.[6] It says neither that the technique of production determines everything else nor that men are exclusively motivated by economic considerations. We must emphasize the concept "mode of production" and understand that Marx interpreted this term rather broadly. The technique of production is important for Marx, but so, too, are the exchange relations. The most characteristic feature of the mode of production in capitalism is seen to be the relation of wage labor to capital, a relation between two—the only two—social classes. This relation expresses itself in the form of exchanges, and exchange therefore is as important as the technique of production. The sum of these relations of production and exchange constitutes the economic structure of society. This economic structure forms, in turn, the real foundation on which rise legal and political superstructures.

These superstructures are very significant for Marx. They are not an automatic and instantaneous expression of the underlying mode of production; they can, indeed, become fetters of production. Social evolution is seen by Marx to arise out of the conflict between the changing material forces of production and the existing and unyielding relations of production. When existing property rights become fetters of production, they must be changed. Although impeded by the existing legal and political superstructure, the change of the entire social system must inexorably come once the material forces of production have undergone a basic change.

BOURGEOISIE AND PROLETARIAT

The following formulations are mostly verbatim quotations from the *Communist Manifesto*, written by Karl Marx and Friedrich Engels in 1848.[7]

The most significant and characteristic feature of capitalism is the relation between wage labor and capital, between proletariat and bourgeoisie. By bourgeoisie is meant the class of modern capitalists, the owners

[6] Schumpeter, pp. 10–13.

[7] Page numbers in parentheses in the text refer to *Capital, the Communist Manifesto, and Other Writings by Karl Marx* (New York: The Modern Library, Inc., 1932).

of the material means of production and employers of wage labor. The proletarians, the modern wage laborers, have no means of production of their own and are reduced to selling their labor power in order to live (321).

Bourgeoisie and proletariat are the product of capitalism. Feudalism had to decline when its relations of production no longer corresponded to the forces of production. The feudal system of industry became inadequate for the growing wants of new colonial markets and the new developments in commerce, navigation, and industry; division of labor between the different corporate guilds vanished in the face of division of labor in a single workshop—the manufacturing system (322). With ever-growing markets, even manufacture no longer sufficed. Steam and machinery revolutionized industrial production. The place of manufacture was taken by the giant, modern industry; the place of the industrial middle class, by industrial millionaires, who were leaders of whole industrial armies, the modern bourgeoisie (322).

The bourgeoisie has performed marvels of productivity. It has been first to show what man's activity can bring about. It has accomplished wonders far surpassing Egyptian pyramids, Roman aqueducts, and Gothic cathedrals. It has constantly revolutionized the instruments of production and thereby the relations of production.

But in revolutionizing the relations of production the bourgeoisie started a development which will eventually put an end to bourgeois society. When the feudal relations of property became no longer compatible with the already developed productive forces, they became so many fetters; they had to burst asunder; they were burst asunder (326). A similar development is going on before our eyes. Modern bourgeois society, that has conjured up such gigantic means of production, is like the sorcerer who is no longer able to control the powers of the nether world whom he has called up by his spells. The history of industry and commerce is but the history of the revolt of modern productive forces against modern conditions of production, against the property relations that are the condition for the existence of the bourgeoisie and of its rule. Bourgeois society is put on trial, each time more threateningly, through the periodical return of commercial crises (327).

The weapons with which the bourgeoisie felled feudalism to the ground are now turned against the bourgeoisie itself. The bourgeoisie have called into existence the men who are to wield those weapons—the modern working class, the proletarians (328). This is a class of laborers who live only so long as they find work and who find work only so long as their labor increases capital. Exposed to all the fluctuations of the market, their wages are restricted almost entirely to the means of subsistence that they require for the propagation of their race (328).

Bourgeoisie and proletariat are eventually the only two classes left to face each other.[8] Society is more and more splitting up into two great hostile camps (322). The bourgeoisie has put an end to all feudal, patriarchal, idyllic relations and has left no other nexus between man and man than naked self-interest, than callous "cash payment" (323).

With the development of industry not only does the proletariat increase in number (because the lower strata of the middle class all sink gradually into it); it becomes better organized, its strength grows, and it feels that strength more. The workers form trade-unions, and while these trade-unions are only now and then temporarily successful, the real fruit of the battle lies not in immediate results but in the ever-expanding union of workers (330). The advance of industry, whose involuntary promoter is the bourgeoisie, ends the isolation of the laborers due to competition. It instead facilitates their combination due to association. The development of modern industry, therefore, cuts from under the feet of the bourgeoisie the very foundations on which this class produces and exploits. The bourgeoisie produces, above all, its own gravediggers. Its fall and the victory of the proletariate are equally inevitable (334).

These quotations from the *Communist Manifesto* provide the necessary framework for a study of Marx's economic theories. Here, long before the publication of *Capital*, Marx's general beliefs and intentions are proclaimed. *It is clear what he wanted to prove.* He wanted to show not only that the whole capitalist process is one gigantic exploitation of one class by another, but also that the logic of this process of capitalist development must lead inexorably to a future classless society.

AN OUTLINE OF MARXIAN ECONOMICS

For the better understanding of Marxian economics it is important to realize the relation of each part of the analysis to the whole, and to draw a rough sketch of the Marxian edifice without any attempt to criticize Marx's assumptions, definitions, and conclusions. Although this discussion will not emphasize at this time the inconsistencies within the Marxian scheme, they may be apparent to the reader even in this rough sketch. A survey serves merely as a map to aid in seeing what significance

[8] ". . . it was a bold stroke of analytical strategy which linked the fate of the class phenomenon with the fate of capitalism in such a way that socialism, which in reality has nothing to do with the presence or absence of social classes, became, by definition, the only possible kind of classless society, excepting primitive groups. This ingenious tautology could not equally well have been secured by any definitions of classes *and* of capitalism other than those chosen by Marx—the definition by private ownership of means of production."—Schumpeter, p. 19.

earlier steps of Marx's analysis have for the conclusions that he draws. Since the outline is immediately followed by a fuller and more critical treatment, axiomatic formulations seem permissible.

1. The Labor Theory of Value. Commodities are products of human labor which are produced for the market. When two different commodities are exchanged, one for the other, they have this and only this in common: they are both the product of the same amount of abstract human labor.

2. Socially Necessary Labor. In determining the exchange value of a commodity, only socially necessary labor counts. Labor is socially necessary when it is of average skill and intensity, uses modern instruments of production, and produces a commodity which is in demand. Skilled labor is a multiple of average labor. Not only "present" labor is socially necessary but also "past" labor—labor needed to produce the raw materials and the machines used in the production of our commodity.

3. The Value of Labor Power. The exchange value of labor power itself is determined (like the exchange value of commodities) by the labor time needed for production of the means of subsistence of the laborer.

4. Surplus Value. The laborer, who does not own the means of production, sells his labor power to the capitalist, who pays a wage equal to the value of labor power. He pays, for instance, a wage equal to 6 labor hours, if 6 labor hours are needed to produce the daily sustenance for the laborer. But the capitalist has bought the whole day's labor power (say, 12 hours of labor power). The exchange value of the commodities produced by the laborer is, therefore, equal to 12 labor hours. We see that the laborer produces 6 hours' worth of commodities over and above the commodities which are needed to cover his means of subsistence. This is the surplus value, which the capitalist keeps for himself.

5. Constant Capital and Variable Capital. The value of a commodity consists of three parts: constant capital, variable capital, and surplus value. Constant capital (c) is the value of whatever part of the machinery is used up in the production process (depreciation) and of the raw materials. This part of a commodity's value is called constant capital because it remains constant and does not produce surplus value for the capitalist. Variable capital (v) is the value of labor power used; it is called variable capital because it produces surplus value (s). The total value of a commodity equals $c + v + s$. We see that total capital is divided into two parts, c and v, of which only v produces s.

6. The Rate of Surplus Value. The rate of surplus value, also called *the rate of exploitation*, is the ratio of surplus value to variable capital (s/v). A part of the whole labor day is needed to produce the means of subsistence for the laborer. If this part is assumed to be 6 hours, although the laborer works a total of 12 hours, the rate of exploitation s/v is 6/6, or 100 percent.

7. *The Organic Composition of Capital.* The organic composition of capital is the ratio of constant capital to variable capital (c/v). It can also be expressed as $c/c + v$, the ratio of constant capital to total capital. The organic composition of capital, owing to technological advance, undergoes a continuous change in favor of constant capital.

8. *The Rate of Profit.* The rate of profit is the ratio of surplus value to total capital: $s/c + v$. It is determined by the rate of exploitation s/v and by the organic composition of capital c/v.

9. *The Falling Rate of Profit.* Since the organic composition of capital undergoes a continuous change in favor of constant capital, the rate of profit must have the tendency to fall, because only the variable part of total capital produces surplus value.

10. *The Effect of Machinery on the Rate of Surplus Value.* The increased use of machinery increases the rate of exploitation, because it now takes less time to produce a laborer's means of subsistence; besides, these means can now be earned by several members of the laborer's family, because the machine permits the use of laborers of slight muscular strength. It also becomes possible to lengthen the labor day or to increase the intensity of work. When the rate of sulplus value increases, the rate of profit tends to rise.

11. *The Reserve Army of Labor.* The most important effect of machinery is to make a portion of the labor class superfluous, to create a reserve army of unemployed men and to exert a continuous downward pressure on wages. The reserve army is also called the relative surplus population.

12. *The Equalization of the Rate of Profit.* Since the organic composition of capital differs from industry to industry, the rate of profit $(s/c + v)$ must also differ. But the rate of profit tends, nevertheless, to be equal throughout the economy. Firms will leave low-profit industries (which have a "high" organic composition of capital) and enter high-profit industries (with a "low" organic composition of capital). Finally, all capitalists will receive an average rate of profit according to the size of their capital $(c + v)$. The price of commodities now differs from the value of commodities, because the s in $c + v + s$ has been replaced by an average s for all industries.

13. *Equalization of the Rate of Exploitation.* Competition among laborers, their movement from industry to industry, makes the rate of surplus value the same everywhere.

14. *The Antagonistic Conditions of Distribution.* The antagonistic conditions of distribution reduce the consuming power of the masses to

a minimum. The productive power of the economy finds itself at variance with this narrow basis of consumption.

15. Periodical Crises. The fall of the rate of profit and the growth of the reserve army are periodically interrupted. A crisis eliminates the smaller capitalists, concentrates capital in fewer hands, and lowers the value of constant capital. Furthermore, the reserve army grows during a crisis, and the increased rate of exploitation raises profits for the surviving capitalists. Then follows a period of increased accumulation and increased demand for labor power. But rising wages cut again into the surplus value. This explains the phenomenon that crises are preceded by high rather than by low wages.

16. Immiserization [9] *and Breakdown.* Since the commercial crises are superimposed on a downward trend, they return each time more threateningly. Real wages and the standard of living must fall (immiserization) as the capitalist class shrinks (concentration) and the proletariat grows. The existing property relations (the antagonistic conditions of distribution) turn into such fetters of production that social revolution will finally usher in the classless society.

[9] This is Schumpeter's suggestion for the proper translation of the Marxian concept *Verelendung*. P. 34.

CHAPTER 11

Marx's Theory
of Surplus Value

RICARDO'S LABOR THEORY OF VALUE

Marx wanted to show that the capitalist process involves exploitation of one class by another and that the economic consequences of this exploitation will eventually destroy capitalism.

The economic theory which explains this process of exploitation is the theory of surplus value, which, in turn, rests on the labor theory of value. Because of its fundamental importance, Marx's labor theory of value must be carefully studied, even though it is untenable and Marx himself had to discard it in the end.

Marx's attitude can be understood much better after a brief review of David Ricardo's [1] labor theory of value, which had a profound influence on Marx. In the preface to his *Principles of Political Economy and Taxation* Ricardo said that the principal problem in political economy is to determine the proportions of the whole produce of the earth that will be allotted to the different classes in the form of rent, profit, and wages. This starting point led him directly into the theory of exchange value. After

[1] *The Works of David Ricardo*, ed. J. R. McCulloch (London: McCulloch, 1846), preface, pp. 9, 10, 15.

having said that utility is not the measure of exchangeable value, although it is absolutely essential to it, Ricardo made a statement that was to influence the development of economic theory for generations: "Possessing utility," he wrote, "commodities derive their exchangeable value from two sources: from their scarcity, and from the quantity of labor required to obtain them."

This statement contains a basic mistake. Reference to scarcity would have been correct; reference to the quantity of labor led Ricardo (and Marx) into a labor theory of value which was unnecessary, awkward, and incorrect. Why did Ricardo believe that he had to add to scarcity this reference to the quantity of labor?

Ricardo admitted that there are some commodities whose value is determined by scarcity alone (such as rare books and coins, or wines of peculiar quality) because no labor can increase their quantity; but he pointed out that these commodities form a very small part of the mass of commodities daily exchanged in the market. "By far the greatest part of those goods which are the objects of desire, are produced by labor; and they may be multiplied . . . almost without any assignable limit, if we are disposed to bestow the labor necessary to obtain them." Ricardo obviously felt that the principle of scarcity did not apply to these products of labor and that another principle for the determination of their value had to be found. This principle, he believed, was the quantity of labor required for the production of commodities, whose production could be increased "almost without any assignable limit."

Ricardo was wrong. We can, of course, produce more shoes or more shirts, but we cannot (at full employment) increase the production of all commodities "almost without limit." Expansion of one industry requires, as a rule, the contraction of another. To solve the problem of exchange value, the principle of scarcity should have been applied to the factors of production rather than to individual products. On this basis a general theory of prices could have been worked out. We have already studied the modern version of this theory in Chapter 3.

Ricardo acknowledged the existence of three factors of production: labor, land, and capital. How could he then maintain that commodities are exchanged according to used-up labor alone? How, furthermore, did he account for different kinds of labor that have different exchange values?

1. Ricardo exluded the influence of the factor land by assuming that the price of commodities is determined on marginal land which is free. The owner of better-than-marginal land receives a rent, to be sure; but the price of the product produced on marginal land determines the rent, and not the other way round; in other words, the rent does not influence the price.

2. As far as the factor capital is concerned, Ricardo simply assumed

that capital and labor are always employed in the same proportion. This same argument appears again in the discussion of Marx's concept of the organic composition of capital. For Marx, too, it is essential to assume a uniform proportion of constant and variable capital throughout the economy if the rate of profit is to be equal in different industries and if the value theory of labor is to be maintained.

3. Concerning the problem of different kinds of labor, Ricardo merely stated that "the estimation in which different qualities of labor are held, comes soon to be adjusted in the market with sufficient precision for all practical purposes, and depends much on the comparative skill of the laborer, and intensity of the labor performed." Since this estimation in the market obviously depends on the exchange value of the product that a given kind of labor is able to produce, Ricardo is guilty to circular reasoning. He wants to explain the exchange value of commodities via the quantity of labor, but needs the value of the commodities to reduce different kinds of labor to normal labor. "He completely overlooks that in arguing in this way he appeals to another principle of valuation and really surrenders the labor-quantity principle which thus fails from the start, within its own precincts, and before it has the chance to fail because of the presence of factors other than labor." [2]

Ricardo's labor theory of value was a misconception. It appealed to Marx because it emphasized the factor labor so much more than a general price theory would have done. However, Marx goes much further than Ricardo; where Ricardo suggested that goods exchange *in proportion to* the labor used in their production, Marx considered labor *the substance of* value.

MARX'S LABOR THEORY OF VALUE

Marx begins his labor theory of value with an analysis of the commodity because "the wealth of those societies in which the capitalist mode of production prevails, presents itself as 'an immense accumulation of commodities'" (1:41).[3] He defines the commodity as an article which has utility, is the product of human labor, and is produced for the market. We note how narrow this definition is. Since the commodity must be the product of human labor, Marx excludes from commodities such gifts of nature as the soil, wood in trees, water power, coal beds, and so forth, just as Ricardo excluded all goods whose quantity could not be increased by

[2] Joseph A. Schumpeter, *Capitalism, Socialism, and Democracy* (New York: Harper & Row, Publishers, 1950), p. 24.

[3] Volume and page numbers in parentheses refer to Karl Marx, *Capital: A Critique of Political Economy*, vol. 1, *The Process of Capitalist Production*; vol. 2, *The Process of Circulation of Capital*; vol. 3, *The Process of Capitalist Production as a Whole* (Chicago: Charles H. Kerr & Company, 1906, 1909, 1909).

labor.[4] These gifts of nature command exchange value; an explanation of exchange value that is not able to account for them is inadequate.

Marx argues that because, as use-values, commodities are of different qualities, the exchange value cannot contain "an atom of use-value" (1:44) to arrive at a completely uncalled-for conclusion: "If then we leave out of consideration the use-value of commodities, they have only one common property left, that of being products of labor" (1:44).

There are, of course, other qualities that commodities have in common: for instance, that they are all scarce or that they are all products of scarce factors of production, though not necessarily of labor alone. Emphasis on scarcity would have permitted the inclusion of the categories of commodities which Ricardo and Marx had to eliminate, those whose scarcity is obviously not determined by the labor that went into their production.

Böhm-Bawerk suggests that, in first defining commodities as products of labor and then saying that commodities only have this one common property left, Marx acted like a man "who urgently desiring to bring a white ball out of an urn takes care to secure this result by putting in white balls only."

Why did Marx ignore the obvious fact that commodities that were not the product of labor had exchange value, and those which were made by labor exchanged at ratios permanently diverging from the ratio of labor contained in them? Why did he not discard the whole labor theory of value with its embarrassing contradiction of obvious facts?

Marx was a disciple of Ricardo, and it is not surprising that he was not skeptical of a view that was so well designed to support his own preconceived economic theory. Marx needed the labor theory of value as a basis for the theory of surplus value; he needed it to prove the existence of exploitation and all the rest; he needed it to keep "insistently before the mind of the reader a picture of the capitalist process as a system of piracy, preying upon the very life of the workers." [5]

Marx obviously did not realize that the labor theory of value is quite unnecessary to support a conviction that capitalism is essentially a system of exploitation. But, as Lerner rightly says, it is "an unfounded dogma that, unless we go in for all this rigmarole about 'value,' we cannot say that capitalists get part of the social product without working." [6]

---

[4] See Eugen von Böhm-Bawerk, *Karl Marx and the Close of His System* (New York: Crowell-Collier and Macmillan, Inc., 1898), pp. 134, 135.

[5] Joan Robinson, *An Essay on Marxian Economics* (New York: St. Martin's Press, Inc., 1947), p. 22.

[6] Abba P. Lerner, "Marxism and Economics: Sweezy and Robinson," *Journal of Political Economy*, vol. 53 (March 1945), p. 81. Modern economists know how to distinguish between "personal" and "functional" distribution of income, and they also know that the connection which exists between the two in capitalism can be dissolved under different, that is, noncapitalist arrangements.

That the problem of exchange value could be discussed quite realistically, without prejudice to the social justice of the outcome, had already been indicated by Adam Smith. "In that original state of things," Smith wrote, "which precedes both the appropriation of land and the accumulation of stock, the whole produce of labor belongs to the laborer." Then he went on to show how, as soon as land becomes private property, the landlord's rent "makes the first deduction from the produce of the labor which is employed upon land" and how the capitalist's profit "makes a second deduction" from the produce of labor. Both the landlord and the capitalist are able to extract their share because they are in the bargaining position to do so. "A landlord, a farmer, a master manufacturer, or merchant, though they did not employ a single workman, could generally live a year or two upon the stocks which they have already acquired. Many workmen could not subsist a week, few could subsist a month, and scarce any a year without employment." [7]

Adam Smith's approach shows that Marx could have accepted the determination of commodity prices according to the relative scarcity of the different factors of production that went into the production of these commodities and still have protested against the income distribution which is characteristic of capitalism.

Marx's assertion that the exchange value of commodities is determined by the only property common to all, abstract human labor, is entirely arbitrary. Its fallacy is revealed by even the most superficial observation of how prices are actually determined on the real markets of the private enterprise economy. Nowhere do commodities exchange according to the amount of abstract human labor contained in them. The exchange value of commodities is determined by conditions of demand and supply and, in equilibrium, by production costs, provided that the commodities in question are the result of production. Production costs do not consist of wages alone; they consist of anything that is needed, is scarce, and commands a price. Labor itself is a factor supplied in an infinite variety of qualities, reducible to "abstract human labor" only by market forces, as we shall presently see.

Regarding the influence of demand upon the exchange value of commodities, Marx wavers somewhat between the statement that exchange value does "not contain an atom of use-value" (1:44) and the admission that "in order that a commodity may be sold at its market-value, that is to say, in proportion to the necessary social labor contained in it, the total quantity of social labor devoted to the total mass of this kind of commodities must correspond to the quantity of the social demand for them, meaning the solvent social demand" (3:226–227).

[7] Adam Smith, *An Inquiry into the Nature and Causes of the Wealth of Nations*, ed. E. Cannan (London: Methuen & Co. Ltd., 1925), vol. 1, pp. 66–68.

Marx, like Ricardo, returns to market conditions of supply and demand whenever his labor theory of value offers no solution.

SOCIALLY NECESSARY LABOR TIME

In elaborating his basic postulate, that the exchange value of a commodity depends on the human labor embodied in it, Marx points out that only socially necessary labor time may be counted, considering the following points:

1. The socially necessary labor time is the time spent by labor possessing average skill and working with average intensity. Skilled labor has to be reduced to average labor.

2. Normal conditions of production must be given. Labor must be supported by modern machinery. Today, for instance, it would be labor done with the bulldozer and not with the hand shovel.

3. The product must be in demand. Labor could not be counted as socially necessary if too much of its product has been produced in relation to solvent social demand.

4. The labor time to be counted includes "past" as well as "present" labor. Past labor is the labor that went into the raw materials and also what Marx calls the "wasted" or "used-up" portion of the machinery.

In the reduction of skilled labor to normal labor Marx meets the same difficulties which Ricardo had to face, and like Ricardo, he suggests that these difficulties are solved by the market:

> Skilled labor counts only as simple labor intensified, or rather, as multiplied simple labor, a given quantity of skilled labor being considered equal to a greater quantity of simple labor. Experience shows that this reduction is constantly being made. . . . The different proportions, in which different sorts of labor are reduced to unskilled labor as their standard, are established by a social process that goes on behind the backs of the producers, and, consequently, appear to be fixed by custom (1:51–52).

Marx illustrates the "normal conditions of production" by the following example. Should the capitalist "have a hobby, and use a gold instead of a steel spindle, yet the only labor that counts for anything in the value of the yarn is that which would be required to produce a steel spindle, because no more is necessary under the given social conditions" (1:210).

It is very important to stress this point in the Marxian system: once a new machine is introduced, the working time which is considered socially necessary is the working time of a man equipped with the new machine. This fact explains why the capitalist will not necessarily invest in variable capital rather than in constant capital, in spite of Marx's insistence that only variable capital produces surplus value.

In defining socially necessary labor time Marx says that there must be enough solvent social demand for the product. If more of a commodity has been produced than can be sold at a price that corresponds to the socially necessary labor time, production must be contracted; on the other hand, if the exchange value of the product exceeds the value of abstract human labor time contained in it, production must be expanded. Speaking of the labor of a weaver, Marx points out that "if the community's want of linen . . . should already be saturated by the products of rival weavers, our friend's product is superfluous, redundant, and consequently useless. . . . If the market cannot stomach the whole quantity at the normal price of 2 shillings a yard, this proves that too great a portion of the total labor of the community has been expended in the form of weaving" (1:120).

Here we find Marx again in the closest neighborhood of the theory of supply and demand. That Marx did not pursue this argument, or did so only apologetically in Volume 3 of *Capital*, is obviously due to the fact that the argument endangers the labor theory of value. The exchange value of labor must not be derived from the exchange value of its product if the labor theory of value and the theory of surplus value are to be maintained. As soon as the relative scarcity of the product and of the factors of production are admitted as determining factors, the whole labor theory of value becomes superfluous and is exposed as an excessively weak foundation of the theory of capitalist development.

Materials and machines are the product of labor and "transfer value to the new product, so far only as during the labor-process they lose value in the shape of their old use-value" (1:229). "The whole of the labor in the yarn is past labor; and it is a matter of no importance that the operations necessary for the production of its constituent elements were carried on at times which, referred to the present, are more remote than the final operation of spinning" (1:209).

We note here that capital goods are merely considered so much past labor and that Marx denies that they can transfer more value to products than corresponds to their own production costs in terms of socially necessary labor time. This means that Marx denies that capital goods are value-producing, that they are characterized by a special scarcity which raises the price of their products over and above the cost of past and present labor. In other words, Marx denies the existence of that special problem which the theory of interest explains.

THE VALUE OF LABOR POWER

Since the surplus value is the difference between the value of the product of labor (which belongs to the capitalist who bought the labor power) and the value of labor power (the price paid by the capitalist for labor power), it is necessary to inquire into the determination of the value of labor power.

According to Marx, "the value of labor power is determined as in the case of every other commodity, by the labor-time necessary for the production, and consequently also the reproduction, of this special article . . . . in other words, the value of labor-power is the value of the means of subsistence necessary for the maintenance of the laborer" (1:189–190). Marx insists that labor power is a commodity like every other commodity. We remember that he defined a commodity as an article which has utility, is the product of labor, and is produced for the market. But in a private enterprise system labor is not produced for the market, as it might be in a society of slave owners; and it is, therefore, quite unjustified that Marx applies the laws which determine the value of commodities to the "commodity," labor power.

The necessary means of subsistence are to be understood as a cultural rather than a physical minimum, and they must include the means necessary to bring up the laborer's replacements, his children, in order that this peculiar commodity may perpetuate its appearance in the market (1:191). Likewise included in the value of labor power are the costs involved in learning the skill and dexterity requisite for a given branch of labor.

But why is labor condemned to subsist permanently on the minimum of existence? Why is labor continuously exploited?

The laborer, according to Marx, is "free in the double sense, that as a free man he can dispose of his labor-power as his own commodity, and that on the other hand, he has no other commodity for sale, is short of everything necessary for the realization of his labor power" (1:187–188). "Marx's idea is that there is no essential difference, though there are many secondary ones, between the wage contract and the purchase of a slave—what the employer of 'free' labor buys is not indeed, as in the case of slavery, the laborers themselves but a definite quota of the sum total of their potential labor." [8]

Marx obviously wants to show that the labor market is a buyer's market where labor, lacking the essential material means of production, has to sell itself at any price offered, as long as the price is just high enough to permit labor's own reproduction.

This pessimistic conclusion was well known in Marx's time and therefore easily accepted by his readers. In his *Essay on the Principle of Population*, written in 1798, Robert Malthus had taught that population tends to increase, when unchecked, in a geometric progression, whereas the supply of food increases at best in arithmetic progression. When more capital and labor are applied to a given piece of land, the law of diminishing returns makes itself felt. Population, therefore, will eternally press upon the means of subsistence, and wages can only temporarily exceed the minimum needed

[8] Schumpeter, p. 26.

for existence. If wages are higher than this, population will grow, real wages will fall, and famine and pestilence will reduce the population once more to the number which is able to subsist.

Marx never accepted the Malthusian doctrine. Referring to Ferdinand Lassalle's "iron law of wages," he declared:

> If I take the law with Lassalles' stamp and, therefore, in his meaning, then I have to take it also with his explanation. And what is this explanation? The Malthusian population theory. However, if this theory is correct, then again I cannot abolish the law even if I abolish wage-labor a hundred times, because then the law rules not only the system of wage-labor but any social system.[9]

A *natural* law clearly was not acceptable to Marx. He relies instead on the capitalist relation and on the reserve army. The capitalist relation is the relation between the capitalist who owns the instruments of production and the wage laborer who owns nothing but his labor power:

> Capitalist production . . . of itself reproduces the separation between labor-power and the means of labor. It thereby reproduces and perpetuates the condition for exploiting the laborer. It incessantly forces him to sell his labor-power in order to live, and enables the capitalist to purchase labor-power in order that he many enrich himself. It is no longer a mere accident that capitalist and laborer confront each other in the market as buyer and seller. It is the process itself that incessantly hurls back the laborer onto the market as a vendor of his labor-power, and that incessantly converts his own product into a means by which another man can purchase him (1:632–633).

This argument is not convincing enough. Although it is true that the laborer has to sell his labor power, it is equally true that the capitalist has to buy labor power in order to make use of his machinery. That many laborers face few capitalists and that the laborer, as a rule, lacks private means, are important facts, but they are not sufficient to establish another "iron law of wages." As Eduard Heimann puts it, Marx's theory would be faultless only if capital could, if need be, get along without the laborer.[10]

Marx needs a stronger argument to prove that the comparative bargaining power of labor is extremely weak. He believes that he has found such an argument in the theory of the reserve army, the army of the unemployed, which creates a labor market in which more men are constantly looking for jobs than jobs for men.

But even the theory of the reserve army is unable to prove that wages will not rise in the short or in the long run. In fact, within the logic of

[9] Karl Marx, *Kritik des Gothaer Programms* (Berlin: Dietz Verlag, 1955), p. 29.
[10] Eduard Heimann, *Soziale Theorie des Kapitalismus* (Tübingen: J. C. B. Mohr, 1929), p. 15.

Marx's own theory the following possibilities exist: (1) The reserve army may be depleted through capital accumulation. In this case wages, relieved of competitive pressure, will rise above the subsistence minimum. (2) The law of the equalization of the rate of profit induces industrialists to enter fields of industry that use relatively large amounts of variable capital. This tendency increases the demand for labor, and, consequently, wages. (3) If the rate of profit tends to fall while efficiency of production increases, wages can rise permanently because labor gets a larger share of an increasing pie.

SURPLUS VALUE

The theory of surplus value rests on (1) the labor theory of value and (2) the assumption of capitalist production, the social process in which the material means of production are owned by capitalists. The capitalist purchases labor power for a wage equal to its value, that is, the value of the means of subsistence required for the reproduction of labor power. If it requires half a day's labor to produce the goods and services needed to keep the laborer and his family alive during a 24-hour period, the capitalist must pay the laborer the product of half a day's labor or its monetary equivalent. Once the capitalist has bought a worker's labor power, "the right to use that power for a day belongs to him" (1:206):

> The fact that half a day's labor is necessary to keep the laborer alive during 24 hours, does not in any way prevent him from working a whole day. Therefore, the value of labor-power, and the value which that labor-power creates in the labor process are two entirely different magnitudes; and this difference of the two values was what the capitalist had in view, when he was purchasing the labor-power (1:215–216).

The commodities produced during 12 hours of normal labor are worth 12 hours. However, to purchase the work of 12 hours (that is, one whole labor day) costs the capitalist in Marx's example a wage equal to the product of only 6 normal labor hours (half a day's labor). The difference accruing to the capitalist is surplus value equal to 6 normal labor hours.

It should be noted that Marx does not blame the individual capitalist for the exploitation of labor. "What he wanted to prove was that exploitation did not arise from individual situations occasionally and accidentally; but that it resulted from the very logic of the capitalist system, unavoidably and quite independently of any individual intention." [11]

The reader of *Capital* cannot escape the impression that Marx conceived the idea of surplus value before he worked out his theory. His labor

[11] Schumpeter, p. 26.

theory of value *implies* the surplus value. "He knew the result he wished to obtain, and must obtain, and so he twisted and manipulated the patient ideas and logical premises with admirable skill and subtlety until they actually yielded the desired result in a seemingly respectable syllogistic form." [12] Those who have studied Marx's theory of value will find it hard to believe that the theory of surplus value was the result of unbiased research. Marx knew what he wanted to prove. He knew it as early as 1848 when he and Friedrich Engels wrote the *Communist Manifesto*. He wanted to unmask exploitation.

Marx's "terminology derives its force from the moral indignation with which it is saturated." [13] Of this terminology the term "surplus value" was the most powerful and impressive. It had to stand out clearly as the incarnation of everything that was wrong in capitalism, as the source of all evil. Profit, interest, rent—all income that was not earned by labor— merged into one huge gain from exploitation: surplus value.

[12] Böhm-Bawerk, p. 152.
[13] Joan Robinson, p. 22.

CHAPTER 12

Marx's Theory
of Profit

VARIABLE CAPITAL AND CONSTANT CAPITAL

The capitalist is driven by the profit motive. In order to make profit he spends money (M) on labor, transforms labor into commodities (C), and sells these commodities for a larger amount of money (M'). The difference between M' and M is the surplus value, the result of exploitation. It is attributable to the variable capital alone, that is, to the wages paid for labor. This fact accounts for the name "variable" capital, because this part of capital is continually being transformed from a constant into a variable magnitude (1:233).[1]

"Constant" capital, by contrast, "does not undergo . . . any quantitative alteration of value" (1:232) and derives its name from this fact. Constant capital consists of materials and machines. Marx calls the machines "fixed capital" in contradistinction to "circulating capital" in the form of raw and auxiliary materials. The value of these materials is fully

---

[1] Volume and page numbers in parentheses refer to Karl Marx, *Capital: A Critique of Political Economy*, vol. 1, *The Process of Capitalist Production*; vol. 2, *The Process of Circulation of Capital*; vol. 3, *The Process of Capitalist Production as a Whole* (Chicago: Charles H. Kerr & Company, 1906, 1909, 1909).

imparted to the commodity. Fixed capital is not so easily handled. Marx does not include in the value of a product more than that part of the instrument which was "wasted" during the process of production, that is, replacement costs. "Suppose a machine to be worth £1000, and to wear out in 1000 days. Then one thousandth part of the value of the machine is daily transferred to the day's product" (1:227).

Marx's statements are correct but incomplete. The final product must, of course, pay for past labor in addition to present labor, that is, it must pay for materials and the replacement cost of machinery used in its production. But this is not all that ought to be counted. The interest on the invested capital must enter into the cost calculations, since capital has a specific scarcity and commands a special price: but this price, the rate of interest, is not included by Marx as a cost factor.

When Marx tries to figure the value of past labor he is not interested in capital as a whole. Wear and tear amount to only a small fraction of the constant capital invested. It is, however, the *total* amount of constant capital which, together with the variable capital, should be used to determine interest as a cost factor. Marx himself uses this concept of total capital in the determination of the rate of profit.

Joan Robinson has pointed out that "both the organic composition of capital and the rate of profit are connected with the stock of capital employed, not with the depreciation of capital." [2] She distinguishes stock of capital or total capital, depreciation (d), and raw materials (r). As we already know, v stands for variable capital or wages. "Then $r + v$ and d must each be multiplied by the appropriate period of turnover. Suppose, for instance, that working capital represents on average 6-months outlay on wages and raw materials, and that the average life of plant is 10 years. Then $r + v$ must be divided by 2, and d multiplied by 10, in order to reduce $c + v$ to the stock of capital." Marx himself was quite aware of the importance of the rate of turnover, as is shown in Chapters 7 and 8 of Volume 2 of *Capital*. Some confusion arises, however, because in determining the value of the commodity he is interested in a magnitude different from the one which he has in mind when he discusses the rate of profit, but refers to both magnitudes as total capital.

The value of the commodity is $c + v + s$. In this case c stands for

[2] Joan Robinson, *An Essay on Marxian Economics* (New York: St. Martin's Press, Inc., 1947), p. 7. If the fixed capital has an average life of 10 years, only one tenth of it is "wasted" during the year. If we assume depreciation per year to be $10,000, the value of the stock of fixed capital is $100,000. Suppose that, in addition, payments for raw materials and labor $(r + v)$ amount to $50,000 per annum. Since one production period is 6 months, the capital can be used twice within one year, so that a capital *stock* of $25,000 suffices for these payments. In our example, total capital (c) is $125,000; depreciation (d), $10,000; and payments for raw materials and wages $(r + v)$, $50,000.

depreciation and materials. The value of the constant capital *used up* is imparted to the value of the product.

Paul M. Sweezy [3] suggests that the formula $c + v + s$ could be extended to take in the entire economy:

> If we use capital letters to designate aggregate quantities, we can say that modern theorists, when they speak of gross national income, commonly include V + S plus that part of C which represents depreciation of fixed capital, but exclude the rest of C. By net national income, they mean simply V + S, which includes all payments to individuals plus business savings.

We note that this aggregation is not an addition of all commodity values. To avoid double counting, only products which enter the gross national income are counted.

If V + S is net national income, S/V determined labor's share in the national income, V being the wage payments during the year and S the source of all incomes not derived from wage labor (profit, interest, rent).

THE RATE OF EXPLOITATION
(THE RATE OF SURPLUS VALUE)

Mark explains the rate of surplus value as follows: During one portion of the labor day the laborer produces only the value of the means of subsistence which he and his family consume. Though he does not directly produce these necessaries himself, he produces a product equivalent to them in value. "The portion of his day's labor devoted to this purpose, will be greater or less, in proportion to the value of the necessaries that he daily requires on an average, or, what amounts to the same thing, in proportion to the labor-time required on an average to produce them" (1:240). Marx calls this portion of the working day *necessary labor time*. "During the second period of the labor-process . . . the workman . . . creates no value for himself. He creates surplus-value which, for the capitalist, has all the charms of a creation out of nothing" (1:240). Marx calls the labor time so spent *surplus labor time*.

The rate of exploitation, as a division of the labor day into necessary and surplus labor time, is determined by (1) the length of the working day and (2) the time required to produce the means of subsistence for the laborer.

In the process which increases the rate of exploitation, machinery

[3] Paul M. Sweezy, *The Theory of Capitalist Development* (New York: Oxford University Press, 1942), p. 63. Copyright 1942 by Oxford University Press.

plays an important part. It "is intended to cheapen commodities, and, by shortening that portion of the working-day, in which the laborer works for himself, to lengthen the other portion that he gives, without an equivalent, to the capitalist" (1:405). The machinery, in short, is "a means for producing surplus-value" (1:405).

The machine has the following effects:

1. The machine cheapens the commodities by which labor subsists and thereby reduces the necessary labor time.

2. The machine becomes a means of employing women and children, that is, laborers of slight muscular strength (1:431). This increases the rate of exploitation. Not only is the supply of labor power greatly increased, but the necessities of life for the whole family can now be earned by the combined effort of several members of the family. "In order that the family may live, four people must now, not only labor, but expend surplus-labor for the capitalist" (1:431–432).

3. The machine lengthens the working day and "the lengthening of the working day . . . allows . . . production on an extended scale without any alteration in the amount of capital laid out on machinery and buildings. Not only is there, therefore, an increase of surplus-value, but the outlay necessary to obtain it diminishes" (1:442–443).

4. The machine increases the rapidity and intensity of labor (1:447). This effect will be particularly strong if the labor day should be shortened by social legislation. When the shortening of labor hours becomes compulsory, "machinery becomes in the hands of capital the objective means, systematically employed for squeezing out more labor in a given time. This is effected in two ways: by increasing the speed of the machinery, and by giving the workman more machinery to tend" (1:450).

5. The machine becomes the competitor of the laborer. "That proportion of the working class, thus by machinery rendered superfluous . . . floods all the most easily accessible branches of industry, swamps the labor market, and sinks the price of labor-power below its value" (1:470).

There is in operation, according to Marx, a "law of the progressive increase in constant capital, in proportion to the variable" (1:682). The capitalist must increase his constant capital because of competitive pressure. We remember that the capitalist cannot hope to gain more surplus value by employing more men through the use of antiquated machinery, since he may count, as socially necessary labor, only labor equipped with modern instruments. A capitalist who cannot increase his constant capital as required by technological progress will soon be unable to compete. Thus he will cease to be a capitalist and will join the ranks of the proletariat. Accumulation therefore will result in the concentration of wealth in fewer and fewer hands.

When the organic composition of capital undergoes a continuous change in favor of constant capital, the mass of the material means of production grows faster than the mass of labor power employed. Suppose that the organic composition of capital c/v changes from 1:1 to 2:1, 3:1, 4:1, and so forth. As total capital increases, a smaller and smaller proportion of the total is transformed into labor power (1:690). "Since the demand for labor is determined not by the amount of capital as a whole, but by its variable constituent alone, that demand falls progressively with the increase of the total capital" (1:690). "An accelerated accumulation of total capital, accelerated in a constantly growing progression, is needed to absorb an additional number of laborers, or even, on account of the constant metamorphosis of old capital, to keep employed those already functioning" (1:690). Thus, "it is capitalist production itself that constantly produces . . . a relatively redundant population of laborers, that is, a population of greater extent than suffices for the average needs of the self-expansion of capital, and therefore a surplus-population" (1:691). This surplus population may take the more striking form of a repulsion of laborers already employed, or the less evident, but not less real, form of more difficult absorption of the additional laboring population through the normal channels (1:691).

The surplus population is Marx's famous industrial reserve army "that belongs to capital quite as absolutely as if the latter had bred it at its own cost" (1:693), that "creates, for the changing needs of the self-expansion of capital, a mass of human material always ready for exploitation" (1:693).

These effects of the machine all work in the same direction—they tend to increase the rate of exploitation. The Marxian system, though, also contains elements that may explain a tendency toward a lower rate of exploitation. The tendency toward an increasing rate of exploitation seems, at first, to be more consistent in the Marxian scheme. But if the final aim of the Marxian analysis is to prove the eventual downfall of capitalism, mainly in consequence of the tendency toward a lower rate of profit, the increasing rate of exploitation becomes embarrassing, because the tendency of the rate of profit to decrease, caused by a changing organic composition of capital, may be overcompensated by an increasing rate of exploitation.

THE FALLING RATE OF PROFIT

The rate of profit is the ratio of surplus value to total capital or $s/(c + v)$. However, $c + v$ signifies in this case the stock of capital and not only replacements, raw and auxiliary materials, and wages. The surplus value springs exclusively from variable capital. A higher organic composition of capital will consequently reduce the rate of profit. Since Marx believes in a law of the progressive increase in constant capital in proportion to the variable (1:682), he seems to be justified in the assumption of a gradual fall of the average rate of profit (3:248).

These assumptions, however, lead Marx into difficulty. A higher organic composition of capital would tend to reduce the rate of profit only if the rate of exploitation stayed the same. An increasing rate of exploitation, however, tends to increase the rate of profit and, perhaps, to overcompensate the effect of the higher organic composition of capital.

The assumption of a constant rate of exploitation is inconsistent with other parts of Marx's system. Paul Sweezy [4] points out that:

> . . . Marx was hardly justified, even in terms of his own theoretical system, in assuming a constant rate of surplus value simultaneously with a rising organic composition of capital. A rise in the organic composition of capital must mean an increase in labor productivity, and we have Marx's own word for it that higher productivity is invariably accompanied by a higher rate of surplus value. In the general case, therefore, we ought to assume that the increasing organic composition of capital proceeds *pari passu* with a rising rate of surplus value. If both the organic composition of capital and the rate of surplus value are assumed variable, as we think they should be, then the direction in which the rate of profit will change becomes indeterminate. All we can say is that the rate of profit will fall if the percentage increase in the rate of surplus value is less than the percentage decrease in the proportion of variable to total capital.

It is necessary for Marx to assume a *constant* rate of exploitation in order to maintain his theory of a "gradual fall of the average rate of profit." This necessary assumption, however, leads Marx into a fatal contradiction with the rest of his system. "For if the rate of exploitation tends to be constant, real wages tend to rise as productivity increases. Labor receives a constant proportion of an increasing total. Marx can only demonstrate a falling tendency in profits by abandoning his argument that real wages tend to be constant." [5]

Joan Robinson points out that the law of falling profits made sense in orthodox economic theory, which had no objection to the conclusion "that real wages are equated to the marginal productivity of labor" and that "the marginal productivity of labor rises as capital per man increases." Marx, however, believes that real wages must remain constant (apart from minor fluctuations) because they are determined by the socially necessary labor time required for production of the means of subsistence necessary for the maintenance and reproduction of labor power. In assuming a constant rate of exploitation, however, Marx discarded one half of the theory of surplus value, the part that makes the value of labor power generally equal to the minimum reproduction cost of labor power.

[4] Sweezy, p. 102.
[5] Robinson, pp. 36, 37.

He discards the other half, the labor theory of value as it applies to commodities, in his theory of the equalization of profit.

THE EQUALIZATION OF THE RATE OF PROFIT

If the rate of exploitation were the same everywhere, different fields of industry could, according to Marxian analysis, have the same rate of profit only if they had the same organic composition of capital. In practice, however, different industries have both different organic compositions of capital and, nevertheless, rates of profit that tend, in the long run, to be equal. Realism thus prevents Marx from maintaining his labor theory of value according to which the exchange value of a commodity equals the socially necessary labor time contained in the commodity. Marx tries here to cope with the difficulty which Ricardo excluded by the assumption that capital and labor are always employed in the same proportion. Marx states his dilemma clearly as follows:

> We have demonstrated, that different lines of industry may have different rates of profit, corresponding to differences in the organic composition of capitals, and, within the limits indicated, also corresponding to different times of turn-over; the law (as a general tendency) that profits are proportioned as the magnitudes of the capitals, or that capitals of equal magnitude yield equal profits in equal times, applies only to capitals of the same organic composition, with the same rate of surplus-value, and the same time of turn-over. And these statements hold good on the assumption, which has been the basis of all our analyses so far, namely that the commodities are sold at their values. On the other hand there is no doubt that, aside from unessential, accidental, and mutually compensating distinctions, a difference in the average rate of profit of the various lines of industry does not exist in reality, and could not exist without abolishing the entire system of capitalist production. It would seem, then, as though the theory of value were irreconcilable at this point with the actual process, irreconcilable with the real phenomena of production, so that we should have to give up the attempt to understand these phenomena (3:181–182).

Marx "solves" the problem by giving up the labor theory of value, which was the basis of his theory of surplus value.

Competition brings about an equalization of the rate of profit in the different fields of industry:

> Capital withdraws from spheres with low rates of profit and invades others which yield a higher rate. By means of this incessant emigration and immigration, in one word, by its distribution among the various spheres in accord with a rise of the rate of profit here, and its fall there, it brings about such a proportion of supply to demand that the average profit in

the various spheres of production becomes the same, so that values are converted into prices of production (3:230).

To explain this conversion of values into prices Marx uses the following numerical example. He assumes five industries with different organic compositions of capital. The rate of surplus value is uniformly 100 percent throughout the economy. Thus the labor day is divided into two equal parts, that is, 6 hours necessary labor time and 6 hours surplus labor time. The surplus value is therefore always equal to the variable capital. Furthermore, since the total capital is always assumed to be 100, the rate of profit is simply expressed by percentage figures equal to the surplus value. For instance, the first industry's total capital of 100 is divided between 80 c and 20 v. With a surplus value of 20, the profit is 20, or 20 percent of the invested total capital. The "used-up" c refers to that portion of c which was used up as material and depreciation (the "wasted" part of the machinery). These figures (50, 51, and so forth) are arbitrarily chosen. The value of commodities is equal to the socially necessary labor time spent in producing the commodities; that is, $c + v + s$, where c, however, is only the used-up portion of constant capital ("past" labor), while v stands for variable capital ("present" labor) and s, for surplus value ("present" labor spent during the surplus labor time). For industry I, $c + v + s$ is 50 + 20 + 20, or 90; for industry II, 51 + 30 + 30, or 111, and so forth.

Capitals	Rate of surplus value: s/v (percent)	Surplus value s	Rate of profit: $s/(c+v)$ (percent)	Used-up c	Value of commodities: used-up $c+v+s$	Cost-price: used-up $c+v$
I. $80c + 20v$	100	20	20	50	90	70
II. $70c + 30v$	100	30	30	51	111	81
III. $60c + 40v$	100	40	40	51	131	91
IV. $85c + 15v$	100	15	15	40	70	55
V. $95c + 5v$	100	5	5	10	20	15
TOTAL $390c + 110v$		110	110			
AVER. $78c + 22v$		22	22			

We note that the *value* of commodities is not the *cost price*. The cost price is the value of the commodity minus the surplus value, or "used-up" $c + v$.

The situation shown in these examples leads to different rates of profit in the different industries and cannot exist in reality "without abolishing the entire system of capitalist production." Capital, therefore, begins to withdraw from the spheres with low profits (such as industries V and IV) and to enter those with high profits (such as industries III and II). After competition has done its work,

> . . . one portion of the commodities is sold in the same proportion above in which the other is sold below their values. And it is only their sale at such prices which makes it possible that the rate of profit for all five capitals is uniformly 22 percent, without regard to the organic composition of the capitals. The prices which arise by drawing the average of the various rates of profit in the different spheres of production and adding this average to the cost-prices of the different spheres of production, are the *prices of production* (3:185).

The numerical example is now changed as follows:

Capitals	Surplus value	Value of commod- ities	Cost-price of commod- ities	Price of commod- ities	Rate of profit (percent)	Deviation of price from value
I. 80c + 20v	20	90	70	92	22	+ 2
II. 70c + 30v	30	111	81	103	22	− 8
III. 60c + 40v	40	131	91	113	22	− 18
IV. 85c + 15v	15	70	55	77	22	+ 7
V. 95c + 5v	5	20	15	37	22	+ 17

If we add the capitals used in the five industries and divide them by five, we find that on the average 78 *c* were combined with 22 *v*. With a rate of surplus value of 100 percent, the average surplus value is 22 and the average rate of profit 22 percent.

After competition has done its work, after capital has withdrawn from the industries with a lower-than-average rate of profit (I, IV, V) and entered those with a higher-than-average rate of profit (II, III), the prices of the commodities have changed and no longer correspond to the values of the commodities. The price of commodities is determined by the cost price of commodities (used-up *c* plus *v*) plus the average rate of profit. For instance, in industry I the *price* of the commodity will be 70 plus 22, or 92. The *value* of the commodity, according to the labor theory of value, was 70 plus 20 (or 90) and the deviation of price from value is therefore 92 minus 90 (or plus 2).

We see that the "different rates of profit are equalized by means of competition into a general rate of profit, which is the average of all these special rates of profit. The profit allotted according to this average rate of profit to any capital, whatever may be its organic composition, is called the average profit. That price of any commodity which is equal to its cost-price plus that share of average profit on the total capital invested (not merely consumed) in its production which is allotted to it in proportion to its conditions of turn-over, is called its price of production" (3:186).

Marx has finally given up the labor theory of value. Commodities do not exchange in proportion to the socially necessary labor used in their production. On the contrary, their prices deviate basically and permanently from the value which corresponds to past and present labor employed in their creation. Only if, by chance, an industry's organic composition of capital happens to be the average composition, do price and value correspond. Nevertheless, Marx upholds "that, from the point of view of the total social capital, the value of the commodities produced by it . . . is equal to the value of the constant capital plus the value of the variable capital plus the surplus-value" (3:196). Therefore, and since the total surplus value still determines the average rate of profit, the law of value regulates prices at least indirectly.

This argument is not satisfactory. Since *relative* prices or exchange values are decisive, it is no help that in an *average* figure the deviations from the average cancel each other. Marx admits that the individual capitalist cannot see that his profit is determined by the amount of unpaid labor, because this is only accidentally true for an individual commodity (if his capital happens to have the average organic composition of capital).

Even according to Marx we are only reminded in a "vague and meaningless form" of the fact that the value of the commodities is determined by the labor contained in them. Nevertheless, he still maintains the labor theory of value as shown in his assertion that the labor theory would determine values in a planned economy. "Only when production will be under the conscious and prearranged control of society, will society establish a direct relation between the quantity of social labor time employed in the production of definite articles and the quantity of the demand of society for them" (3:221).

While this cryptic passage is hard to interpret, it proves that Marx adheres to the labor theory of value in spite of the fact that it is admittedly not able to explain existing price relations in capitalism. It would be equally inadequate as a basis for socialist calculation and control in a planned economy.

EQUALIZATION OF PROFIT AND THE DEMAND FOR LABOR

Consider now an important consequence of the competitive process that tends to equalize the rate of profit. Since it is true that the rate of profit is originally high in fields of low organic composition of capital (for example, 60 c and 40 v) and low in fields with a high organic composition of capital, 95 c and 5 v), to equalize profits, capital withdraws from fields with low profits and invades fields with high profits (3:230). Fields with high profits are those that use relatively large amounts of variable capital, in other words, industries that employ a relatively large mass of labor power. The tendency to equalize profits therefore leads to an increasing demand for labor power—a tendency that the student of Marxian economics suspected from the very beginning, as soon as he was told that only variable capital produces surplus value. Marx's argument for the contrary assumption, his "law of the progressive increase in constant capital, in proportion to the variable" (1:682) rested on technological reasons and on the assumption that only labor power equipped with modern machinery could be counted as socially necessary. Competition forces the capitalist to increase more than proportionally the constant part of his total capital. This relative increase of constant capital in a given sphere of production lowers the rate of profit, in this particular sphere, below the average rate and therefore creates an opposite competitive change—the transfer of investment funds from industries of high organic composition of capital to those of low organic composition. Thus labor, which has just been set free by the introduction of a new machine tends to be in greater demand than before in industries that capital newly invades in quest for higher profits.

Labor power will also move on its own accord. The rate of exploitation tends to be the same in all industries, as well as the rate of profit. This result is also brought about by competitive "withdrawals" and "invasions." Marx suggests that it must be assumed "that the intensity of exploitation, or the rate of surplus-value, are the same" and that this presupposes "a competition among the laborers and an equilibration by means of their continual emigration from one sphere of production to another" (3:206).

The law of progressive increase in constant capital has its counterpart in the law of the equalization of profit. Technological progress destroys the equilibrium again and again. The equality of the rate of profit is continuously disturbed. But, as Heimann [6] has shown:

> Incessantly capital is on its way to re-establish equilibrium; disturbance and re-establishment face each other every moment . . . : the dynamic law [of the industrial reserve army] throws the laborer on the street, and the static law [of profit equalization] draws him again into the labor process; the stronger the shift towards constant capital caused by progress, the stronger the instantaneous counteraction which transfers capital into the spheres with relatively much wage capital.

[6] Eduard Heimann, *Mehrwert und Gemeinwirtschaft* (Berlin: Robert Englemann, 1922), p. 33.

Heimann reminds us that Marx's whole theory presupposes the validity of the theory of the reserve army. This theory, however, can scarcely be maintained if the very technological change that sets labor power free causes a compensating change in the organic composition of capital in favor of variable capital, that is, an increased demand for labor.

CHAPTER 13

Crisis, Breakdown, and Socialism

INTRODUCTION

Up to now the discussion of the Marxian system has dealt with details that Marx had carefully worked out, but there are other parts that remained in an embryonic state, even though they were crucially important: the theories of commercial crises, the breakdown of capitalism, and the theory of socialism. Because the interpretation of these theories is so difficult, there is a schism in the Marxist camp: "Orthodox" Marxists believe, as did Marx, in the eventual breakdown of capitalism as the final result of the ever more threatening return of commercial crises. The "revisionists," on the other hand, do not believe in this implicit self-destruction of capitalism; they believe that socialism can be reached gradually through a process of continuous, deliberate improvements; they are not prepared to draw radically pessimistic conclusions, which would condemn them to inactivity throughout the lifetime of capitalism. Socialism, for them, is not the automatic result of the final breakdown of capitalism, but rather the goal of a conscious reconstruction of the social system. With fundamentally different interests in mind, the "orthodox" and the "revisionist" Marxists came to entirely opposite explanations of the system.

CRISES

Marx never worked out a theory of business cycles, but many remarks about crises and, indeed, periodical fluctuations of the economy are scattered throughout his writings. They center around two distinct lines of argument. Crises in capitalism are seen to result either from the tendency of the rate of profit to fall or from underconsumption caused by the antagonistic conditions of distribution.

This second line of reasoning is indicated in the following passage:

> The last cause of all real crises remains the poverty and restricted consumption of the masses as compared to the tendency of capitalist production to develop the productive forces in such a way, that only the absolute power of consumption of the entire society would be their limit (3:568).[1]

The connection of crises to the falling rate of profit is suggested in the statement:

> The barrier of the capitalist mode of production becomes apparent . . . in the fact that the development of the productive power of labor creates in the falling rate of profit a law which turns into an antagonism of this mode of production at a certain point and requires for its defeat periodical crises (3:303).

We shall first try to construct a cycle theory on the basis of the falling rate of profit. Then the more powerful argument concerning general underconsumption will be discussed.

Why should the falling rate of profit be the cause of cyclical fluctuations? If the rate of profit really falls (in spite of an increasing rate of exploitation), this decline could explain a downward trend in economic activity. Commercial crises must be explained differently.[2] They are related to *oscillations* of the rate of profit. Marx provides an explanation of such oscillations in his assumption that the industrial reserve army is formed, absorbed, and re-formed periodically (1:694) and that real wages fluctuate accordingly. These changes in real wages, in turn, affect the rate of profit. What causes these pulsations of the reserve army is not quite clear.

---

[1] Volume and page numbers in parentheses refer to Karl Marx, *Capital: A Critique of Political Economy*, vol. 1, *The Process of Capitalist Production*; vol. 2, *The Process of Circulation of Capital*; vol. 3, *The Process of Capitalist Production as a Whole* (Chicago: Charles H. Kerr & Company, 1906, 1909, 1909).

[2] ". . . Marx's mechanical process of accumulation going on at an even rate—and there is nothing to show why, on principle, it should not—the process he describes *might* also go on at even rates; as far as its logic is concerned, it is essentially prosperityless and depressionless."—Joseph A. Schumpeter, *Capitalism, Socialism, and Democracy* (New York: Harper & Row, Publishers, 1950), p. 40.

Marx obviously assumed, as did many cycle theorists after Marx, that the introduction of new techniques is not an even and continuous process but occurs intermittently. Perhaps a sudden increase in investment (accumulation) leads to an increased demand for labor and absorbs part or all of the reserve army. Pressure on the labor market is reduced and real wages rise. But the increase in wages (which means a decreasing rate of exploitation) cuts into surplus value and reduces profits. With less surplus value earned, there is less surplus value to accumulate; and with falling profits, there is less inducement to invest. Thus the demand for labor decreases again.

The explanation of revival and upswing rests on the following considerations. Crisis and depression have led to the re-formation of the reserve army. As the "surplus population" grows, the rate of exploitation increases. Wages fall and profits rise once again. The rise of profits is aided by the fact that the crisis has depreciated the value of existing constant capital. While the mass of constant capital has grown, its value has fallen; and the rate of profit, figured on the lower value of the constant capital, increases for those capitalists who managed to survive.

This theory sounds plausible. As a matter of fact, it could be accepted even by non-Marxists. But does it explain what Marx wanted to explain, that crises become increasingly worse?

If Marx were correct in his assumption of a long-run decline in the rate of profit, we could argue that business cycles, as explained above, are oscillations around a falling trend. This would, indeed, emphasize the depression phase of the cycles. But we have already seen that the rate of profit will fall only if the rate of exploitation remains the same, that is, if real wages increase in the long run. Thus the falling rate of profit as foundation of a pessimistic cycle theory precludes the very explanation which Marx wants most to stress—that of underconsumption.

UNDERCONSUMPTION

Marx believes that capitalism's basic trouble is that capitalist production is limited by the consuming power of society. He says:

> The entire mass of commodities . . . must be sold. If this is not done, or only partly accomplished, or only at prices which are below the prices of production, the laborer has been none the less exploited, but his exploitation does not realize as much for the capitalist. . . . The conditions of direct exploitation and those of the realization of surplus-value are not identical. . . . The first are only limited by the productive power of society, the last by the proportional relations of the various lines of production and by the consuming power of society. This last-named power is not

determined either by the absolute productive power nor by the absolute consuming power, but by the consuming power based on antagonistic conditions of distribution, which reduces the consumption of the great mass of the population to a variable minimum within more or less narrow limits. The consuming power is furthermore restricted by the tendency to accumulate, the greed for an expansion of capital and a production of surplus-value on an enlarged scale. . . . To the extent that productive power develops, it finds itself at variance with the narrow basis on which the condition of consumption rests. On this self-contradictory basis it is no contradiction at all that there should be an excess of capital simultaneously with an excess of population. For while a combination of these two would indeed increase the mass of the produced surplus-value, it would at the same time intensify the contradiction between the conditions under which this surplus-value is produced and those under which it is realized (3:286–287).

This theory fits Marx's system with its emphasis on exploitation. When labor is being constantly exploited (whether it gets a subsistence wage or slightly more), the surplus population has no income at all, and the capitalists consume only a tiny fraction of the surplus value, then it is indeed difficult to see to whom the constantly increasing output of commodities should be sold.

But was Marx really entitled to draw these pessimistic conclusions, even within the logic of his own system? For an answer to this question (which is important because the breakdown of capitalism depends on it), we have to consider the following points.

1. Was Marx justified in using the underconsumption theory in spite of his own criticism of the "naive" underconsumptionists? Marx calls it a tautology to say "that crises are caused by the scarcity of solvent consumers, or of paying consumption," (2:475), and he continues:

> But if one were to attempt to clothe this tautology with a semblance of a profounder justification by saying that the working class receive too small a portion of their own product, and the evil would be remedied by giving them a larger share of it, or raising their wages, we should reply that crises are precisely always preceded by a period in which wages rise generally and the working class actually get a larger share of the annual product intended for consumption (2:476).

Marx wanted to make it clear that the difficulties could not be overcome, as some underconsumptionists argued, by simply raising wages. This is a persistent problem found in all wage discussions: that wages are the main source of demand, but that they are, at the same time, a cost factor. Marx was, of course, interested in barring this simple remedy for capitalism's death struggle. Nevertheless, he was right in rejecting wage increases as a simple recipe.

2. Marx's underconsumption theory conflicts, as we saw, with his theory of the falling rate of profit. The rate of profit will fall only when, with the relatively faster growth of c in relation to v, the rate of exploitation stays the same. Then real wages will rise with an increase in productivity and capitalists will have a market for their products to realize their surplus value.

3. Independently of the theory of the falling rate of profit we must reject Marx's argument that labor cannot get more than the means of subsistence. We remember that this theory rests on the presence of the reserve army and on the pressure it exerts on the labor market. But it is circular reasoning to make the reserve army (the result of crisis and depression) the foundation of the theory of surplus value, which explains the antagonistic conditions of distribution and, through underconsumption, crisis and depression.

4. If we follow the interpretation of orthodox Marxists, like Rosa Luxemburg, we are given such an extremely pessimistic estimate of consuming power that it is, indeed, difficult to see how capitalism could possibly have developed "the colossal productive forces" that Marx admired. If only v and a tiny portion of s are consumed, how can the accumulation of more and more s (under conditions of constantly increasing exploitation) proceed without running from the outset into "realization" trouble? Why was capitalism, under such conditions, not stillborn from the very beginning?

5. Paul Sweezy [3] answers this apparent paradox (that capitalism expanded prodigiously in spite of the fact that it tends always toward stagnation) by drawing our attention to certain "counteracting forces" to underconsumption. They are (1) new industries, (2) faulty investments, (3) population growth, (4) unproductive consumption, and (5) state expenditures.

Sweezy points out that "during the formative period of a new industry there is no clearly defined relation between additions to means of production and additions to the output of finished products." From this he concludes that the process of industrialization counteracts the tendency toward underconsumption, as during the eighteenth and nineteenth centuries.

That industrial expansion for over a century and a half should be possible before capitalists notice that the antagonistic conditions of production do not permit them to sell their products is hard to believe. Only if at reduced costs the increased output can be sold at reduced prices, thus increasing real wages, can the process of industrialization grow beyond the very first beginning.

[3] Paul Sweezy, *The Theory of Capitalist Development* (New York: Oxford University Press, 1942), pp. 217–218, 222, 236. Copyright 1942 by Oxford University Press.

Faulty investments would, indeed, absorb accumulation without adding to the output of consumer goods, but are hardly of sufficient quantitative importance to explain why underconsumption did not stop capitalist growth a long time ago.

Population growth, according to Sweezy, permits a rapid growth of variable capital "without any upward pressure on the wage level and hence without an adverse effect on the rate of profit." But Sweezy forgets to mention that this rapid growth of the labor force takes place within the existing antagonistic conditions of income distribution and thus cannot help to solve the problem of underconsumption.

The reader may have noticed that the arguments concerning new industries and population growth are Marxist adaptations of the stagnation theories of the 1930s.

Sweezy's last two points, unproductive consumption and government expenditures, are known as devices to maintain a sufficient amount of aggregate expenditure in the private enterprise economy. But orthodox Marxists must beware of this argument. Sweezy himself asks:

> If the drift to economic stagnation can be successfully countered, then why must we assume that unemployment, insecurity, sharper class and international conflicts are in prospect for capitalism? Why not, on the contrary, a "managed" capitalist society, maintaining economic prosperity through government action and perhaps even gradually evolving into a full-fledged socialist order?

6. Still another difficulty arises in connection with the theory that capitalists cannot "realize" surplus value. Even if Marx's underconsumption theory is acceptable, it does not provide a theory of *cyclical fluctuations*. Sweezy's counteracting forces could perhaps be used to show why the downward trend can be interrupted. But Sweezy's argument does not fit the logic of Marx's system. And the falling rate of profit argument, enriched by reference to the formation, absorption, and reformation of the reserve army, also cannot help. If we have settled on underconsumption as the main argument, we are exposed to the same criticism which Marx used against the "naive" underconsumptionists, in other words, why should the main trouble be found in underconsumption if wages rise during prosperity? It is true that wages have to be viewed not only from the demand but also from the cost side. But if insufficient demand is the *main* cause of the trouble, it does seem strange that the economy should suffer most when, for once, demand has grown.

BREAKDOWN AND IMPERIALISM

Chapter 8 showed how modern non-Marxian theory can explain economic fluctuations, and Chapter 9, how monetary and fiscal policies can be employed to maintain a reasonably high employment level. Decisive is the fact that we *can* deal successfully with recession and depression *within the framework of the private enterprise system.*

This optimistic conclusion discredits modern cycle theory in the eyes of orthodox Marxists. As Sweezy [4] puts it:

> If crises are really caused by nothing more intractable than disproportionalities in the productive process, then the existing social order seems to be secure enough. . . . Not only need there be no collapse of capitalism, but much can be done even under capitalism to iron out the disproportionalities which are the cause of much needless suffering.

We know what Marx wanted to prove. He wanted to show how existing property relations turn from forms of development of the forces of production into their fetters, so that eventually social revolution develops by necessity. But while Marx's aim was unmistakable, his economic theories did not always support his pessimistic preconceptions. Obviously, Marx found it impossible to gather together the different strands of his economic theory into a unified breakdown theory. If all his arguments had clearly pointed to this coveted result, he certainly would not have hesitated to formulate this climactic conclusion. But Marx's arguments are highly contradictory, even when taken on Marx's own terms, that is, even when we leave out those criticisms which invalidate the theory of surplus value from the start. Here the door stood wide open for those who did not want to follow Marx's pessimistic philosophy. A conflict among Marx's disciples was unavoidable.

The orthodox Marxists were right in their interpretation of Marx's philosophy. Marx was convinced that the capitalist relations of production will turn into fetters of production, that the proletariat will eventually overturn the existing relations of production, and that this change will be brought about in a final crisis, the last and worst in a series of crises which had become increasingly threatening. Marx's way to socialism is inexorable and dismal:

> The modern laborer . . . instead of rising with the progress of industry, sinks deeper and deeper below the conditions of existence of his own class. He becomes a pauper, and pauperism develops more rapidly than population and wealth. And here it becomes evident that the bourgeoisie is unfit any longer to be the ruling class in society, and to impose its conditions of existence upon society as an overriding law.[5]

If this interpretation of capitalist development is accepted, it is impossible, and therefore unwise, to try to improve the conditions of the masses under capitalism. It is impossible, at least in the long run, because

---

[4] Sweezy, pp. 160–161.
[5] *The Communist Manifesto, and Other Writings by Karl Marx* (New York: The Modern Library, Inc., 1932), pp. 327, 330, 333.

higher real wages lead only to depression; it is unwise because it is a wasted effort to try to improve a system that is entirely beyond repair. That workers should form increasingly powerful unions is important in view of the final struggle that is shaping up between bourgeoisie and proletariat. Material improvements for the working class, however, can be reached only for short periods. The real fruit of the workers' battle "lies not in the immediate result but in the ever-expanding union of workers."

But in trying to support Marxian philosophy with Marxian economics, the orthodox school was bound to run into difficulties. How was it possible for capitalism to maintain itself as long and as well as it did, in spite of all the dire predictions?

The main answer to this question was the theory of imperialism.

If capitalism suffers from underconsumption, if surplus value cannot be realized, capitalism can maintain itself only by sales outside the capitalist system. "Outside" refers to other countries, but it may also mean segments of the same country which are not yet part of the capitalist process.

The *Communist Manifesto* makes an implicit reference to imperialism when, in answering the question, "How does the bourgeoisie get over these crises?" it points to "the quest of new markets" and "the more thorough exploitation of old ones."

Marx did not follow up this idea. To simplify his analysis, his model considered the whole commercial world as one nation under the assumption that capitalist production would be characteristic for the whole world (1: Chap 22). He expressly stated that consideration of international trade would only confuse the issue without adding a new element either to the problem or to its solution.

Marx's disciples were less wise. They refer again and again to additional markets that must be found in order to get rid of the surplus product. Some Marxists, however, like Heinrich Cunow, Karl Kautsky, and L. B. Boudin, were rather skeptical about the efficacy of this safety valve. The rest of the noncapitalist world would, after all, soon be absorbed; and in the process more and more countries would become, via industrialization, subjects rather than objects of imperialism.

Most consistent and therefore most vulnerable was Rosa Luxemburg's [6] theory of imperialism. Because it is impossible to dispose of the total social output within the capitalist system, she observes, surplus value can be realized only through sales to noncapitalist consumers. Unfortunately, Rosa Luxemburg was not able to tell us how the noncapitalist consumer is able to buy the products that he imports from capitalist countries. The correct answer is simple enough. He can buy only if he is

---

[6] Rosa Luxemburg, *Die Akkumulation des Kapitals. Ein Beitrag zur ökonomischen Erklärung des Imperialismus* (Berlin: Vereinigung Internationaler Verlagsanstalten, 1922).

able to sell, that is, export. Thus in the capitalist country foreign products take the place of home-produced commodities, but the total mass of value that has to be sold remains the same. As a matter of fact, since the profits of trade with the underdeveloped areas will be particularly great, the realization at home is made even more difficult.[7] To put it differently: if the laborers in the colonial areas are even more exploited, and exploitation is the core of "realization" difficulties, imperialism must make matters worse rather than better. It is obvious that international lending would not solve this problem in the long run.

Rosa Luxemburg's theory was not well received by her fellow Marxists. That the revisionists had no use for it is easily understood; those who did not believe in underconsumption as the basic difficulty of capitalism had no reason to subscribe to this weak subterfuge. More interesting is the fact that Luxemburg's theory of imperialism did not find favor with "orthodox" authors. N. I. Bucharin [8] made the reason for this negative attitude quite clear. "If the theory of Rosa Luxemburg were even approximately correct, then truly the cause of revolution would be in a bad way since with the existence of such a huge reservoir of 'third persons,' as it de facto exists, we could not speak of a breakdown in a practical sense." We see that it was not only the revisionists who were disinclined to wait for the eventual downfall of capitalism. Orthodox Marxists, too, favored an interpretation of the breakdown that would not bind their hands for too long.[9]

REVISIONISM

The pessimistic orthodox viewpoint was unacceptable to Marxists who wanted to achieve immediate and permanent economic improvement and found Marx's breakdown theory unconvincing, both on theoretical grounds and also in light of the undeniable, steady, long-run improvement in the standard of living of the working classes during the second half of the nineteenth century.

The revisionists did not want to deny the existence of exploitation or the desirability of socialism, but they arrived at totally different conclusions concerning the approach to socialism. Characteristic is the following statement taken from the *Economic Democracy Program* of the German socialist labor unions in 1928:

[7] See Werner Alexander, *Kampf um Marx* (Postdam: Alfred Protte Verlag, 1932), p. 128.

[8] N. I. Bucharin, *Der Imperialismus und die Akkumulation des Kapitals* (Wien-Berlin: Verlag für Literatur und Politik, 1926), p. 117. "Third persons" are those who do not belong either to the bourgeoisie or to the proletariat, they are outside the capitalist system, whether at home or abroad.

[9] We will not discuss in this context Lenin's theory of imperialism, since it is not directly connected with Marx's underconsumption theory. See V. I. Lenin, *Imperialism* (New York: International Publishers Co., Inc., 1933), p. 81.

The aim of socialism remained unchanged in the modern labor movement, but the ideas about the way that leads to this aim have undergone a change with the growth of the movement and the change of capitalism. What once appeared a distant dream has become for the present day a visible process of development, a practical task of realization, divided into a large number of single tasks. . . .[10]

It is doubtful whether the term "revisionism" is really appropriate. Revision means an altered interpretation. But the term can hardly be used any longer when nothing of the original doctrine is left. This is true not only for the quoted document but even for the originator of the revisionist movement, Eduard Bernstein, whose real aim, according to Sweezy,[11] "was to eradicate Marxism, root and branch, from the socialist movement," though he may not have been fully conscious of it.

Both the revisionist and the orthodox Marxist were willing to disregard Marx where his theory of capitalist development did not suit their impatience to get down to business, the business of evolution through gradual improvements, or of revolution before capitalist development has run its full course.

MARX AND KEYNES

S. S. Alexander and others [12] have pointed out that certain similarities exist between Marx's and Keynes's theories. Both Marx and Keynes emphasize that a state of under- rather than full employment is characteristic of the private enterprise economy. But their explanations differ. Keynes's theory is based on the assumption that investments may fall short of intended savings, in which case aggregate expenditure, national income, and employment decrease. In Marx, the falling rate of profit seems to make accumulation less attractive. Only when profits rise again because of falling real wages will accumulation improve. This somewhat Keynesian interpretation is incorrect, however. The competitive struggle forces capitalists to invest irrespective of the prospects of profit.[13] Thus one of the main difficulties on which Keynes blames unemployment could not arise since investment of the unconsumed part of surplus value is assured. Marx himself belittles the case of accumulation of surplus value as a mere hoard of money (1:401–403). We must conclude that a dangerous decline in

[10] *Wirtschaftsdemokratie* (Berlin: Verlagsgesellschaft des Allgemeinen Deutschen Gewerkschaftsbundes, 1928), p. 10.

[11] Sweezy, p. 193.

[12] S. S. Alexander, "Mr. Keynes and Mr. Marx," *The Review of Economic Studies*, vol. 3, 1939–1940, pp. 123–135; Joan Robinson, *An Essay on Marxian Economics* (New York: St. Martin's Press, Inc., 1947), especially chaps. 4, 6, and 8.

[13] Joan Robinson, p. 29.

investment and expenditure is not so much caused by a decreasing attractiveness of investment as by a decrease in the amount of surplus value which is available for accumulation. Similarly, v, the amount earned as wages, is all spent on consumption. But the capitalist system does not permit the laborer to buy his own product. There is always a scarcity of "solvent consumers" or of "paying consumption" (2:475). Therefore, while both s and v tend to be fully spent, trouble arises when s and v are too small relative to the productive power of capitalism. With a given technique of production the amount of employment depends on the available capital. If a lot of capital is accumulated employment and wages will tend to rise. This, again, means a falling rate of profit (owing to increased wages) and a decreasing rate of accumulation. Also, the capitalist will substitute capital for labor and the demand for labor will fall.

The antagonistic conditions of distribution play a major part in Marx's system. In Keynes's theory, unequal income distribution leads to trouble only if it results in an amount of intended savings that cannot be absorbed by investment. The two theories, therefore, have only one point in common: that permanent unemployment can exist and the national product may be much smaller than it could be. But Keynes's theory rests on assumptions that permit policies aiming at full employment within the framework of the private enterprise economy. Marx, on the contrary, explains the deficiency in demand as an *inherent* feature of capitalist production and accumulation. According to orthodox Marxism, unemployment cannot be abolished as long as capitalism exists. The very increase in consumption that would create sufficient demand to enable the capitalist to "realize" his surplus value would cut into surplus value, accumulation, and demand for labor. These difficulties do not arise in Keynes's theory because adequate expenditure can be secured without having to raise wages above the level of efficiency.

Both Marx and Keynes are convinced that the actions of individuals may lead to results contrary to their intentions. With Keynes, for example, the intention to save more may lead to decreased savings for the economy as a whole. Uninvested savings reduce expenditure and the national income and with a reduced income less is saved. With Marx, the actions of the capitalists are aimed at increased surplus value but lead, via the antagonistic conditions of distribution, to exploitation without full realization of the surplus value.

SOCIALISM AND COMMUNISM

Marx says very little about future economic systems and what he says is vague. The future economy will be a planned economy. "The point of bourgeois society consists precisely in this, that a priori there is no conscious social regulation of production." [14]

But how will the plan operate? Which problems are to be solved and which solution is proposed?

In an interesting passage on Robinson Crusoe (1:88), Marx points out that necessity itself compels Robinson "to apportion his time accurately between his different kinds of work." Like a trueborn Briton he keeps a set of books in which he keeps account of the labor time that definite quantities of different objects have cost him. Marx continues to show how "all the characteristics of Robinson's labor" are repeated in a community of free individuals "carrying on their work with the means of production in common." One portion of the social product serves as fresh means of production and remains social. Another portion is consumed by the members as a means of subsistence. Marx assumes,

> . . . that the share of each producer in the means of subsistence is determined by his labor-time. Labor-time would, in that case, play a double part. Its apportionment in accordance with a definite social plan maintains the proper proportion between the different kinds of work to be done and the various wants of the community. On the other hand, it also serves as a measure of the proportion of common labor borne by each individual and of his share in the part of the total product destined for individual consumption (1:90–91).

He emphasizes the fact,

> . . . that this necessity of distributing social labor in definite proportions cannot be done away with by the *particular form* of social production, but can only change the *form it assumes*. No natural laws can be done away with. What can change, in changing historical circumstances, is the *form* in which these laws operate. [15]

Marx expresses similar ideas in Volumes 2 and 3 of *Capital*, where he points out that bookkeeping is more necessary in cooperative (perhaps he should have said collectivist) than in capitalist production (2:153). Value in terms of labor time will be the governing principle, and book-

[14] *Letters to Kugelmann* (New York: International Publishers Co., Inc., 1934), p. 74. A collection of the few references in Marx's writings to the problem of economic calculation in socialism can be found in K. Tisch, *Wirtschaftsrechnung und Verteilung im zentralistisch organisierten sozialistischen Gemeinwesen* (Wuppertal-Elberfeld: 1932), pp. 110–115; Oskar Lange and Fred M. Taylor, *On the Economic Theory of Socialism* (Minneapolis: University of Minnesota Press, 1938), Appendix; M. M. Bober, "Marx and Economic Calculation," *American Economic Review*, vol. 36 (June 1946), pp. 344–357.

[15] *The Correspondence of Marx and Engels* (New York: International Publishers Co., Inc., 1934), p. 246. Oskar Lange says of this passage that it disproves "the generally accepted view that Marx regarded *all* economic laws as being of a historico-relative character."—Lange and Taylor, p. 132.

keeping in units of labor time will establish a direct relation between the quantity of social labor time employed and the demand of society for commodities (3:221).

That Marx returns here to the labor theory of value (in contradistinction to the concept "price of production") might seem to rescue the labor theory of value and to prove the superiority of the collectivist economy. In reality these passages prove only that Marx did not see the main problem facing the socialist economy. The socialist economy not only has to allocate labor to its proper uses but has to determine the most economical use of *all* the scarce factors of production—natural resources and capital goods as well as human labor. This problem will be discussed at length in the following chapters.

Marx distinguishes two stages in the development of the future society. Between the capitalist and the communist society lies the period of revolutionary transformation of one into the other. This period, sometimes referred to as socialism, corresponds to a period of political transition in which the state can be nothing but an instrument of the revolutionary dictatorship of the proletariat. Socialism, in contradistinction to communism, is characterized by the fact that the laborer is still rewarded in proportion to his contribution. He is no longer exploited but instead receives an income in proportion to labor rendered. And since different laborers contribute different quantities of socially necessary labor, incomes will differ. Then Marx continues:

> In a higher phase of communist society, after the tyrannical subordination of individuals in the division of labor and thereby also the distinction between manual and intellectual work, have disappeared, . . . after the productive forces have also increased and all the springs of social welfare are flowing more freely, along with the all-round development of the individual, then and then only can the narrow bourgeois horizon of rights be left far behind and society will inscribe on its banner: "From each according to his capacity, to each according to his need." [16]

Marx had rather fantastic ideas about the degree of productivity that could be achieved once the antagonistic conditions of distribution were finally abolished. Not only would it no longer be necessary to limit consumption, it would also be unnecessary to allocate labor, since the practice of increasing productivity through division of labor could be discontinued. Then the time would come when the individual could hunt in the morning, fish in the afternoon, rear cattle in the evening, and criticize after dinner, without specializing in any one of these occupations.[17]

[16] Karl Marx, *Critique of the Gotha Program* (London: Martin Lawrence, 1933), p. 31; quoted in the slightly revised translation of M. M. Bober, pp. 352–353.

[17] Marx-Engels, *Die Deutsche Ideologie* (Berlin: Historisch-kritische Gesamtausgabe, 1927–1932), part I, vol. 5, p. 22. Quoted in Bober, p. 351.

M. M. Bober correctly remarks that the contradictions in these statements need no elaboration:

> The loss of the advantages of the division of labor; the expenditure of resources to train each individual in several trades; the huge amount of bookkeeping required for the functioning of such a scheme; and the incompatibility of the one criterion, production and utility, with the other criterion, the development of the physical and intellectual capacities of the worker—these are some of the considerations that come to mind. The fact that Marx is unimpressed by such considerations argues that labor-value is not what he has in mind as the guide to the productive organization under communism.[18]

Marx's earlier concession that in any social system labor would have to be distributed in definite proportions now seems forgotten. Perhaps this statement actually only referred to the socialist interval between capitalism and communism. As far as communism is concerned, Marx assumes a degree of productivity that would eliminate altogether the necessity of economizing. This "solution" of the economic problems of communism, however, is purely utopian.

[18] Bober, p. 352.

PART 4

The

Liberal

Socialist

Economy

CHAPTER 14

Introduction
to the Economics
of Socialism

AN "UNDERDEVELOPED" THEORY

With the growing importance of socialism as *political* power
there should be a substantial body of doctrine referring to the *economics*
of socialism. If a new social-economic order is to be constructed, the proponents should be busy drawing up various detailed outlines of the
advocated order. Criticism of the private enterprise system is not sufficient
for this purpose. Surprisingly, however, the economic theory of socialism
is still in a rudimentary state of development. The considerations listed
below may help explain this strange situation.

1. It has been shown that Karl Marx was much to blame. Economic
Marxism is a critique of capitalism, which has practically nothing to say
about the structure and the working principles of the centrally planned
economy. Marx's severe criticism of the capitalist system, furthermore,
made it impossible for orthodox Marxists to base their blueprints of
socialism on principles similar to the pricing process of the private enterprise economy; on the contrary, market prices had to be abolished to make
room for the application of the labor theory of value.

2. "Bourgeois" economists, too, were to blame for neglecting the important problem of how a socialist economy could function. The classical economists assumed that the institutional setup of the private enterprise system was the only logical and possible framework for their studies.

3. A few modern writers tried to transcend the institutions of the private enterprise system and to prove the general applicability of the principles of the market economy. Although this attitude promoted the economic theory of socialism, it proved detrimental to further development when it overlooked essential practical problems that had to be solved. A case in point is Cassel's theory, which has been discussed in the Appendix to Chapter 3. Frank H. Knight [1] holds the more extreme view that the economic theorist has little or nothing to say about socialism because the bare fact of substituting a collectivist for a competitive individualist form of organization "does not logically or necessarily imply any particular change whatever, in the empirical course of social economic life." Considering that such a change concerns the abolition of private property in the material means of production and all that this implies, this is an extreme statement with weaknesses that will be revealed in the following chapters.

4. As Friedrich A. Hayek [2] rightly pointed out, the fact that in a market economy most social-economic problems are solved without conscious decision by anybody "has the effect that most people are not conscious of their existence." People are often willing to criticize their system and change or abolish some of its features, but at the same time they take for granted that the regulating forces of the market economy will go on working in spite of these changes. To assume that they can change the institutions of a given social order at will and still retain all the features which they do not expressly want to change is dangerous. The institutions and working principles of an economic system are so closely interrelated that one change may necessitate other changes that they did not bargain for.

5. Perhaps classical economics often neglected the particular institutional characteristics of an economic system, but the opposite attitude, the exaggerated emphasis on historical and institutional data, did not help the development of the economic theory of socialism either. The historical and institutional schools of economics often did nothing but record and describe institutional changes, sometimes even denying the existence of any economic laws. [3] This attitude could not draw conclusions

---

[1] Frank H. Knight, "The Place of Marginal Economics in a Collectivisit System," *American Economic Review*, vol. 26 (March 1936), pp. 255–266.

[2] *Collectivist Economic Planning: Critical Studies on the Possibilities of Socialism*, ed. with Introduction and Concluding Essay by F. A. Hayek; contributors, N. G. Pierson, Ludwig von Mises, George Halm, Enrico Barone (London: Routledge & Kegan Paul Ltd., 1935), p. 7.

[3] See Hayek, p. 10.

concerning a collectivist economy of the future and contributed to the strange result that no blueprints for a socialist economy were developed before World War I.[4]

After World War I the economics of socialism could no longer be treated as a problem of the distant future. Socialist and Communist parties came to power and socialist ideas were put to the test. This was particularly true for Russia and Germany. In both countries it could now be seen that the parties of the left were ill prepared for the difficult tasks they had promised to undertake. In Soviet Russia, the new system went through chaotic, dangerous, and painful years of experimentation before the central plan began to emerge. Some of the transition difficulties were, of course, independent of the new social experiment. But we have Lenin's own word for it that much of the chaos then existing in Russia was due to the fact that the Bolshevists had been utterly unprepared for the gigantic task they undertook. "Experience has convinced us," wrote Lenin, "that it is impossible to reach even the lowest stage of communism, without having passed through a period of socialist accounting and control." [5]

In Germany, revisionist Marxists came to power. Without a theory of the socialist economy they had no basis for a program of action in the economic field. Finally, after long years of silence, the socialist labor unions published a program called *Economic Democracy*,[6] in which they enumerated carefully whatever they considered progress in the direction of socialism: autonomous boards, government-owned enterprise, cartels (!), social insurance, labor legislation, consumers' cooperatives, labor unions, and so forth. The nationalization of large-scale industry was envisaged under the influence of wartime experiences. But no radical changes were desired; the existing system was to be altered only gradually. The one novel idea, that representatives of labor should participate in the management of industry and not only in the handling of labor relations, did not prove very fruitful, since management of industry in the private enterprise system does not lend itself to decisions slowly arrived at by a body whose members represent opposing interests.

No change occurred in the basic economic structure of Germany deserving the name socialism. The German economy remained a private enterprise economy—a situation repeated in England after World War II.

Today we find *centrally* planned industrial economies only in countries under communist dictatorship. No centrally planned liberal socialist econ-

---

[4] But see the papers by N. G. Pierson (1902) and Enrico Barone (1908), which are included in *Collectivist Economic Planning.*

[5] Quoted in Friedrich Pollock, *Die planwirtschaftlichen Versuche in der Sowjetunion 1917–1927* (Leipzig: Verlag C. L. Hirschfeld, 1929), pp. 101–102.

[6] *Wirtschaftsdemokratie, Ihr Wesen, Weg und Ziel,* herausgegeben im Auftrag des Allgemeinen Deutschen Gewerkschaftsbundes von Fritz Naphtali (Berlin: Verlagsgesellschaft des Allgemeinen Deutschen Gewerkschaftsbundes, 1928).

omy exists as yet that would conform to the definition of liberal socialism that we find in socialist literature. The economies of the democratic countries are market economies in which the ownership of the material means of production is still predominantly in private hands. But since some governments *aim* at socialism through evolution, there are economies of a hybrid character. These we shall have to discuss later.

But first we shall study a *blueprint* of liberal socialism that makes it easier to understand the problems of the mixed systems. Strong theoretical guidance is needed to see how central economic planning can be applied in an economic system that tries to combine government ownership with free choice of occupation and consumers' sovereignty.

MISES' CHALLENGE

After World War I, when socialist parties had a chance to prove, if they could, the superiority of socialism as an economic system, Ludwig von Mises tried to show that any attempt to create a rational, workable socialist economy was doomed to failure.[7]

Mises assumes that in the socialist economy all production goods are communal and, therefore, *res extra commercium*. Because production goods are state-owned they cannot become objects of market exchanges. Therefore it is impossible to determine their monetary value. Calculations of costs in monetary units are impractical, and without cost calculations there can be no economic behavior "in our sense of the word." The socialist community will have to "cross the whole ocean of possible and imaginable economic permutations without the compass of economic calculation."[8] Mises then continues:

> Unfortunately . . . it is not possible to divorce the market and its functions in regard to the formation of prices from the working of a society which is based on private property in the means of production and in which, subject to the rules of such a society, the landlords, capitalists and entrepreneurs can dispose of their property as they think fit. For the motive force of the whole process which gives rise to market prices for the factors of production is the ceaseless search on the part of the capitalists and the entrepreneurs to maximize their profits by serving the consumers' wishes. Without the striving of the entrepreneurs (including the shareholders) for profit, of the landlords for rent, of the capitalists for interest

[7] Ludwig von Mises, "Die Wirtschaftsrechnung im sozialistischen Gemeinwesen," *Archiv für Sozialwissenschaften*, vol. 47, 1920, translated under the title "Economic Calculation in the Socialist Commonwealth," in Hayek, *Collectivist Economic Planning*, pp. 87–130; *Die Gemeinwirtschaft, Untersuchungen über den Sozialismus* (Jena: Verlag von Gustav Fischer, 1932), translated under the title *Socialism: An Economic and Socioligical Analysis* (New Haven, Conn.: Yale University Press, 1951).

[8] Mises, *Socialism*, pp. 122, 137–138.

and the laborers for wages, the successful functioning of the whole mechanism is not to be thought of. It is only the prospect of profit which directs production into those channels in which the demands of the consumer are best satisfied at least cost. If the prospect of profit disappears the mechanism of the market loses its mainspring, for it is only this prospect which sets it in motion and maintains it in operation. The market is thus the focal point of the capitalist order of society; it is the essence of Capitalism. Only under Capitalism, therefore, is it possible; it cannot be "artificially" imitated under Socialism.

The importance of Mises' argument was acknowledged on the socialist side. Oskar Lange [9] begins his Economic Theory of Socialism with the remark that socialists "have certainly good reason to be grateful to Professor Mises . . . . for it was his powerful challenge that forced the socialists to recognize the importance of an adequate system of economic accounting to guide the allocation of resources in a socialist economy" and the Marxist Otto Leichter wrote: "To Max Weber and Ludwig Mises belongs the merit of having so energetically drawn the attention of socialists to this question. However little it was the intention of Mises to contribute by his criticism to the positive development of socialist theory and praxis, yet honor must be given where honor is due." [10]

Since the discussion of economic calculation in socialism started, in the main,[11] with Mises' challenge, it is advisable to specify the assumptions and implications of his criticism:

1. Mises' assumptions are extreme. He discusses an authoritarian centrally planned economy rather than a liberal socialist economy with free choice of occupation and consumers' sovereignty.

2. He insists that the planned economy needs consistent factor allocation which, he says, is only feasible when it is based on an all-inclusive pricing process. The government must act economically and must know what to produce, how much in each case, and by which methods. The means of production are not less scarce than before simply because they are now owned by the state.

3. Economic calculation does not rest on labor costs alone. Investment funds and natural resources have specific scarcity and are in need of the same careful and consistent allocation as are the different kinds of labor.

4. Cost accounting in physical terms is impossible. There must be exchange values in monetary units, that is, prices, for consumer goods, intermediate goods, investment funds, and labor.

[9] Oskar Lange and Fred M. Taylor, On the Economic Theory of Socialism (Minneapolis: University of Minnesota Press, 1938), p. 57.

[10] Otto Leichter, Die Wirtschaftsrechnung in der Sozialistischen Gesellschaft (Wien: 1923), p. 74. Quoted in T. J. B. Hoff, Economic Calculation in the Socialist Society (London: William Hodge and Company Limited, 1949), p. 3.

[11] But see footnote 4 to this chapter.

5. Private ownership of the means of production and the profit motive are indispensable. Only on the basis of private property is it possible to establish real exchange relations between private economic units, the precondition for the formation of genuine market prices.

THE SOCIALIST ANSWER

Mises' challenge was answered by liberal socialist writers in ways which emphasized the fundamental difference between the economics of liberal and authoritarian socialism. Basically, the liberal socialist answer was the assertion that the principles of consistent factor allocation *could* apply to an economy in which the state had taken over the material means of production. That the need for consistent allocation was seen and admitted was, of course, no real answer to Mises' argument, which had already assumed that consistent factor allocation was indispensable for any social-economic order. Indeed, the question had admittedly been overlooked or neglected in socialist circles until Mises' pertinent questions made it impossible to ignore the issue any longer.[12]

To answer Mises, the liberal socialists had to show how consistent factor allocation could be achieved in real life once state ownership of the material means of production had eliminated genuine markets. The following chapters try to show to which extent liberal socialists have succeeded or failed in this task.

The reaction of authoritarian socialists was different. Most communist writers ignored the whole controversy for many years. Where notice was taken it was only to suggest that the liberal socialists, in trying to answer Mises, had sacrificed the advantages of central planning for an imitation of the pricing process of the private enterprise system. Authoritarian socialists reject consumers' sovereignty and the complications it creates. They also feel that it is wrong to aim for a static equilibrium through continuous price adjustments when it means giving up the advantages of *ex ante* planning. Prices, they believe, can support planning when financial "balances" are used or a comprehensive auditing apparatus has to be set up. But they reject the idea that prices could guide the plan.

Therefore the authoritarian socialist attitude to the liberal socialist imitation of the pricing process of the private enterprise system was, at least at first, entirely negative. Marxist orthodoxy forbade for many years any unbiased research in this direction. Recent developments in Soviet Russia and its satellites suggest, however, that understanding for the importance of factor allocation and the profit motive is growing. This de-

[12] See F. A. Hayek, "Socialist Calculation: The Competitive 'Solution,'" *Economica*, vol. 7, New Series (May 1940), p. 127.

velopment constitutes a very belated acknowledgement of the existence of the problems which Mises had formulated.

But it should also be pointed out that Soviet Russian experiences with central planning have shown that the centrally planned system need not "degenerate into a meaningless chaos in which the whole of our civilization would disappear." [13] No doubt, Mises exaggerated. A centrally planned system can achieve a modicum of bureaucratic integration. But this does not prove that consistent economic factor allocation, if it could be achieved, would not greatly improve the performance of a centrally planned system in terms of its own aims.

DEFINITIONS

To prepare for a discussion of liberal and authoritarian socialism we must try to disentangle some confused terminology. It is impossible to separate social-economic systems cleanly, to find the exact notch where the knife should slice down. This statement applies not only to the distinction between the main types of socialism but equally to the distinction between the private enterprise system and liberal socialism, between liberal and authoritarian market economies, and between different authoritarian systems.

1. Collectivism. The collectivist economy is characterized by the conscious setting of aims for the economy as a whole and implies an authority which sees to it that these aims are reached. We may call "collectivist" all programs, institutions, and measures which consciously regulate, control, or plan the economy so that predetermined results are achieved. These regulations, controls, or plans may concern aggregate demand, full employment, satisfaction of communal demand, allocation of factors of production, distribution of the national income, the amount of capital accumulation, economic development, the building-up of a war machine, and so forth.

Collectivism, therefore, is clearly distinguished from the private enterprise sector of the market economy where production and distribution are the automatic results of market forces. Collectivism, nevertheless, is not clearly distinguished from the private enterprise system. The two overlap in the following cases.

(a) The private enterprise economy has a public sector to satisfy collective wants and to regulate where necessary the private sector. This public sector corresponds to our definition of collectivism: aims are consciously set and the automatic forces of the market are either not at play or have no commanding influence on our decisions. However, no sharp

[13] Mises, *Socialism,* p. 137.

line can be drawn between economic systems merely according to the size of the public sector. It is impossible to say that the private enterprise economy ends and socialism begins when more than, for instance, 50 percent of a country's resources are used to satisfy collective wants.

(b) The government can attempt to plan total aggregate spending to maintain a high level of employment and to keep both inflation and deflation in check. Monetary and fiscal policies are our system's main answer to socialism's more far-reaching requests.

(c) Wartime experiences show that the private enterprise economy can be subjected to a degree of centralized control which establishes a planned economy in all but name and achieves results of an essentially collectivist character regarding both aims and means.

A term like "collectivism" can become dangerous when used in a slovenly way. Many social systems can be called collectivistic and yet may not have more in common than public ownership of the material means of production, or a central plan. In other respects they may be as different as socialism is from fascism. Suppose that an author uses the term collectivism alternately for socialism and fascism, in order to prove that all the shortcomings of one are equally the shortcomings of the other. The term serves here as a terminological turntable, which is used to shift the argument from one system to the other, and unsuspecting readers may soon come to believe that liberal socialism is exposed to all the vices of fascism.

2. *The Authoritarian "Private Enterprise" System (Fascism).* Many controls are temporarily applied and accepted in a private enterprise economy during total war. If such controls are made permanent for the achievement of collective peacetime purposes, we establish an authoritarian "private enterprise" system. Superficially it maintains private property in the means of production, has essentially the same income distribution as the real private enterprise system and maintains, on paper, the same economic freedoms to consume and to work, together with private initiative and competition. Nevertheless, fascism implies a totalitarian collective plan because social aims are consciously set by the leader and because these ends always take precedence over the private ends of individuals ("Gemeinwohl geht vor Eigenwohl"). Achievement of the ambitious aims of the dictator necessitates establishment of a system of controls which in scope and degree of integration amounts to a central plan and destroys "private enterprise" in its full meaning. (This is the reason why quotation marks have been used.)

3. *Central Planning.* This term, too, has to be used with care. In a discussion of socialist systems we are concerned with *central* planning. The individual economy in a private enterprise system also "plans." It employs systematic thinking, allocates its resources with a given end in mind, and wants to achieve this end with the least costly expenditure of

scarce resources. But this is not central planning that concerns the economy as a whole. In this sense all collectivist economies (and all collectivist sectors of market economies) are centrally planned, implying an authority which decides what goals have to be reached and what resources are available.

H. D. Dickinson [14] adopts the following definition of planning: "Economic planning is the making of major economic decisions—what and how much is to be produced, how, when and where it is to be produced, and to whom it is to be allocated—by the conscious decision of a determinate authority, on the basis of a comprehensive survey of the economic system as a whole." This definition does not state by what method the allocation of the factors of production is to be accomplished or how much room will be given to managerial decentralization. Later, Dickinson suggests that "we may apply the term planning to schemes of economic control that deal with the broad outline of economic activity, without regulating details, provided that, so far as they go, they treat the economic system as a whole." As an example of this type of planning Dickinson mentions "schemes for deliberate control of the price level."

Following Dickinson, we must come to the conclusion that the planned economy and the collectivist economy are identical. But it would be better to reserve the term central planning for Dickinson's first definition and to refer to those broad policies of a monetary and fiscal character merely as indirect controls.

Where the material means of production are owned and operated by the state, it seems obvious that they should be allocated in a predetermined way. No doubt, most socialists think of socialism as a centrally planned system. Yet, if we stress the centralist character of the plan we are in danger of ignoring the crucial difference between liberal and authoritarian socialist economics. Socialist writers often soft-pedal this difference. The authoritarian socialist sometimes wishes to create the impression that the central plan could be combined with a great deal of freedom for consumers, workers, and managers. Liberal socialists, on the other hand, while emphasizing freedom and decentralization, nevertheless want to create the impression that their economy would enjoy all the advantages of central planning. We shall have to study this difficult problem of personal freedom and decentralization under central economic planning. Both liberal and authoritarian socialists profess that freedom and planning can be combined but differ substantially in emphasis. The authoritarian central planner often shows little concern for individual liberties; and for the liberal socialist the central plan is a convenient device, used when the liberal socialist blueprint threatens to deteriorate into a mere replica of

[14] H. D. Dickinson, *Economics of Socialism* (New York: Oxford University Press, 1939), p. 14.

the private enterprise economy. In our study of the economics of socialism we must concentrate on this crucial problem: the planned character of the economy and its implications for individual freedom of action.

4. Liberal Socialism. Liberal (or democratic) socialism is characterized by public ownership of at least the strategically important material means of production, but also by free choice of occupation and consumers' sovereignty. To simplify the discussion we shall assume that *all* material means of production are state-owned and that the producing units are managed by public officials who follow certain rules of behavior. These rules will be discussed in Chapter 16.

The decisive difference between liberal socialism and the private enterprise system lies in the existence of state-owned industries that are not operated for *private* profit. If they exist at all, private firms will be enclaves in the socialist economy, just as nationalized industries are enclaves in the private enterprise economy.

Public management of all productive and distribution processes stamps the liberal socialist economy as a collectivist economy. Liberal socialism wants to supplant the present private enterprise economy, because the latter's individualistic production is assumed to be "fundamentally blind, purposeless, irrational, and incapable of satisfying many of the most urgent human needs." [15] Most liberal socialists agree with this criticism, but there is less agreement on the positive aims of the liberal socialist economy or on the ways by which these aims can be reached.

The liberal social economy needs an authority that can set and accomplish social-economic ends—an authority that must have the power to allocate the means of production according to some plan. In this respect the blueprint of the liberal socialist economy is centralistic, though it need not be totalitarian. The liberal socialist system wants to permit consumers' sovereignty in its full meaning. This point is of major significance for differentiating various forms of collectivism. Communism and fascism will not make the preferences of consumers the main criterion in production and in the allocation of resources. They do not want unpredictable actions of consumers and workers to endanger the functioning of the plan. Free individual choices must, in case of conflict, give way to the plan. Liberal socialism is in a more difficult position. It must prove that consumers' sovereignty is compatible with the collectivist character of its economy, that individual freedom can be combined with state ownership of the material means of production, and that central planning can and will follow the preferences of the consumers.

Not all writers who consider themselves liberal socialists are equally sanguine concerning this important point. R. L. Hall, for instance, says that the collectivist character of the socialist economy "involves the aban-

[15] Dickinson, p. 9.

donment of free choice of the individual, at any rate as a fundamental liberty: consumption and production must fit into a central scheme." [16]

Liberal socialism wants to achieve substantially greater equality of income distribution than is possible under the private enterprise system. The abolition of private property in the material means of production leads to greater equality through the elimination of unearned income. As a rule, socialists do not ask for complete equality; they realize that wage differentials are a necessary feature of an economy that wants to maintain free choice of occupation.

Capital accumulation and investment are the main areas of liberal socialist planning. Investment in overhead capital and initial investment would not be guided solely by consumers' preferences, but care would have to be taken lest consumers' sovereignty got lost in this process of investment planning. In the last analysis, the demand for investment goods would have to remain a "derived" demand, that is, a demand induced by the demand for consumer goods.

This enumeration of the characteristic features of the liberal socialist economy shows that, as an economic system, liberal socialism finds its place somewhere between the private enterprise and the authoritarian system. With the private enterprise system it shares freedom of occupational choices and consumers' sovereignty, the use of prices to direct production and to allocate productive resources, a certain amount of inequality of income distribution, and belief in the necessity of decentralization in the management of production. With authoritarian socialism it shares the more pronounced collectivist character of the system (that is, the conscious pursuit of social-economic aims), state ownership of the material means of production, a more equalitarian income distribution, and the existence of a central economic authority that determines the rate of capital accumulation and somehow provides necessary guidance where automatic market forces cease to operate.

The liberal socialist economy hopes to combine the features of conscious planning with individual freedom, so that a large social product can be more equally distributed according to the wishes of the consumers. Although these aims are fairly clear, it is less clear how the different features of liberal socialism are to be combined in a working order. What compromise is to be struck between freedom and planning, market exchange and public management?

5. Authoritarian Socialism (Communism). In the authoritarian socialist economy the central authority owns and controls all the means of production (labor, natural resources, capital), autocratically determines the aims of the economy, directs production in an all-inclusive plan, and

[16] R. L. Hall, *The Economic System in a Socialist State* (New York: St. Martin's Press, Inc., 1937), pp. 41–42.

regulates distribution accordingly. The freedoms enjoyed in the liberal socialist economy are abolished wherever they collide with the plan. Authoritarian socialism resolves the conflict between freedom and planning at the expense of freedom. Thus it offers a more simple working model of socialism. If consumers can be forced to take what is produced and if the members of a totalitarian socialist society can be made to work where the plan requires their services, the general scheme of things is less complicated.

However, even the authoritarian socialist economy needs a comprehensive accounting process and consistent factor allocation. If plan figures are expressed in monetary terms in a financial plan, do these prices guide the plan or does the plan arbitrarily determine prices with the sole intention of aggregating? We shall try to answer these questions after we have studied the allocation process in the liberal socialist economy.

The authoritarian socialist economy can be less extreme than this model. It may, for example, permit free choice of consumption or the allocation of labor by means of wage differentials. However, should consumers' preferences become the guide of production, the authoritarian socialist system would change into a liberal socialist system.

CHAPTER 15

Liberal Socialism
and Factor Allocation

INTRODUCTION

The following paragraphs try to show that a socialist economy faces difficult problems of factor allocation. Public ownership of the material means of production and government control of all investment funds do not erase these problems. Investment funds, in particular, must be allocated consistently, whether the economy is liberal or totalitarian, consumer-oriented or centrally planned.

Emphasis will, at first, be placed on the liberal socialist economy because, in its consumer-oriented production, it is more similar to the private enterprise economy than to authoritarian socialism. But our results will be applicable to some extent to authoritarian socialism as well. In changing from liberal to authoritarian socialism the assumption changes regarding aims and methods, but the problem of factor allocation must be solved in either case.

PRESENT AND PAST LABOR

It is assumed that in liberal socialism production is to follow the wishes of consumers as they express themselves in prices on consumer goods markets. These markets are *real* markets where consumers spend their income in government stores freely and without rationing. Changing prices indicate changes in demand or supply. But these price movements alone are not a sufficient guide for production. Commodity prices are relevant only in relation to costs; only a comparison of prices and costs can tell whether production should expand or contract in given industries.

Costs are determined by factor prices and techniques of production. Ideally, the price charged for a unit of a particular homogeneous factor must be the same for all industries using that factor if a rational factor allocation is to be achieved. An hour of labor of a given kind, for example, must be paid the same wage wherever used; otherwise equilibrium is not yet achieved and labor should be moved.

In the private enterprise economy factor prices are determined by demand and supply on factor markets. How would they be determined in a liberal socialist economy?

If "present" labor [1] were the only factor of production the answer would be quite simple. Since liberal socialism wants to maintain free choice of occupation, there must exist a *real* labor market on which the public managers of plants or industries compete for different kinds of labor, and where laborers try to find the best-paid jobs for which they qualify. In equilibrium the wage rate for each (noncompeting) group will balance demand and supply.

If wages of present labor were really the only cost item that had to be considered, product prices would be determined by labor costs alone. In equilibrium, commodity prices would just cover these costs and simultaneously equate demand and supply. Production in different industries would expand and contract, and labor would shift until these results were achieved. In equilibrium, furthermore, the total wage bill would suffice to enable workers, as consumers, to buy the whole national product; for total wages, national income, national product, total costs, and the total of all commodity prices would all be equal. The distribution of income, the allocation of labor to different industries, and the production of commodities would be determined by (1) the relative scarcities of different kinds of labor, (2) techniques of production, and (3) tastes (and incomes) of consumers.

The only difficulty encountered in this simple model concerns the monopolistic position of government managers in commodity markets and their monopsonistic power in labor markets. The element of arbitrary price determination implied in the state's position as the single buyer of labor and the single seller of commodities can perhaps be overcome by establishing a rule that public managers must behave as if they were acting under

[1] As contrasted with "past" labor. See above, chap. 11.

real competitive pressure; or real competition could possibly be permitted to exist among decentralized, semiautonomous government agencies.

Let us now remove the assumption that only present labor need enter our cost calculation. We assume that labor uses instruments and materials of production that are scarce, since they are the result of earlier production processes and have to be accounted for at least as past labor in the Marxian sense.

It would be naïve to assume that a socialist economy could disregard these capital goods in its accounting processes merely because the state owns them already and, accordingly, does not have to buy them from private sources. Certainly, Karl Marx would not have drawn this wrong conclusion. His labor theory of value counts past as well as present labor and it does not make any difference to him how long ago a unit of labor was used. If all materials and instruments of production were the result of labor alone, raw materials and depreciation allowances would still be included in cost calculations. Decisive would be the production costs in terms of socially necessary labor time, together with the periods of turnover.[2] Marx also points out that a portion of the social product serves as fresh means of production and remains social in the socialist society. This is capital accumulation at the expense of present consumption. Because both the replacement of old and the construction of new capital goods are necessary in socialism, part of the working force must be employed in the investment goods industry. This means that the workers in the consumer goods industries must share their product with their comrades who produce raw materials and replace or create fixed capital. Obviously, then, the prices of consumer goods must rise above their cost in terms of present labor if equilibrium between demand and supply is to be maintained. To put it differently, the aggregate value of consumer goods prices must be substantially higher than the total wage bill in consumer goods industries.

But not even the consideration of capital replacement and capital accumulation is sufficient if a proper allocation of the factors of production is to be achieved. Up to now we have acknowledged only that capital goods are as scarce as is the socially necessary labor used in their production, that capital goods are in need of amortization, and that resources have to be diverted from consumer goods production to investment goods production if the economy is to grow. Now the *specific* scarcity of capital must be accounted for by a specific price over and above the amortization of the original production cost of capital goods. This price is the rate of interest. To admit the need for an accounting process that uses an interest rate to allocate capital means, of course, that we must deviate from Marxian ideas of socialist accounting.

2 See above, chaps. 11 and 12.

THE SCARCITY OF INVESTMENT FUNDS

But is the assumption justified that a liberal socialist economy requires a rate of interest for the consistent allocation of its resources? Is not the rate of interest a typical phenomenon of the private enterprise system, which could be discarded in a socialist economy with public ownership of the material means of production?

First consider a problem whose solution in the private enterprise economy depends, at least partly, on the rate of interest. The socialist economy does *not* have to use interest payments to elicit a sufficient supply of savings, that is, funds set aside for the production of investment, rather than consumption goods. The socialist government can arbitrarily decide how much it wants to accumulate, how much of the total national product shall take the form of producers' goods.

Whether such an arbitrary decision on the part of the government would violate the principle of free choice of consumption depends on the interpretation of this freedom. If free consumers' choice is to include the option between present and future consumption, the freedom to save must be maintained, even though it implies private accumulation of capital, at least in the form of claims to future income. A socialist economy with state ownership of the material means of production could still permit the purchase of government securities or of life insurance. It could even employ the inducement to save that the private enterprise economy uses, that is, pay interest on savings. It must make sure, however, that private ownership of securities does not imply the right to control the use of capital goods.

But a socialist economy would be unlikely to permit the total amount of capital accumulation to depend upon the willingness of its members to save. The state, as the owner of capital and land and the producer of all commodities, would receive part of the national income as interest, rent, or profit and could either invest or distribute these earnings. Investment could be smaller or greater than the state's share in the national income. If it were smaller, a "social dividend" would be paid to each member of the community; if it were larger, the government would have to take away part of the income of the citizens through taxation, monopolistic pricing, or inflationary credit creation. Capital accumulation rests, in a full employment economy, on the reduction of consumer goods production in favor of an enlarged production of capital goods.

If we say that the government of the socialist state decides arbitrarily on the volume of capital accumulation, this is not meant as a value judgment. This decision can be the result of democratic processes. The socialist can point out, moreover, that it is the unequal income distribution in the private enterprise system that largely determines the amount of voluntary individual and corporate savings, and that this determination is in no way less arbitrary than when the rate of capital accumulation is chosen by a socialist government.

The discussion has shown that the essence of capital formation or accumulation is not so much the production of capital goods as it is the setting aside of factors of production for investment rather than for consumption. Within the framework of the private enterprise economy this generalized purchasing power, which can be used to buy whatever is necessary for any conceivable production process, has been referred to as loanable funds. Since we are not certain that actual lending and borrowing would take place in a socialist economy, we shall use the term investment funds instead. Investment funds are not yet committed to any particular investment project. They merely embody the power to use productive resources for the production of investment goods.

It is of the greatest importance for any economic system that this generalized purchasing power, called loanable or investment funds, be put to the best possible use to achieve the aims of the economy. In the private sector of the private enterprise economy these funds are mainly distributed, according to the willingness and ability of borrowers to pay for their use, that is, to pay a sufficiently high rate of interest. The interest rate, therefore, does not merely have the function of inducing the supply of savings. Even if individual savers were willing to forgo their income from interest —even if they would save at zero rates of interest—interest would still be forced upon them by entrepreneurs competing to obtain the use of loanable funds. Normally, the demand for loanable funds for investment purposes would far exceed the supply at zero rates. Whether this specific scarcity, which causes the price phenomenon called interest, is characteristic only for the private enterprise economy or applies equally to other economic systems must be determined.

The socialist may be tempted to argue that there is no such thing as a special scarcity of capital goods or of investment funds in socialism. Capital goods can be produced in increasing amounts if only more labor can be allocated to their production. The only primary factor of production, the socialist might say, is labor, and capital goods produced by labor are therefore only as scarce as the labor used in their production. This throws us back once again on the labor theory of value.

There is, however, a serious flaw in this argument. It is by no means possible to requisition any desired quantity of labor (and of already produced capital goods and natural resources) for the manufacture of new investment goods. Assuming full employment, the output of consumer goods has to be restricted in order to increase the output of capital goods. Of course, as more investment goods are produced, the productive power of the economy grows; therefore, it is able *in the long run* to produce more consumer goods. It is indeed mostly for this reason that we are always eager to introduce newer and better machines. But the increase in productivity from new investment does not occur until *later*, and in the meantime we must forgo the satisfaction which could have been derived from spending the funds which we chose to save and invest.

Modern production processes are time-consuming and roundabout. The construction of capital goods takes time. In addition, many capital goods are durable and render their full services only over long periods. Therefore some time must elapse before there can be any increase at all in the satisfaction of consumers' wants, and a much longer time must pass before a given durable capital good has rendered all the services of its lifetime. In other words, the satisfaction of wants must be *waited for*. There will be more consumer goods in the future, but at present there are fewer than would otherwise be possible.

Obviously, it would be absolutely impossible to allocate all our available resources to the production of capital goods. As indicated in Chapter 2, this is a basic truth that is independent of the economic organization of our society, independent even of whether an indivdual lives in isolation or as a member of a social economy. This can be demonstrated for several different economic systems.

An isolated farmer spends a large part of his time carrying water from the water hole. He wants to dig a well but can never spare enough time to do the job. The capital good, though very useful and in the long run laborsaving, is beyond his reach because of the constant pressure of his daily struggle for existence.

This farmer's economy is isolated and not part of a social economy, but his case is repeated by the economies of *poor countries*, like India, where millions live on a starvation level simply because they are not productive enough to be able to set aside savings for the production of other than immediately needed goods. This is one of the most crucial problems of economic development.

In *a private enterprise economy* total savings are determined by many factors, such as income level and income distribution. As total income increases, consumption, though increasing in absolute figures, tends to decrease relatively, so that a greater proportion of the growing national income is being saved. A higher level of consumption carries with it a growing willingness to forgo some consumption in the present in the hope of bettering the opportunities for consumption in the future.

In *an authoritarian economy* the rate of accumulation is determined by the dictator, who can arbitrarily divide the available factors of production between consumer goods and capital goods industries. He may enforce a starvation level of consumption, but even he cannot ignore consumer goods production altogether.

The liberal socialist economy, too, will have to decide on a rate of accumulation, that is, it must somehow choose between present and future consumption. It may desire both a more equal income distribution and a higher rate of capital formation and economic growth than would prevail under a private enterprise system. Here it faces a dilemma because a higher real income for the masses militates against a high rate of accumulation.

Therefore, the problem of capital accumulation is essentially the same in all systems. It is a conflict between the reluctance to cut down a possible present consumption level and the desire to raise the standard of living in the future via increased production of capital goods. Assuming full employment, it is not difficult to find the reason for that specific scarcity which leads, in our market economy, to the payment of a special price for the use of loanable funds.

LIBERAL SOCIALISM AND INTEREST

It is time to return to the question of whether the liberal socialist economy would also have to make use of interest charges for the purpose of adequate calculation and factor allocation.

Since the rate of interest is a price, it must, like any other price, rest on the fact that the commodity or service for which it is paid is both useful and scarce. Investment funds would be scarce in any social economy. Similarly, capital goods are useful, and the efficiency of production increases when labor is supported by tools and machines. This fact has never been denied by socialist writers. If anything, socialists want to use more capital goods than the private enterprise economy manages to produce. We are therefore entitled to say that capital goods increase labor's efficiency, that it is desirable to have more capital goods, that investment funds are always relatively scarce, and that this situation is independent of the institutional framework of the economy, applying therefore to socialism quite as much as to the private enterprise system.

Since the liberal socialist economy cannot have all the capital goods that it would wish to employ, it has to be very careful to produce those that are the most useful. The question is not only how *many* capital goods should be produced during a period but also *which* capital goods should be selected, which industries should enjoy the advantage of being able to support their labor force with newer and better equipment. This second question is not yet solved when the central authority of the liberal socialist economy has decided on the total amount of capital goods production. The *total* can be determined arbitrarily, but the *allocation* of investment funds to different industries should not be decided in an arbitrary fashion. We have to know whether more steel, tractors, automobiles, roller bearings, or printing presses ought to be produced, and how far the expansion of production should go in each case. A *consistent* solution to this problem is possible only when we make each user of investment funds pay, or account for, the same rate of interest. This rate must be high enough to equate demand and supply both in the economy as a whole and in each industry.

It could perhaps be thought that a socialist government simply allocates funds according to plan. But this does not solve the question of the most economical use of a limited supply of investment funds. Mere reference to a plan is not sufficient or it leads only to the question of how the plan itself can be so designed that it allocates resources in the best way to secure the ends of the collectivist economy. Will not the planners themselves need to be guided by a uniform rate of interest?

The most economical allocation of investment funds is a problem that must be solved in all economic systems. Whether the aim of production is to satisfy the changing wants of sovereign consumers or the preferences of a dictator—the investment funds must be allocated in conformance to these wishes or preferences. The difference between liberal and authoritarian socialism lies in the fact that liberal socialism sets itself the more difficult task of adjusting the direction of production constantly to the changing demand of consumers, whereas the authoritarian system eliminates this complication.

The only way to establish an orderly priority of production, which accurately reflects the intensities of consumer demand, is to compare, for each commodity, the price which consumers are willing to pay and the cost of its production. However, costs must include not only labor costs, past and present, and expenditures for scarce natural resources, but also interest on the invested capital. No production that is unable to cover interest charges should ordinarily be undertaken.

But how is the rate of interest to be determined in an economic system where a genuine market for investment funds does not exist, where the state bank alone can furnish these funds and the demand for them comes exclusively from state-owned industries and firms?

The authorities could set an interest rate of, say, 5 percent and rule that industrial managers, using investment funds, would have to pay this rate. But a manager could pay the rate only if, in turn, he were able to sell his product for a price high enough to pay for this special charge in addition to all other production costs. The unique uniformity of the rate of interest (as a percentage, per period of time, of a sum of money) lends itself conveniently to central regulation. It has done so for many years in the monetary policies of private enterprise economies. In spite of the fact that the private enterprise economy can establish a market rate of interest, it has often been found desirable (for better or worse) to change this rate artificially. The rate of interest, for example, has been kept artificially low to stimulate private investment or to reduce the cost of servicing the public debt; or it has been artificially raised to stop inflation and to balance the international accounts.

Certainly, a price that has been subject to constant public management in the private enterprise economy could also be subject to public regulation in a socialist economy. Nevertheless, there is a difference: whereas in our type of market economy a cheap-money policy constitutes a deviation from a market price that would establish itself without the government's interference, in a liberal socialist economy an arbitrary setting of the interest rate would always be necessary. In both the private enterprise and the liberal socialist economy, money creation can augment the normal supply of funds out of private or public savings and thereby lower the rate of interest that equalizes supply and demand; and in both systems inflation and deflation can be used *ex post* to determine whether the rate is too low or too high.

The government can in either system maintain an inflationary low rate of interest and counteract inflationary effects through price controls, rationing, and investment priorities. But such action implies interference with consumers' sovereignty and thus violates the basic premises of the two systems. If with a given rate of accumulation the noninflationary rate should be 8 percent but the government decided to set a ceiling of 3 percent, the following consequences can be expected in both the private enterprise and the liberal socialist economy:

1. If the gap between the demand for and the supply of investment funds is being filled by credit creation, price inflation will develop even before "full" employment has been reached.

2. To prevent price inflation, price ceilings may be imposed and consumption may be limited by rationing.

3. Since at artificially low rates of interest there are many more investment opportunities than available factors of production, the allocation of investment funds must also be controlled. Where the rate of interest no longer makes the selection, a central plan tries to make a reasonable allocation of investment funds, both in the economy as a whole and in individual industries and plants.

Later the question of whether or not a consistent central plan can be worked out without the basis of a correctly chosen rate of interest will be considered. If the conclusion is reached that a correct rate is essential for the plan to be economical on its own terms, reference to a central plan offers no escape from the present problem.

That a liberal socialist economy can set rates of interest just as they are set by central banks of private enterprise economies does not prove that the allocation of investment funds can be solved satisfactorily. Only when the managers of state-owned industries and plants, who can secure these funds, are the ones who should receive them, can this allocation problem be considered solved. But even then, how can the managers be induced to make the most economical use of the investment funds that they received? In other words, we meet the problem of the allocation of investment funds both in the macro- and microeconomic field.

INTERMEDIARY GOODS

The uniformity of the rate of interest as price and the possibility of setting this price seem to indicate that the liberal socialist economy would not face a particularly difficult allocation problem as far as investment funds are concerned. But we must reserve judgment until we have seen convincing proof that the system knows which managers ought to get the funds, particularly where entirely new investment projects are concerned.

In the private enterprise economy, the allocation of loanable funds rests on the comparison of rates of profit with rates of interest. Would this comparison also apply to the liberal socialist economy? Before turning to this problem we must deal with Mises' main argument, namely, that a genuine pricing process is not possible in the absence of private property. The assumption of state ownership of capital goods and land implies that real markets for intermediate goods do not exist and that a *complete* pricing process would have to rest on artificially set prices as far as these commodities are concerned. Artificially set prices, subject only to occasional adjustments, tend to become wrong prices during most of the period of their validity. They will then misguide production and, in case of price adjustments, lead to abrupt changes in the production processes. A pricing process that rests, in part at least, on temporarily fixed prices will be inferior to a real market process which permits instant price reactions to changing market forces.

The state would face a formidable task in trying to set (and frequently adjust) the prices of all intermediate goods, many of which cannot be sufficiently standardized. The managers on the spot would have a much better knowledge of what the prices ought to be than the men in the central planning agency, and the managers would be reluctant to base their economic calculations on (what they know to be wrong) official prices. The planning authorities, on the other hand, would often not be able to check the actions of the managers. The tendency toward decentralization of management in liberal socialism rests, at least in part, on the acknowledgment that the detailed know-how lies with the men on the spot rather than with the planners in the center.

Artificial pricing of capital goods, which are not subject to genuine market processes, would tend to be jerky and inexact and subject to constant controversy between planners and managers. If it is argued that the set prices would become more accurate as equilibrium is approached in a series of trial-and-error processes, this would hold true only for an approach to static equilibrium, whereas it is the main function of the market processes to provide constant adjustments under dynamic conditions.

PROFIT AND RISK

In order to understand the role of profit in the liberal socialist economy, we must first analyze the different meanings of profit, profit motive, and profit maximization in the private enterprise economy.

A. C. Pigou [3] stresses the difference between profit and profit motive. Profit is the margin between outlay and receipt; profit motive is simply synonymous with the desire for personal gain, the attitude which we called acquisitiveness. In this sense everybody would tend to "maximize his profits." Even in liberal socialism the worker or manager who would leave his job to accept a better one in another plant or industry would be acting in response to the profit motive. But this is not what is usually referred to when speaking of maximization of profit. We are then speaking of profit as an entrepreneurial income, and the desire to make this difference between outlay and receipt as large as possible.

What will happen to profit maximization in this narrower sense in a liberal socialist system? Will public managers be told to maximize profits, that is, to use the publicly owned land and capital at their disposal to earn the greatest possible returns for the state? Since all profits are the state's, the proposal would not be incompatible with the socialist character of the system. Neither, however, would it serve the best possible allocation of the means of production with reference to consumers' preferences. Maximization of profit certainly cannot be an end in itself in the liberal socialist economy. The state does not need a maximum profit for purposes of capital accumulation; it can raise the necessary funds through taxation or other methods.

But the fact that profits are made in a plant or industry is, in itself, an important indicator that production in this plant or industry should be expanded. As production expands, profits will disappear. Public managers should therefore use profits as an indicator to prove that their particular plants or industries are entitled to further expansion.

[3] A. C. Pigou, *Socialism Versus Capitalism* (New York: St. Martin's Press, Inc., 1939), pp. 3–5.

Profits as indicators perform a necessary function in the liberal socialist economy. They lead to the most desirable allocation of the nation's productive resources and are constantly eliminated by continuous reallocation of the factors of production. For the managers of plants and industries, the principle of profit maximization is actually reduced to the effort of keeping costs as low as possible. Profits, *however they originate*, should lead to an increased allocation of loanable funds for expansion. Even if profits are caused by a monopolistic position, this rule would apply, since expansion of production would eliminate the basic objection against monopoly—its artificial limitation of production.

In the private enterprise system, profits are an indicator that equilibrium has not yet been fully achieved, and that competition should lead to equilibrium of demand and supply at cost prices. Although liberal socialism may aim more directly at equilibrium at cost prices, temporary profits will appear in the process of approaching equilibrium. Indeed, such profits are the gauges necessary for steering the allocation of resources.

Legitimate (that is, nonmonopolistic) profits may appear for two reasons. Either the managers concerned have encountered greater demand than they had foreseen, or they have developed methods of reducing costs. In both cases they can claim additional investment funds; they have the means of servicing the loan of additional funds, in other words, to pay the rate of interest.

Often the reduction of production costs is impossible without the introduction of labor-saving machinery. In these cases investment funds must be obtained *before* the anticipated cost reduction can be achieved. Doubts may here arise whether the claimed increase in labor efficiency will actually materialize. In other words, the proposed investment is risky. Similarly, the *anticipation* of a growing or entirely new demand will involve risk. Where a growing demand must be met, it should first be seen in the form of higher product prices, an excess of demand over supply. In the case of anticipated demand for a *new* product, however, this is not possible, and risks will have to be taken.

In the case of new production methods and new products it is conceivable that a "risk-premium" might be added to the rate of interest. Then only managers who believe they can cover this additional premium in their products' sales price (or through lowered costs) will be given the necessary funds. Certainly the liberal socialist economy cannot employ scarce resources in an entirely speculative way; on the other hand, it cannot stop probing new techniques and new markets.

If these decisions are difficult in consumer goods industries, they are even more complex in all earlier stages of production, which are far removed from the ultimate consumer goods that they help to produce. Therefore a demand for investment funds may come from managers who produce only parts of capital goods, and the capital goods, in turn, may not yet be used in the final stages of production. Furthermore, we know that the demand for investment goods in the private enterprise system is subject to a "magnification" that can create substantial cyclical movements.[4] The explanation of this phenomenon does not suggest that it is limited only to the present system.

PRICING AND PLANNING

Socialists say that the instability of the private enterprise economy is caused by its reliance on the "blind" forces of the market, by the decisions of people who can see only a tiny section of the whole. The implication is, of course, that the socialist economy would enjoy the advantage of central planning.

But does central planning provide a substitute for market prices where no markets exist? Liberal socialists are for *de*centralization; they believe in as much freedom of management as can be made compatible with public ownership; and they are aware that the necessary detailed knowledge of technological and other important data lies only with the men on the spot.

We should therefore assume that managers in a liberal socialist economy are *not* just fulfilling predetermined production quotas. Predetermined central planning is already excluded by the fact that production is ultimately to be guided by the consumer. But between consumers' demand and investment decisions in capital goods industries lies a big gap, which must be bridged either by planning an integrated production program or by consistently extending the pricing process from *real* consumer and labor markets (via a somewhat artificial capital market) into the area of capital goods production.

The theory of liberal socialism has to show how central planning can be squared with consumers' sovereignty and how consistent pricing is compatible with artificial markets where public managers deal exclusively with other public managers. Liberal socialists want to combine planning and pricing. From this combination they hope to derive a system that promises the advantages of both freedom and conscious collectivist planning.

The crucial economic problem of liberal socialism is the substitution of new methods of cost calculation and factor allocation for those that were removed by the abolition of the private enterprise system. If it is impossible to maintain an adequate pricing process, *liberal* socialism may be doomed, because production can no longer follow the command of the consumer, and the central authority will have to rule by arbitrary decision.

[4] See above, chap. 8.

If, on the other hand, a comprehensive pricing and accounting process can be created within a socialist framework, most problems indicated in this chapter will have found an answer, at least on the theoretical level. The most essential question is therefore whether or not the liberal socialist economy can reproduce the pricing process without the foundation of several typically "capitalist" institutions: private property in the material means of production, market exchanges between independent firms, actual competition, risk taking, and the profit motive.

But even if these attempts were successful, could the liberal socialist economy then still claim for itself the advantage of central planning?

CHAPTER 16

Blueprints
for a Liberal
Socialist Economy

ABSTRACT SOLUTIONS

Socialist writers who have dealt with the problems which were discussed in the preceding chapter can be divided into four groups.

A *first* group suggests that money be abolished and necessary calculations carried out *in natura*, that is, in work hours, tons, kilowatts, and so forth. Only writers who are completely bewildered will try to "improve" the social-economic system by depriving it of the services of a common unit of account, the *sine qua non* for consistent factor allocation. These proposals are not worth studying.[1]

A *second* group proposes abstract solutions in the hope that its proposals can work in the real world. A brief discussion will show that these blueprints have not managed to bridge the gap between theory and reality.

A *third* group recommends a practical trial-and-error solution, a proposal that will be discussed in the present chapter.

[1] See, however, the criticisms of the following: T. J. B. Hoff, *Economic Calculation in the Socialist Economy* (London: William Hodge and Company, Ltd., 1949), chap. 4; Franz Haber, *Untersuchungen über Irrtümer moderner Geldverbesserer* (Jena: Gustav Fischer, 1926); Arthur W. Cohn, *Kann das Geld abgeschafft werden?* (Jena: Gustav Fischer, 1920).

The *fourth* group also suggests a practical approach, but since it is emphasizing central planning at the expense of consumers' sovereignty, its proposals will be discussed later as an authoritarian solution.

The first proposals to be considered are the abstract schemes that merely indicate the problem but do not offer any really convincing recommendations for a practical solution.

Some socialists think it possible to provide for adequate calculation in socialism by reference to the possibility of an "imputation of quantitative significances." Eduard Heimann,[2] for example, says that the valuation of consumption goods is "reflected" in the valuation of the factors of production, that market prices of consumer goods are "transmitted" through all the stages of production, that the values of consumer goods and of the factors of production are connected by an "elastic string," and that it is consequently possible, even if private property in the means of production is abolished, to "calculate the significance of each factor in the manufacture of goods if the prices of the products are given."

This is not a solution of the allocation problem; it is not even a correct statement of the issue. What we need is not an *ex post facto* imputation of commodity prices but an answer to the question of what costs are to be incurred in view of a given demand for consumer goods. Cost data can be obtained only from an *independent* and consistent valuation of the separate factors of production, which can be combined in an infinite variety of ways. T. J. B. Hoff[3] rightly points out that factor values cannot be imputed exclusively from the values of the final products. "This could only be done if the factors of production were always used in fixed proportions and they were only used to produce a single product."

For a practical solution it is also not enough to *imagine*, as Carl Landauer[4] suggests, "each good changed from one employment to another until it has actually obtained its highest attainable significance." Robinson Crusoe can perform this task because he knows all the relevant data and his mind registers instantly all the changes of these data. But when the aggregate demand in the social economy rests on innumerable individual priority scales, when the division of labor is carried to the extreme, when the enormously complex process of production and distribution is beyond the power of comprehension of any individual or even of a central planning board, then any imputation other than through a comprehensive pricing process is impractical.

---

[2] Eduard Heimann, *Mehrwert und Gemeinwirtschaft: kritische und positive Beiträge zur Theorie des Sozialismus* (Berlin: Robert Engelmann, 1922); *Kapitalismus und Sozialismus* (Potsdam: Alfred Protte, 1931).

[3] Hoff, p. 123.

[4] Carl Landauer, *Planwirtschaft und Verkehrswirtschaft* (Munich: Duncker und Humblot, 1931), p. 119.

It has been suggested that the factor allocation could be handled by a system of simultaneous equations which could be solved and would, in one tremendous comprehensive calculation, determine the interrelated prices of consumer goods, intermediate goods, and the factors of production. For instance, Gustav Cassel's equations have been used for this purpose.[5] But it is quite obvious that these equations do not provide us with a practical solution of the allocation problem in liberal socialism. Cassel knew that his equations could not be solved, for the demand functions are unknown.[6]

Enrico Barone [7] uses a system of equations to show that the Ministry of Production in a collectivist state would have to use "all the economic categories of the old regime . . . : prices, salaries, interest, rent, profit, saving, and so forth." He comes to the conclusion that "it is conceivable . . . that with a vast organization for this work it would be possible to collect the individual schedules for every given series of various equivalents, including the premium for deferred consumption." But, he continues, "it is frankly *inconceivable* that the *economic* determination of the technical coefficients can be made a priori, in such a way as to satisfy the condition of minimum cost of production. . . ."

Vilfredo Pareto,[8] who like Cassel and Barone, uses a system of simultaneous equations, says:

It may be mentioned here that this determination has by no means the purpose to arrive at a numerical calculation of prices. Let us make the most favorable assumption for such a calculation, let us assume that we have triumphed over all the difficulties of finding the data of the problem and that we know the ophélimités of all the different commodities for each individual, and all the conditions of production for all the commodities, etc. This is already an absurd hypothesis to make. Yet it is not sufficient to make the solution of the problem possible. We have seen that in the case of 100 persons and 700 commodities there will be 70,699 conditions (actually a great number of circumstances which we have so far neglected will still increase that number); we shall therefore have to solve a system of 70,699 equations. This exceeds practically the power of algebraic analysis, and this is even more true if one contemplates the fabulous number of equations which one obtains for a population of forty millions

[5] See below, Appendix to Chap. 3. For a solution based on the Casselian equations, see Klaire Tisch, *Wirtschaftsrechnung und Verteilung in zentralistisch organisierten sozialistischen Gemeinwesen* (Wuppertal-Elberfeld: 1932).

[6] See Appendix to Chap. 3, footnote 3.

[7] Enrico Barone, "The Ministry of Production in the Collectivist State," in *Collectivist Economic Planning*, ed. F. A. Hayek (London: Routledge & Kegan Paul Ltd., 1935), Appendix A, pp. 287, 289.

[8] Vilfredo Pareto, *Manuel d'économie politique*, 2d ed., 1927, pp. 233–234. Quoted in F. A. Hayek, "Socialist Calculation: The Competitive 'Solution,'" *Economica*, New Series, vol. 7 (1940), pp. 125–126.

and several thousand commodities. In this case the roles would be changed: it would not be mathematics which would assist political economy, but political economy would assist mathematics. In other words, if one really could know all these equations, the only means to solve them which is available to human powers is to observe the practical solution given by the market.

It is interesting to note that the three authors, Cassel, Barone, and Pareto, whose equation schemes have been used to prove the feasibility of adequate accounting in socialism, are convinced that their schemes do *not* offer a practical solution for the problems of socialist factor allocation.

H. D. Dickinson,[9] too, suggests a mathematical solution. "Given, at each end of the chain of production," he says, "a free market for finished goods and for productive services, the prices and the quantities that would exist if the intermediate goods were sold in a market, could, theoretically, be determined." What does "theoretical" mean in this case? Since Dickinson's book wishes to prove only "that, as far as pure economics is concerned, a socialist economy is at least theoretically possible," we cannot contradict him. However, Dickinson tries to show in detail how a socialist economy would work and how it would be quite superior to capitalism. Furthermore, like Cassel, he abandons the abstract nature of his system by letting his equations rest on the data produced by actual markets "at each end of the chain of production." Obviously, then, "theoretical" does not mean "abstract," and Dickinson asserts that we could solve our problem by solving thousands or millions of equations.

When Lionel Robbins[10] expressed doubts that this method was workable, he was told by Oskar Lange that the central planning board of the socialist economy would not have to solve millions of equations, because this task, obviously considered too big by Lange,[11] would be made unnecessary through a method of trial and error.

Dickinson[12] admits that the method of trial and error, which will be discussed below, would not be "replaced entirely by centralized price determination, based on the solution of thousands of simultaneous equations. . . . The reason is that the data themselves, which would have to be fed into the equation-machine, are continually changing." In other words, the expressions for consumers' decisions as a function of commodity and factor prices, as well as technological coefficients, cannot be ascertained through the equations themselves.

[9] H. D. Dickinson, *Economics of Socialism* (New York: Oxford University Press, 1939), pp. 13, 104.
[10] Lionel Robbins, *The Great Depression* (New York: St. Martin's Press, Inc., 1935), p. 151.
[11] Oskar Lange and Fred M. Taylor, *On the Economic Theory of Socialism* (Minneapolis: University of Minnesota Press, 1938), p. 88. Copyright 1938 by the University of Minnesota.
[12] Dickinson, p. 104.

These considerations are of importance for the theory of socialism because they show that pricing in socialism has to rest on actually known prices, whether they are supplied by the functioning of real markets or are set by the government.

THE TRIAL-AND-ERROR METHOD

If the liberal socialist economy is to rest on a comprehensive pricing process, this pricing process must be more than an abstract scheme. Each person—consumer, worker, plant manager, industrial manager— must have data on which to base his decisions. Such a pricing process must be very similar to the price mechanism of the private enterprise economy. The basic problem of liberal socialism in the economic field is the creation of such a pricing process within the structural environment of socialism. Where real markets exist we can expect to find equilibrium prices which equalize demand and supply. Where no real markets exist prices can be set arbitrarily by government authorities.

On the basis of a complete set of prices the different members of the liberal socialist economy can make their decisions. They will buy whichever commodities they desire to buy, they will work where their skills are offered the highest wages; and managers will produce only commodities whose prices cover the costs of production, and will try to keep these costs as low as possible.

Once all these decisions have been carried out, it is inevitable that the original prices must change. Real market prices change automatically, while set prices have to be adjusted by the central authority. Where it becomes obvious that at the set price the amount demanded exceeds the amount supplied, the price must be raised; where unsold goods prove that the price was set too high, the price must be lowered.

After these changes have been made, the members of the liberal socialist scoiety act once more on the basis of these new prices according to their interests or, in the case of managers, according to rules of behavior prescribed by the government. This time the result should be more satisfactory, unless changes in the basic data have occurred (for instance, technological changes). Without such exogenous changes the system would gradually find an equilibrium position in which all factors of production are employed, consumers get the commodities they desire, factors of production are correctly allocated, and demand and supply are everywhere equated at prices which cover costs of production.

This interesting proposal, which was made by Oskar Lange, D. H. Dickinson, and other liberal socialists, has been attacked from two sides. Some writers contend that a system of partially artificial pricing would not lead to the desired results. The private enterprise economy, they argue, rests on the profit motive and on competition, and these driving and check-ing forces could not be reproduced by the socialist economy. The other attack comes from authoritarian socialists, who emphasize central plan-ning. A system of trial and error implies, according to these critics, a degree of decentralization that would not leave enough room for planned action.

Basically, the trial-and-error system is very simple and seems to answer Mises' criticism. Mises argued that (1) a comprehensive pricing process is necessary for rational economic behavior, (2) the pricing process has to rest on markets for all goods and for all the different factors of production, and (3) markets can exist only under conditions of private property, characterized by the buying and selling of independent private consuming and producing units who are driven by the acquisitive motive and kept in check by a sufficient amount of competition.

Dickinson, Lange, Dobb, and others content that Mises and his fol-lowers used the term "price" in the narrower meaning of *market* price, whereas it can also be used in the wider sense of "terms on which alterna-tives are offered." [13] We are told that only prices in this wider sense are indispensable for the choice between alternatives. Maurice Dobb [14] criti-cizes both Mises and the present writer for a "confusion between two distinct things: between the process of calculation and the source of the data for calculation."

Before we continue our study of the trial-and-error blueprint we must emphasize that liberal socialists do not want to set up a highly centralized system. On the contrary, they favor decentralization because they are aware that no central authority can possibly know, and comprehensively interrelate, all the relevant data. If it could, it would not need a compre-hensive accounting process; it would act like Robinson Crusoe. Prices mean nothing to Robinson because he can compare the intensity of his wants and allocate the means of production in one mental process. The problem of allocation in a modern liberal socialist economy, however, is far too complex to be solved without a pricing process and a sufficient degree of decentralization.

L. D. Trotsky [15] stated the problem as follows:

> If there existed the universal mind, that projected itself into the scientific fancy of Laplace; a mind that would register simultaneously all the proc-esses of nature and of society, that could measure the dynamics of their motion, and could forecast the results of their interactions, such a mind, of course, could a priori draw up a faultless and an exhaustive economic plan, beginning with the numbers of hectars of wheat and down to the

[13] Lange and Taylor, p. 60.

[14] Maurice Dobb, Review of *Collectivist Economic Planning*, ed. F. A. Hayek, in *Economic Journal*, vol. 45 (1935), pp. 532–535.

[15] L. D. Trotsky, *Soviet Economy in Danger* (New York: Pioneer Publishers, 1933), pp. 29–33.

last button for a vest. In truth, the bureaucracy often conceives that just such a mind is at its disposal; that is why it so easily frees itself from the control of the market . . . ; but in reality the bureaucracy errs frightfully in this appraisal of its spiritual resources. . . . The innumerable living participants of economy, State as well as private, collective as well as individual, must give notice of their needs and of their relative strength not only through the statistical determinations of plan commissions but by the direct pressure of supply and demand. The plan is checked and, to a considerable measure, realized through the market. The regulation of the market itself must depend upon the tendencies that are brought out through its medium. The blueprints produced by the offices must demonstrate their economic expediency through commercial calculation.

The trial-and-error blueprint of the liberal socialist economy establishes a decentralized system with genuine markets for consumer goods and for the services of labor (including managerial labor). Since there is no market for producers' goods and for productive services except labor, "the prices of capital goods and productive resources outside of labor are thus prices in the generalized sense, that is, mere indices of alternatives available, fixed for accounting purposes." [16]

The working principles of this system are as follows: Consumers, workers, and managers make their decisions on the basis of given prices. Consumers and workers will act very much as they act under present conditions. The principles and motivations of their actions are therefore known to us. Self-interest will be sufficiently strong, and acquisitive tendencies will express themselves through price movements on *genuine* markets—provided that the managers who sell consumer goods and buy the services of labor are duty-bound not to use their monopolistic and monopsonistic powers. This brings us to the most important problem of decentralization in a liberal socialist economy—the behavior of production managers.

HOW ARE THE PUBLIC MANAGERS TO ACT?

The designers of liberal socialist blueprints are disappointingly vague when they discuss the rules of behavior for public managers. This vagueness is understandable, however, because this is the crucial point of conflict between pricing and planning, between freedom and central command. Here, also, it becomes obvious that the socialist economy can no longer follow the private enterprise model. State ownership of the material means of production eliminates private enterprise wherever it exists, and public management must, therefore, be substituted for the activities of the private entrepreneur.

[16] Lange and Taylor, p. 73.

Liberal socialist writers like to argue that the difference between state management and private management is not as great as it may appear and that public managers actually behave much like the managers of the large corporations in a private enterprise system. Chapter 4 already emphasized the importance of the division of ownership and control. Paul Sweezy concisely describes the resulting change in leadership as follows:

> The typical capitalist enterprise outgrew the personal entrepreneur. His functions and responsibilities were now split up among a number of more or less separate groups. The function of the capitalist—to provide capital —was assumed by shareholders whose only concern was the state of the corporation's profit-and-loss account and the price of its shares. The functions of employer of labor, organizer of production, and salesman of commodities were taken over by a hierarchy of salaried officials, engineers, and accountants, who became increasingly specialized and expert in their respective spheres of activity. Final authority in a corporation of this sort lies with a board of directors, nominally elected by the body of shareholders but actually chosen by a complex process in which not only those who exercise capitalist and entrepreneurial functions but also outside groups (such as bankers and important customers) normally play a part.[17]

This is a realistic description of the situation prevalent in parts of the private sector of the private enterprise economy. The internal structure of a socialist production unit can, therefore, be modeled after the bureaucratic setup of the large corporation. For this reason we assume that the problems of the *internal* functional division of labor can be solved in a liberal socialist plant or industry. No doubt, many specialized functions can be performed by hired experts, who need no more incentive for competent work than what the labor market can provide in form of attractive salaries. This statement is true for engineers, production managers, accountants, and so forth. As for the function of the stockholder, we have already seen that it must be performed by the government of the liberal socialist economy. We should note, however, that in the private enterprise economy the stockholder has not only performed the function of saving; he has, in addition, decided *where* to invest his funds and what risks to take. Although the state can arbitrarily determine the total amount of accumulation, arbitrary decisions are no longer permissible when we come to the problem of allocating investment funds to different industries. This allocation has to be consistent. Investment funds must go to those industries where the productivity of capital is thought to be greatest. In the end, the marginal productivity of capital should be the same in all branches of industry.

This problem of allocation cannot be waived aside by mere reference to

[17] Reprinted from *Socialism*, by Paul M. Sweezy, p. 209. Copyright, 1949. Courtesy of McGraw-Hill, Inc.

the *internal* structure of the modern corporation. It is the most crucial problem—the problem of which industry is to expand and which to contract.

Whoever makes these most fundamental decisions in the private corporation supposedly acts according to the profit motive. The answer to the question of expansion and contraction will be provided by those who decide to purchase or produce additional capital goods and those who are willing to risk their funds in the venture. Characteristic of this solution is, in any case, the absence of a central investment plan.

The problem of the liberal socialist economy is to substitute for the profit motive certain rules of behavior that the public managers of plants and industries have to follow.

Chapter 15 showed that public managers will not be told to maximize profits; they are to use profits as a signal that production is to be expanded. But this rule is deceivingly simple; it cannot easily be applied where *new* products and *new* techniques are in question. In these cases it is impossible to request allocation of loanable funds on the basis of known, demonstrable profits. Allocation of resources in expectation of *future* profits and for the elimination of *anticipated* gains is a difficult matter; it involves risks. These difficulties and uncertainties are particularly great in the large area of intermediate goods production, which is precisely the area where genuine market prices have to be replaced by the setting of accounting prices, and where private initiative and risk taking must first give way to public management. Here, too, will be found the greatest emphasis on central development planning.

Liberal socialist writers are exceedingly vague when they come to the question of whether public managers are to follow a predetermined development plan or whether decentralization can be carried far enough to permit independent investment decisions by these managers.

Liberal socialists are aware of the fact that detailed allocation of every bolt and screw by the central planning board is an impossibility, that decentralization is of vital importance, and that the managers on the spot must have leeway to make whatever adjustments in production are necessitated by changes in techniques, demand, and factor supply. Those who advocate the trial-and-error method want to express the effects of these changes in price changes and, temporarily, in profits and losses.

The *industrial* manager is a socialist functionary who has no counterpart in the private enterprise economy. Under normally competitive conditions we do not find corporations that control a whole industry. The economic unit in the private enterprise economy is the firm, and it is to be assumed that the firms in an industry act independently and competitively.

The liberal socialist economy, on the other hand, must have industrial managers. The question of whether a new plant should be added to already existing producing units in a given industry cannot be decided on the basis of profit expectations of independent firms. The request for new producing units in an industry must come from the specialist who, on the basis of cost-price calculations, can establish a claim to allocation of further funds. The manager of an industry must know the cost schedules of the different plants; he must be able to decide whether it is better to enlarge existing plants or to build a new unit; he must be able to control the actions of the plant managers; his interest must transcend that of an individual producing unit. The plant managers will be permitted to handle problems of a more local character, but the basic economic unit of the liberal socialist economy is the industry.

QUESTIONS OF COST ACCOUNTING

Oskar Lange proposes that the managers of socialist plants and industries should act *as though* they were private entrepreneurs in a competitive market. We recall that the conditions of pure and perfect competition are that (a) the seller cannot influence the market price, and (b) everybody is free to enter the industry.[18] Lange requests, accordingly, that the central planning board should impress on managers, as an *accounting* rule, that "all accounting has to be done *as if* prices were independent of the decisions taken. For purposes of accounting, prices must be treated as constant, as they are treated by entrepreneurs on a competitive market."[19] The industrial manager must see to it that the industry produces "exactly as much of a commodity as can be sold or 'accounted for' to other industries at a price which equals the marginal cost incurred *by the industry* in producing this amount." This rule performs "the function which under free competition is carried out by the free entry of firms into an industry or their exodus from it: that is, it determines the output of an industry." The plant managers must choose the methods of production "which minimize average cost" and "equalize marginal cost and the price of the product."

[18] See Chap. 7, footnotes 3 and 10.

[19] Lange and Taylor, pp. 77, 78, 81. Hayek criticizes Lange as follows: "The force which in a competitive society brings about the reduction of price to the lowest cost at which the quantity saleable at that cost can be produced is the opportunity for anybody who knows a cheaper method to come in at his own risk and to attract customers by underbidding the other producers. But if prices are fixed by the authority this method is excluded. . . . Since the man with the new idea will have no possibility of establishing himself by undercutting, the new idea cannot be proved by experiment til he has convinced the Supreme Economic Council that his way of producing the things is cheaper. Or, in other words, every calculation by an outsider who believes that he can do better will have to be examined and approved by the authority, which in this connection will have to take over all the functions of the entrepreneurs." Hayek, "Socialist Calculation," p. 139.

To explain Lange's request, we have to recall how production adjusts under conditions of pure and perfect competition in the private enterprise system. At first we assume a *constant cost industry* in which production can be expanded through the addition of new plants whose average and marginal costs are the same as those of already existing producing units.

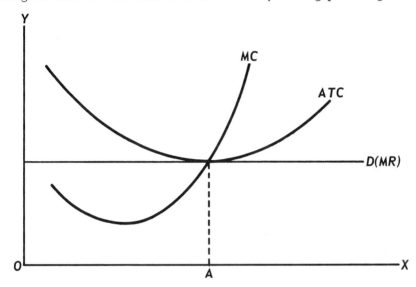

Figure 2 illustrates the production costs incurred by a firm (plant). ATC, the average total cost of production, or cost per unit of output, is the total cost divided by the number of units. Without entering into a detailed cost analysis, we assume that the typical producing unit has one production volume (OA) where average total costs are at a minimum. This is, technically speaking, the optimum. The reason for this assumption is *the law of diminishing returns*, which can be summarized as follows:

> An increase in some inputs relative to other comparatively fixed inputs will cause output to increase; but after a point the extra output resulting from the same additions of input will become less and less; this falling off of extra returns is a consequence of the fact that the new "doses" of the varying resources have to work with less and less of the constant resources.[20]

It should be noticed that this law of diminishing returns is entirely independent of the economic system in which it operates.

The marginal cost curve MC is derived from the same set of data as the average total cost curve ATC of Figure 2. If we produce 10 units at a total cost of $200 and 11 units at a total cost of $209, the average total cost

[20] Paul A. Samuelson, *Economics*, 6th ed. (New York: McGraw-Hill, Inc., 1964), p. 27.

changes from $20 to $19 as we expand production. The marginal cost, or the cost of producing an extra unit, is in our example, $9, namely the total cost of producing 11 units ($209) minus the total cost of producing 10 units ($200).

Whenever marginal cost is lower than average total cost, average total cost decreases as production expands, because the inclusion of this extra (or marginal) unit lowers the average; but as soon as it costs more than the average to produce an additional unit, that is, as soon as the marginal cost exceeds the average total cost, average total cost will rise. From this we must conclude that marginal cost and average total cost are identical at the volume of output that minimizes average total cost. To put it differently, the MC curve must intersect the ATC curve at the latter's lowest point; and to say that an entrepreneur or manager should produce at lowest cost means that he should choose as his output (OA), the quantity shown at the intersection of the MC and ATC curves.

The intersection of the MC and ATC curves also happens to be the point at which the MC curve intersects the straight line D or MR. D stands for demand and is shown as a straight line parallel to the OX axis because we assume a condition of pure competition, which exists "if the seller thinks that at the market price he could sell as much as he wanted." Demand as seen by the seller, therefore, is perfectly elastic. But if the seller can sell any unit he cares to produce at this price, the D curve constitutes simultaneously his marginal revenue curve MC. He will produce up to point A, the intersection of the MC and MR curves because his profit will not be maximized as long as the marginal cost remains below the marginal revenue while in the opposite case (when the MC curve lies above the MR curve) he will reduce his profit. Lange's managers, therefore, do not only have to produce up to the point where average total cost is minimized. They must, in addition, equalize marginal cost and the price of the product. In Figure 2 they have obeyed this rule because the price (D or MR) just covers the lowest average cost of production. Since it is assumed that cost curves are identical for all plants that constitute an industry, the conclusion reached is that, in equilibrium, the price must correspond to the lowest average total cost. Where it is higher, profits would appear; where it is lower, losses would be incurred; and expansion or contraction of production would lead back to equilibrium. This would be the result of pure and perfect competition in the private enterprise system where perfect competition means that anybody can enter any field of production that looks promising. In liberal socialism the industrial managers would have to see to it that the needed adjustments are made. Obviously, in all plants production will be carried to the point where average total cost, marginal cost, and price are identical; and in the industry the number of producing units and total output will be so chosen that, with a given demand for the product, the price corresponds to the lowest average total cost in all the identical plants. The choosing of the right number of plants by the industrial manager is substituted for the effect of perfect competition in the private enterprise system.

The case of an *increasing cost industry* is more controversial. Here costs will differ from plant to plant. Take, for example, the case in which land is of varied quality and the best land has been used first. As more producing units are added, their average total costs are higher than those of the older producing units. In the private enterprise system the entry of new high-cost firms is possible only if and when the price of the product covers the minimum costs of these *marginal* firms. At this price, already existing firms will be able to expand production. They will produce up to the point where their marginal cost is equal to the higher marginal revenue as illustrated in Figure 3. Since the minimum average total cost of the already existing firms is lower than the market price, total revenue will be higher than total cost in these firms. If the advantages which the older firms enjoy cannot be duplicated by the newcomers, these "profits" cannot be eliminated. Because of their permanent character we call them "rent."

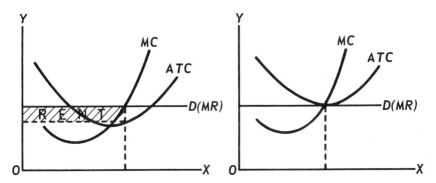

Rent is the result of certain permanent advantages that enable some firms to produce a given output with less labor and capital than the marginal producer.

If the same situation exists in a liberal socialist economy, how are industrial managers to act? Two solutions suggest themselves:

1. The industrial manager can follow the private enterprise model and lay down the rule that the plant managers should produce up to the point where marginal costs are equal to price. Only in the marginal plant would marginal cost at this output be equal to average total cost. All other plants would earn an extra revenue, rent, which would be turned over to the government.

2. The industrial manager could treat the whole industry as a unit, with costs figures as industrial averages. In this case the low-cost units

would permanently subsidize the high-cost units and, in equilibrium, total cost and total revenue would be the same *for the industry as a whole.*

Unquestionably the liberal socialist system could use method (2) and instruct the managers of increasing-cost industries to pass on to consumers through lower prices the rent income from those unique advantages that some of the producing units enjoy. At first this may seem the logical thing to do. The industry is the economic unit in the socialist economy and is treated as such in this method of accounting in terms of industrial averages.

Nevertheless, method (1) should be used for the following reasons: If we assume full employment of the factors of production throughout the economy, we see at once that the consumer does not necessarily gain, because production in the individual industries concerned is driven further under method (2) than under method (1). Since we assume full employment, less of something else will have to be produced in such a case. The rent which goes to the government under case (1) will either lead, through increased accumulation, to production of producers' goods or it will be distributed via social-dividend payments or lower taxes and will therefore cause increased consumption. The question of accumulation need not interest us at the moment. Let us assume, therefore, that the consumer may choose either a higher money income, according to method (1), or lower prices for articles produced under increasing-cost conditions, according to method (2). The basic principle of free consumers' choice clearly favors method (1). This method also recommends itself because it makes the consumer pay a price equal to marginal cost and therefore equal to the alternatives sacrificed. Rent can be interpreted as the price paid for scarce production advantages that enable us to save labor and capital. Finally, method (1) is useful because it leads to the application of one and the same principle to all industries and plants. A system in which many industries would have to use sliding cost averages would present formidable problems of cost accounting.

When industrial output can be increased under *decreasing-cost conditions,* the lower costs should be the deciding ones, even if the average total costs of smaller, older, and obsolete plants cannot be fully covered. This case is the opposite of the situation just discussed. Again two policies are possible. In policy (1) production is continued until marginal cost in the new plants is equal to price. Since marginal cost is now lower than average total cost in the older plants, losses will be incurred in these plants. In policy (2) production would stop when average cost *for the industry* equals price. In this case the low-cost plants subsidize the high-cost units. To be consistent, we again have to choose policy (1). Socialist writers, as well as A. C. Pigou, have argued that the negative rents or accounting losses incurred under rule (1) should be covered by permanent subsidies. These subsidies could be taken from a "marginal cost equalization fund" into which would be paid all positive rents arising in increasing-cost industries.[21]

Lange's suggestions are based on the assumption that pure and perfect competition can be *imitated* by providing rules of behavior for socialist managers. However, the theory of monopolistic (or imperfect) competition has shown that the case of pure and perfect competition is not too often found in the private enterprise economy. This means that many entrepreneurs know quite well that they can sell more at lower prices, that the demand curve, as they see it, is not of perfect elasticity, and that the demand and marginal-revenue curves are not identical. Furthermore, in many cases the producing units are too big and prevent a competitive solution, as indicated above; that is, the question of how much to produce is not solved by the addition or subtraction of small producing units but rather by changes in the output of existing industrial plants.

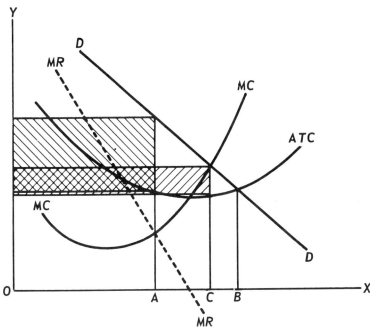

Figure 4 illustrates this case. The private businessman will, of course, produce up to the point where the marginal revenue curve (which is no longer identical with the demand curve!) intersects the marginal-cost curve, since the firm's profits are increased (or losses reduced) as long as each new unit produced and sold adds less to total cost than to total revenue.

How is the industrial manager in liberal socialism to behave? We may assume that he is fully aware of the situation, knowing that his sales

---

[21] Dickinson, p. 108; Lange and Taylor, p. 77; A. C. Pigou, *The Economics of Welfare*, 4th ed. (New York: St. Martin's Press, Inc., 1938), Part 2, chap. 11.

depend on the price and, also, that his producing units are too big to permit the infinitesimal adjustments under Lange's *as-if* method.

Figure 4 seems to suggest three possibilities for the manager's course of action: (1) He can imitate the private enterprise solution, produce amount OA, and hand the monopoly profit over to the government; (2) he can expand production to point B, that is, until the ATC and DD curves intersect, thus achieving equality of total cost and total revenue; (3) he can produce OC determined by the intersection of the MC and DD curves.

For the reasons given above, he will choose the third solution (output OC), steering a middle course between the monopolistic private enterprise case (OA) and the artificial lowering of the commodity price through output OB. The consumer pays at output OC a price equal to marginal cost and, therefore, equal to the alternatives sacrificed. The enterprise's profit is either being invested or used for social dividend payments. The latter uphold the principle of free consumer choice compared with the case of artificial price reduction at output OB which does not constitute an advantage in a fully employed economy. Finally, since the government is free to determine the rate of taxation and accumulation, nothing speaks for the imitation of the monopolistic private enterprise decision to reap the highest possible profit.

Far more important than these cost accounting rules are practical problems of management concerning the relation between managers and the planning authorities; the psychological practicality of the proposed "as if" behavior; protection against monopoly power; the degree of decentralization; the initiative of managers; dangers of bureaucratization; the possibility and importance of auditing; and so forth. Next to (and connected with) the questions of accounting, allocation, and pricing, these management problems are the most controversial issue of liberal socialist economics.

Lange solves all the problems facing industrial managers by his breathtakingly simple request that managers should behave *as if* prices were unalterably given. This rule is to establish conditions of pure competition under liberal socialism. However, is it not highly doubtful that the managers can be induced to follow rules of behavior which every entrepreneurial impulse must urge them to reject? The manager cannot offer higher prices for raw materials, cannot try to borrow larger investment funds through his willingness to pay higher interest rates, and cannot sell larger amounts by lowering the price of his product. He has to adjust his behavior, against his better judgment, to price signals that he knows were inaccurately set by the authorities. In short, Lange's rules prevent the manager from making use of his more precise knowledge, from carrying through the necessary adjustments as fast as possible, from letting the economy enjoy the advantages of greater elasticity which can be gained from real decentralization.

FUNCTIONS OF THE CENTRAL PLANNING BOARD

The central planning board of the liberal socialist economy has the following functions:

The planning board determines the rate of accumulation; that is, it draws the dividing line between producers' goods and consumer goods production. Saying that this decision is an arbitrary one does not imply that the political processes by which it is made could not be democratic. "Arbitrary" means only that the decision to accumulate is no longer dependent on the willingness of individual members of the community to save. Accumulation can take several forms: (1) Individuals may still be free to postpone consumption, in other words, to save. (2) Money earned by the government in form of interest, rent, or profit can be set aside for accumulation. (3) Government revenue from taxation may exceed the cost of current communal services. (4) The creation of new money may cause price inflation and thus decrease the purchasing power in the hands of consumers. From all these sources may flow investment funds, which are available for capital goods production. In addition, the government will receive amortization funds, which do not necessarily have to be invested in the plant or industry from which they came; rather, they should be added to the total fund and allocated according to the same general principles that apply to the distribution of investment funds among different industries.

Closely related to the problem of accumulation is the problem of income distribution. If the government paid its expenses and financed accumulation exclusively out of interest, rent, and profit, no taxation need be required, and citizens would receive their wage income in full. While this situation would establish a very simple model, it would be just as arbitrary as any other method of determining the relative proportions of accumulation and consumption.

As far as the distribution of income among members of the liberal socialist society is concerned, the central planning board could not act entirely arbitrarily. The labor market fulfills an important function, and the income distribution established by demand and supply on the labor market must not be "corrected" to such a degree that the labor market would cease to function. If a social dividend is paid, it must *not* be distributed with the intention of leveling the inequalities which the labor market creates. Nobody would greatly care what wages were paid in a given field if he could expect relatively low wages to entitle him to a relatively larger share in the social dividend. That partial equalization of wage incomes is possible, however, is clearly indicated by the application of progressive taxation in the private enterprise system.

The central planning board must perform a very important function in the pricing process. Many prices are only accounting prices that are set and subsequently changed when demand exceeds supply or supply exceeds demand. Even consumer goods prices and wages may be influenced by the central planning board. The demand for labor comes from public managers, and consumption goods are sold exclusively in public stores. Perhaps the managers of these stores are permitted to change prices frequently, but it is possible that this right is reserved for the planning board. The blueprints are not clear on this point. Probably, Lange's artificial system of pure competition will extend to the still existing "genuine" markets of the liberal socialist economy, because in these markets, too, the state enjoys a monopolistic or monopsonistic position. Are we to assume, then, that even in the commodity and labor markets the managers are required to act as if the given prices and wages could not be changed?

The central planning board, having been made responsible for *all* price changes, must adjust prices rather frequently to avoid dangerous discrepancies of demand and supply. How long set prices are to remain unchanged we are not told, nor how the central planning board will integrate into a consistent pattern the tremendous number of price changes urged upon it by the managers.

A particularly important function of the planning board is the allocation of investment funds. This allocation will be based upon the rate of interest in comparison with real or anticipated profits. The function of the central planning board will consist of weighing expansion claims of different industries against one another. Such a survey can be made consistently only in general monetary terms and through a uniform price for the means of expansion. This price, the rate of interest, must be raised high enough to check sufficiently the total demand for available investment funds.

The central planning board cannot prescribe the exact amount of production for each industry, unless it is assumed that board members have the knowledge to predict what, under changing conditions, marginal costs and marginal revenues in each industry will be. We assumed decentralization precisely because such universal knowledge is not at the disposal of the board. Yet many socialist writers emphasize that the central planning board has "a much wider knowledge of what is going on in the whole economic system than any private entrepreneur can ever have, and, consequently, may be able to reach the right equilibrium prices by a *much shorter* series of successive trials than a competitive market actually does."[22] Dickinson points out that the organs of the collective economy will have incomparably more exact knowledge of one another's actions than enterprises under capitalism, since all enterprises work, as it were, within glass walls.[23]

This glass-wall character of the liberal socialist economy should not be overstated. Although the planners have more data available than the entrepreneurs of the private enterprise economy, they also need much more information. Private entrepreneurs need to know only the prospective demand for their products and the probable costs of production. The planners, on the other hand, must adjust the whole price system continuously on the basis of an immense amount of statistical data while the industrial managers must act as if the prices set according to these data were correct. Better information does not help them in this case. The knowledge of the private entrepreneur may be more limited, but so is his task; and he is permitted to make the most of what knowledge he has and to act promptly.

The glass-wall quality of liberal socialist enterprise does not eliminate the need for genuine decentralization because the superhuman mind who could register and integrate the enormous amount of information that is constantly pouring into the central planning office is simply nonexistent. The question is not how many facts are available; crucial is the ability of the men in the center to interpret the reports, accounts, claims, and counterclaims of the men on the periphery. And against this mass of largely indigestible material must be held the lack of automatic regulation through genuine competitive markets.

Only when the system can shift the main burden of economic decisions to managers who can operate on the basis of correct prices and can act instantly according to their superior factual knowledge, can liberal socialism hope to achieve a high degree of productivity and successfully combine consumers' sovereignty with state ownership of the material means of production.

[22] Lange and Taylor, p. 89.
[23] Dickinson, p. 213. See also his article "Price Formation in a Socialist Community," *Economic Journal*, vol. 43 (1933), pp. 237–250.

CHAPTER 17

Liberal
Socialism's Claims

BETWEEN CAPITALISM AND CENTRAL PLANNING

The trial-and-error system studied in the preceding chapter is in
many respects similar to the private enterprise economy. "There is," says
Lionel Robbins,[1] "a certain aesthetic attraction in the contemplation of a
project which, setting out to eliminate the institutions of a 'planless'
society—the 'chaos of competitive enterprise'—arrives at an attempt to
reproduce them."

The main question seems to be whether under these conditions the
change from private enterprise system to liberal socialism is worthwhile.
Is it not a rather roundabout exercise to abolish private enterprise through
state ownership of the material means of production and then rely on
prices to such an extent that the whole economy becomes a mere replica of
the present system? Even Oskar Lange[2] asks, ". . . but if competition en-

[1] Lionel Robbins, *The Great Depression* (New York: St. Martin's Press, Inc., 1935),
p. 153.
[2] Oskar Lange and Fred M. Taylor, *On the Economic Theory of Socialism* (Minneapolis: University of Minnesota Press, 1938), pp. 98–99. Copyright 1938 by the
University of Minnesota. Lange answers his question as follows: "The *formal* principles
are the same, but the *actual* allocation may be quite different. This difference is due to

218

forces the same rules of allocating resources as would have to be accepted in a rationally conducted socialist economy, what is the use of bothering about socialism? Why change the whole economic system if the same result can be attained within the present system, if only it could be forced to maintain the competitive standard?"

The importance of this question is increased by the possibility, on the one hand, of maintaining a high level of employment in the private enterprise economy, plus the danger, on the other, that liberal socialism might develop into an authoritarian system. Liberal socialism must be compared with the regulated private enterprise system that can develop if we are willing to do all that is necessary to maintain a high level of aggregate spending, deal prudently with the problems of monopoly, and aim at the greatest amount of equality that is feasible in this economy. Against this type of private enterprise economy we have to set the advantages promised by liberal socialism. In investigating these promises, the liberal socialist assumptions should be consistently maintained, that is, authoritarian solutions should be excluded. After all, trial-and-error procedures are artificial creations in a system that is basically collectivist. The appeal of authoritarian solutions is enhanced by the fact that the authoritarian system is more simply structured than a system which indulges in the luxury of broad civil and economic liberties.

INCOME DISTRIBUTION IN LIBERAL SOCIALISM

In Chapter 5 we concluded that the possibilities for greater equality of income distribution are limited within the institutional framework of the private enterprise system. Private property in the means of production, the connection of personal with functional distribution, private capital accumulation, and the importance of the profit motive—all these features make a more equal personal distribution difficult and, in some instances, capable of more harm than good. However, in the case where investment opportunities are lacking, a more equal distribution could actually increase the national income by increasing aggregate expenditure. A more equal income distribution can be achieved by making social services available gratuitously. Among these services free education was seen to be particularly important as a means of reaching a more equal distribution in the future and of increasing the productivity of the economy.

No doubt, liberal socialists can claim that their system will establish a more equal income distribution. This claim is based on the fact that

---

two features." One is the distribution of income, the other the comprehensiveness of the items entering into the price system. See pp. 99 and 103.

public ownership of the material means of production eliminates the so-called unearned income of private persons. Interest, rent, and profit go to the state. However, much of the unearned income in the private enterprise system is either taxed away or saved and invested; it then serves to finance tasks that would also have to be financed in socialism. This part of the unearned income, therefore, will not be available for distribution to consumers if the socialist economy is to grow at least as fast as the private enterprise economy.

As far as wages and salaries are concerned, most modern socialists do not aim at complete and rigid equality. It is now generally understood that the maintenance of free choice of occupation implies wage differentials. If functional and personal distribution are to be one on the labor market, liberal socialists will have to accept a substantial degree of inequality.

H. D. Dickinson [3] points out that "in a socialist system there is no essential connection between the value of labor and the payment of a sum of money to a laborer." In other words, wages might be used for accounting purposes only, while the national income would actually be divided up according to such principles as perfect equality or payment according to need. Dickinson's remark refers, however, to authoritarian rather than to liberal socialism. Free choice of occupation makes it imperative that wage differences be used to guide workers into industries where their particular skills can be most productively used. Aside from compulsory assignment there exists no method of labor allocation other than the offer of pecuniary or other advantages. Compulsory assignment violates the principle of free choice of occupation. In liberal socialism wage differences are therefore used for more than accounting purposes; they are essential if labor is to be allocated without compulsion to the production of commodities that consumers demand or the state decides to produce.

Oskar Lange [4] believes that these wage differentials would be negligible in view of the fact that "the choice of an occupation offering a lower income, but also a smaller disutility, may be interpreted as the purchase of leisure, safety, agreeableness of work, etc., at a price equal to the difference between the money earned in that particular occupation and in others."

But are income differences in the liberal socialist economy really "only apparent"? In some cases a lower income may be offset by nonpecuniary advantages, such as leisure. In many cases, however, jobs that are disagreeable are also badly paid. The cause of low wages in spite of great "disutility" is, of course, a relatively large supply of certain kinds of labor; and as far as this large supply is caused by more modest requirements in terms of

[3] H. D. Dickinson, *Economics of Socialism* (New York: Oxford University Press, 1939), p. 119.
[4] Lange and Taylor, pp. 101–102.

the laborer's natural endowments, the liberal socialist economy will not be able to equalize incomes, even in the meaning of Lange's broader interpretation.

T. J. B. Hoff [5] has pointed out that Lange is really contradicting himself when "he starts by requiring differentiated income, but arrives at the conclusion that the incomes are in reality the same. . . ."

Of course, in the long run it may be possible to increase the supply of labor in the better-paid fields, once expensive education and training are no longer dependent on private means. We can agree with Dickinson [6]:

> If obstacles to the mobility of labor were removed and if education and vocational training were really free and available to all who cared to take advantage of them, the supply of kinds of labor that are to-day scarce (skilled and professional labor) would probably increase and its economic value fall, so reducing the inequality in personal earnings.

But we can hardly share Dickinson's fantastic conclusion that,

> in a socialist community it is possible that the dirty and unpleasant occupations would come to be the best paid, instead of, as at present, the worst; that a cabinet minister or a bank director might elect to serve for a few months as a dustman or a lavatory attendant in order to get enough money for a holiday trip.

Some writers argue, perhaps correctly, that differences in income need not be so great that they correspond to differences in producticity,[7] and they ask why "the game cannot be continued just as well with counters of small size—why the difference between an income of $3000 and $4000 should not be at least as strong an incentive as the difference between $3 million and $4 million." [8]

There is some justification for this argument in view of the arbitrariness of determining very high salaries in the private enterprise economy. R. L. Hall may be right in saying that "the experience of companies and of the public service shows us that if the men in responsible positions are getting enough to mark them off from their subordinates, they will feel some duty to perform their functions conscientiously and will find their work interesting for its own sake." We must be careful though. Chapter 5

[5] T. J. B. Hoff, *Economic Calculation in the Socialist Society* (London: William Hodge & Company, Ltd., 1949), p. 73.

[6] Dickinson, p. 133.

[7] See, for example, J. M. Keynes, *The General Theory of Employment, Interest, and Money* (New York: Harcourt, Brace & World, Inc., 1965), p. 374; R. L. Hall, *The Economic System in a Socialist State* (New York: St. Martin's Press, Inc., 1937), pp. 160–161.

[8] Abba P. Lerner, *The Economics of Control* (New York: Crowell-Collier and Macmillan, Inc., 1946), p. 42.

showed that progressive taxation can severely interfere with productivity. Similarly, the allocation of scarce labor skills could be distorted and their supply reduced if the wage differences that a free labor market tends to bring about were greatly diminished.

The limitations of progressive taxation will be the same in liberal socialism, except that there is no prospect that private capital accumulation will be adversely affected. In liberal socialism, as in the private enterprise economy, taxation must not eliminate the differentials upon which the working of the price mechanism rests.

This statement is equally true for the distribution of a social dividend. Lange [9] emphasizes that,

> the distribution of the social dividend must be such as not to interfere with the optimum distribution of labor services between the different industries and occupations. . . . *The social dividend must be distributed so as to have no influence whatever on the choice of occupation.* The social dividend paid to an individual must be entirely independent of his choice of occupation. For instance, it can be divided equally per head of population, or distributed according to age or size of family or any other principle which does not affect the choice of occupation.

By referring to a social dividend, socialist writers sometimes create the impression that socialist citizens, instead of paying taxes, would receive a share in the state's income. However, only the consumed part of unearned income under the present system is available for distribution, and even this part will be available only if the socialist economy does not aim at a higher rate of accumulation. Since the unearned income of the state (interest, rent, profit) must finance the public sector of the economy *and* take care of capital accumulation, it is most unlikely that *without taxation* anything would be left for the distribution of a social dividend. But if taxes have to be imposed to supplement the state's income from ownership of the material means of production, the social dividend, as a kind of reverse taxation, becomes a superfluous complication.

BUREAUCRACY AND PRODUCTIVITY

In discussing some conflicting opinions about the productivity of liberal socialism, it is necessary to postpone (as in Chapter 6) the consideration of monopoly and unemployment. How would liberal socialist and private enterprise economies compare if both were working on a sufficiently competitive basis and at high levels of employment? Modern socialists have shown greater modesty than have their predecessors in claim-

[9] Lange and Taylor, pp. 83–84.

ing superior productivity for socialism, but they still assert that the socialist would be superior to the private enterprise economy in productive efficiency.

Some aspects of productivity in socialism were briefly discussed in Chapter 6. It is impossible, for instance, to contend that scientific research is dependent on the private enterprise system. World War II and the utilization of atomic energy have inaugurated an era of government research projects that are, in scope, beyond the reach of even the largest private corporation. Since these government projects are feasible within the framework of the private enterprise system, socialism's criticism can be only that not *all* research is carried on in government laboratories. Paul M. Sweezy [10] says:

> Each firm or industry seeks competitive advantage through research and can neither relinquish responsibility to the government nor pool resources with its rivals. Hence it is inevitable that under capitalism work of this kind should be undertaken on a comparatively limited scale and in an uncoordinated fashion. The advantages enjoyed by socialism in this respect are too obvious to require elaboration.

In addition, socialist writers suggest that such scientific results as are forthcoming may be more readily used in socialism than in monopoly capitalism, where new techniques may be suppressed to prevent the depreciation of invested capital.

Critics of socialism, on the other hand, express doubts that socialist managers will make the same prompt use of new methods of production which is characteristic of private enterprise under sufficiently competitive conditions.

We know already that the comparison between socialist and corporate managers does not lead to a clear-cut distinction between bureaucrat and businessman. We must admit that the private enterprise system is no longer exclusively characterized by the entrepreneur-capitalist who singlehandedly makes all the important decisions, bears the risk, and earns the profit. It is true, that "when ownership and control are united in a single hand there is greater freedom of action, more scope for initiative, a greater readiness to attempt untried ways and to take risks, a quicker response to changing conditions, probably more drive, than are to be found either in joint stock companies or in any socialized industrial form." [11] Under present conditions, however, the comparison must be between the public manager and the manager of the large private corporation. Socialists contend that in this comparison the private enterprise system cannot maintain its claim to higher efficiency.

[10] Reprinted from *Socialism*, by Paul M. Sweezy, p. 213. Copyright, 1949. Courtesy of McGraw-Hill, Inc.

[11] A. C. Pigou, *Socialism Versus Capitalism* (New York: St. Martin's Press, Inc., 1939), p. 78.

Yet many socialists are, nevertheless, quite conscious of the problem of lacking incentives under bureaucratic management. Oskar Lange,[12] for instance, asserts "that *the real danger of socialism is that of a bureaucratization of economic life,* and not the impossibility of coping with the problem of allocation of resources." But he makes this concession to the critics of socialism only because he believes that the same, or even greater, danger cannot be averted under monopolistic capitalism. "Officials subject to democratic control seem preferable to private corporation executives who practically are responsible to nobody."

Lange's argument can be accepted where private monopolies are guilty of exploitation, inefficiency, and the obstruction of economic progress. Where a sufficient degree of competition exists, however, Lange cannot demonstrate the greater bureaucratic inefficiency that he attributes to private enterprise as compared to socialism. True, the private corporation is responsible to nobody except for the fulfillment of contracts freely entered into. But this independence promotes efficiency and initiative rather than bureaucratic slowness.

The essential difference seems to be as follows: the private corporation is related to other firms only through the market; it buys and sells according to price-cost relations; it expands and contracts as profit expectations dictate. In all these actions there is no red tape as there is in a liberal socialist plant or industry. The manager of the socialist plant is responsible to the manager of the industry who, in turn, is responsible to the planning authorities. *The bureaucratic impediment lies in the external relations of plant or industry and not in their internal structure.*

Let us assume that a liberal socialist plant manager has a scheme to reduce costs. The scheme requires the investment of a considerable amount of capital. In the private enterprise system the scheme would be introduced without difficulties and delays if it might be profitable; no bureaucratic delay would be involved. In the liberal socialist economy investment funds can be obtained only from the state, and the manager does not have an opportunity to prove his claim by experiment "till he has convinced the supreme economic council that his way of producing the thing is cheaper." Any proposed change must, together with potential changes in other plants, "be examined and approved by the authority, which in this connection will have to take over all the functions of the entrepreneur." [13]

Therefore, decisions that should rest on intimate knowledge of all existing circumstances are not made by those possessing this knowledge, namely, the men on the spot, but rather by those in the upper strata of the socialist bureaucracy. The planning authorities, supposedly, act according

---

[12] Lange and Taylor, pp. 109–110.

[13] F. A. Hayek, "Socialist Calculation: The Competitive 'Solution,'" *Economica*, New Series, vol. 7 (1940), p. 139.

to advice coming from the producing units, but the higher authorities cannot rely exclusively on the counsel of those whom they are to direct and control. As a rule the requests for additional funds will exceed the available supply, and the competing claims of many industries will have to be rated according to their relative merits. Or, to put it differently: as individual producing units are no longer integrated by the market, what is not accomplished by the market has to be achieved by bureaucratic action.

When Oskar Lange says that the problem of bureaucracy is a greater danger to socialism than the problem of allocation, he separates problems that are closely related. Bureaucracy may flourish in liberal socialism precisely because real markets no longer exist for intermediate goods and the actions of the managers no longer *automatically* adjust themselves to changing circumstances. Free and prompt guidance through market prices must be supplanted by bureaucratic guidance via accounting prices set by the planning board. It is clear that the relations *among* different industries rather than the relations *within* individual producing units will be most endangered by bureaucratic arthritis.

True, the liberal socialist wants to use the trial-and-error system in order to avoid too much bureaucracy and to give to consumers and to labor the greatest possible amount of freedom. If the system works, decentralization will avoid some of the pitfalls of bureaucratic planning. If it does not work, if the planned character of the economy must be stressed more and more, then the bureaucratic apparatus must grow; and liberal socialism may change into authoritarian socialism. The problems of bureaucracy and allocation are, therefore, very closely related.

It has been argued that, as the private enterprise system matures, the state plays a more active part in the economic process, but private corporations frequently consider such action "interference" and attempt to render it ineffectual. "The result is that there is a tendency for two bureaucracies, each swollen by the necessity of fighting the other, to be built up where one would be sufficient to do all that is required from a strictly economic point of view." [14] A. C. Pigou,[15] referring particularly to public utilities, suggests that public ownership might be preferable to public control because it would "obviate expense, overlapping and, above all, friction, if, instead of there being a controlling authority *plus* a controlled one, control and operation were united, as under socialism they would be, in the same hand." Nevertheless, Pigou does not want to create the impression that socialism would be less bureaucratic than capitalism, for he continues: "*Pro tanto* this consideration provides a valid argument for extending the range of socialization. But that is not the same thing as

[14] Sweezy, p. 215.
[15] Pigou, pp. 45–46, 90, 91.

substituting for the present system general socialism with all-round central planning." Pigou, in other words, refers to what may be called "partial socialization," which does not alter the basic structure of the market economy. A publicly owned corporation is embedded in the market mechanism. The main problems of central planning do not appear. It is therefore quite possible that partial socialization will reduce the degree of bureaucratization without proving socialism's superiority in this respect.

Chapter 6 showed that productivity and profitability tend to coincide when the utility of a product is increased by producing a larger or better product with given means of production, or by adjusting production more readily to the wishes of the consumers. On the other hand, activities which increase the scarcity of products or waste productive resources cannot be called productive, though they may be very profitable.

Liberal socialists may well claim that certain cases of profitability, which are detrimental to productivity, are excluded by the very nature of socialism. As Pigou convincingly states:

> A consumers' association for providing itself with raspberry jam will be under no temptation to manufacture pips for it out of wood; a capitalist jammaker may do this. A municipal authority will be under no temptation to slaughter animals for food under insanitary conditions to escape the expense of making them sanitary: a private butchering concern may do this. This is a very important matter, so important, indeed, that in industries closely associated with public health it is customary in this country [England] to insist on rigorous inspection, and, when, as in the construction and operation of sewers, that is, for technical reasons, difficult, on public ownership and operation.

Pigou adds that in these cases of control the degree of freedom of private enterprise is weakened and the cost of control "ought to be reckoned as a negative element in measurements of its efficiency." In this case, therefore, the cost of bureaucracy has to be charged to the account of the private enterprise system.

The socialist economy can to a large extent avoid the wastes of competition that were indicated in Chapter 6. Milk may then be distributed as mail is delivered today; one efficient gas station may do the work of three or four competing ones; cutthroat competition among giant firms will be excluded; natural resources will not be wasted by exploitative methods; and excessive advertising may be supplanted by an attempt to educate the consumer. However, *authoritarian* socialism may circumvent free consumers' choice by educating consumers to like what the government has produced.

Oskar Lange [16] mentions among the advantages of liberal socialism

---

[16] Lange and Taylor, pp. 103–104.

the comprehensiveness of the items entering into the price system. Following Pigou he shows that,

> . . . there is frequently a divergence between the private cost borne by an entrepreneur and the social cost of production. Into the cost account of the private entrepreneur only those items enter for which he has to pay a price, while such items as the maintenance of the unemployed created when he discharges workers, the provision for the victims of occupational diseases and industrial accidents, etc., do not enter, or, as Professor J. M. Clark has shown, are diverted into social overhead costs. On the other side, there are the cases where private producers render services which are not included in the price of the product . . . A socialist economy would be able to put *all* the alternatives into its economic accounting. Thus it would evaluate *all* the services rendered by production and take into the cost accounts *all* the alternatives sacrificed; as a result it would also be able to convert its social overhead costs into prime costs. By so doing it would avoid much of the social waste connected with private enterprise.

Pigou [17] suggests that, theoretically, "these maladjustments are capable, under capitalism, of being set right by an appropriately devised system of bounties and duties" though the difficulties in practice would be quite formidable:

> How for example, are we to ascertain to what extent the social cost, as measured in money, of the marginal unit of beer exceeds the private cost by making necessary the provision of extra policemen; how are we to make the corresponding calculation for a factory industry the smoke of which increases the expenses of the public in washing and cleaning? How, *per contra*, are we to reckon up the indirect benefits that the planting of a forest may have on climate?

In referring to these statements, Lange forgot to tell the reader that Pigou [18] is of the opinion that "a central planning authority would find it no more easy than the government of a capitalist State to obtain the data required for these calculations."

LIBERAL SOCIALISM AND MONOPOLY

In discussing the problem of monopoly within the framework of a liberal socialist system we must remember that socialist industrial managers enjoy a *de facto* monopoly, that a real, competitive market economy does not exist, that for this very reason a trial-and-error system with accounting prices has to be introduced, and that pure and perfect competition are replaced by rules of behavior for managers.

[17] Pigou, p. 42; see also his *The Economics of Welfare*, 4th ed. (New York: St. Martin's Press, Inc., 1938), pp. 192–193.
[18] Pigou, *Socialism Versus Capitalism*, p. 43–44.

The following remarks are not meant as an attempt to deny the disadvantages of private monopoly, which have already been enumerated in Chapter 7. If, however, these disadvantages are to be used as a justification for liberal socialism, two questions must be asked: First, whether there are no solutions other than full-fledged socialism; and next, whether liberal socialism will eliminate the dangers of monopoly. On both counts the answers are not as obvious as some writers think.

If an industry is in a position to exploit the consumer, or if the competitive struggle is excessive, such an industry can be nationalized, particularly if nationalization would be more efficient and less bureaucratic than mere public control. History offers many examples of this type of partial nationalization. As we have seen, partial nationalization is basically different from total nationalization, which alone would establish a socialist economy. It must be clearly understood that nationalization of single industries does not create the allocation problem typical of the socialist economy. The pricing process is kept intact while the problem of monopolistic exploitation is solved, at least in principle. Either monopolistic prices are reduced or the monopolistic profit goes to the state.

The second question—whether the dangers of monopolistic abuses are eliminated in liberal socialism—is more difficult to answer. Undoubtedly, there will be no *private* monopoly in liberal socialism. But the socialist economic unit is the industry rather than the plant, and there is therefore only one seller of each product. Even the consumer goods market is characterized by the monopolistic position of the industrial manager, just as the labor market finds him in a monopsonistic position. It can be argued, of course, that state agencies will not try to exploit the citizens as consumers or workers. It is possible, however, that industrial managers might make use of their *de facto* monopolistic (or monopsonistic) position. They might, for instance, charge higher-than-cost prices in order to accumulate capital. Furthermore, to avoid the derangement caused by innovation, which might be rather formidable in a bureaucratic system, a manager may be satisfied to leave conditions as they are, being able to do so because he is not exposed to *real* competition in his field.

Although liberal socialist managers are supposed to "play at competition," they may not play the game conscientiously, because they can simplify their problems by using their sheltered monopolistic position. For this reason, the auditing apparatus of the central planning board must act as an efficient umpire in the game. But, since the relevant technical knowledge rests with the industrial managers, it will be difficult for the auditors to tell the men on the spot what they ought to have done. Socialist managers may be mainly interested in avoiding personal risks. Although they may not use their monopolistic powers for the purpose of exploitation, the results for the economy might be similar to those of monopolistic restrictions by private enterprise. While socialist misuse of monopoly power might be less dramatic, it could be more widespread and insidious.

LIBERAL SOCIALISM AND FULL EMPLOYMENT

Mass unemployment is perhaps the greatest evil that can befall the private enterprise economy (Chapter 8). Chapter 9, however, demonstrated that there are methods by which aggregate expenditure can be controlled to maintain a reasonably high level of employment and at the same time retain the essentially private enterprise character of the system.

Socialists criticize the unplanned character of the private enterprise economy. We are told that since consumption, production, saving, and investment rest on innumerable independent, individual decisions, it is not at all surprising that mass unemployment occurs frequently. The socialist economy would much better coordinate the actions of the various producing units, prevent discrepancies between saving and investment, and make full use of available resources.

In these assumptions the socialists are basically correct. Not that occasional overproduction in socialist investment goods industries is impossible. Most likely, substantial mistakes can be made. But the socialist economy is able to localize overproduction and avoid a general deflationary trend. "Concretely: a crisis centering in the cotton industry may in the capitalist order put a stop to residential construction; in the socialist order it may of course also happen that the production of cotton goods has to be drastically curtailed at short notice, though it is not so likely to happen; but this would be a reason to speed up residential construction instead of stopping it." [19]

Full employment is not identical with the most economical use of the available resources. Full employment through make-work rules or labor camps is not necessarily preferable to open unemployment. Even if all who want to work are "gainfully" employed, the national income is not always greater than if the same economy were exposed to mild cyclical fluctuations. Dynamic growth cannot always be perfectly steady. It is possible that the liberal socialist regime might maintain its favorable employment level through avoiding disturbing changes, which, in the long run, would prove to be productive. This danger has already been suggested in the discussion of the monopolistic and bureaucratic character of socialist production.

[19] Joseph A. Schumpeter, *Capitalism, Socialism, and Democracy*, 3d ed. (New York: Harper & Row, Publishers, 1950), p. 195.

In addition, the liberal socialist economy shares with the private enterprise system the difficulties that result from free choice of consumption. If individual freedoms are the cause of disturbances, liberal socialism may be tempted to use the simplified formula of authoritarian socialism. For the same reason, however, a private enterprise system may be in danger of resorting to fascist solutions. Both liberal systems may yield to authoritarian temptations; neither can claim complete immunity.

Liberal socialism would also be exposed to some of the difficulties that full employment creates in the private enterprise economy. If, with Lord Beveridge,[20] we define full employment as "having always more vacant jobs than unemployed men," this means that the labor market would be a seller's market with labor in a favorable bargaining position. Lord Beveridge lists among the difficulties of a liberal, rather than authoritarian, solution of the unemployment problem the fact that labor's bargaining strength may lead to a vicious spiral of inflation.

If this inflationary development is "repressed" by price control and rationing, it may easily have detrimental effects on the efficiency of labor. Where higher wages cannot buy more, or can buy more only at exorbitant black market prices, efficiency will decline.

Even in normal times, without repressed inflation, full employment can be detrimental to labor discipline and efficiency. Paul M. Sweezy [21] believes that the abolition of unemployment in socialism "may, especially in the early stages of socialist development, seriously complicate the problem of maintaining labor discipline." He thinks that socialism "will have to develop a code of labor law which ensures the maintenance of labor discipline, in much the same way that capitalism has evolved a code of commercial law which ensures the maintenance of discipline in such matters as payment of debts, fulfillment of contracts, and the like."

HOW MUCH PLANNING?

When liberal socialists claim superiority for their order, they do so on the assumption that theirs is a centrally planned system, whereas the market process is blind, haphazard, and chaotic. Yet liberal socialists waver in their emphasis on central planning. Supposedly the planners, with a wealth of knowledge at their disposal, can integrate different production processes by a shorter series of trial-and-error attempts and we hear of such grand development schemes that we temporarily forget that the consumer was supposed to guide production. At other times, however, the

[20] William H. Beveridge, *Full Employment in a Free Society* (New York: W. W. Norton & Company, Inc., 1945), pp. 18, 22, 199.
[21] Sweezy, pp. 205–206.

consumer seems to be in full command; and the central planning board, after having set rules of behavior for socialist managers, seems to limit itself to making price adjustments and decisions about capital accumulation. But to authoritarian economists this appears to be a defeatist attitude and a very anemic kind of plan. Indeed, this emasculated form of socialism is so disappointing to most socialists that the liberal socialist blueprint is unlikely to be followed in practice.[22] According to Sweezy:

> Lange's Board is not a *planning* agency at all but rather a *price-fixing* agency; in his model production decisions are left to a myriad of essentially independent units, just as they are under capitalism. Such a system is certainly conceivable, but most socialists will probably feel that it reproduces some of the worst features of capitalism and fails to take advantage of the constructive possibilities of economic planning.

The weak and ambiguous nature of liberal socialist planning is indicated by Dickinson's attitude. Although Dickinson's *Economics of Socialism* is a book of 237 pages, only on pages 219 to 225 do we find a discussion of planning, and this discussion begins apologetically as follows:

> So far, the reader will say, there has been little talk of planned economy. The S.E.C. [Supreme Economic Council] has been described as a mere statistical board, collecting and publishing data of output, cost, price, capital and income, calculating demand and supply schedules, but not exerting any real directive functions. All that has been done is to set up within the socialist community a sort of simulacrum of a capitalist economy, purged from the latter's grosser errors, but, like it, actuated by the blind choice of millions of unco-ordinated consumers and producers. This is now the place to make clear the proper relation of economic planning to the price-process. The two are not opposed, but complementary, principles of economic regulation.

According to Dickinson, planning in liberal socialism is only marginal. It supports the pricing system and does so in four different ways. "The first is to give general directives to socialist economy. The second is to make decisions where market indications are lacking. The third is to eliminate cyclical fluctuations in economic activity. The fourth is to deal with special emergencies."

General directives, according to Dickinson, will be necessary when the government has to rebuild the economic life of society out of the ruins left by revolution and civil war. In this stage "the first thing to do would be to ensure a supply of bare necessities to the people without any consideration of the rights of property and without much consideration for the niceties of an elaborate system of pricing and costing." Later on, however, as a more normal level of productivity is again reached, "the great majority of

[22] Dickinson, p. 17; Paul M. Sweezy, *op. cit.*, p. 233.

lines of production would be carried on automatically within the framework of costs and prices so as to supply goods to consumers according to their preferences as indicated in the market." Dickinson believes that finally "a stage would be reached in which the economic machine would practically run itself. The planning authority would need only to lay down a few very general leading principles, and to make definite decisions regarding the allotment of resources to new capital construction and to communal consumption."

Since all governments of modern capitalist countries are committed to maintain high employment levels and to act in emergencies, it is doubtful whether Dickinson has enlarged our concept of planning beyond that which is either equally possible under private property or clearly implied in the very definition of liberal socialism. But the weak nature of their central planning deprives liberal socialists of some claims they have made. Indeed, liberal socialism and a regulated private enterprise economy could be so similar that the change to socialism might hardly be worthwhile, particularly in view of the still unsolved problems of factor allocation and bureaucratic management indicated above.

PART 5

Authoritarian

Socialism

CHAPTER 18

Authoritarian Socialism and Central Planning

INTRODUCTION

In Chapter 14 the authoritarian socialist (or communist) economy was characterized by state ownership of all means of production, autocratic determination of the aims of production, and an all-inclusive central plan. It was pointed out, however, that authoritarian socialism could be less extreme, that it could permit free choice of consumption and allocation of labor through wage differentials. Since this freer system resembles the present structure of the Soviet economy, we shall use it for our theoretical discussion of the authoritarian socialist economy.

In studying the private enterprise system and *liberal* socialism, we assumed consumers' sovereignty. In both systems production is consumer-oriented and not harnessed into the shafts of a pervasive central plan. To follow the changing wishes of consumers means to permit continuous alterations in the allocation of productive resources; to follow a central plan means prearranged production to meet the state's preference schedule. The authoritarian central plan may permit free consumers' choice among the commodities and services which the planners decided to supply. However, price changes, necessary to maintain equilibrium between supply and demand, would not influence future production. The question remains whether it is possible to combine central planning with such guidance through consumer goods prices, by introducing consumers' sovereignty into a centrally planned economy. For the present, there is little indication that those in charge of planning in Russia would be willing to have their difficult task made even more complicated by continuous adjustments to price changes emanating from changing consumer demand. Central planning approaches the problems of the social economy from the opposite end: the road does not lead from consumers' choices, via market prices, to production processes and factor allocations guided by these prices; it leads from planned targets, via bureaucratic integration of all industries, to results that the consumers have to accept.

If it were possible to introduce consumers' sovereignty through guidance of the managers by price signals, the authoritarian economy would have changed, according to our definitions, into a liberal socialist economy. The discussion of liberal socialism has shown, however, that the pricing process would have to be more genuine than the one suggested by Lange and Dickinson.

CENTRAL VERSUS MARGINAL PLANNING

The liberal socialists' attitude toward central planning is not shared by authoritarian socialists. Paul M. Sweezy,[1] for instance, does not like this milquetoast version of planning. He believes that a socialist economy needs real central planning rather than a mere price-fixing agency. He starts from the investment problem, not from consumers' preferences, and consistently arrives at the conclusion that planning must become all-inclusive:

> In an unplanned economy—whether capitalist or collectivist—investment decisions are made by many independent units. . . . It is this circumstance that accounts for the irrational behavior of an unplanned economy: the alternation of booms and slumps, the coexistence of gluts and shortages, the paradox of unemployed workers with unsatisfied wants. . . . It is scarcely conceivable that the socialist state will so decentralize the making of investment decisions as to recreate the blindness and uncertainty of unplanned capitalism. Moreover, it is not hard to see that the centralization of investment decisions makes comprehensive economic planning all but inevitable. Assume, for example, that the government of a socialist society makes a basic policy decision to invest a certain percentage of the national income over a period of, say, five or ten years and lays down certain general goals such as the building up of heavy industry, the re-

[1] Reprinted from *Socialism*, by Paul M. Sweezy, pp. 234–236, 238–239. Copyright, 1949. Courtesy of McGraw-Hill, Inc.

housing of a specified proportion of the population, and the development of hitherto backward regions. The next step would naturally be to charge the Central Planning Board with the task of drawing up an investment plan for carrying out these decisions. This investment plan will begin by translating the general goals laid down by the government into quantitative terms: so many new factories, railroads, power plants, mines, apartment houses, schools, hospitals, theaters, and so forth. The dates at which these various construction projects are to be started and finished will then be specified. From these data it will be possible to draw up schedules of the different kinds of materials and labor which will be required. At this point the investment plan may be said to be complete. But would it be sensible for the Central Planning Board to stop here and to rely on price and income controls to ensure that what is needed will be ready at the right time, at the right place, and in the right quantities? The answer is surely that it would not be.

After the requirements of investment are taken into account,

> . . . the Central Planning Board will find it necessary to estimate consumer demand for all products which compete for resources with the investment plan and to draw up a second set of schedules showing the different kinds of materials and labor which will be required. It should now be possible, by consolidating the investment and consumption schedules and by comparing them with current and prospective supplies, to work out a general plan for the development of the economy over the period in question. . . . When a consistent and practical plan has finally been adopted, it cannot be left to the discretion of individual industry and plant managers whether or not they will conform to it; rather it must be their first duty, imposed by law, to carry out their part of the plan to the best of their ability— just as, for example, it is the duty of corporate managers under capitalism to make profits for the owners.

Here, finally, we have the full picture of a centrally planned economy —the price system no longer encompasses the plan, consumers no longer decide what is to be produced, and managers no longer act independently on the basis of price-cost relations. The central planning board does not rely on prices to ensure that what is needed will be ready "at the right time, at the right place, and in the right quantities." The plan controls everything, and prices, if used, are subservient to the plan.

That we have moved away from the liberal socialist models of Lange and Dickinson is admitted by Sweezy, who regards it "as established by both theoretical reasoning and practical experience that a socialist economy will be centrally planned in a sense very different from that in which Lange's model may be said to be centrally planned."

In moving away from the trial-and-error model Sweezy feels obliged to ask whether rational accounting and allocation, which are possible in Lange's model, are also possible in a comprehensively planned economy. "Is it possible," he writes, "that in going from one to the other we have unwittingly fallen into the clutches of Mises and his followers?" Of course, he is of the opinion that this is not the case,

> . . . that rational accounting and allocation are still possible under comprehensive planning. . . . As the experience of the Soviet Union proves, there is no conflict between comprehensive planning and money calculation. . . . The crucial difference between Lange's model and the comprehensively planned economy lies in the location of the authority to make decisions about production. In the one these decisions are made by many independent units; in the other by the Central Planning Board. . . . This shift in the location of the authority to make production decisions in no way disturbs the logic of Lange's argument.

Why, however, did Sweezy not tell his readers that Lange believes the trial-and-error method to be just as applicable to authoritarian as to liberal socialism? Probably Sweezy wanted to detract his readers from Lange's [2] description of a comprehensively planned system because Lange feels that such a system must clearly be an authoritarian one,

> . . . where freedom of choice in consumption and freedom of choice of occupation are non-existent and where the allocation of resources, instead of being directed by the preferences of consumers, is directed by the aims and valuations of the bureaucracy in charge of the administration of the economic system. In such a system the Central Planning Board decides which commodities are to be produced and in what quantities, the consumers' goods produced being distributed to the citizens by rationing and the various occupations being filled by assignment. In such a system also rational accounting is possible, only that the accounting reflects the preferences of the bureaucrats in the Central Planning Board, instead of those of the consumers.

Lange rejects this system because of its undemocratic character and its "incompatibility with the ideals of the socialist movement."

Lange also discusses a compromise between central planning and free choice of consumption. He suggests that free choice of consumption need not imply that production is actually guided by the preferences of consumers:

> One may well imagine a system in which production and the allocation of resources are guided by a preference scale fixed by the Central Planning Board while the price system is used to distribute the consumers' goods produced. In such a system there is freedom of choice in consumption, but the consumers have no influence whatever on the decisions of the managers of production and of the productive resources. There would be two sets of prices of consumers' goods. One would be the market prices

---

[2] Oskar Lange and Fred M. Taylor, *On the Economic Theory of Socialism* (Minneapolis: University of Minnesota Press, 1938), pp. 90–91, 95, 96. Copyright 1938 by the University of Minnesota.

at which the goods are sold to the consumers; the other, the accounting prices derived from the preference scale fixed by the Central Planning Board. The latter set of prices would be those on the basis of which the managers of production would make their decisions.

Lange does not believe that such a system would be tolerated by the citizens of a socialist community.

In Sweezy's description of central planning, investment decisions are made by the central planning board according to the state's preference scale and the operation of the plan is not based on a pricing process. Production targets are targets *in kind* and resource allocations are *physical* allocations. Accounting prices and monetary transfers are used, but the importance of these financial phenomena must not be exaggerated. Money performs the function of a unit of account where aggregates of dissimilar things are in need of a uniform expression. Transfer payments offer an opportunity for keeping check on plan-fulfillment by the managers. All transactions between administrative units must be paid for by checks drawn on accounts in the state bank. The sums involved must correspond to the number of physical units delivered, multiplied by their accounting prices. Finally, there are markets for consumer goods and labor and the planning board must see to it that, for example, the total supply of consumer goods times their sales prices equals the aggregate purchasing power of the consumers, or that the value of output equals the value of input plus planned profits in a given industry or enterprise.

While these functions of money and prices are important, they are not *guiding* functions. Major decisions and allocations are made irrespective of these prices—fortunately so, because the accounting prices are artificially set and rarely changed. Reliance on these prices would lead to results that would be undesirable in every respect. We shall try to find out whether, after a thorough reform of the price structure, prices could be used for consistent accounting and allocation within the central plan and what the conditions of this reform might be.

THE CASE FOR CENTRAL PLANNING

The case for central planning is expressed eloquently in Maurice Dobb's *Soviet Economic Development Since 1917.*[3] It rests on the following premises:

1. The importance of consumers' sovereignty has been greatly overstressed by bourgeois and socialist writers. Consumer goods may be distributed through the market, but production need not be directed by the consumer. Consumers' sovereignty can and should be abolished.

[3] (New York: International Publishers Co., Inc., 1948.)

2. The choice among different production patterns is far less formidable than it is made to appear in bourgeois literature. The question is not how to find an optimum combination of factors among an *infinite* variety of possible combinations. Historical, technological, and social conditions limit the practical choices of the central planning board to manageable proportions.

3. The longer the contemplated planning period, the greater is the number of possible investment patterns. Such long-run plans cannot be made by *independent* producing units, because they rest on parallel developments of *interdependent* industries.

4. Economic development through long-run planning is more important than the question of how a perfect static equilibrium can be achieved.

5. Equilibrium in the development process can be maintained through so-called balances by which the internal consistency of the plan is constantly checked.

6. Through these balances the interrelationships of the different industries are known and planned *ex ante*, in contrast to the tardy way of *post facto* coordination through the price mechanism. However, the plan has to be constantly reshaped and adjusted as it is carried out because of inconsistencies or recent changes in priorities and technology. Only in this sense can it be said that a trial-and-error procedure is used.

THE ABOLITION OF CONSUMERS' SOVEREIGNTY

Socialist writers have pointed out that consumers' sovereignty has little meaning in the private enterprise economy for two reasons: (1) because the inequality of income distribution leads to "plural voting," [4] and (2) because in any complex economic system the choice lies with the producers rather than with the consumers.[5]

The first point is well taken as long as it is assumed that authoritarian socialism leads to a much more equal income distribution, an assumption that becomes more difficult to make once free choice of occupation and allocation of labor through wage differentials are permitted. Abba Lerner,[6] furthermore, is quite right when he points out that the authoritarian socialist's "urgency for exact equality of voting goes ill with the bureaucratic contempt for the intelligence of the voter." Equal voting rights

[4] See, Maurice Dobb, "Economic Theory and the Problem of a Socialist Economy," *Economic Journal*, vol. 43 (December 1933), pp. 588–598.

[5] Barbara Wootton, *Plan or No Plan* (London: Victor Gollancz, Ltd., 1934), p. 173.

[6] A. P. Lerner, "Economic Theory and the Socialist Economy," *Review of Economic Studies*, vol. 2 (1934–1935), pp. 51–61.

would be important if consumers were to guide production. But this function is to be taken over by the central planning board of the authoritarian socialist economy.

The second point argues that consumers never direct production anyway, that they merely choose among goods *that are already there.* Owing to the law of large numbers, the producer can foresee the wants of a multitude with more ease and accuracy than a consumer can foresee his own wants.[7] This does not mean, however, that production for the market eliminates the consumer as final arbiter. Barbara Wootton,[8] after emphasizing that the initiative must always lie with the producer, admits that in the unplanned economy it is impossible "to go on persevering with a wrong guess, pretending that it is right." In the planned economy, on the other hand, "there is no such definite limit, since mistakes can be covered up by subsidizing one article out of the profits of another, or manipulating the purchasing power of consumers, or by similar devices which are open only to those who control virtually the whole economic life of the community, and not merely certain industries."

Dobb[9] argues correctly that "with regard to new commodities and varieties of a commodity catering for new wants, in no economic system can the market afford any automatic index to guide production." Nevertheless, he forgets that it does make some difference whether the producer must be anxious to please the consumer and to anticipate his wishes or whether a central planning board decides arbitrarily on the variety and quantities of the commodities to be produced.

Dobb believes that the number of different commodities whose production must be considered is fairly small. "The items which compose consumers' aggregate demand to any large extent form a closely interrelated set, bound together, that is, by social convention or by links of complementarity between particular wants into 'modes of life' or patterns of behavior which assume the character of organic wholes." In addition, commodities must be produced on a sufficiently large scale, and this reduces drastically "the number of different things that it is practicable to put simultaneously into production."

Both arguments are rationalizations of the natural tendency of the authoritarian planner to bring about a much higher degree of standardization of individual behavior and of production. While this makes the authoritarian economy less complex—and conceivably more productive in physical units—it tends to make it less productive in terms of satisfaction of human wants. Those who believe in consumers' sovereignty suggest that we leave it to consumers to decide what price they are willing to pay for

---

[7] See Chap. 3.
[8] Wootton, p. 173.
[9] Dobb, *Soviet Economic Development since 1917,* pp. 5, 377.

diversity in want satisfaction. They also believe, with J. M. Keynes,[10] that the loss of personal choice "is the greatest of all losses of the homogeneous or totalitarian state."

It is true that for a country that is still poor, the problem of choice is not a very difficult one; the planners could decide what the bare necessities of life are. But "as primary wants are satisfied and variety is multiplied, the alternatives become more numerous and choice between them more controversial and less calculable." Dobb [11] believes, however, that by that time "the difference to be made to human welfare by the difference between two alternative solutions of the puzzle will have become a quantity of a relatively small order." This is exactly what the advocate of consumers' sovereignty denies. He wants *his* solution and not the solution of the central planning board.

Dobb points out that,

> the nearer that a society approaches to an equality of income-distribution, the more likely it is that market-demand for a very wide range of articles will be characterized by this sort of discontinuity: above a certain price the article (let us suppose it is some new commodity like bicycles, wristwatches, radio sets or refrigerators) will have scarcely any purchasers at all, because few or none can afford it; while immediately below this price the demand for it may become almost infinitely elastic because everyone will now wish to acquire it, until the supply has become adequate for all, when the demand may once more become quite inelastic.

On the basis of experiences of the Soviet-type economies, Stanislaw Wellisz [12] comes to conclusions that contradict Dobb's theorizing. Wellisz points out that under free choice of consumption the use of prices as an equilibrating device is made particularly difficult where income differentials are very small, because small price cuts, which put commodities within the range of the low-income worker, cause "demand avalanches." Wellisz also says that the planned economy will meet with serious difficulties in the setting of thousands of commodity prices. Not knowing the elasticities and cross-elasticities of demand, the price-fixing authorities will change prices only rarely. This means that consumer goods prices cannot perform even the modest function of maintaining equilibrium between demand and supply. The still existing commodity markets, therefore, are not real markets with genuine price formation. Prices are set by the authorities, rarely changed, incapable of maintaining equilibrium, and worse than useless for the purpose of guiding production.

[10] John Maynard Keynes, *The General Theory of Employment, Interest, and Money* (New York: Harcourt, Brace & World, Inc., 1965), p. 380.

[11] Dobb, *Soviet Economic Development since 1917*, pp. 19–20.

[12] Stanislaw Wellisz, *The Economies of the Soviet Bloc* (New York: McGraw-Hill, Inc., 1964), pp. 88, 89.

A similar situation prevails in the labor market. While wages may mirror roughly the scarcity of certain kinds of labor and guide labor to different occupations, the demand for labor on the part of the managers is determined by output targets and production norms. Normally, therefore, the managers are not competing for labor and there is no genuine price formation on the labor market.

THE CHOICE OF PRODUCTION PATTERNS

Dobb believes that the task of the central planning board is far less formidable than some economists seem to think. The planned system does not have to cross a "whole ocean of possible and imaginable economic permutations" as Ludwig von Mises [13] assumes. The choice of production patterns is rather narrowly limited, at least in the short run, by the following facts:

1. Productive resources cannot be shifted at will; they are not very tractable.

2. Technical considerations impose a minimum scale of production for many products.

3. At any given time the productive resources are woven into a given pattern which cannot be changed suddenly or without considerable cost.

4. Technical coefficients of production require production processes to be internally consistent and forbid the combination of factors unless all required elements are available in the right quantities.

5. Expansion of production A without contraction of production B depends on the existence of reserve productive capacity.

6. The pattern of production is partly determined by the pattern of consumption discussed above.

If Dobb wants to argue that we are limited in what we can do in the short run, no one will disagree with him. Nor has anyone suggested that the planning board would have to choose anew in every planning period among infinite possibilities. Any social economy will base most of its decisions on past patterns. Dobb himself argues that the number of possible investment patterns increases with the length of the planning period. Obviously, then, *ex ante* planning is not the mere sum of those minor changes that are permissible under the constraints he has enumerated; the more drastic changes will conflict severely with the set pattern of the present instead of being helped by it.

The conflict between change and the status quo is well known to central planners. It has divided them into two groups: those who are sat-

[13] Ludwig von Mises, *Socialism: An Economic and Sociological Analysis* (New Haven, Conn.: Yale University Press, 1951), p. 122.

isfied with minor revisions of past trends (the so-called "genetic" planners) and those (the "teleological" planners) who do not want to be bound by the constraints of the patterns of the past. Dobb, who supports teleological planning, is unwittingly supplying the genetic planners with strong arguments when he emphasizes the difficulties involved in extricating the plan from its constraints, although he wanted to prove that the choices would be very narrow and, accordingly, much easier than envisaged in bourgeois economics.

Actually, the constraints may be more formidable in the authoritarian socialist than in a private enterprise economy because the former relies on a bureaucratic integration of production, which is very difficult to achieve, and which the bureaucrats will not want to destroy. This fact accounts for the strong support of gradualism among bureaucrats and managers (the genetic planners), in spite of the fact that teleological planning can make a strong case for itself, if it can break through the constraints of interdependent limiting factors.

TARGET PLANNING

The strongest argument for central planning says that independent producing units cannot plan far ahead because they are not in a position to predict the actions of others with sufficient accuracy. Modern industrial production is a complicated and intricate process where every industry rests on instruments and materials made by other industries, and products can be sold only if other industries or the consumers need them. The individual producer in a private enterprise economy can anticipate the actions of others for the near future only, and, even then, there is a degree of uncertainty. He must wait and see whether subsequent price developments justify his actions; whereupon he may proceed another step.

The planned economy depends on the same *technical* interrelation as the unplanned economy. But it makes *conscious* use of the knowledge of this interrelation and would,

> substitute *ex ante* co-ordination of the constituent elements in a scheme of development for the tardy *post facto* co-ordinating tendencies that are operated by the mechanism of price movements on a market in a capitalist world—tendencies, moreover, which in the presence of substantial time-lags may merely achieve extensive fluctuations. In this the essential difference between a planned economy and an unplanned evidently consists.[14]

Dobb points out that such *ex ante* coordination, by eliminating much uncertainty, not only permits a given objective to be attained more

[14] Dobb, *Soviet Economic Development*, pp. 2–3, 9.

smoothly but also makes possible developments that the private enterprise economy cannot undertake at all because the independent producer cannot be certain "that others will follow suit and take parallel action which coordinates with, and justifies, his own."

Dobb emphasizes the importance of planned *development* in contradistinction to the achievement of perfect *equilibrium* at any given point of time. Bourgeois as well as liberal socialist theories are, according to him, preoccupied with equilibrium analysis. They want to find "an *optimum* allocation of resources between alternative uses, with both resources and uses treated as given." He suggests that "a more crucial test of the contribution made by an economic system to human welfare" is to be found in the system's ability to develop successfully from one situation to another. And in this respect he believes the centrally planned economy to be far superior to the unplanned economy.

However, the theory of central planning cannot discard the concept of economic equilibrium altogether. Any social economy must try to reach a position in which the currently available productive resources are employed and distributed among different industries so that the production processes gear into one another without much friction. All industries in need of a particular factor of production must get a sufficient amount to fulfill their production quotas, and all intermediate industries must produce enough to enable others to reach their targets. Because all industries are interrelated in the most intricate manner, the centrally planned economy must see that they cooperate smoothly and avoid bottlenecks or unemployment—danger signals that disproportions may have developed in the economic process. Bottlenecks occur when whatever is needed is not ready at the right time, the right place, or in sufficient amounts. These bottlenecks prevent the use of complementary means of production; therefore unemployment develops, which leads to underfulfillment of plan figures and to new bottlenecks in an ever-widening circle.

Coordination of the production processes can be achieved by use of so-called balances, that is, "a complex system of equations between the various magnitudes in a plan as the tests of internal consistency or coherence between its various elements." [15] These balances can be real, material, or physical balances. For example, all quantities of a given material used in all production and consuming units during a given period of time can be added together, and this sum can then be compared with the forthcoming supply of the material or with the total of each of the various factors of production needed to produce the given material in such quantities.

The production plan of the authoritarian socialist economy is "a complex of output-programmes for all the main products of the economic system, embracing real expenditure and real product, input and output in

[15] Dobb, pp. 331, 348, 355.

each case." Not all the balances in this production plan can be real or physical balances, however. Where dissimilar things are to be added together, we need equations or balances in monetary terms. Monetary balances are necessary, furthermore, where money incomes are earned and spent on consumer goods and where wage differentials are used to regulate the supply of labor for different industries.

When factor and product prices are introduced, real balances are changed into monetary balances and the production plan into a financial plan. Producing units must be supplied with enough purchasing power to be able to buy necessary means of production. The quantities of the various factors needed in different production processes are indicated by technological coefficients and plan quotas. These quantities have to be multiplied by factor prices to determine the planned cost of production. Planned profit may be added, and greater-than-average economy in the use of factors may lead to higher than planned profits. This extra margin may possibly be used as collective incentive.

Once a producing unit is supplied with the necessary funds, it should be able to maintain its liquidity through the sale of its product. Obviously, the state bank, which carries the accounts of all producing units, can trace all their receipts and disbursements, and check whether funds were spent in accordance with the aims of the plan. The operations of the state bank, therefore, will serve as a comprehensive auditing apparatus.

Against Dobb's theoretical picture of central planning as a conscious effort to determine the development of the economy as a whole and to specify the role that each part is to play in this effort, we must hold the fact that central planning will prove to be extremely difficult in practice. If it could function well, the authoritarian planned economy might indeed be superior to the private enterprise economy, except for the amount of individual freedom that it is willing to grant. But the question remains, will central planning work well, only tolerably well, or, perhaps, not well at all? It must at least provide a minimum of bureaucratic integration of the production processes of the social economy. Since the socialist managers are no longer driven by the profit motive and not guided by market prices, they must be told what to produce and how; in other words, they have to follow commands. The system must be centrally planned since it could not function without plan. The central plan is an alternative to the market mechanism. Where the pricing process is abolished, the plan exists as a necessity and not as conclusive proof of economic superiority.

Long-run plans are always target plans and not operational plans. They are long run because only over a lengthy period is it possible to sufficiently change the production pattern. Yearly plans effect only minor changes. However, extension of the plan period to 5 or 10 years does not permit the exactness required of operational plans. Long-run plans, therefore, are little more than broad outlines, a framework for the yearly operational plans. They must stay elastic enough to permit revisions in the light of practical experience gained in the execution of the yearly plans.

The most basic decision in target planning concerns the line drawn between consumer and producers' goods production. The authoritarian economy has the power to press for a high growth rate by expanding investment goods production at the expense of consumption. The private enterprise economy, by contrast, relies on the free decision of its members to postpone present for the sake of future consumption.

The determination of production targets (in both investment and consumer goods production) depends on the state preference function. Obviously, the targets are chosen with some consideration of costs involved, though sometimes the goals are so important they must be reached "regardless of cost." In the private enterprise economy this situation occurs in wartime when priority claims are so obvious they are outside the realm of economics. The special problem of the authoritarian economy, however, is that costs cannot be expressed in monetary terms and planners cannot limit themselves to setting just a few priorities. Prices, set by the authorities themselves, cannot decisively influence the choice of targets because the authorities would consider it absurd to be bound by price guidelines of their own making. Therefore costs play only a minor part in the target plans of the command economy, though, ideally speaking, the targets should be the result of choices made after careful consideration of numerous alternative plans. The authorities should be able to select those investment expenditures that promise the best possible satisfaction of the state's preference schedule.

Once acquainted with the difficulties of putting even one target plan into operational figures, we see that it is impossible to prepare within a short time a whole series of alternative plans. We must conclude that long-term planning is not an exercise in economic calculation and factor allocation, but an arbitrary determination of physical production goals that are consistent enough to permit a bureaucratic integration of the needed production processes. However, if and when this aim is accomplished, we would be still far from an allocation in which the factors of production are used in the most economical way (that is, so that the marginal productivity of the factors would tend to be approximately the same in all industries).

The reasons for the planners lacking interest in a more refined system of economic factor allocation are several: adherence to Marx's labor theory of value (which can be made to fit whatever resource distribution is chosen); aversion to exact cost accounting for priority projects; unwillingness to complicate the planning process; and, finally, fear of the degree of managerial decentralization and freedom implied in more sophisticated allocation schemes. To put these thoughts into more general terms: teleological planners are not willing to sacrifice their commanding power for an improvement of factor allocation (an advantage that some of them are not even able to comprehend).

THE OPERATIONAL PLANS

The target plan must be translated into a series of operational plans. Obviously, the central planning board cannot make all the detailed decisions which are necessary to implement a comprehensive central plan. The needed technical knowledge for this purpose rests with the managers of enterprises and industries. How, then, does authoritarian socialism propose to combine centralized target planning with the activities of local managers so that the latter's initiative and special knowledge are used to the best advantage?

The results of the target plan are "preliminary indicators," which undoubtedly contain many inconsistencies and disproportionalities. Only the men nearer the periphery will be able to correct these errors. The preliminary indicators (or "control figures") are, therefore, distributed downward through the administrative network with the request for correction and information. Now the enterprises and industries draft or redraft sections of the plan on the operational or working level. They establish, for example, what physical and financial resources are needed when given output figures are to be reached. These activities have nothing in common with the reactions of managers to price changes in market economies. In the authoritarian socialist economy the manager of an industry will point out, for instance, that it is technically impossible for him to reach expected output figures unless, say, 20 percent more of a given material is allocated, that the proposed time schedule cannot be met, that transportation facilities are inadequate, or that more skilled labor is needed. These criticisms do not question the output quota as such, they only want to make one section of the plan more realistic.

Planning on the industrial and enterprise level must follow certain production norms set by the central authorities. Furthermore, the inputs are allocated from above and the managers have little leeway in factor substitution. This setup has the weakness that those who have the know-how have little to say while the men in the center must decide on questions which they cannot properly handle.

When the managers send their corrections back to the planning board, the latter is once more faced with the immense task of producing a consistent input-output network in which all managers get the allocations that they need to produce what all other managers must have. As one enterprise's output is part of another's input, the achievement of even the roughest bureaucratic integration is a great accomplishment. Furthermore, this integration cannot be assumed to be the result of a slow trial-and-error process. The essence of teleological planning is change. Not only must still existing imbalances in past performance be ironed out, changes in the state preference function will demand continuous adjustments. Suppose that industry A's productive capacity is suddenly to be expanded. Obviously A needs larger allocations of whatever is technically required and these resources must (under the implicit assumption of full employment) be taken from industries B or C. A wave of change will spread throughout the economy whose force and impact can best be grasped if seen in the light of the Casselian equations of the Appendix to Chapter 3.

If each factor could be transferred at will until the desired new pattern of production emerged, the task would have its theoretical solution and a new state of balance would be established. In practice we must use a trial-and-error process of successive approximations whose frictional shortcomings are costly even if our aim remains the achievement of mere bureaucratic consistency, that is, a pattern of production in which all enterprises supply each other with the specified inputs. This solution is still a far cry from a consistent economic factor allocation as demanded by Cassel, Mises, or Lange.

CENTRAL AUTHORITY AND PERIPHERAL MANAGEMENT

The greatest difficulty faced by the authoritarian socialist economy lies in the enormous dimensions of the task that the central planners have to solve and in the fact that, even under the most favorable assumptions, the managers cannot be made to shoulder much of this burden.

Suppose that the managers try wholeheartedly to support the central plan. Within their small range of freedom, that is, in the "interstices" of the system,[16] they do their utmost to make the plan work: they give honest information, follow output figures and production norms in the best interest of the economy as a whole, try to lower cost through factor substitution wherever feasible, and demand scarce investment funds only where a substantial increase in productivity can be expected. Even in this ideal case the full burden of the major investment decisions would be resting on the men in the planning board. A virtual avalanche of reports and requests will be pouring in and the various claims and demands will often conflict. For example, without the benefit of a rate of interest there will be investment demand that will far surpass the supply of investment

[16] See David Granick, "An Organizational Model of Soviet Industrial Planning," *Journal of Political Economy*, vol. 47, no. 2 (April 1959), p. 110.

funds. Obviously, then, the investment decisions cannot be made locally where the technical know-how is available because the aggregate of the requested investments would far exceed the output capacity of the investment goods industry. The center, on the other hand, can allocate investment funds only arbitrarily, with rough bureaucratic consistency, which is the *minimum* condition for the functioning of the authoritarian socialist economy.

If the managers do not do their utmost to support the center in its agonizing task, the picture becomes still darker. The price system of the private enterprise economy can easily be combined with the profit motive, but there is no reliable incentive system that grows naturally out of an all-inclusive plan. Reference to command is not enough. The authorities in the center depend on the support of the managers who alone have the needed know-how. Production plans, developed exclusively in the center, are often not detailed enough (and give too much leeway to the managers) or they are taut and rigid but inconsistent because of insufficient knowledge on the part of the planners.

If, then, the authorities must rely heavily on the managers, both in the preparation and execution of the plan, how can they induce the latter to cooperate for the benefit of the economy rather than for their own benefit? While the enterprise is at the low end of the chain of command, cooperation on the local level is indispensable; therefore, the managers often have a strong bargaining position.

In a command system with tightly drawn input-output plans and production norms, managers may easily be induced to misinform the central authorities. The manager who succeeds in convincing the planners that he needs more inputs to reach stated output figures protects himself against the accusation of having disobeyed the central command—he has made sure that his enterprise or industry will be able to meet the quota. By consciously understating the capacity of his unit he avoids the embarrassing consequences of inconsistencies in the plan figures (for which he was not responsible) or the impact of a sudden curtailment of his input as consequence of sudden priority changes. Every manager will desire to build up reserves of material and labor and he can do this by misinforming the planners. Considering the incompetence of the center in technical matters and the absence of competition, the managers are likely to be successful. If, in addition, overfulfillment is rewarded through bonuses, the manager has the more reason to see to it that his output quota is set low and his input quota high. He may gain profit and security, a combination hard to achieve even in the private enterprise system.

Since interest rates on long-term investments are not charged in a system that prides itself in following Marx's labor theory of value, the manager will always consider additional investment goods worth having if, at no cost, they facilitate the reaching of given output goals. On the other hand, the manager may easily shy away from undertaking revolutionary new investments (even though they be free of interest charges) if they imply uncertainties and risks in terms of interruptions of the production process or stepped-up quotas and output norms. Therefore, the managers may not be helpful to the center when it tries to solve the huge problem of distributing a limited supply of investment funds throughout the economy.

Nor is it certain that the managers will try to reduce the cost of production. This is already implied in the assumption that they will tend to understate their production capacity and to accumulate excessive reserves. In addition, they cannot be expected to act economically since they do not have the benefit of a reliable accounting system. Prices, set for aggregating and auditing purposes by the central authorities, would be worse than useless for the economic allocation of productive resources. Furthermore, since the enterprises' factor supplies are determined by the plan, allocations in a given enterprise will be determined by the artificially created scarcities of these factors within its confines. Under these conditions it is perfectly possible that a given factor may be considered a "free" good, deserving no economic consideration, though the same factor may conceivably be a bottleneck item in another industry.

An output program in quantitative terms may have the effect of tending to lower the quality of the product or leading to an undesirable output-mix unless the most detailed specifications are used by the center. But in this, as in the previous cases, the tightening of the program by the center is impracticable because a really taut program can only be achieved if the enormous burden on the central authorities is increased even more, which makes the so-called bureaucratic bottleneck even worse.

As a means to relieve the central authorities one could suggest the opposite route, namely, to decentralize, to give the managers leeway to solve those problems that they are better qualified to handle. But decentralization raises grave new problems for the center. The freer the managers, the more important it is that their actions be guided by motivations other than blind obedience to command from above. With decreased emphasis on central planning there would be increased stress on guidance by prices and motivation by some incentive akin to the profit motive.

We have already studied the problems that exist under liberal socialism when the Lange-Dickinson suggestions are applied. These recommendations could possibly be changed to fit the authoritarian socialist economy but it is doubtful that the abolition of consumers' sovereignty would eliminate the questions raised in the study of liberal socialism.

If the managers were given freedom to determine input and output according to profit expectations based on cost-and-price calculations, the minimum condition would be a price system where the prices and costs mirror correctly the relative scarcities of the available factors of production in the light of the state's preference schedule. If all prices were *set* by the center and not automatically *formed* on markets under conditions of real competition, the planning authorities would be free of the present problem of bureaucratic integration but would face an infinitely more difficult task —the problem of setting and continuously adjusting millions of prices, consistent with the results that the free actions of the managers were supposed to achieve within the framework of the plan!

Creation of a genuine system of real price formation (in contradistinction to mere price setting) was not proposed by the liberal socialists and must be considered entirely incompatible with teleological planning.

SUMMARY

The crucial difference between liberal and authoritarian socialism is the abolition of consumers' sovereignty in the latter and the replacement of the pricing process by *ex ante* coordination. Taking the abolition of consumers' sovereignty for granted, is it possible to reach a combination of aims that is preferable to other combinations on strictly economic grounds? Should we, for example, make use of the services of experts, let medical doctors draw up a comprehensive health plan, make teachers redesign the educational system, and have physicists and generals control the output of atomic energy? Obviously, the central authorities must secure the opinions of experts in setting aims for the economy, just as they need the help of managers in the formulation and execution of the central plan. But this reference to expert opinion leaves the main problem unsolved, for "someone must coordinate the experts." [17] The claims of different committees of experts surely would overtax the available resources. If this is true, according to which principles are we to decide how much weight is to be given to different objectives that compete for the limited resources of the economy?

We are interested in questions concerning the authoritarian socialist *economy*. The *political* power behind the state's preference function is not the subject matter of this study. Conceivably, this power could be in the hands of representatives chosen by democratic methods.[18] Nevertheless, we assume that the centrally planned economy is a command economy in the sense that production follows a predetermined course, which cannot

[17] H. D. Dickinson, *Economics of Socialism* (New York: Oxford University Press, 1939), p. 48.

[18] See Barbara Wootton, *Plan or No Plan*, p. 311; Joseph A. Schumpeter, *Capitalism, Socialism, and Democracy*, 3d ed. (New York: Harper & Row, Publishers, 1950), pp. 296–302.

be materially altered by individual members of the economy, be they managers, wage earners, or consumers.

Concerning the basic policy decisions that shape the structure of the plan, we have no way of showing that one set of preferences is superior to another. In making these decisions a comprehensive pricing system would be very useful because it would permit the determination of opportunity costs. Even in a centrally planned economy the authorities should think in terms of alternatives sacrificed. After all, the intention of acting rationally is implied in the very concept of planning. Opportunity cost calculations, however, are not practical in terms of physical units and of little value when they are based on prices that have been artificially set by the authorities themselves.

In the translation of targets into operational programs the minimum requirement is bureaucratic integration. The production processes must be made to gear into each other without too much waste or friction. Bureaucratic integration can be achieved through approximation by trial and error. However, this bureaucratic integration, while permitting operation of the system without total breakdown, does not offer a solution in terms of truly economical factor allocation. Even if we substitute the state's for the consumers' preferences, we should see to it that the factor allocation is consistent in an economic rather than a bureaucratic sense. All scarce means of production, and in particular investment funds, should be subject to uniform and consistent pricing.

That this economic factor allocation is not possible in a centrally planned authoritarian system is the strongest argument that can be used against it. A second argument shows that even bureaucratic integration of production processes is hampered by the magnitude of the problem and the fact that a proper division of labor between planners and managers is not possible. In the absence of a genuine price system and without real decentralization it will always be the central authorities who have to make all the important decisions. This is true partly because only the center can coordinate expert opinions and decide between competing claims, and partly because the managers cannot be fully trusted to do their best. It is impossible to replace the command system by simple incentives. Since the target plans will be full of inconsistencies, the managers will be eager to soften the impact of these errors on their industries or enterprises. But they can do this only at substantial cost for the economy by setting the sights low, accumulating unproductive reserves, lowering the quality of the products, and fighting any disturbance of the status quo.

Against these negative features we must weigh the system's power to force the economy into an investment program that a private enterprise economy could not afford because it leaves the rate of growth to capital formation out of private and corporate savings. The high rate of accumulation which the authoritarian system has the power to enforce can compensate or overcompensate the loss through inconsistent factor allocation and bureaucratic friction. In any case, the consumption level is drastically reduced by the combination of an ambitious investment program and a relatively low productivity, particularly in the consumer goods industry.

The fact that consumers' sovereignty is replaced by mere free choice of consumption can be counted against the authoritarian system. However, though the economist may argue that sovereignty would give the consumer more satisfaction, we are dealing here with issues that, in the last analysis, exceed the competence of economics.

CHAPTER 19

The Soviet
Road
to Central Planning

INTRODUCTION

In studying the liberal socialist blueprint we had to limit our-
elves to theoretical considerations because a practical application of these
blueprints has not yet been tried.[1] In the case of authoritarian socialism
it is fortunate that we can now look back on nearly half a century of Russian experimenting in central planning.

The very existence of the Soviet economy seems to indicate that Ludwig von Mises' predictions have been proved wrong.[2] We recall that Mises
asserted that "in a socialist state, there can be—in our sense of the word—
no economy whatever" and that, in the absence of rational accounting,
"hopeless chaos" would prevail. The Soviet economy was able to show
that even in the absence of genuine markets a modicum of bureaucratic
integration of the production processes can be evolved by trial and error

[1] We shall see later that the experiment in Yugoslavia does not correspond to the
Lange-Dickinson proposals.
[2] See Chap. 14.

and that the planned economy need not be "floundering in the ocean of possible and conceivable economic combinations without the compass of economic calculation." [3] However, this rejection of Mises' contentions is only justified if directed against obvious exaggeration. The basic argument that a system without genuine price formation would suffer from misallocation of the factors of production remains intact. As we shall see, the Soviet economy is not chaotic, but it is far less productive than it could be if economical factor allocation were possible.

Mises' exaggerations are not worse than the Marxist claim that the private enterprise system is anarchic. Mises did not mean to deny that some form of bureaucratic coordination of production was possible; he only wanted to point out that the centrally planned economy would have to forego the great advantage of economical factor allocation and accordingly be far less productive than it otherwise could be. Two additional reasons for his pessimistic appraisal of socialist economic behavior were the following: first, the overwhelming magnitude of the task of directing all economic activities from the center, that is, to substitute for the invisible hand of the market the visible hand of bureaucratic control of an incredible amount of detail; second, the problem of human motivation. Clearly, central planning is impossible without the closest cooperation between the central planners and the managers on the spot. But when the profit motive disappears together with private property, Mises can not find a reliable motivation on the part of the managers. "If the prospect of profit disappears, the mechanism of the market loses its mainspring." [4] Socialist managers are then reduced to the execution of commands, in other words, the whole burden of central planning is borne by the central authorities alone.

For many years the problem of economic factor allocation was not discussed in Soviet Russia since adherence to Marx's labor theory of value precluded its very mentioning. Some who violated the taboo paid with their lives. Only overwhelmingly strong indications for the malfunctioning of the system could change this situation, and the present Russian discussion of economic motivations, against the background of the Marxist taboo, is proof that the Soviet economy suffers from deep-seated difficulties. These difficulties are the very problems that Mises had in mind.

---

[3] *Collectivist Economic Planning, Critical Studies on the Possibilities of Socialism*, ed., with Introduction and Concluding Essay by F. A. Hayek; contributors, N. G. Pierson, Ludwig von Mises, George Halm, Enrico Barone (London: Routledge & Kegan Paul Ltd., 1935), p. 110.

[4] Ludwig von Mises, *Socialism: An Economical and Sociological Analysis* (New Haven, Conn.: Yale University Press, 1951), p. 138.

MARX AND THE BOLSHEVIST REVOLUTION [5]

Did the Russian revolution correspond to the teachings of Karl Marx? The answer to this question is of more than academic interest since it can throw light on Soviet economic thinking and explain some past actions.

We have already seen that Marx did not develop a theory of the socialist economy. Socialism was expected to emerge ready-made from the wreckage of monopoly capitalism, with the latter's advanced methods of centralized control in working order. Marx envisioned socialism as a society that comes into the world out of the womb of capitalism and bears the birthmarks of the old society. It is characterized by the dictatorship of the proletariat, and the laborer, though no longer exploited, is still rewarded in proportion to his contribution. Only later, in a higher phase of communist society, does productivity increase enough so that the "narrow bourgeois horizon" can be left far behind, when each can work according to his capacity and be rewarded according to his needs.

Marx's theory suggests that the major organs of the socialist economy are complete before the act of birth. From this idea it is obvious that the state of the capitalist economy immediately preceding the revolution was of great importance to the Marxist. We may therefore ask: Was the Russian economy ready in this sense? Was Russia one of the most advanced countries in terms of monopoly capitalism? Obviously, this question can only be answered in the negative. Russia was a poor agrarian country, not ready for socialism even if socialism had been introduced simultaneously in all other capitalist countries. Accordingly, the revolution in Russia came as a shock to some orthodox Marxists who saw in it a violation of the basic tenets of Marxian dogma.

The Bolshevists explained their seemingly heretical behavior by pointing out that the Marxian revolution was meant to be a world-wide chain of simultaneous revolutions in different countries, and that a gap of a few years would hardly count in historical perspective. Indeed, there is little doubt that the Russian revolution was undertaken in the hopeful conviction that other revolutions would quickly follow. Had these revolutions materialized, it would not have mattered where the series of revolutions began, for the chain of capitalism had to be broken by smashing the weakest link. While the most advanced countries would provide the centralized organization of the new socialist society, the poorest and most backward

[5] See Boris Brutzkus, *Die Lehren des Marxismus im Lichte der russischen Revolution* (Berlin: Hermann Sack, 1928), pp. 9–15; Joseph S. Berliner, "Marxism and the Soviet Economy," in *Problems of Communism*, vol. 13, no. 5 (September-October 1964), pp. 1–11.

country could provide the greatest revolutionary élan, the pressure that would start things going. The Russian revolution was assumed to be the prologue to world revolution. That other countries would follow the Soviet example was extremely important, owing to the one-sidedly agrarian character of the Russian economy. It was generally believed at the time that socialism in one country was politically and economically impossible. When the expected world revolution did not come, the question of the feasibility of socialism in one country was much discussed in Soviet Russia but it remained an academic issue inasmuch as both Trotsky and Stalin were firmly determined "to hold the socialist fortress." While Stalin believed that socialism could be established in one country alone, he admitted, nevertheless, that such a country could only regard itself safe against foreign intervention after the revolution had been victorious in a number of other countries.[6]

Lenin believed that socialism had to rest on capitalism, that the industrial proletariat and not the peasantry was the bearer of the socialist movement, and that capitalist organization should be used in the development of the socialist economy. He was fully aware that the Bolshevist textbooks did not contain a blueprint of the socialist economy and that *faute de mieux* one had to use some of the facilities capitalism had created. The monopolistic organization of industry had to be strengthened; the amalgamation of all banks into a single bank had to serve as all-inclusive auditing apparatus. Full-fledged socialism did not have to be introduced all at once, provided only that the government held the so-called commanding heights and private production could be controlled.

Whether this slow approach was compatible with Marxism of strict observance is a question that will never be decisively answered because Marx did not state clearly how the socialist economy was to work. In one respect, however, no doubt is possible. The Soviet economy finds itself today still in the first or socialist phase of development, though Russian writers will, of course, deny that dictatorship of the proletariat still exists. The state has not "withered away." The Soviet economy still makes use of the labor market, wage differentials are substantial, and the national income per capita is low. Soviet Russia is still far from communism in the Marxian sense of the word, though it has a communist economy if by communism we mean authoritarian socialism.

WAR COMMUNISM

Lenin believed in state capitalism as a link between bourgeois capitalism and socialism. By state capitalism he meant state control over

[6] See Paul M. Sweezy, *The Theory of Capitalist Development* (New York: Oxford University Press, 1942), p. 354.

private production, the state holding the commanding heights both politically and economically.

We cannot say what the outcome would have been if Lenin could have followed this cautious approach to socialism. In Germany and England a hesitant approach left capitalism basically intact. The more violent revolution in Russia did not permit state capitalism to establish itself. The situation was politically too unstable, too elemental, to permit Lenin to work out an orderly cooperation between the state on the one side and small industrial producers and peasants on the other.

Even before the outbreak of the civil war, an orderly experiment in state capitalism proved to be impossible. To win the political support of the peasantry, the landed estates had to be given to the peasants, and the state became dependent on the surplus product of the private sector of the economy. In industry, direct action by the proletariat threatened to lead to a deterioration of the socialist experiment into syndicalism (the takeover of industrial plants by their workers), the most naïve and primitive form of collectivism. Syndicalism's aim is decentralization, without regulation through either market or central plan. Where syndicalism was strong, productivity declined to very low levels. Where private enterprise still existed, the cooperation by private managers was half-hearted and hampered by lack of authority.

Syndicalism and the elimination of the private manager would have enforced a high degree of nationalization in industry even under otherwise normal conditions. The outbreak of the civil war hastened the process still further. But the disorganizing elements were stronger than central control. Production declined disastrously. Regular revenues all but disappeared and the government had to use the printing press to finance its expenditures. Hyperinflation destroyed the monetary system so completely that barter methods were used and a growing number of wage earners were paid in kind. This gradual repudiation of money was hailed by some communist writers as the transition to communism. In reality the introduction of barter was most dangerous because it destroyed the cooperation between industry and agriculture on which everything depended.

A strong alliance between industrial proletariat and peasantry was the indispensable foundation of the Soviet economy. This alliance was gravely threatened by the destruction of the market economy through inflation and by the decline of industrial production. What industry could supply was largely needed for the war, so there was little left to barter for food and materials which the peasants were expected to supply. The peasants were most reluctant to exchange food for industrial products at unfavorable barter rates, but they were even more reluctant to part with their surplus without any compensation. When the government "solved" this problem by requisitioning with armed detachments, the peasantry answered the challenge by reducing the cultivated area, thus making sure that there would be no surplus to confiscate.

The peasants' dissatisfaction with the regime was shared by the industrial proletariat, which was ill-fed, hemmed in by innumerable regulations, thwarted in its syndicalist ambitions, and unemployed for lack of materials. War communism was not an economic success, even though the Red Army remained victorious and the Soviet economy managed to survive. A reversal of economic policies was unavoidable. Mere requisitioning of agricultural surplus was abortive; and since there was no apparatus to force the cooperation of millions of peasants, the government had to revert to the incentives of the market economy. But barter transactions proved to be too clumsy. Although some communist writers had prematurely hailed the "dying-out of money," it became obvious that the socialist economy needed a stable currency nearly as much as a private enterprise economy. War communism showed that socialism needs markets, exchanges, prices, monetary incentives and other paraphernalia of capitalism until it has reached a more sophisticated state of central control.

The world took the failures of war communism in the economic field as proof that communism and socialism were impossible. We know now that these conclusions were premature. The circumstances surrounding the first experiment with communism had been severely unfavorable; the result was inconclusive. A peasantry with no incentive to work and produce the vitally needed agricultural surplus, an industry without managers, an undisciplined labor force, an inexperienced bureaucracy, a barter system without industrial commodities to trade, the abolition of the market without its replacement by planned coordination—all this inevitably led to chaos. The result was neither a planned system nor a market economy. War communism was not even an experiment, it was a struggle to survive the impact of the elemental forces of revolution and war.

This first period of Soviet history can tell us little about the socialist economy. However, it can serve as a warning to all revolutionaries who, preoccupied with political problems, believe that they can accomplish a direct transition from the market economy to some centrally organized system of direct coordination. In a social economy millions must integrate their efforts. Their cooperation must rest either on market exchanges, or on a central plan, or, finally, on a workable mixture of these two principles. But the problems of social production will not be solved if we destroy one organizing principle before we have developed the other. This the Russians had to learn by bitter experience. Many perished during the famine of 1921.

The organizational details of this early period are not very interesting. A Supreme Economic Council was created to direct the nationalized enterprises in the key industries, but it did not even attempt to develop a central plan for the country as a whole. On the contrary, characteristic of this period is the lack of coordination between separate activities of the various bureaucratic institutions.

War communism teaches that in the absence of motives of personal gain the government has to command, if a given production program is to be fulfilled. But a command economy was not practicable. Because of the individualized character of production in a peasant economy, half of the population would have had to watch over the other half. In industry, too, it became obvious that mere membership in a socialist commonwealth could not substitute for monetary incentives. Not even free choice of occupation could be maintained under war communism. Syndicalism and lack of authority on the part of the managers had lowered labor discipline. It became necessary to extend militaristic principles to the labor market. Laborers were "soldiers" who were not permitted to "desert." Labor was "mobilized" for the "labor front." "Shock brigades" were used in critical stages of the "battle of production" and "labor victories" were celebrated when a given production quota was reached. But the peasant could not be forced to produce and went on strike, which necessitated the return or partial return to the profit motive.

THE NEW ECONOMIC POLICY

The New Economic Policy (NEP) was based on the following facts and considerations: It was vitally necessary that production should be increased, both in agriculture and in industry. The small peasants could be made to produce more only if they were organized in collective farms with mechanized equipment. This development would take a long time and would depend on an industrial output that could not yet be reached. In the meantime it was necessary to increase production in agriculture through monetary incentives. The peasants were permitted to sell their surplus on the market after a fixed proportion of the crop had been paid to the government in kind. This arrangement implied not only markets for agricultural products but also the possibility of buying industrial products with the proceeds. Accordingly, industrial enterprises were permitted to sell their products on markets and to buy the needed raw materials rather than to wait for bureaucratic allocations. This reintroduction of market exchanges, of money and of monetary incentives was a partial return to capitalist methods. Industrial enterprises, though state-owned and organized in trusts, were expected to be managed on commercial principles. But the state retained control over the economy by occupying the commanding heights. Controlling heavy industry, transportation, the credit system, and international trade, the Soviet government could feel reasonably sure that the capitalist forces would be kept within bounds.

The NEP experiment was meant to be a temporary expedient, a

transitional stage between bourgeois capitalism and socialism, a method of increasing productivity to the point where central planning could begin.

Agricultural production increased as soon as the system of food requisitioning was replaced by monetary incentives. The peasants were permitted to lease land and to hire labor. The demand for agricultural products was strong. The industrial enterprises needed raw materials and food for their workers but had, at first, little to give in exchange. In this emergency, when working capital had to be found at all costs, state enterprises sold their stocks and even part of their equipment. This was the period of "squandering" in 1921–1922 which led to terms of trade between agriculture and industry which were favorable to the peasants. For a short period the peasants enjoyed a sellers' market. This was soon to change, however.

From the summer of 1922 to the fall of 1923 the price relationship between agricultural and industrial products changed sharply in favor of the latter. This was the so-called "scissors" crisis. It was a crisis because it endangered the alliance between peasants and industrial proletariat. After all, the NEP had been introduced to appease the peasant!

The scissors crisis was caused by the fact that recovery proceeded faster in agriculture than in industry. The latter had suffered from the effects of squandering, from the still persisting lack of working capital, from poor management, from a shortage of skilled labor, and from the uncertain results of the kaleidoscopic changes during this transition period. It is unlikely, however, that the unequal rate of recovery was a sufficient explanation for the sharp change in the terms of trade. The scissors was not entirely the result of competitive market forces. The markets were not free. The peasants bought and sold under competitive conditions but they were faced, as sellers and buyers, by monopsonistic and monopolistic state trusts. Where private traders endangered this privileged position of the trusts, they were soon eliminated. And since a central plan was not yet in operation, the different trusts were independent in their production and price policies. Basing their decisions on commercial principles, they made the most of their monopolistic position, which enabled them to restock, to accumulate working capital, and to cover up inefficiency and resulting high costs.

The government tried to close the scissors through credit, price, and commercial policies. Credits to industry were restricted to force the trusts to sell, while credits to grain purchasing organs were increased; grain prices were raised simultaneously with an introduction of maximum selling prices in industry; and grain exports were encouraged while the industrial trusts were threatened with a possible "goods intervention"—the importation of low-priced manufactured products.

Long-run policies to move the terms of trade in favor of agriculture could have been (1) a reduction in industrial costs and (2) a more moderate rate of capital accumulation. Industrial costs were high for several reasons. Shortage of working capital made it impossible to use plant and equipment at optimum capacity, labor was unskilled, and the managers, often suspect because they were members of the former bourgeoisie, were handicapped in their decisions by the representatives of labor unions and of the Communist Party.

INDUSTRIALIZATION

The second long-run policy that could have been used to satisfy peasants and consumers conflicted with the main objective of the Soviet regime. This objective was the quickest industrialization possible, in other words, investment in heavy rather than light industry. Investment in light industry would have led to an increased output of consumer goods that could have been exchanged for agricultural surplus at terms satisfactory to the peasants. Investment in heavy industry, on the other hand, made it practically impossible to close the scissors fully. The terms of trade remained unsatisfactory to the peasants throughout the rest of the NEP period. To close the scissors for good would have implied concessions to the well-to-do peasants (kulaks). The industrial sector of the economy would have been weakened in favor of the most capitalist element of the peasantry. To accumulate capital for purposes of industrialization, the terms of trade had to be favorable to industry rather than to consumers and peasants.

The basic difficulty of the Soviet economy was the desire to hasten industrialization and to appease the peasants simultaneously, that is, the desire to follow conflicting policies. Industrialization was necessary because world revolution had not materialized. Russia had to provide her own capital goods out of her own resources. Only on the basis of an enlarged heavy industry, furthermore, could agricultural production be mechanized, and only in this way, it was believed, could the socialist island be defended against capitalist attack.

Toward the end of the NEP period the price relationship between agricultural and industrial products seemed so unfavorable to the peasants that they were, once more, reluctant to deliver their surplus grain to the state purchasing agencies. To overcome this reluctance, compulsory confiscation of grain from well-to-do peasants was introduced. The NEP, therefore, ended just as war communism had ended—with confiscation of the agricultural surplus. But now the economy had reached its prewar production figures and could afford to embark on the experiment of central planning.

Another reason for the insufficient supply of agricultural products became evident as the economy returned to more normal production levels under the NEP. It turned out that the distribution of the landed estates among small peasants (the first agrarian revolution) had reduced the marketable surplus of agricultural products. The market supply had formerly come from the estates and from the larger farms. Now that the estates had been split up into small peasant holdings, the poorer and middle peasants, who accounted for 85 percent of the grain production, consumed a large share of their own growth. It was doubtful, therefore, whether even more favorable terms of trade could have achieved the desired result of creating a sufficiently large agricultural surplus in the face of the changed structure of Russian agriculture. Maurice Dobb [7] believes that large scale farming on cooperative lines appeared as "the only release from that closed circle of interdependent limiting factors within which the discussion of the last four years had revolved." He quotes the following passage from Stalin's report to the Fifteenth Congress:

> The way out is to turn the small and scattered peasant farms into large united farms based on the common cultivation of the soil, to introduce collective cultivation of the soil on the basis of new and higher technique. The way out is to unite the small and dwarf peasant farms gradually and surely, not by pressure but by example and persuasion, into large farms based on common, co-operative cultivation of the soil, with the use of agricultural machines and tractors and scientific methods of intensive agriculture. There is no other way out.

Dobb points out that once,

> the transformation of peasant agriculture on to an entirely new basis had been placed on the agenda, and had justified its claim to be regarded as a practicable solution, the situation was radically changed. A new qualitative element had been introduced, providing a break in the closed circle and altering the pattern of "causal-genetic" determination. There was now no more reason to assert the one-way dependence of industrial growth on the growth of agriculture than to assert the contrary (for example, the dependence of agricultural production on the supply of tractors and of chemical manures).

In other words, real central planning would become possible as soon as the government succeeded in drawing agricultural production firmly into the plan rather than letting it remain an uncontrollable limiting factor.

Throughout the NEP period the question had been discussed whether

[7] Maurice Dobb, *Soviet Economic Development since 1917* (New York: International Publishers Co., Inc., 1948), pp. 222, 330.

"genetic" or "teleological" planning should be used. With agriculture still outside the plan, the genetic method *had* to be used, which amounted to an extrapolation of the past development of the different branches of the economy over the next few years. Planned action was limited by the unpredictable actions and reactions of a huge private sector. In particular, eliciting greater efforts in agriculture would have required major concessions in the form of increased production of consumer goods—which was contrary to the aim of the Soviet authorities.

On the eve of the decisive change from "commercial considerations" to a centrally planned command economy the Soviet economy had recovered from the effects of war communism: its productivity was restored; its industry was firmly in the hands of the government; foreign trade was relatively small and channeled exclusively through the organs of a state monopoly; the monetary, credit, and fiscal systems were re-established; and a labor market was operating. Many consumer goods, however, were rationed, and it could certainly not be said that production was following the wishes of the consumers. On the whole, the NEP had done its job.

Some aspects of this picture are far from clear. These are caused by the dual character of the period, by its gradually changing mixture of free market pricing, monopolistic policies, government interference, and central planning. Many difficulties arose that must be attributed to the hybrid character of this period. In industry, for instance, the dual character of the economy affected the quality of management. The position of the manager was extremely difficult. Often he had no clear-cut directives, was dependent on the market, yet, subject to commands from the Supreme Economic Council; he was limited in his actions by other members of the management triangle (the trade-union committee and the communist cell), had little authority over labor, and was afraid of his responsibility, which he therefore tried to shirk.

That the NEP worked as well as it did can be attributed to several factors: The statistical figures are impressive, mainly because they start from an unbelievably low level. The NEP generally did no more than restore pre-war productivity. Much of this was accomplished by market forces, as was intended. Probably these forces would have operated better if the speed of capital accumulation had not interfered with the monetary incentives for both peasants and industrial workers. Real income was low in comparison with the effort expended. That the integration of the different production processes did not encounter greater difficulties was partly because, in times of a goods famine and under the impact of ambitious long-run investment schemes, anything produced could be sold without much difficulty. Nobody cared about equilibria or optima in this reconstruction period.

THE SECOND AGRARIAN REVOLUTION

We have already shown that collective farming seemed to be the only way by which the centrally planned economy could rid itself of the limitations imposed upon it by the market and by the actions of millions of peasants supplying the market. Yet the goal was at first quite modest. Only about one seventh of the cultivated area was to be operated under the new system by the final year of the first Five Year Plan (1928–1933). Huge state farms were created and it was hoped that they would lead to a quick increase in agricultural surplus production. However, these giant units were too unwieldy for efficient management and their production was too specialized to correspond to sound principles of farming.

Generally, grain production was still dependent on the poor and middle peasant. "We would be deceiving ourselves," said the authors of the Five Year Plan, "if we asserted that the socialized sector—at least within the limits it will have reached by the end of the five-year period—could enable us to disregard the production of those groups of middle peasants who produce marketable surpluses." [8]

While the Soviet government favored the poorer peasants as the proletarian element in agriculture, it treated the rich peasants, the kulaks, very harshly, imposing upon them heavy additional taxes and insisting on the immediate repayment of loans. Since the kulaks answered these attacks by decreasing production, it was decided to eliminate them and to step up the process of collectivization. It became imperative to depend to a larger extent on the socialized sector if the most productive farmers were to be liquidated.

The poor peasants were willing to join the collectives since they had little to lose. The cruel process of the liquidation of the kulaks was organized by industrial workers who had been sent into the provinces with orders from Moscow. The confiscated property of the kulaks was turned over to the new collectives. The kulaks could not become members and were sent to Siberia or shot.

The combination of kulak liquidation and farm collectivization created chaotic conditions. The local administrative authorities started collective farms at such a rate that it became impossible to organize them properly. Membership in the collectives, though officially voluntary, was forced upon the peasants. By January 1, 1930, about five million families had become members; by March 1, 1930, an additional 9.5 million terrorized peasant families had declared their willingness to join.

The process had been much too fast. There were not enough trained

---

[8] Alexander Baykov, *The Development of the Soviet Economic System* (New York: Cambridge University Press, 1946), pp. 189–190.

managerial personnel available; the "Machine-Tractor–Stations" could not be set up and equipped at such a tremendous rate; the new process of cooperative production and distribution could not be organized that fast. Agricultural output was in grave danger. The worst immediate result was the slaughtering of livestock since a peasant would often kill his livestock rather than hand it over without compensation before joining the collective farm.

Once more the government decided to retrace its steps. In his famous article "Dizzy with Success," Stalin put the blame on the local administrations. They had, Stalin said, violated the principle of voluntary collectivization and indiscriminately forced the peasants into the collective farms whether local conditions were ready or not. Actually, it is most unlikely that the central authorities were ignorant of what was happening. The speedy collectivization had, obviously, created such dissatisfaction among the peasantry that the blame had to be shifted to the local authorities.

The proposed change was not a change in direction, as in 1921 when the NEP had appeased the peasants. Only the tempo of the process was to be altered. The voluntary character of the transfer was emphasized (a doubtful item in an authoritarian regime) and peasants who had already become members were permitted to leave the collectives again, together with their belongings. In addition it was made clear that the collective farm intended to socialize production but not consumption. The peasants who joined were permitted to retain their dwellings with an adjoining allotment (garden, orchard, and so forth), small agricultural implements, and dairy cattle for personal use.[9]

By the end of 1932 about 14 million families or nearly 60 percent were organized in 200,000 collective farms which covered two thirds of the total sown area, compared with the one seventh that the original Five Year Plan had set as its goal.

If the rate of collectivization was much higher than scheduled, the growth in agricultural production was smaller. The following factors contributed to this disappointing result:

1. The collective farms were, as yet, inadequately organized. An entirely new system of production had to be worked out. Skilled managers were not available since the kulaks who had been the most efficient farmers had been liquidated.

2. Within the collective farm a conflict developed that produced in miniature the agrarian problem of the entire country: how to have planning and yet induce the peasant to produce. Retaining part of their personal property, the members of the collectives were tempted to devote more time to this personal property than to the cooperative effort.

[9] Baykov, p. 197.

3. Since the output of consumer goods was small, many members of the collective farms thought it hardly worth their while to increase production even for sale in the free farm market.

Nevertheless, collective farms were established whose production goals were determined by the central plan. Agricultural output was no longer dependent on the profit motive of a class that was not considered trustworthy.

CONCLUSION

The development of the Soviet economy has now been outlined up to the point where the experiment in all-inclusive central planning could begin, when the government controlled all productive forces and could replace market mechanism and profit motive by central plan and command. To follow in detail the historical facts of this experiment in central planning would be less rewarding than a theoretical analysis of the command economy after its foundations had been laid and after the disturbing effects of World War II had been overcome. Accordingly, Chapter 20 will attempt to discuss the Soviet economy as it existed up to the present, while Chapter 21 will deal with recent reform proposals.

The Command
Economy
of Soviet Russia

THE MARKETS OF THE SOVIET ECONOMY

The Soviet economy, as it emerged from the collectivization of agriculture, does not correspond to the extreme form of authoritarian socialism that was the object of Ludwig von Mises' criticism.[1] Limiting our study to the barest outlines, and ignoring the kaleidoscopic changes that have occurred during the last 30 years, we can draw a generalized picture of Soviet planning which is still basically correct in spite of the far-reaching reform proposals that are at present under discussion.

The Soviet government either owns outright, or controls decisively, all material means of production. This is true for agriculture as well as for industry. Production in tens of thousands of producing units is carried through in fulfillment of plan figures, not in reaction to price incentives. The managers no longer follow commercial considerations, as under the NEP. The Russian economy is a command economy, not a market economy. However, dissatisfaction with its recent performance has led to reform proposals that amount to the reintroduction of decentralization and price incentives, hopefully within the framework of a central plan.

[1] See Chap. 14.

Consumers are normally free to purchase in government stores without ration coupons. It must be emphasized, though, that free consumers' choice is limited to the commodities that the planners decide to produce. Consumers' sovereignty does not exist, that is, consumers do not direct production as in the private enterprise economy or, supposedly, in liberal socialism. Furthermore, consumers' demand does not instantly influence the prices of consumer goods. Prices are *set* by the planning authorities and remain at given levels until officially changed. It must not be assumed, therefore, that the Soviet economy rests on a genuine consumer goods market in which prices adjust automatically to changing demand-and-supply conditions and managers adjust production accordingly.

To set *equilibrium* prices would imply a knowledge of demand elasticities and cross-elasticities that the planners do not possess. Furthermore, even if the prices were originally correct, they would gradually become false as demand-and-supply conditions change. Since price adjustments for individual commodities shift the demand for other products, the authorities are most reluctant to make price changes and the whole price structure becomes frozen for years. It gives way only under urgent pressures and without establishing a new correct price pattern.

Under these conditions it is obvious that production is not guided by commodity prices. As a matter of fact, guidance through patently false prices would lead to chaotic results. We have to remember, furthermore, that cost prices are either arbitrarily set or ignored (as in the case of interest and rent). A change-over to price guidelines and monetary incentives would involve a complete reconstruction of the whole economic system and, perhaps, the abandonment of authoritarian central planning.

The market most similar to markets in a private enterprise system is the so-called collective farm market where prices are permitted to equate supply and demand. Farm market prices tend to be much higher than corresponding official retail prices. The farm market, therefore, serves the function of absorbing excess purchasing power and inducing the collective farms to increase production as much as possible, in excess of the stated quantities that must be delivered to the authorities at low "procurement prices."

The situation on the labor market is similar to that on the consumer goods market. Again we must beware of the notion that the Soviet labor market is a genuine market that operates much like its counterpart in the private enterprise economy. Free choice of occupation exists and makes it inescapable that the allocation of labor should rest on wage differentials and monetary incentives. But wage differentials are not the automatic result of market forces. Wages are *set* by the planners so that labor flows on its own volition into the production processes that need it to fulfill planned tasks. The demand for labor comes from enterprises who receive funds that permit them to reach their output quotas according to set wages and productivity norms. Usually, enterprises cannot outbid one another by offering higher wages.

Since wages are set and not subject to competitive bidding, they do not determine the demand for labor, although they do influence the supply of labor. Obviously, set wages will differ from wages designed to equilibrate demand and supply, and the allocation of labor will to that extent be arbitrary. If an enterprise has succeeded in convincing the authorities that it needs a larger supply of labor than is actually necessary, the marginal productivity of labor can be very low while the same kind of labor can be critically short in other sectors of the economy.

Within its all-inclusive plan, the government takes care of education and training. This obligation provides an opportunity for steering those newly entering the labor market into occupations and industries favored by the plan. In addition, there are cases of exhortation, of limitation of mobility, and of downright coercion—exceptions to the basic principle of free occupational choice that enable the government to allocate contingents of labor when and where the set wage differentials prove insufficient to channel labor in the right direction.

PRICES IN THE SOVIET ECONOMY

A glance at Soviet markets shows that prices do not perform the same important guiding function as in a private enterprise economy and that the price mechanism must be replaced by a comprehensive central plan. Nevertheless, the Soviet economy cannot dispense with the use of money and prices for the following reasons:

1. The operational units must be controlled for plan fulfillment. Since these units buy one another's products at transfer prices and in prescribed quantities, the state bank, on which all checks are drawn, can serve as an auditing agency.

2. Monetary values serve to translate dissimilar physical units into aggregates which are comparable. For example, the Soviet planners will see to it that total wage income and the total value of consumer goods are equal so that inflation is avoided.

3. Prices may influence the managers' choice of production methods. If the managers have sufficient leeway, they will make a choice of production methods of different capital intensity. But we have to remember that the prices are often false indicators and that the managers are predominantly interested in fulfilling physical output norms.

Supply does not adjust to changes in consumers' demand. On the contrary, since the planners consider consumer goods basically less desirable than investment goods, the latter's production is expanded as much as possible at the expense of the former. The planners know little about consumer demand and care even less. In general, demand has exceeded supply in the consumer goods markets, indicating that consumer goods prices have been set too low with the result that often shortages have appeared and queues have formed. The situation is similar to the phenomenon of repressed inflation in the private enterprise economy.

That the planners should want to underprice consumer goods may seem strange, considering that they desire to keep consumption down and to establish equilibrium between supply and demand. However, an explanation for the Soviet type of repressed inflation is easily found. We have already seen why price adjustments are only rarely undertaken. Since the Soviet economy is a full-employment economy with a constant tendency to overestimate productivity, the total wage bill tends to exceed the total value of consumer goods at set prices. Creeping inflation (to finance higher than estimated wage costs), plus reluctance to carry through price adjustments, leads to the characteristic situation in which prices of consumer goods are lower than market conditions justify. Another reason for the underpricing of consumer goods may be that the regime finds it beneficial to let demand run ahead of supply, because if they are equal at a reasonably high level of consumer goods production, more attention must be paid to the relative price structure. Consumers may then insist on buying only commodities that they really want. Undesired goods or commodities of shoddy quality then may remain on the shelves, and the planners may be forced to adjust both quantity and quality of production to the wishes of the consumers. This introduction of some degree of consumers' sovereignty, in turn, would make central planning much more difficult. Not only would it imply frequent price changes, corresponding to the scarcity of the commodity in question, it would necessitate a change in the output of consumer goods, which could only be accomplished by a highly decentralized system where the managers enjoy a great deal of freedom in their decisions.

Since the aggregate value of all consumer goods must correspond to the total demand of all members of the economic system, consumer goods prices must, as a rule, exceed their production costs by a large margin, considering that nearly all personal income is spent on consumer goods while only a part of this income has been earned in their production. The difference between cost and price is, apart from planned profit, the turnover tax, the most important source of investment funds in the Soviet economy. The rate of the turnover tax varies with the discrepancy of demand and supply.

Industrial wholesale prices are prices at which the enterprises buy from each other. Again, these prices have no allocative function and any attempt to follow them as guidelines would have chaotic results.

As far as the determination of cost prices is concerned, it should be remembered that cost accounting must follow Marx's theory and that costs must contain nothing but past and present labor. Rent and interest have, as a rule, not been considered. As scarcity prices, therefore, all Soviet prices are implicitly false, and not just because they remain frozen over long periods.

While up to now Soviet prices have been rejected as guidelines of production, they have played an important part in the auditing apparatus that performs the important function of checking plan fulfillment. Since transfer payments are made at set prices in accordance with physical allocations, the state bank can determine whether and when an enterprise in its buying and selling operations has followed the commands of the plan. In this context is makes little difference whether or not the prices are scarcity prices; on the contrary, it is important that they should stay the same, at least over the accounting period, which is what real equilibrium prices could not do.

SOVIET PLANNING

The Soviet economy is a command economy. The government's command regulates the interdependent actions of producing units on the basis of one comprehensive plan. Predetermined production quotas and appropriate allocations of productive resources, rather than competitive buying and selling, are the characteristic feature of this new method of integrating the production processes.

The aims of the economy are decided upon by the highest party authorities and not by the consumer. Long-term plans translate these aims into production targets for the different industrial enterprises and agricultural collectives; more detailed short-term or operational plans see to it that the different branches of the economy keep in balance. Authoritarian central planning means more than the setting of broad development schemes; it means the careful enumeration of hundreds of thousands of items which are needed in the life of the nation, from rolling mills to hairpins, from nuclear reactors to school equipment and ballet performances. This task is so formidable that it cannot be solved by the central planning agency alone. "It is impracticable for the central authorities to prescribe physically every product and input, or to prescribe some of them —indeed usually most of them—in completely disaggregated terms." [2] To illustrate by a much ridiculed example from the Polish economy: the plan should not endeavor to name the number of sour pickles or of hares to be shot.[3]

[2] Gregory Grossman, "Industrial Prices in the USSR," *American Economic Review*, vol. 49 (May 1959), p. 59.

[3] Alexander Erlich, "The Polish Economy after October 1956: Background and Outlook," *American Economic Review*, vol. 49 (May 1959), p. 96.

The aims of the plan are competitive. Each production program must be limited so that the total of all targets does not exceed the productive power of the country. And since the factors of production are substitutable only within limits, the production program must be drawn with reference to the given technical possibilities. Each industry's output depends on an input of intermediary goods that are the output of other industries. How can the plan relate all input and output figures and achieve that coordination of production processes that results in the output of all needed goods in the right proportions?

But even this formulation of the problem is incomplete. The gradual achievement of a workable bureaucratic and technical interdependence is not sufficient if we want to make the best economic use of the factors of production. Bureaucratic interdependence guarantees that the system will function without too many breakdowns resulting from bottlenecks; however, it does not guarantee the best combination of factors in an economic sense. To achieve the latter, output figures and factor allocations ought to be chosen so that the marginal productivity of each factor tends to be the same wherever it is used. We remember, furthermore, that the social economy has to solve not only the problem of *what* and *how much* to produce; it must also answer the question of *how* to produce, that is, which technique of production and, in particular, which degree of capital or labor intensity to choose.

We shall see that until recently the Soviet planners have consistently ignored the problem of the most economical factor allocation and limited themselves to the much easier (but still formidable) task of achieving a modicum of bureaucratic consistency. This criticism cannot be answered by reference to the fact that the Soviet system substitutes the state's preference function for consumers' sovereignty. No system can solve the problem of the most economical factor allocation by recourse to bureaucratic integration. Of course, the authoritarian system can pretend that what it produces is exactly what it wanted and that it is in the best long-term interest of the people. Also, it will pride itself that, following Marx's labor theory of value, only the most modern techniques of production are being used. But this, of course, can never be true for all production processes: the use of the most advanced methods in high-priority industries is counterbalanced by the employment of primitive methods in low-priority sectors.

Leaving aside all bureaucratic detail, we can draw the following simplified outline of Soviet planning:

The authorities decide on the relative growth rates of the various main sectors of the economy. These decisions are formulated in the form of target plans that determine the general framework of economic development for the next 5 or 7 years. These target plans cannot be precise owing to unforeseeable developments. But even the target plans must roughly balance. Insistence on balance is a must in a centrally planned system because continuous adjustments through a price mechanism are lacking.

With the targets given, and the restraints through limited factor supply, technology, and production patterns known, experts draw up operational (1-year) plans, which attempt to translate the targets into concrete production quotas and corresponding allocations of productive resources. The interdependence of all production processes and the complete absence of guidance through price variations make it imperative that the operational plan should pass the test of mutual consistency of input and output for all enterprises and collectives. After all, more than anything else, planning means balancing.

The planners cannot know all the technical details and cannot give commands in completely disaggregative terms concerning product mix, input mix, the capital intensity of production methods, labor productivity, and so forth. This kind of specialized knowledge rests with the managers. These men must be consulted. While they will have no right whatever to question the aims of the plan, they must cooperate in the setting of input and output figures for their industries and plants. Otherwise they would later be placed in the impossible position of having to achieve results that cannot be achieved on the basis of planned allocations.

Tentative figures are, therefore, distributed through the administrative channels of the Soviet bureaucracy down to industrial and agricultural producing units. These figures are not yet directives; rather, they are requests for corrections. Corrections and suggestions are then collected through the administrative arteries of the system. Based on this material, a revised plan is drawn up; and this plan, once adopted, becomes the official production program. Its detailed output quotas become compulsory instructions. They are commands.

Of course, the final figures which result from this planning procedure cannot possibly be perfect, not even in the very limited sense of bureaucratic-technical consistency. They rest on assumptions that cannot always be correct. The weather or the terms of foreign trade cannot be ascertained in advance, just as the rise in productivity per man-hour may elude exact estimates. For these and other reasons (such as human failure) it is vitally important that the execution of the plan be watched constantly so that imbalances can be corrected at the earliest possible moment.

It would be wrong, however, to exaggerate the difficulties that the planned economy faces in achieving balance in the limited sense of bureaucratic consistency. No social economic system is perfect, including the private enterprise economy with its overinvestment crises which are huge disproportionalities in the development of different sectors of the economy. We have to remember, furthermore, that it is possible to create flexibility through the accumulation of reserve stocks, that is, inventories that make the supply of strategic materials temporarily independent of current production. Finally, the commands refer to minima for output and maxima for input rather than to rigidly fixed amounts.

Let us assume that this process of bureaucratic integration, as sketched above, works reasonably well, in other words, that the economy has achieved a sufficient degree of consistency in the cooperation of its various sectors. Continuous production without major breakdowns would be possible in this case and the means of production would be fully employed in producing what the planners want to have produced with specified techniques of production. But even a smoothly operating system of bureaucratic integration would not mean that the choice of the state preference schedule or the choice of production techniques or, finally, the allocation of the factors of production had been made in economical terms. Which is to say that even a smoothly functioning Soviet-type economy, with full employment and a high rate of accumulation, could be relatively unproductive in terms of its own preference scale and in terms of human sacrifice demanded.

In reality, however, the Soviet economy, in its present form, is not able to perform well in terms of the relatively modest goal of mere bureaucratic coordination. The main reason for the relatively poor working of the central plan is the enormous size of the task of central planning and the fact that it cannot be made manageable through decentralization—unless we mean by decentralization the reintroduction of guidance through a price mechanism. An additional difficulty lies in the insistence on aims that are mutually exclusive, the overemphasis on industrialization at the expense of agriculture, on whose surplus the continuation of industrial growth depends.

If static equilibrium were desired, the planners could approach it gradually by trial and error, using their powers to prevent any undesired and disturbing changes in form of new technology or variations in preference schedules. But it would be absurd to make this assumption for a centrally planned economy that prides itself in its ability to plan for dynamic economic growth.

Technological changes and alterations in the state preference schedule imply continuous modifications in the whole pattern of production and factor allocation. Suppose that new chemical plants for fertilizer production are to be created. Since employment was full by definition, the allocation of factors must be changed. And since all production processes are interdependent, the shift in the state preference function must affect the whole economy. We saw in the Appendix to Chapter 3 how any change in our demand functions (or in a technological coefficient) tends to change all demand schedules, all prices, all factor prices, all supply schedules, and so forth. Of course, in an authoritarian planned economy we do not operate via price changes. Furthermore, we have simplified the process by eliminating consumers' sovereignty. Still, the needed adjustments must somehow be made. The factors needed in the new or expanded fertilizer production cannot be used any longer where they had been used before. But the reduction of other production processes means the reduction of inputs of still other industries, and so on ad infinitum. In terms of the present Soviet economy this means adjustments of all the physical input and output balances that have become affected. For instance, if more steel should be needed for the erection of the new fertilizer plants, the following steps will have to be taken:

> First it is important to find out how much more input will be directly needed by the steel industry in order to increase output by the desired amount. Let there be need, say, for x more coal, y more iron, and z more transportation units. Now the balances for coal, iron, and transport have to be adjusted. To produce more coal, iron, and transport, one must increase the quantities of other inputs. If one of these inputs is steel, the steel balance must be rebalanced in order to take into account the secondary demand. This adjustment starts a second round of approximations, and a readjustment of the iron, coal, and transport balance. The process continues until the desired degree of accuracy is achieved.[4]

What happens in the case of shifting priorities in the state preference schedule is that the productions with the improved priority rating will dislodge established allocations. This is the substitute for the way in which firms with higher purchasing power outbid others in the factor markets of the private enterprise economy. It is not sufficient, of course, that some other item is stricken from the state preference list to make room for the new priority item since, as a rule, the technical production requirements will differ.

The ideal solution would be an increased supply of factors or a better use of the productive resources. To some extent this can perhaps be achieved by reduced input allocations while the output quotas are maintained or by the substitution of more abundant for scarcer materials. Obviously, however, a full employment economy cannot hope to squeeze enough additional production out of the existing facilities to supply new priority industries without a quantitative or qualitative reduction in other areas of production.

Far from being an economy in which all material balances balance, the Soviet economy is simply separated into two sectors: a high-priority area, characterized by heavy industry, and a low-priority area, consisting of consumption and agriculture, which serves as cushion for the absorption

[4] Stanislaw Wellisz, *The Economies of the Soviet Bloc* (New York: McGraw-Hill, Inc., 1964), pp. 149–150.

of the above-mentioned difficulties.[5] In this system, heavy industry is not only preferred in terms of high targets and allocations that correspond to the most modern techniques of production; they also enjoy the advantage of having the upper hand in unavoidable adjustment processes. Agriculture and consumer goods industries, on the other hand, do not only start out with more modest targets; they are expected to give way whenever reallocations become necessary. Therefore their chances of reaching their originally low targets are much smaller.

The Soviet economy is a rough system of priorities, which performs well only in its high-priority sectors and operates most inefficiently in the low-priority strata. In its present form the Soviet economy does not correspond to Marx's postulate that human labor must always be supported by the most modern machinery. The statement was always invalid, of course, because investment goods are too scarce to be used in all production processes according to the most modern techniques. In excluding the rate of interest from their investment decisions, the Russian planners arrived at a perfectly lopsided factor allocation. In the high-priority fields, investment funds are often treated as free goods while in the low-priority sectors the most primitive, labor-intensive methods are common.

A defender of central planning could perhaps try to justify the priority system by arguing that economic development depends on a high priority for heavy industry as the only way in which future production of consumer goods and agricultural products could be increased. Maurice Dobb's argument that development is more important than equilibrium points in this direction. However, the argument is untenable. The economy must be treated as a whole. To force industrial investment continuously at the cost of other parts of the economy will eventually produce an inconsistency that would slow down growth even in the priority sector. To put it differently: it is impossible to maintain orderly conditions in one sector if the other sectors are not permitted to achieve equilibrium. All sectors of the economy are interdependent. Industry cannot continue to grow normally when agriculture is permitted to lag too far behind; and even consumer goods production will eventually exert its influence via the willingness of labor in both industry and agriculture to support a given output program. Incentive systems must be based on improvements in real income.

A priority system in which the low-priority sector cushions the shocks imparted to the economy through priority changes, is more suited to an early stage of development than to the more complicated interrelationships

---

[5] See the description of this situation in John P. Hardt, Dimitri M. Gallik, and Vladimir Treml, "Institutional Stagnation and Changing Economic Strategy in the Soviet Union," in *New Directions in the Soviet Economy*, Joint Economic Committee (Washington, D.C., 1966), pp. 33–34.

that characterize the more sophisticated production process in a more advanced country. In the beginning of the Russian experiment it may have been permissible to equate industrialization with electrification, as Lenin did. Soon, however, the investment program grew in size and complexity. The cushioning low-priority sector tended to shrink relatively at the very time when it was being called upon to finance an ever more ambitious investment program. Increasingly, therefore, the base for further industrialization narrows until it becomes evident that the whole system suffers from a basic disproportionality that the over-simplified high-priority-low-priority dichotomy permitted to develop. Increasingly, the low-priority sectors will protest against their permanent underdog position. And as the economy becomes rich enough to produce more than the absolute necessities of life, the consumers will become increasingly dissatisfied with a system that continues to ignore their preferences. The very fact that a greater variety of consumer goods can now be offered will lead to the demand for a more sophisticated distribution system and some sort of consumers' sovereignty.

SOVIET AGRICULTURE

Most crucial in this context is the role of agriculture. Throughout the history of the Soviet economy, agriculture was in the anomalous position of being both the basis and the least favored part of Soviet economic development. Agricultural surpluses had to finance industrialization, yet agricultural producers could not count on adequate incentives to make their efforts worthwhile; nor did they have sufficient technical support to keep their output in line with the intended growth of Soviet industry.

In Chapter 19 we had the opportunity to watch two crises in which the ill-treated peasants finally refused to cooperate, thereby bringing about a complete shift in policy: the NEP and the collectivization of agriculture. The latter, however, did not lead to an entirely satisfactory solution. True, agriculture was drawn into the plan and the government could try to determine output figures. But this must not be interpreted to mean that the planners could increase the agricultural production to support just any industrialization program. If they had been willing and able to carry through a program of rapid mechanization and electrification of agricultural production and if they had introduced a well functioning incentive system, the desired results might have been forthcoming. But rapid mechanization would have tried to give agriculture a priority rating that did not fit into the preference scale of a regime bent on pushing heavy industry, and the organization of the collective farm unit, together with imprudent procurement methods, did not establish a good incentive system.

Another cause for relatively poor agricultural performance can be found in the fact that in collectives, as in industrial enterprises, economical use of the available resources was hampered by lacking cost data. Since both rent and interest were excluded in cost accounting, land and capital could not be used efficiently, apart from the fact that the collectives were perpetually shortchanged in the overall allocation of investment funds.

PLANNERS AND MANAGERS

The manager of the Soviet firm differs considerably from his colleague in the private enterprise economy. Lacking the freedom in decision-making that the latter enjoys, he seems at first to be reduced to the role of a mere executor of commands. But this picture is inaccurate. The manager must cooperate in the formulation of the plan because the men in the center lack the knowledge of the men on the spot. In addition, since no central plan can give all the details, the managers must be relied upon to make the right decisions within the remaining interstices, that is, to act in the best interest of the economy as a whole.

The Soviet system tries to motivate the managers to make them personally interested in achieving the ends of the plan. Fixed salary payments are not considered sufficient for this purpose, so the managers' incomes increase according to their progress as they achieve plan fulfillment. A system of bonuses induces the managers to maximize the national product in terms of the state's preference function. Most importantly, the managers must aid the planners with their specialized knowledge. They must inform the center truthfully about the production possibilities of their respective producing units, must strive to reduce costs, and try to develop better production techniques.

The Soviet system has not yet succeeded in designing a satisfactory system of managerial incentives. The managers' actions, elicited by the various bonuses, are often contrary to the interest of optional plan fulfillment. Reasons for the malfunctioning of the Soviet incentive system can be found in the following basic difficulties:

The system suffers because the planners depend upon the managers to formulate the plan as well as the commands that they have to obey. The more knowledgeable manager has the power to determine what he is expected to accomplish. This means that he can use his power, gained by his special knowledge, to make his task less arduous, while earning larger bonuses. The managers possess a monopoly of know-how that the center cannot break unless it can introduce some competition. Thus we come to the conclusion that "the primary data used for planning and decision-making purposes are generated largely by individuals and groups whose performance is evaluated, and whose rewards or punishments are determined, on the basis of the same data." [6]

At present, the Soviet economy does not make use of a uniform incentive system, though changes are planned for the near future. Profit, as the difference between outlay and receipt, is a result of price developments. Where price variations are not possible because prices are fixed, profits can be "planned," or, if "unplanned," the result of either overfulfillment or the saving of inputs. But overfulfillment can be the result of understatements about productive capacity; and the reduction of costs through factor substitution can lead to desirable results only when based on consistent pricing, which, at present, is impossible in the Soviet economy. We must assume that the managers will try to reduce costs if, thereby, they can increase their bonuses, but their efforts will be determined by the marginal productivity of the factors *at their disposal*, which may differ radically from the marginal productivity of the same factors in other enterprises.

But even where cost reduction or increased production is possible, the managers may decide against these improvements, fearing that they would only lead to stepped-up production quotas or reduced input allocations in the next plan period. In the private enterprise economy, similar reluctance would only be possible in the absence of competition.

The impossibility of using the profit motive has led to the use of bonus arrangements that are often too crude to permit desirable results for the economy as a whole. For instance, where output goals are stated in weight units, the production of heavy items will increase the bonus; where plan fulfillment is measured in monetary terms, the production of low-priced items is discouraged; where spare parts are not counted in gross output, their production is neglected with damaging long-run effects.

Theoretically, these undesirable reactions could be avoided by giving the managers no elbowroom whatever, that is, by handing down the most detailed operational plans. But *practically* this solution would make the bureaucratic bottleneck even worse. It would substitute macroeconomic inconsistencies for the microeconomic sins of the managers. We have to remember, furthermore, that the macroeconomic inconsistencies would be unavoidable because of the immensity of the task of central planning and because of the faultiness of the information that the planners receive from the managers. We may assume, therefore, that major improvements cannot be expected from a movement in this direction of more detailed planning.

The opposite approach would try to decentralize planning. The managers would be given leeway to solve all those problems *within the general*

[6] Hardt, Gallik, and Treml, p. 44.

plan, which they are better qualified to handle than the men in the center. But decentralization creates new problems. The freer the managers, the more necessary it is that their decisions rest on reliable calculations and are guided by dependable incentives. Greater stress would have to be laid on costs, prices, and profits. An essential condition for these arrangements would be a price structure that mirrors correctly the relative scarcities of the factors of production, including investment funds, capital goods, and natural resources. This would imply either price formation on real markets —the managers outbidding each other in a competitive process—or a process of price-setting by the planners that would be complete, accurate, and elastic enough to serve as substitute for genuine markets.

MONEY AND FINANCE IN THE SOVIET ECONOMY

Corresponding to the flow of productive resources and commodities in the Soviet economy there is an opposite flow of money, similar to the circular flow of money in the private enterprise economy. The difference between the two systems lies in the fact that in a planned economy with material balances, physical allocations, output quotas, and set prices, the money flow follows these arrangements in kind and serves mainly to check on plan fulfillment, while in a real market economy monetary forces influence prices, and through prices, the flow of production. Basically, therefore, money and monetary policy are of greater importance for the private enterprise economy.

If the material balances of the central plan could be made perfect, it would be easy to envisage a circular flow of money that would have no disturbing effects. The producing units of the Soviet economy would receive their investment funds either from the state budget as grants, or from the state bank as credits in amounts just large enough to finance all necessary input purchases, including the payment of wages, which, in turn, would be spent on consumer goods. The return-flow of money would take the form, firstly, of sales revenues of enterprises and, secondly, of tax payments to, or profit earnings by, the government, and repayments of credits to the state bank. The funds would then be ready to flow out again, perhaps increased by a creation of credit, which would be balanced by corresponding increases on the "goods" side of the economy, owing to rising productivity.

Obviously, bureaucratic integration cannot achieve such perfection, and it is in the real world of inconsistencies, miscalculations, misallocations, bottlenecks, and shortages that monetary problems arise. The managers will have some elbowroom since output and input figures cannot be broken down to the minutest detail. They will have some choice in their input and output "mix," in factor allocation, in purchases, and in sales. But as soon as we move away from the official area of plan figures and clear-cut commands into the shadier areas where "expediters" try to secure some needed but (through regular channels) unobtainable materials, or where labor is attracted to an enterprise not by higher wages but by upgrading or fringe benefits, we enter a grey-market area where the managers can operate if they have the needed monetary balances.

A priori, it is impossible to tell whether these unofficial transactions are, on the whole, good or bad for the Soviet economy. Possibly, the system could not even work without this degree of leeway for the managers. On the other hand, it is obvious that the Soviet system can tolerate these deviations from the planned path only to the extent that some needed elasticity is provided, but not to the point where the plan itself is being endangered. Therefore, it becomes one of the main functions of the state bank to see that the enterprises are limited to minimum balances as required by their official role in the plan. This task is intricate, because some leeway is unavoidable and that elusive factor, the velocity of circulation of money, enters the picture. If, for instance, funds can be repeatedly spent during an accounting period, the enterprise can buy more than it was intended to purchase.

The Soviet economy has been subject to price inflation, a situation that may seem strange in an economy with officially set prices and the ability of the government to regulate the purchasing power of the citizens and the accumulation of investment funds. But we must remember that the Soviet economy is a full employment economy whose planners have sometimes overestimated prospective productivity increases. Owing to these inaccurate guesses a demand pull inflation resulted, an inflation that would not have happened, of course, had the state bank refused to accommodate the situation by permissive credit creation. This it could refuse to do even less than a central bank in a private enterprise economy. However, there can be little doubt that the authoritarian regime can control wage payments and thereby avoid repressed inflation.

The main task of the monetary authority in Soviet Russia is the auditing of plan fulfillment and the prevention of plan distortions via uncontrolled actions of managers who succeed somehow in acquiring purchasing power that is not strictly allowed. In this respect the activity of the state bank resembles the function of a central bank in a private enterprise economy: the state bank prevents dangerous deviations from the plan and the central bank tries to avoid those falsifications in the price structure that accompany any price inflation and have the effect of disturbing the working of the price mechanism (nonneutrality of money). In both systems, therefore, orderly monetary arrangements are supposed to maintain the basic operating principles of the economy.

In the private enterprise economy, investment funds are supplied through private and corporate savings and credit creation by the banking system, while the public sector is financed by taxation and borrowing. The sources of investment funds in the Soviet economy are basically the same but, as it were, with reversed emphasis. Most important are the different kinds of taxation (for example, the turnover tax and the taxation implied in low agricultural procurement prices), while planned profits correspond, roughly, to corporate savings. Amortization quotas are essentially the same in both systems, while private savings play a minor part in the Soviet system, owing to the relatively low individual income level and the broad social security coverage.

No doubt, the Soviet planners can determine the rate of accumulation and investment to a much larger extent and by more direct means than the governments in private enterprise economies. It is in the use of the investment funds that the weakness of the system must be found.

CHAPTER 21

The Liberman
Discussion

INTRODUCTION

An interesting discussion is taking place in Russia, which could lead to a change in the structure of the Soviet economy. The discussion is so lively, and its subject so important, that some observers in the West [1] feel reminded of the Keynesian "revolution," that major change in western economic thinking which taught the governments of private enterprise countries how to maintain high employment levels. It may seem rather farfetched to compare the dramatic events of the great depression, which led to the "new economics," with the growing dissatisfaction in Russia in recent years. After all, the slowing down of growth rates does not have the ring of urgency connected with prolonged mass unemployment. But there are some similarities between the two debates.

When in the early 1930s the downward spiral of falling investment and consumption led to mass unemployment in the United States and other private enterprise economies, it became obvious that market forces

---

[1] See J. P. Hardt, D. M. Gallik, and V. G. Treml, "Institutional Stagnation and Changing Economic Strategy in the Soviet Union," in *New Directions in the Soviet Economy*, Joint Economic Committee (Washington, D.C., 1966), pp. 25–30.

alone could not be relied upon to cope with this situation of self-deflation and, in particular, that a mere reduction of interest rates could not be counted on to maintain investment expenditures, savings, and national income at reasonably high employment levels. Since then, the governments in the developed private enterprise economies have found it necessary to influence aggregate spending through a combination of monetary and fiscal policies. Though we have not learned, as yet, to use the new economic instruments to perfection (to combine "full" employment levels with complete monetary stability), the new economics was a great success; and, most important, the new policy was merely additive: it did not change the working principles of the market economy, it only improved the economic climate in which private enterprise worked, and it thereby eliminated the greatest threat for a continuation of the system of economic freedom.

The present Soviet debate centers around the fact that economic growth has been slowing down disappointingly and that an ossified bureaucratic apparatus seems no longer able to cope with the ever-increasing complexity of the planned system. Whatever the reasons, the dissatisfaction is widespread and the conviction is growing that something in the organization of the Soviet economy is basically wrong. Nobody suggests that authoritarian central planning should be given up. But the general feeling is that the Soviet incentive system is faulty, that the managers do not have enough independence, and that the planners cannot cope with their problems any longer under the existing arrangements. The present debate tries to find the best combination of managerial freedom and central planning: an incentive system which makes the managers support rather than obstruct the plan.

The proposed solution wants to make use of profits, interest rates and accounting prices. These economic levers, as they are often referred to, are to achieve a perfect blending of efficient managerial behavior with central planning. But it may turn out that "two different institutions cannot perform the same function at the same time, and enterprises cannot simultaneously produce the mix of output that the market wants and the one that planners want." [2] As of now, the Russian debate has not been able to produce the equivalent of a Keynesian solution, that is, a solution that promises to work and to leave the system basically intact.

The Soviet controversy centers around proposals by Professor Evsey G. Liberman.[3] Accordingly, it is necessary to be acquainted with the "Liberman Plan" and the Russian reaction to it, which, on the whole,

[2] R. V. Greenslade, "The Soviet Economic System in Transition," in *New Directions in the Soviet Economy*, p. 14.

[3] See *The Liberman Discussion: A New Phase in Soviet Economic Thought*, vol. 1 of *Planning, Profit, and Incentives in the USSR*, ed. Myron E. Sharpe (New York: International Arts & Sciences Press, 1966), quoted below as *Liberman Discussion*.

has been favorable and has led to pronouncements by Government and Party that indicate a willingness to give the proposals a try. We shall, of course, also attempt to evaluate the whole debate in terms of western economic thought.

The Western reader will find the reform proposals difficult to interpret. Marxist verbiage and slogans make tortuous formulations, particularly where a nearly 50 year old ban on capitalist terms is gradually lifted. Furthermore, a Soviet author must still be careful to point out that he does not want to imitate the market economies and intends his reforms to work strictly *inside* the central plan. But the two main reasons for the opaqueness of the whole discussion may be the following: it is quite possible that a system that mixes central planning successfully with real entrepreneurial initiative cannot be found because it is not feasible; and we have reason to suspect that many of the participants in the discussion do not even see, or want to see, the main problem of consistent economic factor allocation, a problem that, after all, has been ignored for half a century.

LIBERMAN CRITICIZES THE PRESENT SYSTEM

Liberman does not attack the central plan, or the state preference function, or the fact that the Soviet system does not rest on consumer sovereignty. He has practically nothing in common with Oskar Lange.[4] The plan remains sacrosanct. Liberman does not criticize the main structure of the authoritarian socialist economy in which planners determine the targets without the benefit of economic calculations in terms of opportunity costs. His disapproval concerns almost exclusively the bonus system of the Soviet economy. According to Liberman, the managers are practically forced into *mis*informing the planning authorities about the true potential of their enterprises. And, since the managers *alone* have the knowledge needed for operational planning, an incentive system must be found which makes it profitable for the manager to reduce costs and improve output strictly in line with the targets of the plan.

A few quotations from Liberman's article "Plan, Profits, Bonuses"[5] will show the weaknesses for which Liberman and many other Soviet authors criticize the present incentive system. We are told that the enterprises' estimates "are usually much lower than their capacities," that the managers must be made to "stop asking for superfluous capital investments and machine tools," and prevented from creating "unnecessary stocks";

---

[4] See Chap. 16.

[5] Pravda, September 9, 1962. See *Liberman Discussion*, pp. 79–87. Reprinted also, in a different translation, in *The Current Digest of the Soviet Press*, vol. 14, no. 36 (October 3, 1962), pp. 13–15.

that they should "be deterred from artificially overstating the norms for the consumption of materials, fuel, tools and power," and from "asking for, and hiring, superfluous manpower." Since the managers cannot be trusted, they must be under strict supervision, and this task of controlling, from the center, tens of thousands of enterprises puts a very heavy burden on the planning authorities. Furthermore, supervision from the center cannot possibly be effective because the planners lack the detailed knowledge that could tell them when and where the managers are wrong. Therefore, it is essential that the planning authorities be relieved from "petty tutelage over enterprises" and that the latter be freed from the fear "that through their own good work they will put themselves into a difficult position in the following year."

LIBERMAN'S PROPOSALS

Liberman [6] proposes the introduction of an incentive system based on profits and on greater managerial freedom. The economy remains centrally planned, but the new arrangements see to it that "what is profitable for society, as represented by the state, must be profitable for every collective of the enterprise and every member of that enterprise." To introduce Adam Smith's "invisible hand" into authoritarian socialism, Liberman makes the following interesting proposals.

"The enterprises are presented with plans only with respect to the volume of output and the assortment and dates of deliveries." The managers, therefore, are still under command to produce what the planners decide. Furthermore, "all the levers of centralized planning—prices, finances, the budget, accounting, large capital investments—and, finally, all the value, labor and major physical indices of rates and proportions in the sphere of production, distribution and consumption will be determined centrally." Nonetheless, the proposed system "will relieve centralized planning of the petty tutelage over enterprises, of the expensive attempts to influence production not by economic measures, but by administrative techniques." This change-over from administrative techniques to "economic levers" is to be accomplished through the use of a profit system in which a "profitability rate" that expresses enterprise profits *as a percentage of production capital* is to be compared with a long-term "profitability norm" that the central authorities will establish "for every branch of production."

"On the basis of the targets for volume and assortment of output,

[6] Liberman, "Once Again on the Plan, Profits, and Bonuses," in *Liberman Discussion*, pp. 79, 82, 217.

the enterprises themselves should work out a complete plan that covers, among other things, labor productivity, quantity of work force, wages, costs of production, accumulations, capital investments, and new machinery." Physical allocations are not mentioned and the reader is left to speculate how inputs are to be procured by the enterprises under the new system. We are forced to assume, however, that specific physical allocations by the center are definitely ruled out since the operational plans are to be drawn up by the enterprises themselves.

Liberman claims that his system will induce Soviet managers to make fullest use of their production potential because the enterprise shares in the profit. Moreover, no enterprise would care to continue the old practice of overfulfilling by first disguising its true potential because overfulfillment would entitle only to a *lower* share in the profit. Failure to carry out plan assignments, on the other hand, would deprive the enterprise of the right to any bonus. To achieve high profitability, an enterprise will use its full capacity, increase the number of shifts, refrain from asking for unnecessary capital goods, and stop building up emergency reserves. The profit incentive, therefore, is expected to do away with most, if not all, malpractices of the present system. The fear that successful performance will only lead to higher output targets and stiffened profitability norms for the following year—and, accordingly to the old practice of consciously lowering enterprise performance—is met by the suggestion that the profit norms should apply for up to 5 years.[7] To encourage the use of new techniques and the introduction of new products, it is suggested that profitability norms might be artificially lowered in priority industries.

These are the main features of the Liberman Plan. It is obvious that Liberman does not try to introduce a liberal socialist system à la Lange. He wants to find a solution for the following crucial problem: "How can the centralized management of the national economy, the need for which is unquestionable, be combined with the greatest possible scope for the undoubtedly significant local initiative and independence at the enterprises?"[8] Obviously, Liberman is of the opinion that his reduction of the antiquated system of a great variety of material incentives to one simple profit formula will solve all the major economic problems. If he were correct, he would, indeed, become the Keynes of authoritarian socialism, the reformer who made his system work without having to alter it basically to any significant degree.

The Soviet authorities are willing to experiment with Liberman's

[7] V. S. Nemchinov proposes that the norms should be standardized over a ten to fifteen year period. See "The Plan Target and Material Incentive," in *Liberman Discussion*, p. 111.

[8] L. Leont'ev, "The Plan and Methods of Economic Management," in *Liberman Discussion*, p. 207.

ideas. The *Resolutions on Industrial Management of the Plenary Session of the Communist Party of the Soviet Union* of September 29, 1965 noted,

> that the existing organizational structure of management, methods of planning and economic incentives in industry do not conform to the present-day conditions and the level of development of production forces. . . . The work of the enterprises is regulated by a large number of plan indices, which limits the independence and initiative of the enterprise collectives and weakens their responsibility for improving the organization of production. . . . It is recognized as desirable to halt excessive regulation of the activity of enterprises, to reduce the number of plan indices imposed upon the enterprises from above, to provide them with the necessary means for developing and improving production and to improve the use of such highly important economic levers as profit, price, bonuses and credit. . . . While expanding the economic independence of the enterprises, the Party and the Soviet government will continue in the future as well to carry out a single policy in the planning of the major trends of development of production, technical progress, capital investment, prices, wages and finance.[9]

This official acceptance, in principle, of Liberman's proposals makes the present Russian debate particularly interesting and important. However, a brief discussion of the issues involved will show that nothing surprising is bound to happen, least of all a *decisive* turn toward decentralization or the introduction of a price *mechanism*.

First of all, Liberman himself does not want to do away with the central plan in the full meaning of the term. He does not see the macroeconomic problem of factor allocation and, accordingly, has no criticism to offer as far as the target plan itself is concerned. All he wants to do is harness the managerial initiate into the shafts of the plan and not abolish the target plan as the best expression of the state's preference function. But even if he and his colleagues were bent on wresting power from the central authorities, they could probably not succeed since "it is difficult to picture the party and the planners presiding over the dissolution of planning" since "neither the economic bureaucracy nor the local party apparatus is likely to accede gracefully to its own withering away." [10]

---

[9] *The Current Digest of the Soviet Press*, vol. 17, no. 38 (October 13, 1965), pp. 16–17. A different translation can be found in *Reform of Soviet Economic Management*, vol. 2 of *Planning, Profit, and Incentives in the USSR*, ed. Myron E. Sharpe (New York: International Arts & Sciences Press, 1966), pp. 277–283. Pages 3–46 of this volume also contain A. N. Kosygin's speech "On Improving Industrial Management, Perfecting Planning, and Enhancing Economic Incentives in Industrial Production" of September 28, 1965, on which the resolutions of September 29 were based. Kosygin follows, in the main, Liberman's proposals but also considers problems of central planning that Liberman ignores. However, while Kosygin insists that disproportionalities between the major branches of the economy be ironed out, he does not indicate how the new proposals concerning profits and cost-accounting can accomplish this end.

[10] R. V. Greenslade, p. 15.

PROFITS AND PRICES

The Liberman discussion has already led to interesting developments. Marxist stereotypes gradually are making room for a debate about the importance of consistent pricing and the absurdity of a system that lets enterprises use capital resources without interest charges.

The most important single issue connected with the Liberman Plan concerns prices. Most Soviet prices are government-set. Some (like wages and consumer goods prices) must come close to genuine market prices because they permit the steering of the labor supply roughly in conformance with the plan and the distribution of consumer goods without rationing. The prices of intermediate goods, however, are more or less arbitrarily set and only very infrequently changed. To follow these prices as guidelines for the integration of production processes and the allocation of the factors of production would bring absurd results. Profit rates must rest on correct prices since they are the difference between product prices and cost prices, expressed as percentages of the value of production capital. Liberman admits that "our prices are too often divorced from their natural basis—the socially necessary production cost" and that "of course, it is not an easy or simple task to combine price stability with flexibility." [11] Considering that all prices have to be set, and set consistently, by the central authorities, Liberman's remark is certainly an understatement. The central planners, whose limitations are obvious when they set production norms, are suddenly considered capable of correctly setting, and continuously changing, many millions of prices. But since it is obvious that the profitability scheme must end in failure if the prices are not correctly chosen, it is understandable that Liberman unconsciously tends to soft-pedal this basic difficulty.

Other participants in the debate have been more candid. L. Leont'ev,[12] for example, writes that "perhaps the most complicated problem arising in connection with the use of profits as the single criterion of an enterprise's efficiency is that of *price formation*" and L. Gatovskii points out that "if prices are not revised for a long time a big disparity in profits will inevitably arise, placing some enterprises in an undeservedly privileged position and artificially increasing their profits." [13] Gatovskii feels that "further adjustment of prices is a prerequisite for elevating the role and significance of profit." That prices must play a primary role in the con-

[11] "Once Again on the Plan, Profits, and Bonuses," in *Liberman Discussion*, p. 214.
[12] L. Leont'ev, "The Plan and Methods of Economic Management," *Liberman Discussion*, p. 211.
[13] L. Gatovskii, "The Role of Profit in a Socialist Economy," *Liberman Discussion*, pp. 98–99.

templated reforms is confirmed by V. Sitnin,[14] Chairman of the USSR's State Planning Committee's Price Committee, who emphasizes the importance of price as a tool of economic management. Referring to the Resolutions of September 29, 1965, which want to give broader scope to economic methods, he argues that a precondition of this change would be a thorough price reform:

> In a number of instances unsubstantiated prices, set without taking objective economic criteria into account, have been in effect in our economy. This led to a loss of authenticity of many economic calculations and opened the way for subjective decisions. Profit, profitability and sales, which are now moving to the forefront as indices of the activity of enterprises, can indicate the effectiveness of their work only if prices for output reflect socially necessary expenditures of labor. Present prices to a considerable extent do not meet this requirement. The last review of prices was carried out 10 years ago in 1955. . . . In setting prices, it is very important to assure their correct correlation for interchangeable output (Coal, oil and gas, for example). The correlation of prices must be such that it promotes technological progress. . . . The main thing consists in determining correct prices for each item, for each product. Otherwise, the output of the enterprise will be divided for no good reason into the profitable and the unprofitable. . . . However, this does not mean that the profitability of production of all items must mandatorily be equal. In setting prices, it is essential to use this highly important economic lever to stimulate the output of technically progressive types of goods that are of high quality and enjoy great demand. . . . The development of economically substantiated prices that are in line with the new conditions of economic management is a very complicated job and has virtually only begun.

While the importance and urgency of a general price reform is admitted by practically all its participants, the present debate has not produced a single suggestion as to *how* the central authorities can achieve a system of correct prices, which, in turn, would permit profit rates to give the right signals to the managers.

Since the present debate was the outgrowth of the admitted inability of the central planners to coordinate the various production processes in a system of bureaucratic integration, it is astonishing that not a single participant in the present debate has expressed doubt about the authorities' ability to create a consistent network of many millions of prices and to adjust these prices continuously to changes in factor supplies, technology, and priorities. Yet they are the same authorities who, until recently, simply ignored the very existence of such cost categories as interest and rent!

A further difficulty arises when profits are expressed as percentages of capital assets. How are these capital values to be found? Obviously, we

---

[14] V. Sitnin, "Price is an Important Tool of Management," *Current Digest of the Soviet Press*, vol. 17 (December 1, 1965), pp. 7–8.

cannot capitalize *known* profits since the profits are to be expressed as percentages of the figure we are trying to find. But if we do not know, or cannot artificially set, capital values, then the determination of profit *rates* is robbed of its basis, even though product prices and variable costs are known.

Perhaps this difficulty of not being able to figure the value of the fixed capital component has led to the request that profit norms should be set individually, not uniformly, for all branches of industry. Indeed, this could counteract the disturbing influence of arbitrary valuations of the fixed capital of enterprises, but only if past mistakes were known in order to compensate for them by varying the profit norms.

A comparison of the profit norms with the long-term rate of interest in the private enterprise economy would argue for norms that are as uniform as possible. A comparison of profit rates and profit norms could improve the allocation of investment funds according to objective criteria. But in the present debate in Russia it seems to be generally understood that the profit norms ought to vary for different branches of industry, so that low profit norms can channel investment funds into priority areas while high norms can discourage the demand for additional capital goods in industries of low priority rank. This rejection of the principle of a uniform interest rate (or profit norm) is strange. Being completely sovereign in the setting of their targets, the authorities would only gain if, through consistent cost accounting, they created a firm base for economic factor allocation under consideration of opportunity costs. Being able to decide supremely which industries they want to expand, they need not fool themselves through artificial cost reductions. Industries whose growth is considered desirable need not be treated to low profit norms. The logical approach would be to offer them correspondingly high prices for their products.

Several participants in the present discussion have suggested that "every possible measure should be taken to reduce to naught, to restrict to special exceptions, the so-called planned operation at a loss, which spreads sentiments of dependence, strikes at cost accounting, and stifles the initiative of enterprises." [15] Consistently applied this would mean that, as a rule, the profit norms should be uniform, with exceptions where the planners consciously want to deviate from the principle of uniform cost accounting. Alternatively, they could increase the price of the product sufficiently to enable the enterprises in question to reach or surpass the same profitability norms as the rest.

If we make the assumption that the managers are able to base their decisions on a set of correct prices (an assumption that we can*not* make),

[15] L. Gatovskii, "The Role of Profit in a Socialist Economy," *Liberman Discussion*, p. 102.

it could be that a replacement of the present incentive system by the profit system would lead to substantial advantages: the managers would try to increase their profits through a reduction of costs and endeavor to keep their capital small to raise the profit rate. This could be accomplished by factor substitution, employment of devices to save material and labor, fullest use of the production potential of given plant and equipment, reduction of reserve stocks to a practical minimum, and request for additional capital only if its marginal productivity will increase the profit rate. But if the managers have to base their calculations on an inconsistent price pattern, their success of reaching a high profit rate might easily harm the economy at large, because what is right for the microcosm of the firm would no longer be good for the macrocosm of the planned economy. This has been generally admitted in the present debate.

Also, it remains doubtful whether under the Liberman system the managers will cooperate wholeheartedly with the planners. Success in reaching high profitability rates will, sooner or later, lead to stiffened profitability norms. A mere promise that norms will not be raised might be considered inadequate protection. Probably, the present bargaining and wrangling about output quotas and input allocations would change into a fight about profitability norms. Furthermore, since the enterprise must reach prescribed output figures and can never be absolutely sure about its command over the needed productive resources, it may well retain some of its previous habits in misinforming the center about its capacity. Also, the managers may want to reduce rather than increase the pace of the growth program, as the less arduous and safer policy in the long run.

We must remember that the managers have a kind of monopoly position in their relations with the authorities since they alone possess the indispensable know-how. To break this monopoly, the central authorities would have to introduce competition among the managers, but nothing in the Liberman Plan points to real competition, though the western observer may, at first, be tempted to interpret the proposed arrangements as if the managers were to get their inputs by outbidding their colleagues. Competitive bidding is clearly ruled out by the fact that all prices are set by the center.

Profits according to Liberman [16] are "a yardstick for production efficiency" since they "follow, in principle, only from technological and organizational improvement." Furthermore, "they are returned to the population in the form of social services and expanded production." Profit norms may be stiffened to encourage enterprises to draw up still better plans but the elimination of profit through increased production plays no

---

[16] Liberman, "Are We Flirting with Capitalism, Profits, and 'Profits,' " *Liberman Discussion*, p. 311.

part in Liberman's proposals. Whether accumulation of capital proceeds via profit revenues or turnover tax is a matter of relatively minor importance.

Soviet authors make much ado about the fact that, in the private enterprise economy, profits can be increased through higher prices, implying that profits are to a large extent monopolistic profits. To some extent this is true, as we have seen. However, profits can also be the result of artificial price setting in the Soviet economy. Referring to the latter, Gatovskii reminds us that "if a price is set too high and automatically ensures the enterprise a big profit, this undermines the stimuli to cut production costs, raise labor productivity, and use resources rationally. An 'easy' life, hothouse conditions, are created for an enterprise which enable it to be highly profitable without any exertion of effort." [17] Gatovskii uses this argument to show that the profit system à la Liberman can function only on the basis of correct prices. But since the central authorities know much less about the conditions in a given industrial branch than the managers on the spot, the latter might easily succeed in talking the former into the setting of favorable prices, just as they misinform them under the present system of material incentives.

THE INCONSISTENCY OF LIBERMAN'S PROPOSALS

Liberman wants to limit the central plan to quantity of output, assortment, and delivery schedules. Commands to this effect are handed down to the enterprises. But the operational plans would be drawn up exclusively by the enterprises themselves. The managers would decide how to use the factors of production and what investment to make in new machinery. Their sole aim would be to fulfill the commands from above at the least cost, thereby increasing profit and their own share in it. The interest of the manager does not transcend the microcosm of his enterprise. He cannot improve the target plan since he must meet output and assortment requirements and is even punished in case of overfulfillment.

Because in the network of interdependent production processes, one enterprise's inputs are the outputs of others and, vice versa, its own output becomes inputs of other industries, it is impossible that all enterprises together should be able to use more or different inputs than are supplied by the output plan. Since all prices are set by the central authority and there can be no price competition, it is difficult to understand how operational plans of different enterprises should be properly integrated and how, in their aggregate, they should not overtax available factor supplies.

[17] L. Gatovskii, "The Role of Profit in a Socialist Economy," *Liberman Discussion,* p. 99.

At this point it is tempting for western economists to substitute managerial reactions to price fluctuations for operational planning. But a careful study of the Liberman proposals shows that price fluctuations due to competitive bidding are not permitted. Thus we are not told whereof, precisely, operational planning consists. Are the managers assigned monetary balances whose size limits their input purchases? Are they permitted to borrow additional investment funds at the risk of lowering their profit rate? Are they free to purchase any input mix that promises to lower production costs? And what happens if, at given prices, they tend to buy more of product A or factor B than corresponds to output plan or factor supply?

The Liberman Plan leads to difficulties that the system of bureaucratic integration tried to avoid *ex ante*. Now there is only an output plan but no corresponding input allocations; there are reactions to prices but no guarantee that these reactions will lead to an aggregate demand that corresponds to the planned supply. In other words, the part of central planning that has been scrapped to achieve greater freedom for the managers has not been replaced by a pricing process.

Both B. Sukharevskii [18] and A. Zverev [19] emphasize these contradictions and come to the conclusion that the Liberman proposal cannot work. They point out that it is not possible to limit the plan indices to quantity-assortment targets alone and that the actions of an enterprise that tries to increase its profits are likely to conflict with the quantity-assortment targets. Furthermore, if the central planners are not as informed as the managers, it is inconsistent to specify volume and composition of production. And finally, balanced development "can best be achieved when the amount and direction of investment are determined by a state plan and not decided by an enterprise." [20] The enterprises "are ignorant of the various national economic interrelations" and "even if they wanted to establish the balance of the economy they could not do it." Zverev concludes: "Even now we have mistakes in planning that result in disproportions in the national economy; what would happen if every individual enterprise would engage in this work?"

These criticisms seem justified from the standpoint of the central planner who sees part of the plan dismantled in order to hand to individual enterprises the function of operational planning. The planner notices that there is no mechanism to coordinate the actions of the enterprises and that the prices that determine enterprise plans are, in all probability, false prices.

[18] B. Sukharevskii, "On Improving the Form and Methods of Material Incentives," *Liberman Discussion*, pp. 114–134.

[19] A. Zverev, "Against Oversimplification in Solving Complex Problems," *Liberman Discussion*, pp. 141–148.

[20] A. Zverev, p. 144.

LIBERMAN AND LANGE

Since the Liberman Plan deals with improved factor allocation, which, admittedly, is to rest on a much improved price system, the reader can get the impression that Liberman is much concerned with the problems of *national* factor allocation in an authoritarian socialist economy. This impression would be wrong. Liberman takes the target plan as given and is not concerned with its improvement on the basis of opportunity cost calculations. Nor is there any indication that he expects any change in the target plan in consequence of a possible divergence of target plan and operational plans. He is not applying the principle of consistent factor allocation to the economy as a whole and does not demand uniform standards for national investment decisions. On the contrary, the profit norms are to differ for different branches of industry.

His supporters and even most of his critics join him in this neglect of the macroeconomic allocation problem.[21] This is strange when we consider that the present difficulties in the Soviet economy are to a large extent the outgrowth of macroeconomic disproportionalities and not exclusively of faulty incentives.

However, greater insistence on cost accounting and the acknowledgment of the importance of interest payments on fixed capital are substantial improvements over previous economic discussions in Russia, although, as of now, the application of cost accounting is limited to the firms, rests on unreliable prices, and does not influence the national allocation of resources.

It is interesting to compare Liberman's proposals with Lange's model. Lange wants his liberal socialist economy to work along the following lines: (1) The consumers are sovereign. (2) While the government determines the dividing line between consumer goods and capital goods production (the rate of accumulation), even capital goods production is, indirectly, guided by the changing wishes of the consumers. (3) The markets for consumer goods and for labor are genuine markets. (4) The prices for investment goods and investment funds are set by the central authority and are changed when they do not lead to equilibrium between demand

[21] An exception is V. S. Nemchinov who points out that "the plans dealing with production, labor, finance, credit, and material and technical supply are uncoordinated" and also remarks, interestingly, that "the abnormality of the existing planning procedure consists in the one-sided character of the obligations" since "our local enterprises are constantly getting from above definite planned percentage assignments (concerning growth of the volume of production, higher labor productivity, lower production costs, etc.), while higher bodies, as a rule, do not bear any responsibility to local enterprises for disproportions in the plans." ("Socialist Economic Management and Production Planning," *Liberman Discussion*), pp. 178–179. See also footnote 9 above on Kosygin's proposals.

and supply. (5) The managers act as if all prices were constant and try to achieve equality of product price and average marginal cost of the plants comprising the industry; they do not try to maximize profits but approach equilibrium directly and *ex ante*. (6) The central planning board has not only the function of determining the rate of accumulation, it also must distribute investment funds among the different industries. This allocation takes place on the basis of a uniform rate of interest. Only those managers whose products will, after an expansion, sell at a price that covers the cost of production, including the interest rate, can count on additional investment funds.

Lange's scheme has been criticized not on the grounds of theoretical inconsistency but because, on the one side, it is highly improbable that managers can be induced to follow rules that every business instinct must urge them to reject, and on the other, it is equally unlikely that the planners can adjust the whole price system continuously and consistently. The behavior of Soviet managers under the influence of various bonus schemes has shown that they will try to further the interests of the enterprise rather than those of the nation. In Lange's system, the managers would enjoy a powerful position as monopolists in the markets and as specialists who alone possess the indispensable technical know-how. Therefore, they could use their market power to reap monopolistic profits and the superior knowledge to hide these violations of the "rules of behavior."

In comparing Lange's [22] model with Liberman's proposals, we find the following differences: Liberman's managers will maximize the profits of their enterprises but their actions will not influence the plan or the state preference function. Lange's managers will try to equalize prices and marginal costs and their actions will lead to corresponding changes in national factor allocation. Lange would probably have criticized the Liberman Plan along the following lines: (1) A system in which the accounting prices reflect the preferences of the bureaucrats instead of those of the consumers is "incompatible with the ideals of the socialist movement." (2) Given a state preference function, economic accounting would still be needed but impossible in Liberman's system, because Liberman pays attention only to creating a profit motive for the individual enterprise but not to the question of factor allocation for the economy as a whole. (3) The system of cost accounting must transcend the limits of the enterprise and, even within the enterprise, will lead to desirable results only if all managers use the same (correct) cost prices for identical factors of production.

From these comparisons we can draw the conclusion that Lange and Liberman do not complement each other. To make the Liberman Plan

---

[22] Oskar Lange and Fred M. Taylor, *On the Economic Theory of Socialism* (Minneapolis: University of Minnesota Press, 1938), pp. 90–91, 95.

work a consistent price pattern plus a coordination of the individual enterprises' efforts into a consistent operational plan are needed. But since Lange's scheme is only a bloodless model, it cannot imbue the Liberman Plan with a realism it does not itself possess. As far as consistent factor allocation on the national level is concerned, the Soviet economists have never fully understood Lange. The Liberman discussion has shown that an escalation of the idea of decentralization to the degree implied in Lange's model is quite unacceptable to Soviet economists and even more so to Soviet bureaucrats.

LIBERMAN AND MISES

Our discussion has shown that the Soviet economy has not solved Mises' problem of consistent factor allocation. We have seen, furthermore, that reforms are blocked in both directions. Neither greater centralization nor greater decentralization promises success. To make the plan more detailed, and thus immune to false price signals and unreliable managerial behavior, would strain the capacity of the central authorities to the breaking point. And even if fullest centralization could be accomplished, it would achieve nothing more than a bureaucratic-technical integration of the productive processes. Factor allocation would still be arbitrary and disproportionalities would develop as they have in the past.

To decentralize would mean to substitute managerial operational planning for detailed central commands. Profits would motivate the managers and prices guide their actions. However, without genuine markets, the central authorities would be responsible for consistent price relationships. That they could not perform the task of correct price determination was precisely Mises' contention.

It is now often taken for granted that Lange had successfully answered Mises' challenge. Therefore, Soviet attempts to use prices as guidelines are discussed in the West with reference to Lange rather than to Mises. But Lange did not show how consistent pricing could be combined with central planning in *real life*. The Lange model cannot rescue the Liberman Plan nor can Liberman's proposals breathe life into Lange's model.

Thus we must come to the conclusion that the Soviet economy suffers from the following basic shortcomings: it cannot achieve economical factor allocation, it permits the development of major disproportionalities, and has not solved the crucial problem of managerial incentives. Against these weaknesses we can weigh the advantages of central capital accumulation and *ex ante* planning for economic growth. However, these advantages are, perhaps, not beyond the reach of the market economies once a democratic system considers them essential and compatible with the working principles of the private enterprise system.

PART 6

Between

Market

and

Plan

CHAPTER 22

Yugoslavia: Symbiosis of Plan and Market?

INTRODUCTION

Originally, the Yugoslav economy was to follow the Soviet model. It was to be centrally planned, with nationalization of industry and collectivization of agriculture. What the Yugoslavs called "administrative socialism" was envisaged as a full-fledged command economy, characterized by minutest interference in local management, planning in physical terms, elimination of market pricing, and disregard of consumers' preferences. Nevertheless, it would be wrong to conclude that the difficulties which plagued the Yugoslav economy during its first 6 or 7 years were the same problems that recently led to the Liberman debate in Russia. Superimposed on the weaknesses that central planning in a command economy might produce in any situation, there were additional troubles. Some were similar to the problems which Russia had to face during the second agrarian revolution, and others were due to the fact that it proved impossible to achieve bureaucratic integration of the productive processes by trial and error in the short span of a few years. Furthermore, out of the economic problems grew a major political crisis. The Yugoslav decision to discontinue the process of collectivization of agriculture led to the Cominform blockade of 1948, which, in turn, required a reorientation of Yugoslav foreign trade. Matters were made still worse by two severe droughts in 1950 and 1952.

The disappointing results of central planning together with the schism in the communist camp pointed the way toward a more liberal form of socialism in Yugoslavia, with decentralization, profit motive, and the use of market prices as important ingredients of the new system. Particularly interesting, however, was the reorganization of the Yugoslav firm, which was to be operated by its workers.

SYNDICALISM, GUILD SOCIALISM, AND PRODUCERS' COOPERATIVES

The idea of a direct participation of a firm's workers in its management is nearly as old as socialism itself. Syndicalism, for example, advocated ownership of the means of production not by the state but by the workers themselves. However, it gave no thought to the problem of how the social economy could function under these conditions. Obviously, the Yugoslav system of workers' management has nothing to do with these naïve suggestions. Nor is it to be compared with the producers' cooperatives on which Louis Blanc (1813–1882) and Ferdinand Lassalle (1825–1864) placed such high hopes.

The essence of a producers' cooperative lies in the idea that the workers of an enterprise, as owners, are willing to let their income be dependent on the profit of the cooperative. Furthermore, the workers are to participate in the management of the firm. Where capital has to be borrowed, interest must be paid before profits can be distributed. The full risk is to be borne by the worker-managers. By contrast, the typical private firm in the private enterprise economy protects the wage earner at least against minor profit fluctuations, although it must be emphasized that he still faces the substantial risk of unemployment.

Louis Blanc advocated producers' cooperatives as a path to socialism. The state would finance these cooperatives, which, owing to their alleged superiority, would successfully compete with private enterprise. After complete elimination of the latter, the cooperatives would be joined in huge industry-wide central cooperatives which would remain independent of the state. They would pay part of their earnings into a mutual fund out of which less successful cooperatives (or central cooperatives) could be financed.

That Ferdinand Lassalle could not adhere to his iron law of wages and, simultaneously, accept Louis Blanc's proposal as a way out, was already shown by Karl Marx with reference to the Malthusian population law as a natural law that could not be changed by a mere improvement of social organization.[1] The Marxist Tugan Baranowsky attacked Blanc's proposal with the criticism that in a cooperative society the means of production would belong to individual groups rather than to the people as a whole. Individual producers' cooperatives, therefore, could exploit favorable market conditions at the expense of the rest of society. The conflict of economic interests would not be abolished but only shifted from private enterprise to organized groups, thereby becoming even more intense. Furthermore, corporate socialism would leave national production, as a whole, unorganized and thus exposed to industrial crises. Support of less successful cooperatives by the state, finally, would only serve to make the management of the cooperatives irresponsible.[2]

Where producers' cooperatives had to face the full impact of competition by private enterprise, they were, as a rule, unable to survive. The reasons usually given are "lacking demand, lacking capital, and lacking discipline." [3] Lacking demand indicates low competitiveness in terms of quality and price. Lacking capital refers to the hurdle which Blanc wanted to overcome through the use of public funds. Basic, however, is the third criticism: lacking discipline. Where the workers were the owners of the enterprise, it proved impossible to maintain discipline. The manager of the producers' cooperative did not have the power of the "sack," he could not get rid of undesirable elements in the labor force and could not adjust employment and production to demand. Furthermore, it was impossible for the manager to make those quick decisions that market conditions necessitate, since he had to use most of his energies to satisfy the worker-owners whom he could not command but who, nevertheless, had the nuisance power of continuous interference. After all, the workers themselves were supposed to have a right of codetermination.

It took many years before the idea of cooperative socialism was sufficiently discredited, probably because direct ownership, direct participation in profit, and codetermination in entrepreneurial decisions had enormous appeal among the working class. Cooperative socialism seemed to promise the end of insecurity, degradation, and exploitation without implying the roundabout way of setting up a system of state ownership and central command.

Decentralization and a minimum of state interference is also the main feature of Guild Socialism as proposed by G. D. H. Cole.[4] As its very name suggests, Guild Socialism has a kind of medieval flavor and appeal. "A National Guild would be an association of all the workers by hand and

---

[1] See Chap. 11.

[2] Tugan-Baranowky, Der moderne Sozialismus (Dresden 1908), pp. 131–132.

[3] See Wirtschaftsdemokratie. Ihr Wesen, Weg und Ziel (Berlin: Verlagsgesellschaft des Allgemeinen Deutschen Gewerkschaftsbundes, 1928), p. 77.

[4] G. D. H. Cole, Guild Socialism Re-Stated (London: Leonard Parsons, 1921).

brain concerned in the carrying on of a particular industry or service, and its function would be actually to carry on that industry or service on behalf of the whole community." However, the guild system would be very decentralized. Greatest emphasis would be placed on local initiative and autonomy for the small group, with the National Guilds playing a coordinating rather than a controlling role. The factory, for example, would be self-governing as the natural and fundamental unit of industrial democracy. The governing principle in the choice of the managers would be election "from below" by those who are cooperating with the manager. The manager, in turn, would lead by persuasian and not by the imposition of his will.

Again, as in the case of the producers' cooperatives, how can labor discipline be maintained under these conditions; how can the managers be trusted to make the right decisions; and, finally, how is the whole social production process to be organized? Concerning the question of the proper coordination of the various branches of the economy, Guild Socialism is almost as naïve as syndicalism. Emphasis on decentralization enables the guild socialists to avoid the mentioning of central planning, but they are not able to show how central planning could be avoided. Since many factories will produce intermediate goods there must, according to Cole, be "close connections established," preferably on the local level. But little is said about price determination and it is assumed that prices would not be the result of competitive processes. Also, factories and guilds are obviously not trying to maximize profits but carry on their business "on behalf of the whole community."

Guild Socialism has nothing to contribute to the problem of planning and pricing, possibly because it suffers from the delusion that the magnitude of these problems is still the same as in a medieval town. For instance, it is impossible to find a clear answer to the basic problem of how major shifts in demand or in priorities would be handled in the proposed system.

THE YUGOSLAV SYSTEM OF WORKERS' MANAGEMENT

The Yugoslav economic system wants to be clearly distinct from the private enterprise system and the command economy of Russia. Its unique new feature is the system of workers' management. To correctly interpret the working of the Yugoslav economy it must be understood, however, that the system of workers' management has little to do with syndicalism, guild socialism, or producers' cooperatives, though there are some similarities.

First of all, the Yugoslav workers do not own the firms in which they work. The state owns the firm's capital goods, the firm has to make interest payments on the capital, and the government exercises its ownership rights in the case of liquidation of the enterprise.

Not being an owner, the worker has no absolute job security: he can become unemployed. This very fact eliminates one of the main weaknesses of the older schemes, which implied that a firm could maintain employment for all its workers under all conditions. On the other hand, the Yugoslav economy shows unemployment more openly than a centrally planned system of the Soviet type.

In comparing the Yugoslav system with Guild Socialism, it is important that the Yugoslav firm is part of a system where profit motive, prices, and government planning lead to some form of coordination of the different branches of the economy. The system may be better or worse than either the private enterprise or the Soviet type, but at least it defines the position of the firm in contrast to Guild Socialism and syndicalism where the interrelationships of the producing units remain entirely vague. When the Yugoslav firms are compared to producers' cooperatives as they existed within the general framework of the private enterprise system, the comparison is wrong on two grounds: the Yugoslav firms do not compete with private corporations, and they are not owned by their workers.

Nevertheless, after these possible misunderstandings have been clarified, we can legitimately ask whether the Yugoslav system of workers' management is subject to the criticism that it could suffer from lack of discipline and entrepreneurship. We must first study the manner in which the Yugoslav firm works.

The Law of June 27, 1950 "transferred the operation and management of all factories and of all economic enterprises in general to the persons employed in such enterprises." [5] The workers select a workers' council and a managing board from their own ranks. The council makes basic decisions that the managing board must carry out. Board or council members cannot be dismissed. The enterprise has also a director, a "top executive responsible for organizing production in accord with the dictates of the workers' council and managing board and consistent with the laws and regulations pertaining to the organization and business of the enterprise." As a representative of the local community, the director "is empowered to set aside or hold up any decisions adopted by the workers' council or the managing board that he considers in violation of existing laws and the regulations of government authorities." In other words, the director has exactly as much power as the government wants him to have. This arrangement can lead to major conflicts since all the potential disagreements between the central and the peripheral forces, and between community and enterprise, tend to focus on the relationship between workers and directors. Indeed, it is possible that the Yugoslav economy

[5] George Macesich, *Yugoslavia. The Theory and Practice of Development Planning* (Charlottesville: The University Press of Virginia, 1964), pp. 69, 70–71, 75.

will prove relatively weak in this respect when compared with the private enterprise system, in which entrepreneurial decisions are free, and the Soviet system, in which commands must be obeyed if they cannot be evaded.

The Yugoslav system of workers' management does not only try to give the workers the satisfaction of codetermination, it actually changes their status as wage earners into that of sharers of the enterprises' profits. "The workers are paid, not by a wage representing in some sense a market price for labor, but rather by a share in the gross profits of the enterprise after deduction of cost of materials, depreciation, and various taxes." [6] The idea behind this arrangement is, of course, to induce both the firm and each individual worker in the firm to strive for excellent performance.

Before judging this incentive system, it must be mentioned, however, (1) that differentiated minimum wages are set by the state for various categories of workers, (2) that, on the decision of the workers themselves, wage income can be increased at the expense of capital formation, and (3) that, unless prices are fixed by the government, profits and incomes can be raised by monopolistic practices. In other words, it is impossible to rely on the workers' council system for maximum development of the productive effort of all members of the firm: the workers may be content to receive the minimum wage when too much of the profit is being taxed away; they may insist on raising wages at the expense of capital formation; and it is possible that the worker-managers may try to raise profits when the absence of price controls makes such policies practical. In May 1962 President Tito criticized workers' councils for "such practices as raising prices without regard to underlying market conditions, using funds earmarked for investment to raise wages" [7] and similar malpractices.

These criticisms concern efficiency and initiative, but they do not yet concern the working of the economy as a whole, the coordination of the production processes, and the inherent conflict between planning and pricing. In this context it may be mentioned that the workers' management system can create difficult employment problems for both the individual enterprise and the national economy. Even though the workers' council has the power to fire employees, it is obvious that it will hesitate very much to use this power and will rather not hire new workers because of difficulties in laying them off, "the result being an increase in the rate of unemployment in Yugoslavia." [8]

[6] J. Marcus Fleming and Victor R. Sertic, "The Yugoslav Economic System," *International Monetary Fund Staff Papers*, vol. 9, no. 2 (July 1962), p. 203.

[7] Macesich, p. 87.

[8] Svetozar Pejovich, *The Market-Planned Economy of Yugoslavia* (Minneapolis: University of Minnesota Press, 1966), p. 77. It could also be that the enterprise is reluctant to hire so as not to reduce the individual worker's share in the profit. However, this might also imply increased efficiency.

PLANNING IN YUGOSLAVIA

Planning in Yugoslavia today is no longer Soviet-style central planning. Detailed planning from the center, by command, and without support by the market, is rejected as dangerously bureaucratic, clumsy, stifling for the enterprises, incapable of coordinating the main branches of the economy, and neglecting the wishes of the consumers.[9] Nevertheless, while rejecting Soviet planning, Yugoslavia wants to retain a planned economy. Planning is to be supported by the pricing process so that a substantial degree of decentralization, both in operational planning and in the management of the enterprises, can be achieved.

The plan on the Federal government level has become a relatively brief document that tries to outline in broad estimates the desired development of the economy as to its direction and growth figures for the main branches. However, Yugoslav planning is not genetic planning; the plan is not a mere projection of past trends. The government has the power to determine the rate of accumulation and thus, at least potentially, the rate of economic growth.

The plan does not hand down more or less detailed figures through administrative channels. Government agencies at the lower level and the enterprises do not have to fulfill set quotas nor do they receive allotments of resources. They are free to formulate their own operational plans within the general framework of the Federal target plan, under consideration of local conditions and profit expectations. Technical knowledge and price signals guide the production decisions of the enterprises and the district governments. The latter are responsible for the creation of new enterprises, and they control, to some extent, the behavior of the directors of the enterprises, old and new.

This combination of planning with freedom permits many mixtures of planning and pricing, of central power and local autonomy, of state preferences and consumers' sovereignty. The picture of the Yugoslav economy, for example, could be painted so as to resemble a western market economy, with the only difference being that the enterprises would be publicly and not privately owned. The central plan would then be reduced to an estimate of output and income, the development of individual branches and sectors, employment conditions, credit supply, and so forth —not too different from the attempt of western governments to inform themselves of the general trend of their economies as basis for efficient

---

[9] See Macesich, chap. 5; Pejovich, chap. 2; Rudolf Bicanic, "Economic Growth Under Centralized and Decentralized Planning. Yugoslavia—A Case Study," in *Economic Development and Cultural Change* (Chicago: University of Chicago Press, 1957), pp. 64–75; Albert Waterston, *Planning in Yugoslavia: Organization and Implementation* (Baltimore: The Johns Hopkins Press, 1962), chap. 2.

monetary and fiscal controls. However, the government would decisively determine the rate of investment. It is possible that the Yugoslav economy may move in this liberal direction. For the present and the foreseeable future, though, this development does not seem likely.

The fact that the Federal plan no longer uses commands, that it speaks, instead, of "anticipations" and leaves leeway to local authorities to follow price-and-profit incentives can be deceiving. We shall see that the Federal government collects and distributes a decisive amount of the investment funds of the nation and does not allocate these funds according to neutral market principles. Furthermore, the prices that determine the actions of those who follow the profit incentive are in many instances set or controlled by the Federal government. The latter, therefore, is able to guide production through the arbitrary allocation of investment funds and through price controls despite the free decisions of the worker-managers. The Federal government thus can make production correspond to the general plan. Since these policies are not unknown in western economies, the difference is a matter of degree rather than of principle, a statement that could not equally be applied to a comparison of Yugo-slavia and Russia.

The true character of the Yugoslav economy can only be established by studying the price, monetary, credit, and fiscal policies of the Federal government.

PRICES IN YUGOSLAVIA

A discussion of prices in Yugoslavia can start from one of the two basic assumptions: (1) that prices are freely determined by demand and supply, but that the government reserves for itself the right to fix, control, or influence prices; or (2) that the system has nearly complete price control but the enterprises have the right to make price adjustments, if these are justified in the eyes of the authorities and expressly permitted.

Production and investment decisions of the enterprises are made on the basis of given prices and with the intention of maximizing profit. In this the Yugoslav system is more realistic than either the Soviet economy or Lange's liberal socialist model. The Soviet system maintains an artificial price pattern, which is not permitted to influence the decisions of the managers. We have seen, furthermore, that the present reform proposals have not indicated how correct prices could be set by the authorities or how the managers could greatly benefit by price changes, being, as they are, still subject to command concerning required output. Lange's imagi-nary price structure is exact—on paper. But the Yugoslav system has the practical advantage of being real and of permitting the worker-managers to act in their own best interest on the basis of price guidelines.

A model of the Yugoslav price system could rest on the following assumptions: Since the economy is to grow, the demand of the government for investment funds must be permitted to compete successfully with the demand of the citizens for consumer goods. Ideally, this competition would have to take place under conditions of monetary stability. The government would not create more new purchasing power than is justified by the economy's increase in productivity. The government, therefore, would have to finance its expenditures through turnover and profit taxes so that the demand for consumer goods would be reduced to the supply of these goods at stable prices. Also, the distribution of investment funds would have to correspond to the division of total production between consumer and producer goods and the intended growth of the different branches of production implied in the state preference function.

It is possible that the Yugoslav economy may gradually develop in line with this model, where price formation, including the rates of interest, would be entirely left to market forces.[10] But the present situation is far more complex and impure. Basically there exist four categories of prices: (1) prices that are free to adjust (however, enterprises can raise their prices only with government permission when increased costs "justify" the move); (2) ceiling prices on such items as copper, aluminum, or oil; (3) fixed prices on electric energy, transportation, utilities, and rents; and, finally, (4) support prices for certain agricultural products and export items.

Since the price policy of the government leads to prices that deviate from those prices that market forces would establish, while the economy is, nevertheless, based on a profit system and on prices as guidelines, it must be assumed that price distortions will often misdirect production even with respect to the preference schedule of the Federal Government.[11]

Wages are, strictly speaking, not prices in Yugoslavia. But the distribution of the wage portion of the profit of the Yugoslav enterprise follows certain wage patterns set uniformly for the whole country, while piece rates try to superimpose individual incentives on the profit incentive for the group. Whether the workers' management system will permit greater wage elasticity in the Yugoslav economy, thus making it somewhat less inflation-prone, remains to be seen. The ambitious investment pro-

---

[10] A considerable step in this direction was recently taken in connection with the devaluation of the dinar and the drastic lowering of customs duties. However, this attempt to return to real market prices led to great difficulties by suddenly revealing the enormous distortions that had been the result of investment and price controls. See "The Jugoslav Experiment," *The Economist*, London, July 16, 1966, pp. 237–240 and "Jugoslavia. Alarm Bells for the Economy," *The Economist*, London, December 3, 1966, p. 1021.

[11] It is interesting to note that Yugoslav authorities, trying to remove distortions in the price structure "have adopted the price pattern prevailing in the economies of Yugoslavia's trading partners as the main standard by which to guide their price policies." See Fleming and Sertic, p. 210.

gram of the government competes with the desire of the worker-managers to increase real wages. In the conflict between these forces the choice may be between inflation and unemployment, just as it is in the private enterprise economies of the West (or even more so, considering the much less developed state of the economy).

THE NATIONALIZATION OF CREDIT

Before discussing the accumulation and distribution of investment funds that play a decisive role in Yugoslav planning, it should be pointed out that here too, as in the case of workers' management, there has been a long evolution of socialist thought. Since Saint Amand Bazard (1791–1832) and Barthélemy Prosper Enfantin (1798–1864) we find, again and again, the view that social production could be uniformly regulated through a nationalization of the whole banking system. These followers of Claude Henri de Saint-Simon (1760–1825) thought of the government as a huge bank that administers all investment funds. A recent advocate of the nationalization of credit, Robert Deumer,[12] describes the advantages of his proposed system as follows: The competitive struggle for capital, which is characteristic of the private enterprise system, would cease. The total demand for capital would be classified according to urgency, necessity, and usefulness in the interest of the country as a whole. The superficial attractiveness of this proposal lies in the relatively minor reorganization of the banking system that produces a complete reorganization of the whole economy. Without the nationalization of individual industries, the economy could be guided according to a central plan via the distribution of credit by a unified, government-operated credit market. Since all producers, it is argued, are dependent on credit, the state can control the whole economy as soon as it has taken charge of all banks.

Those who want to distribute all investment funds in accordance with the state's preference function reject, as a rule, a distribution via a comparison of interest and profit rates. Sometimes they suggest that interest rates could be artificially lowered or even abolished, with the additional advantage of a corresponding reduction in production costs.

If nationalization of credit is combined with the private enterprise system, the result is a mixture of incompatible principles. Once the state decides on the "urgency, necessity, or mere usefulness" of production processes, consumers' sovereignty has been abolished. Yet the consumers are still free to spend their income and business men to follow the profit motive. What will happen to an economy where the government allocates

[12] Robert Deumer, *Die Verstaatlichung des Kredits* (München und Leipzig: Duncker & Humblot, 1926).

investment funds so that the expansion of different branches of industry conflicts with the wishes of the consumers and the motivations of the producers? What if the industries whose products are in demand but are not considered urgent or necessary by the government cannot expand owing to insufficient credit allocations? Obviously, the prices of these products will rise, thereby increasing profits. May these profits then be plowed back? In other words, is self-financing permitted to circumvent the government's banking monopoly?

In a centrally planned command economy, the artificial distribution of productive resources is implied in the general scheme of things, and the banking system becomes a mere auditing apparatus. In the Yugoslav case, however, the nationalization of credit takes on a different meaning. It has the very important function of "putting teeth" into the Federal target plan by distributing credits from the Federal funds according to the preference schedule of the state. Yet, at the same time, the local administrations and the enterprises are free in their decisions, particularly in so far as they can manage to be partly independent of these Federal allocations of credit.

YUGOSLAV INVESTMENT POLICIES

The Yugoslav economy enjoys one of the main advantages of planning: the government decides on the rate of accumulation and growth. About one third of the social product is channeled into investment, a high rate for a poor country. However, only about 60 percent of the investment funds come from the Federal government, indicating possible elbowroom for local administrations and enterprises.

The sources of investment funds are, as usual, different kinds of taxes (including the capital tax, which really amounts to interest payments on Federal loans), profit allocations to investment, amortization funds, and credit creation by the National Bank. The distribution of investment funds at the disposal of the Federal government is managed by the Investment and Agricultural Banks, which follow the preference scale of the government. This means that credit is artificially allocated to the different branches of the economy according to their importance. Within these noncompetitive sectors of the credit market, however, the allocation of investment funds follows competitive procedures.[13] Periodically, the In-

---

[13] Thus the distribution of credit in Yugoslavia is similar to certain exchange control systems in which the foreign exchange market is first cut apart into watertight compartments (the supply depending on the degree of urgency of certain imports) while the allocation within the sectors is left to some form of auctioning. See, for example, the proposal by Robert Triffin in "National Central Banking and the International Economy," *International Monetary Policies. Post-war Economic Studies*, No. 7 (Washington, D.C.: Board of Governors of the Federal Reserve System, 1947), p. 69.

vestment Bank makes it known which industries will receive loans and invites enterprises of these industries to bid for funds. Obviously, the credits cannot simply be given to those enterprises that are willing to pay the highest rate of interest.[14] Instead, the Investment Bank makes loans on the basis of such criteria as profitability, capital output ratios, length of credit period, ability to repay and to meet interest charges, and the balance-of-payments implications of the investment project. In addition, the borrower may be asked to finance part of the investment out of his own resources—an important point where the availability of investment funds on the communal or enterprise level endangers the tautness of Yugoslav planning.

GENERAL APPRAISAL

In a general appraisal of the Yugoslav system we must emphasize the importance of the Federal government's accumulation and distribution of investment funds. The remarkable growth of the Yugoslav economy rests on this planned division between investment and consumer goods production. Total saving is independent of the high propensity to consume, which, otherwise, would be characteristic of a poor economy.

Whether or not central investment planning violates the principle of consumers' sovereignty is a question of interpretation. If, within the consumer goods sector, production follows the wishes of the consumers as expressed by real market prices, consumers' sovereignty can be said to exist in spite of the fact that a very large part of the productive resources is reserved for capital goods production. More critical may be the fact that a consistent pricing process is not permitted to operate and that the decisions of the worker-managers accordingly may lead to misallocations even where it is the government's intention to let production be guided by both consumer and state preference functions.

It seems that Yugoslav authorities consider free market pricing a

[14] This could not even be true for a private enterprise economy of strictest observance. Yet "it was believed in Yugoslavia from December 1953 until sometime in 1955 that the competitive rate of interest was the best possible device for the allocation of investment funds from the General Investment Fund. . . . Yugoslav economists believed that higher interest rates offered should indicate higher prospective rates of return on investment. . . . The high expectations for the system in which the competitive rate of interest was the allocator of funds among competing users within the industry . . . turned to bitter disappointment. In order to get loans enterprises tended to offer higher rates than they could reasonably afford, so that their applications had a better chance to be intramarginal. . . . Since this behavior was more or less common to all enterprises the result was that the marginal rate of interest rose too high relative to the expected net returns." Pejovich, pp. 19–20.

proper method by which to guide production in the consumer goods industries, but feel that the same pricing process could not simultaneously accommodate the state's preferences. According to Macesich [15] the divergence of individual demand and community interests leads to various methods "for influencing the market so that it will behave in a way thought to be in the 'communist interest,' especially in regard to achieving a rapid rate of economic growth." The two most important instruments for this purpose are the artificial compartmentalization of the credit market and direct price controls. However, in a system that is neither all planned nor consistently guided by uniform prices, it can happen that the two policies are applied at cross purposes. An enterprise, for instance, may be kept from expanding by being excluded from cheap Federal credit, but induced to expand by high prices and high profits, particularly when the latter secure independence from the Investment Bank.

There is no real need for this inconsistency. The mere decision of the Federal government to spend given sums on investment goods would lead to sufficient profitability in the desired industries. Here, as in the Liberman proposals, we find the strange attitude that an omnipotent government justifies development expenditures by making them appear cheaper than they are. Where, as in Yugoslavia today, price guidelines are the main prop of operational planning, the enterprises and communes must make their decisions on the basis of profit considerations. Thus the tampering with prices becomes potentially more dangerous than in an economy of the Soviet type.

If consistency is essential for economic factor allocation, it is wrong to falsify the process through noncompetitive credit markets. No wonder the Yugoslav economy is still characterized by some of the major disproportions that plague the Soviet economy. But while a fully planned economy can rely on its bureaucratic integration and can go on pretending that the uneven development of its branches corresponds to the intentions of the planners, the Yugoslav economy will expose itself to more visible dangers. Having entrusted its functioning to a considerable degree to markets and the profit motive, it will be exposed to the twin evils of unemployment and inflation.

Price inflation often results from trying to reach a combined level of consumption and investment that overtaxes the available resources. Once this overheating of the economy has begun, stabilizing monetary policies can be applied only at the cost of unemployment. But not even inflation is an absolutely sure means to avoid sectional unemployment. As in the western economies, monopolistic forces in Yugoslavia can produce inflation and it is doubtful that the workers' council system will provide that wage elasticity downward which the market economies have largely lost. A

[15] Macesich, p. 64.

system with watertight sectional divisions of the credit market could very well produce a combination of unemployment and inflation, particularly when the enterprises are hesitant to employ workers who are difficult to fire and who would be sharing in the profit.

The compartmentalized credit markets and the other forms of Yugoslav price control prevent the Federal government from achieving its target planning under full consideration of opportunity costs. Mises' problem has not been solved in Yugoslavia, but a solution is perhaps more possible than in either the Soviet economy or in a system that follows the Lange blueprint. However, a development which would follow Mises' suggestions could easily put the workers' councils into a dangerously strong position. Even today the system has no reliable competitive brakes when we consider the great incentive that the enterprises have to increase profits if they want to gain independent investment funds.

The Yugoslav economy has the merit of having shown that a socialist system, decidedly different from the Soviet model, can be made to operate. It has used ideas that had enjoyed acclaim for many years but had not been practical before. The Yugoslav economy has the attractive feature of being a "mixed" system, a "market-planned" economy,[16] and has been hailed as a liberal socialist economy, though it cannot be interpreted as proving the feasibility of the Lange blueprint. It is a hybrid, ambiguous and ambivalent, whose proper classification is impossible on the basis of the few available stereotypes. Yugoslavia has gone much farther in decentralizing than Liberman and his colleagues dared. Yet the Yugoslav economy remains a planned economy and it is doubtful whether we can see in it the long sought-after symbiosis of central plan and market mechanism.

---

[16] The title of S. Pejovich's book is *The Market-Planned Economy of Yugoslavia.*

CHAPTER 23

The Economics
of Central
Administration
(Germany 1933-1945)

WAR ECONOMICS

During World War II democratic market economies were subjected to a degree of central planning that would be impossible in peacetime. Strange as it may seem, total war simplifies the economic problem. Consumers' sovereignty and even free choice of occupation can be abolished if they interfere with the one and only aim of winning the war.

Theoretically, a market economy at war could still rely predominantly on the price system. It could reduce consumption, not by rationing and priorities, but simply by transferring sufficient consumers' purchasing power to the hands of the government. The government could then successfully compete for the factors of production by outbidding consumers. We could maintain free choice of occupation as long as the industries that produce war materiel were enabled to compete successfully in the labor market against industries engaged in peacetime production. Needless to say, the government could make the production of weapons profitable enough.

Why, then, are the principles of the market economy not applied in times of total war? Three main reasons can be cited:

1. The change-over to war production cannot be left to the slow-

working processes of the market. The sudden creation or enlargement of a military establishment belongs to the category of tasks where *ex ante* integration of the production processes becomes imperative. It may be that market forces could do the job more economically, but they would take too much time.

2. The tremendous change that total war necessitates in the pattern of production would lead to enormous changes in the structure of prices. The ultimate importance of winning the war would justify paying the most exorbitant prices imaginable for strategic materials. Different industries, though technically cooperating, would bid against one another for scarce labor and scarce investment funds. Exorbitant price changes would lead to extreme shifts in the distribution of the national income. Simultaneously, consumer goods would become increasingly scarce as a growing share of the national product is diverted to war production. The combination of a changing income distribution and an acute scarcity of consumer goods would lead to changes in consumer goods prices which would be considered socially unbearable.

3. The situation just described would develop even if the government succeeded in collecting all the revenue it needed through normal, that is, noninflationary, channels. Historical experience, however, has shown that this is practically impossible. Even where the operation of market forces has been replaced by direct controls, it has been impossible to avoid inflation. Were the government to compete for the needed resources on a free market, the inflationary impact of total war would become much greater. Inflation would eventually become the main instrument by which to reduce consumption in favor of armament production. The distribution of the national income, in both monetary and real terms, would become even more unbearable.

This is common knowledge. We have only to add that war production itself needs planned integration. The general staff has to think in terms of production priorities, of coordination, of distribution of available equipment among the different theaters of war, and so forth. This task could not be handled by the price mechanism. It is doubtful that thinking in terms of opportunity costs will influence the major decisions of the military leaders. A rise in interest rates, for example, would hardly induce a less capital-intensive production of missiles.

Once we dispense with the market mechanism, we have to replace it by the expedient of direct controls. Take the case of gasoline. If its price were permitted to increase drastically, the lower income groups would be without adequate transportation facilities. But as soon as a ceiling price for gasoline has been established, demand will exceed supply. Ceiling prices, therefore, must be accompanied by rationing. Now that only *less* than formerly can be bought at *lower* prices, unused purchasing power piles up in the hands of consumers and looks for outlets in other markets, where newly developing scarcities will soon call for further controls. It should also be noticed that ceiling prices reduce the willingness of producers to supply more of the scarce article. Production of the more important commodities, therefore, must be guided by central administration rather than by the profit motive.

Therefore, in the case of a national emergency the private enterprise system tends toward central controls and eliminates, to a large extent, the pricing process. But this does not entitle us to draw the conclusion that central control is superior to the profit system. Whenever we try to satisfy the wishes of consumers we must revert to a comprehensive system of cost accounting that only the market economy can provide. Central control is superior when it is necessary to reach one overriding aim, which is so predominant that the economic freedoms normally characteristic of the market economy are willingly dispensed with—even in a democracy. In trying to accomplish this common aim people stop taking their own wishes too seriously. "Freedom is in such danger that, paradoxically, it no longer matters." [1]

Thus we are not entitled to conclude that what was right and possible in war must be right and possible in peace. Nevertheless, war experiences are important for the student of social systems. They prove, first of all, that central administration can be successful if we subordinate our economic freedoms to a single purpose; second, they acquaint us with methods of allocation that can be substituted for the price mechanism; third, they impress upon us that something can be done to achieve full employment; and, fourth, they help us understand some of the basic features of authoritarian capitalism.

AUTHORITARIAN CAPITALISM (FASCISM)

In the preceding chapters we have seen how authoritarian socialism established a centrally planned economy. We shall now discuss the National Socialist economy in Germany (1933–1945) as the most outstanding example of authoritarian capitalism. We are interested in only the main structural features of this economy, which maintained the exterior façade of a private enterprise system. References to administrative detail will be kept to a minimum.

Even less than in the Soviet case can we indicate a point of time at which this authoritarian economy emerged. Hitler's system of central administration grew gradually and, to some extent, even without the intention

---

[1] Barbara Wootton, *Freedom under Planning* (Chapel Hill, N.C.: University of North Carolina Press, 1945), p. 89.

of the responsible leaders. As in Russia, there was no blueprint available. Certainly, the program of the National Socialist German Labor party (NSDAP) cannot be considered a blueprint. In spite of the party's promise that "unearned" income would be abolished, that land would be confiscated without compensation for communal purposes, and that the bondage of interest slavery would be broken, nothing very revolutionary happened when Hitler came to power. When the National Socialist economy developed into a command economy, it did so via an entirely different route than was suggested in the party program. In outward appearance the German economy remained a private enterprise economy. Nevertheless, it changed gradually and imperceptibly until it was centrally directed even before World War II broke out.

Whether an economy of central administration should be referred to as capitalism is a matter of terminology. Marxists may claim that National Socialism was the logical development of monopoly capitalism, in other words, that a change in the political superstructure was necessitated by a change in the mode of production. The protagonists of the market economy, on the other hand, are not willing to consider Hitler's command economy a private enterprise system. They point out that the National Socialist economy resembled the private enterprise economy only superficially, while in essence it was much more like the Soviet system—a centrally directed economy whose production process was no longer guided by market forces.

HITLER'S FULL-EMPLOYMENT POLICIES

Upon coming to power Hitler [2] proclaimed a Four Year Plan for a "concerted and all-embracing attack on unemployment." The measures to be employed to that end differed only in degree from those adopted by democratic governments. The gist of the German recovery policy, "initial ignition" via government deficit spending, had the express purpose of stimulating *private* investment. Government spending and tax remission were to taper off as soon as private consumption and investment became strong enough to guarantee a high level of employment. [3]

In 1933–1934 Hitler was opposed to direct government interference. His aim was to increase aggregate spending and to put to work forces that are now referred to as multiplier and accelerator. [4]

The initial ignition program was a failure as far as the effects of deficit

[2] *The Speeches of Hitler: April 1922–August 1939*, ed. Norman H. Baynes, vol. 1 (New York: Oxford University Press, 1942), p. 114.
[3] See Chap. 9.
[4] See Chap. 8.

spending on private investment were concerned. Business did not react favorably; it did not trust a regime that had come into power on a socialist program. Indeed, the radical wing of the National Socialist party interpreted the whole recovery policy as a short-run concession to momentarily indispensable capitalist forces.

There was a more important reason for the recovery program's failure: it was too inflation-conscious and therefore, not courageous enough. This cautious attitude expressed itself throughout the whole period 1933–1945. Wages were kept at the very low levels to which they had fallen during the preceding depression. Increasing consumer purchasing power was supposed to result from increasing employment and not from increasing wage rates. The wage-price spiral was to be avoided at all cost.

Here we meet a decisive difference between the German recovery policy and the full-employment policies which were followed in democratic countries. Only a totalitarian regime can combine a low-wage policy with general economic expansion. Democratic governments have to accept the results of collective bargaining. But a low-wage policy does not go well together with the intention of stimulating private investment via the multiplier effect. Inflation-conscious Germans saw the multiplier as that dangerous velocity of circulation of money that had played a decisive part in the German hyperinflation of 1923.

An interesting detail of the German work-creation program was the establishment of a special committee, under H. Schacht, with dictatorial powers in all financial matters. The committee determined the extent of credit creation, being empowered to halt the whole employment program at the first signs of price inflation.

As a result of its cautious nature the early Nazi recovery program mostly benefited *primary* employment, that is, employment created in industries and on projects where government funds were directly expended and in industries that supplied them with raw materials. As has been mentioned, *secondary* effects on private investment were at first highly desired but were not readily forthcoming. Much of the money earned was not spent again but was used instead for the repayment of debt or for building up new savings; this constituted a leakage in the multiplier effect.

Since private investment was not willing to take over, the government had to shoulder an ever-increasing investment burden in an effort to reach, and maintain, full employment. However, the situation could have been saved by any large-scale investment program and not only by rearmament. As a matter of fact, such investment programs (in housing, road construction, and so forth) competed with armaments up to the beginning of World War II.

By 1935 the National Socialists realized with satisfaction that the failure of private business to recover was not so bad after all. Increasing private investment in the consumer goods industries would soon have been incompatible with the regime's growing ambitions.

ELIMINATION OF THE PRICING PROCESS

During the beginning of the recovery period (1933–1934) Hitler still emphasized the importance of economic freedom. The economy had to be liberated "from the chaos of oppressive regulations and of restrictive measures" that were "stifling economic life." He also said that "the initiative thus taken by the State had always solely as its aim and purpose to awake private economic initiative, and thus slowly to set economic life once more on its own feet." [5]

But as early as 1935 Hitler admitted that the National Socialists had taken the path to a planned economy, "a perilous adventure; for planned economics lead to bureaucratic control and thus to the suppression of individual creative effort." In the same speech he gave a good picture of the planned character of the German economy in 1935:

> What we have achieved in two and a half years in the way of a planned provision of labor, a planned regulation of the market, a planned control of prices and wages, was considered a few years ago to be absolutely impossible. . . . In order to guarantee the functioning of the national economy it was necessary first of all to put a stop to the everlasting oscillations of wages and prices. It was further necessary to remove the conditions giving rise to interference which did not spring from higher national economic necessities, i.e., to destroy the class organizations of both camps which lived on the politics of wages and prices.

Although the measures used at that time were still mild in comparison with what was to follow, one cannot miss the authoritarian attitude in the passage quoted above. It had not taken much time to move from a policy of stimulating private enterprise to a policy in which any expression of economic freedom by citizens was frowned upon as "interference."

Hitler was probably indifferent concerning which methods were used, as long as his aims were achieved. By 1935 he was politically ready to start his armament program, and to make a great effort to become as independent as possible from foreign supplies. Hitler was aware that these programs were another big step in the direction of central planning, but he argued that it was "a question of existence or nonexistence."

When Hitler declared that "in order to guarantee the functioning of

[5] *The Speeches of Hitler*, vol. 1, ed. Baynes, pp. 886, 910–911, 927–928.

the national economy it was necessary first of all to put a stop to the ever-lasting oscillations of wages and prices," he rejected, perhaps unconsciously, the very basis of the market economy. For guidance through prices he substituted a constantly growing number of direct controls, which, after some coordination, amounted to a system of central economic administration.

The wishes of the people (whether as consumers, workers, industrialists, or farmers) were considered "interfering" when they tended to clash with the aims of the "nation." And since the wishes of the people found expression in price and wage movements, these market reactions were suppressed and replaced by administrative procedures through which the economy could be made to conform to the dictator's wishes.

Such price and wage controls suggested themselves also as a direct method to stem price inflation. Fear of monetary disorders was an obsession with Hitler. It is worth remembering that his first bid for power on November 9, 1923 was made 6 days before the stabilization of the German mark and that, when, nearly 10 years later, he was appointed Chancellor, in January 1933, the German economy was again grievously suffering from monetary disorders; only this time it was severe deflation with concomitant depression and mass unemployment.

Gustav Stolper [6] said rightly "that no historical experience, not even the defeat in the [first] World War and the Treaty of Versailles, left such deep impression on the minds of the German people as the utter collapse of the German currency."

The strange phenomena of hyperinflation had impressed the early Nazis: the increasing use made of the printing press, the fantastic rise of the velocity of circulation of money, price increases by more than a trillion times, and an even worse depreciation of the mark in terms of foreign currencies. While most people lost their savings and those living on fixed incomes their whole livelihood, persons who had access to bank credit grew rich overnight. This gigantic reshuffling of income and wealth caused bitter resentment. That the National Socialists could rouse the anger of the dispossessed was not astonishing. It was strange, however, that the party's own monetary and fiscal program was extremely inflationist.

In point 11 of the party program "abolition of the thraldom of interest" is demanded. This was to be accomplished by issuing money for purposes of residential and public construction, the money being backed by the capital goods so created. The government could finance its expenditures without having to pay interest. The most fantastic assumption

---

[6] Gustav Stolper, German Economy 1870–1940 (New York: Reynal & Hitchcock, 1940), p. 235. After the inflation, the author of the present volume asked many Germans which they would rather go through again, the war or the inflation. The answer was, without exception, "the war."

was that, while the creation of too much paper currency would create price inflation, the creation of checkbook money was innocuous.[7]

These theories gave hopes to those opposed to the National Socialists that, if Hitler ever got into power, he would ruin the German economy and thereby lose his hold on the German people. However, when the National Socialists did get into power they adopted, *volte face*, a policy that was extremely inflation conscious. Some economic policies can be understood only when we keep in mind that Hitler feared inflation perhaps more than anything else.

The National Socialists managed, indeed, to "forbid" inflation, that is, to repress it by command. The great disadvantage of repressed inflation in a private enterprise economy, namely, that it freezes the price pattern, was actually welcomed by the Hitler regime. Since price variations were considered interfering, they were sacrificed without regret.

We cannot discuss in detail the frequently changing price regulations by which the National Socialist government tried to combine anti-inflation policies with central production control. The policy was not uniform and grew in scope and rigidity as full employment and rearmament made the German economy more vulnerable to price inflation. The freezing of the price pattern proved so stifling that it necessitated more and more direct controls if production was to continue. We have already seen that repressed inflation can be even worse than open price inflation. In an open inflation, price relations, though distorted, are still the result of market forces, while the frozen prices of a repressed inflation gradually lose all connection with reality.

To prevent private firms from producing for wrong markets (guided, as they were, by wrong prices), price controls had to be accompanied by direct allocations of productive resources and by stringent investment controls.

We turn now to some of the more important controls that replaced the working of market forces in the National Socialist economy.

WAGE CONTROLS AND THE ALLOCATION OF LABOR

We saw that Hitler maintained a low wage level as a basis of inflation-proof expansion to full employment. The achievement of full employment did not lead to a change in this policy. On the contrary, his

---

[7] For a discussion of this theory see Franz Haber, *Untersuchungen über Irrtümer Moderner Geldverbesserer* (Jena: Gustav Fischer, 1926). In a discussion that the author of the present volume had with Rudolf Hess on problems of inflation in 1923, Hess, too, insisted on the different effects of pocketbook and checkbook money. A better argument was that, once in power, the National Socialists would stabilize prices by decree. However, had the National Socialists followed their original ideas of eliminating inte░░░░

determination to keep wages low was strengthened by the realization that labor's position in a sellers' market would be too strong if collective bargaining were permitted. On the whole, wages were kept at the depression level of 1933, but increasing employment led to increasing total earnings.

The Law for the Regulation of National Labor (1934) eliminated collective bargaining and established the "leadership principle" in each enterprise. The owner or manager of the firm was the "leader," who cooperated with his employees as "followers" for the benefit of the people and the state. The "leader" determined the conditions of work, including wages. In this task he was advised by a "confidential council" selected from, but not elected by, the "followers." Although the council could not overrule the decisions of the "leader," it could, in case of conflict, appeal to the so-called "trustee of labor," a government official.

Thus it seemed as though the breaking-up of labor unions and the abolition of collective bargaining had indeed established the employer as the decisive figure in labor relations. This impression supported early beliefs that Hitler's aim was the revival of capitalism in its most conservative form.

In reality, however, the trustee of labor had unlimited power to dictate the conditions of work, including wages, hours of work, the right to fire, and so forth. Any regulation issued by the trustee for his district superseded existing agreements or decisions made unilaterally by the leader-manager. The trustees, of course, had to carry out Hitler's instructions.

The government's complete control of labor relations was not restricted by the Labor Front, a party organization that included both employers and employees. By no stretch of the imagination could the Labor Front be interpreted as a labor union. It was supposed to foster mutual understanding between employers and employees, it supervised vocational training, and it took over some of the cooperative and insurance functions of the defunct labor unions. Indeed, it had even less influence than do Russian workers' organizations, which can at least try to influence the plan in its formative stage.

Since wage rates were no longer determined on the labor market, labor could not be expected to be automatically guided into the industries that needed it most. Labor had to be allocated by command: free choice of occupation was abolished. In 1935 the so-called labor book, a kind of passport that contained a description of the training and career of the worker, was introduced. This book had to be handed over to the employer, who, under certain conditions, could refuse to hand it back, thus freezing the worker in his job. Labor offices had complete files that enabled them to guide labor according to the government's priorities. The Labor Draft

ough money creation, no ceiling price policy could have stemmed the inflationist

Law of 1938, which eventually applied to all inhabitants of Germany, enabled the government to shift individual workers as well as whole gangs of workers from one place to another. It should be remembered that these regulations originated in a peacetime economy.

INVESTMENT CONTROLS

It is obvious that investment must be centrally regulated in a command economy. But how was investment to be controlled where private enterprise was left in charge of production? No attempt was made to nationalize even the most strategic industries. Nevertheless, the national resources had to be used according to the production pattern which Hitler's priority scheme demanded.

Since private property in the material means of production was maintained, government investment in armaments, synthetic raw materials, and so forth, took the form of an expansion of the productive capacity of private enterprise. Private firms produced what the government wanted, and the government, in turn, saw that the firms got sufficient allocations. An attractive margin between costs and prices was permitted. These profits did not guide production, however, and their reinvestment was subject to government control.

The coordination of industrial production was entrusted to representatives of the business community rather than to a bureaucracy unacquainted with the problems of industry and trade. Since the concentration of economic power had gone far in Germany, this arrangement was relatively easy. Former cartel leaders could now become chairmen of "Economic Groups." Many industrialists were quite willing to wield the additional power conferred upon them as representatives of the government. Private monopoly and public power merged. The aims, however, continued to be those of the National Socialist command economy.[8]

As in Russia, the whole production process of the nation had to be coordinated in one comprehensive plan once guidance through market prices had been abolished. How was this coordination accomplished?

First, it was necessary to collect statistical data for all industries and groups of industries. From these figures the physical balances of input and output had to be derived.

Secondly, these figures and balances had to be used to accomplish the needed over-all integration. Each industry's output had to be seen as the input of other industries. Or, to put it differently, the physical balances for the different economic groups had to be coordinated—an extremely difficult task, as we saw in the discussion of authoritarian socialism. In the National

[8] See Heinz Paechter, "Recent Trends in the German Command Economy," *Journal of Political Economy*, vol. 52 (1944), pp. 217–233.

Socialist economy it became customary to concentrate on bottlenecks, that is, on those spots where severe shortages endangered the plan.

Thirdly, the individual firms were told what, how much, and when to produce. Simultaneously, they were given priorities for the purchase of the materials needed to fulfill these orders and an attractive margin between costs and price.

Finally, constant check had to be kept on the fulfillment of the plan.[9]

The basic similarity between planning procedures in the National Socialist and Soviet economies is not surprising. With the elimination of the price system as automatic allocation procedure, it is necessary to design a conscious process of bureaucratic-technical integration of the production processes. That the German planning procedure was less ponderous, less visible and, perhaps, somewhat more elastic, may be due to the fact that the task was handed to the leading businessmen in each industrial branch. Also, the Hitler regime had inherited a better-proportioned industrial structure than the Soviet planners were able to evolve.

Had Hitler's economy remained a peacetime economy, our criticism would have to be the same as in the Soviet case, namely, that a system of bureaucratic integration does not lead to the most economical use of the means of production. Since, however, Hitler's economy was geared, practically from the beginning, to the simple priority scheme of all-out war, the advantages of *ex ante* planning overshadowed this disadvantage.

FINANCIAL ARRANGEMENTS

The outwardly capitalist character of the National Socialist economy implied financial arrangements that differ from those of the Russian plan. The principles were simple. Private industry was required to use its profits to finance investments desired by the government. In order to pay for armaments, road construction, synthetics production, and so forth, the government collected a substantial part of the nation's income. Whatever additional funds were needed for government-planned projects could be borrowed in the credit market, whose organization ensured smooth compliance with the government's will.

The work-creation program was financed by so-called work-creation bills. These bills were issued by private firms, accepted by the authorities in charge of the projects, discounted by the commercial banks and rediscounted by the Reichsbank. In these arrangements we can detect the government's desire to imitate as closely as possible the creation of money on the basis of commercial paper.[10] National Socialist financial experts

[9] See Walter Eucken, *Grundsätze der Wirtschaftspolitik* (Hamburg: Rowohlt, 1959), pp. 61–63.

[10] See George N. Halm, *Economics of Money and Banking* (Homewood, Ill.: Richard D. Irwin, Inc., 1961), pp. 109–111.

argued that, with the success of the work creation program, the bills could be redeemed out of increasing public revenues. Indeed, it was correct to assume that increasing economic activity would permit a substantial amount of credit creation without price inflation. The imitation of short-term commercial paper was mere rigmarole, however.

More straightforward were two other measures. The Dividend Limitation Law of 1934 demanded that dividends above 6 percent be invested in Government bonds; while the Law for the Regulation of Credit (also of 1934) made the whole banking system subject to complete government control.

In the spring of 1938 the government stopped using short-term bills for fear that credit creation would cause too much inflationary pressure. By now the government had full control of the credit market, could enforce the purchase of its bonds, and could restrict the private issue of bonds and shares. There was considerable purchasing power, which could no longer be spent on consumer goods and could instead be mopped up for yet another round of Government spending—a typical sign of repressed inflation.

It would be interesting to know to what extent the financial arrangements of the National Socialists were mere window dressing. Possibly they were meant seriously. The preservation of the capitalist framework of the economy made it necessary to use the financial apparatus of the private enterprise economy. Furthermore, Hitler was deeply concerned about possible inflationary developments. It is possible that the National Socialists, underestimating the economic powers of a totalitarian regime, were overconcerned about monetary problems and that Hitler was much more timid in the field of finance than in his political and military ventures. Thus, by the irony of fate, Hitler's monetary scruples may have helped to win the war for his enemies.[11]

In connection with the discussion of financial matters it should be mentioned that, once in power, Hitler did nothing to abolish the interest rate as unearned income, that is, to abolish the "thraldom of interest." However, the system of central administration deprived the rate of interest of its important function of allocating investment funds in the most economical manner.

AGRICULTURE AND FOREIGN TRADE

Next to the creation of full employment, Hitler most wanted to improve the position of the farmer. "Within four years," said Hitler on February 1, 1933, "the German peasant must be rescued from the quag-

[11] See Burton Klein, "Germany's Preparation for War: A Re-Examination," *American Economic Review*, vol. 38 (March 1948), p. 73.

mire into which he has fallen." [12] Furthermore, Germany's supply of food and raw materials was to be made as independent as possible of foreign sources.

As early as 1933 the whole agricultural sector of the German economy had been organized in the so-called Reichs Food Estate, a "self-administered" statutory corporation, which included all persons connected in any way with the production, processing, and distribution of agricultural products. The term "estate" gives to this and other organizations an aura of medieval glory but hinders rathei than increases our understanding, for it implies an autonomy which the estates did not enjoy. They were organs of the central administration.

It was relatively easy to eliminate price fluctuations in the field of agriculture. Strict regulation of agricultural imports and exports could largely adjust supply to demand, while remaining domestic oscillations in supply could be offset by government sales and purchases. The farmer paid for this protection against price fluctuations by having to accept innumerable bureaucratic controls. The nation as a whole paid for increasing self-sufficiency through sharply increasing production costs, in other words, through loss of the advantages of international division of labor.

A centrally directed economy with price and production controls cannot permit freedom of international trade. The planned economy must be protected against unforeseeable changes in exports and imports. In Russia the needed insulation against the vagaries of world trade is accomplished through a state monopoly that controls all exports and imports. The National Socialist economy achieved virtually the same result through foreign exchange controls. Foreign trade was left in private hands, but what the private traders were permitted to do was strictly and minutely regulated by the government.

The foreign exchange control measures of the National Socialist economy were fantastically complicated. The major principles of foreign exchange control, however, were quite simple to understand. Essentially, exchange control is a combination of ceiling prices and rationing on the foreign exchange market. The government establishes a price (in terms of its own currency) for the basic unit of each foreign currency. For all or most of these currencies, however, the rate established is lower than the equilibrium rate, just as the price of gasoline, in wartime, is kept much lower than the market situation justifies. The demand for foreign currencies exceeds the supply at the official rate and must be artificially restrained. The allocation of foreign exchange through the government leads to imports in conformance with the requirements of the plan. Regarding imports, the administration has to make four major decisions: "(1) how much to allot for different *purposes* (commodity imports, debt

---

[12] *The Speeches of Hitler*, vol. 1, ed. Baynes, p. 114.

service, tourist traffic); (2) how to distribute the exchange available for imports among different *commodities*; (3) how to ration exchange among different *firms*; and (4) how to distribute the total among different *countries*." [13]

In order to be able to allocate foreign exchange to the uses it considers most important, the government must get hold of incoming foreign exchange. All exporters must be made to sell their foreign exchange earnings to the government at the official price. Since this price is artificially low, exporting is not attractive to private traders and must be stimulated by subsidies that improve the exporter's competitive position on the foreign market.

Hitler developed foreign exchange controls into an instrument for the monopolistic control of international trade, the circumvention of commercial treaties, and the establishment of bilateral clearing agreements under which the accumulation of German debts could by itself be used to exert pressure on foreign creditors.

THE NATURE OF THE NATIONAL SOCIALIST ECONOMY

Was the National Socialist economy a capitalist or a socialist system? Probably it was neither; it wanted to be quite different from both. The Hitler economy can, perhaps, be understood best as a kind of war economy able to operate in peacetime. What democratic countries could do only under the impact of war, the dictator could undertake to do 6 years before the outbreak of hostilities. The totalitarian regime can dissolve labor unions, abolish collective bargaining, freeze wages and prices, control the distribution of resources—can do all this and more without having to wait for a national emergency in which the people are ready to forego important economic liberties.

Let us see what remained of the private enterprise character of the German economy under Hitler.

1. The outer shell was preserved. The new organizations and controls were not overtly against private enterprise; they were designed to overcome difficulties connected with depression, dependence on foreign supplies, shortages of foreign exchange, inflation, and rearmament. All deviations from the straight market system seemed to be as temporary as the emergencies requiring direct controls. It is understandable that many Germans held the belief that sometime in the future all these various controls would be removed to make room again for the operation of market forces.

2. It would have been possible for Hitler to go back to a system with fewer controls and an increased emphasis on price fluctuations. The basic

[13] League of Nations, *International Currency Experience*, 1944, p. 173.

institutions of private property and private enterprise were still preserved. The success of the German "social market economy" after 1948 is proof of the fact that the price system was able to take over.

3. In several instances the National Socialist economy prided itself as representing a return to a free economy rather than a movement toward central planning. The destruction of the labor unions, the increasing power of the employer as "leader" in all labor relations, the emphatic refusal to nationalize the banking system, and the importance of big business in the administration of industrial production—all these were interpreted as evidences of a "purer" form of capitalism, purer in the sense of being more uncompromising and more extreme. Of course, such policies were also more in conformance with the Marxist idea of what capitalism would be like before its downfall.

4. For many years the leaders of the National Socialist economy continued to think financially in terms of private enterprise. Indeed, they were unaware of all the economic implications, possibilities, and potentialities of the system of controls that they had created. They learned faster in some instances than in others. Exchange control measures, for example, were exploited to the utmost. Domestic monetary problems, on the other hand, seemed to have worried these leaders more than the facts warranted.

The above points, then, might be used to argue that National Socialism was either a kind of monopolistic supercapitalism or an essential market economy reluctantly forced to use controls. On the other hand, one might contend that the totalitarian, centralist character of Hitler's economy indisputably deprived it of the right to be called a private enterprise system. It depends, of course, on what is considered the essence of a private enterprise system. If, instead of emphasizing its monopolistic features, we stress the unplanned character of the market economy, consumers' sovereignty, and free choice of occupation, then increasing controls would be alien and dangerous. While each individual regulation may appear comparatively unimportant, all controls together may amount to a complete change in the economic climate.

The following points can be made by those who believe that National Socialism must not be identified with the private enterprise system:

1. The forces of the market were replaced by direct controls.

2. Much of the capitalist appearance of the National Socialist economy was mere window dressing designed to make the crude fact of a command economy less obvious. Its leaders tried to create the impression of a maintenance or even a revival of free enterprise, while the facts pointed clearly in the other direction. The regime was eager to maintain the appearance of personal freedom when, in reality, its citizens had no choice whatever. Although membership in the Labor Front, for example, was voluntary, it was impossible to get employment without membership.

3. The regime theoretically could have reverted to the principles of a market economy, but it also could have shed its capitalist skin to show its true nature as a command economy. Private ownership of the means of production is of doubtful significance if production is centrally planned. The government could have fulfilled its promise to abolish income unearned by work. Since prices, wages, and profits had lost their guiding functions, there was no need to maintain the income distribution that had been inherited.

4. The more we emphasize the element of economic freedom, the less can the National Socialist system qualify as a private enterprise economy. The question of free choice loses all meaning in a regime that, through its propaganda ministry, controls the minds of the people until they can no longer distinguish what they themselves want from what the government wants them to want. Such a system has reached its aim when the people are so thoroughly indoctrinated or intimidated that they "freely" act as the government expects them to act.

CHAPTER 24

Social Market Economy and British Socialism

INTRODUCTION

Chapters 24 and 25 deal with economies that are predominantly consumer-oriented private enterprise economies, not centrally planned (like the Soviet economy), not centrally administered (like the German economy under Hitler), and not primarily based on government ownership. The discussion is limited to developed industrial economies, leaving the economic systems in developing countries to Chapter 26.

Since a survey of all developed market economies would be too large a task,[1] the study will concern only three cases of special interest for comparative economics: the West-German social market economy during the reconstruction period, the British economy under the first postwar Labor government, and the French experiment in indicative planning. All three had the main purpose of fostering recovery; therefore, the examples compare three approaches to economic problems that were roughly similar. Existing differences concerned attitudes and emphases rather than basic economic issues. We are dealing with diverging ideas about the market

[1] See, however, *Economic Systems of the West* (Basel: Kyklos Verlag, Tübingen: J. C. B. Mohr, vol. 1, 1957, vol. 2, 1959).

and its regulation rather than with different economic systems. The postwar reconstruction period is emphasized because it underlines some basic positions that would be less noticeable in more normal times.

In addition one major difficulty will be considered that the market economies have unnecessarily created for themselves, and which still persists. Chapter 25 will deal with problems that result from trying to combine fixed exchange rates with currency convertibility and full employment. It will also be shown that a so-called "incomes policy" cannot provide a solution for problems that are unavoidable when we follow incompatible policies.

To understand the problems facing the European market economics after World War II, we have to look back to the interwar period when the private enterprise economies went through the cataclysm of the Great Depression. Out of this catastrophe grew Hitler's economy of central administration and, in democratic countries, a deep distrust in the efficacy of market processes. Confidence in the reliability of free market forces was not regained before the outbreak of World War II, and war experiences, in turn, fostered the opinion that emergency periods could or should not be handled by the price system. War destruction, demobilization, retooling of industry and excess purchasing power (the "monetary overhang") were new problems superimposed on the still unsolved difficulties of the 1930s. After the relative security of full employment under wartime controls, most economists and politicians dreaded the jump into the insecurity of a "free" market system. Baffling contradictions caused alarm. Would pent-up purchasing power lead to inflation or would lacking investment opportunities and mass unemployment have deflationary effects? Should the interest rate be kept low to stimulate private investment or raised to maintain monetary stability after the removal of price controls? Some countries, refusing to rely either on free markets or on central planning, temporized as best they could, with a host of direct controls; others abolished price and production controls before they had reconstructed their monetary systems, and, consequently, paid the price of inflation; while still others dealt decisively with the monetary problem, dismantled controls and trusted the market and private initiative.

WEST GERMANY'S SOCIAL MARKET ECONOMY

We saw that at the end of World War II the impression prevailed that emergencies have to be met by special measures, the market cannot be trusted to adjust production to sudden changes in demand, and the greater the emergency that must be met, the more is the need for direct controls. Applied to postwar Germany, this recipe would have meant maintenance of a centrally controlled economy and, at best, a very gradual transition back to the principles of a market economy. What actually happened was the opposite.

Nowhere in the western world was the economic situation so desperate, and apparently so hopeless, as in Germany between 1945 and 1948. The cities were heaps of rubble; the transportation system was destroyed; production and distribution were almost at a standstill. Even when, with the aid of the occupation authorities, a semblance of order was established, the situation was still bleak. The country was partitioned, and the Western part was the aim of an endless stream of refugees from the East. Inflation could no longer be repressed. Food rations were insufficient. Work at official wage rates offered little incentive when barter transactions in black markets were more profitable and necessary for survival. Even industry had to employ barter methods—at tremendous cost in terms of productivity. The mark had ceased to function as a unit of account and was practically repudiated as a means of payment.

This situation was changed overnight through the currency reform of June 1948, in which the supply of money was cut down decisively to match the supply of goods without excessive price inflation. A currency reform would have been necessary in any case: even a system of central control would have needed reconstruction on the basis of a new monetary unit, though it is difficult to see how a new pattern of official prices could have been found without the aid of free markets. Whether a currency reform would have been successful within a system of central administration we do not know, for the currency reform in West Germany was connected with a basic change of economic philosophy: the return to a market system.

Why did West Germany return to the principles of a market economy, and what kind of economic system was to be constructed?

It should first be stated that the choice was by no means unanimous. The Social Democratic party was vehemently opposed, and the occupation authorities were cool and skeptical. But the country at large had had enough of controls. Controls had characterized the Hitler regime, which had gone down in defeat; after the war, controls had failed to achieve their purposes and instead had led to an unbearable psychological situation, where, in the face of a tremendous reconstruction job, all personal initiative was blocked. The population was willing to give the market system a try. Nevertheless, great courage was required of the political leaders responsible for undertaking an experiment that ran counter to the nearly unanimous opinion of politicians and economists throughout the world. How did these German politicians reason?

Alfred Müller-Armack,[2] who coined the term "social market economy," argued as early as 1946 roughly as follows:

2 Alfred Müller-Armack, *Wirtschaftslenkung und Marktwirtschaft* (Hamburg: Verlag für Wirtschaft und Sozialpolitik, 1947).

The market economy antedates the philosophy of laissez faire. The essence of the market economy is that all economic processes serve the consumer, whose preferences guide production via price signals. But liberalism (which in the European sense means a philosophy close to *laissez faire*) is not acceptable anymore. It made the mistake of regarding the market process as a satisfactory order of a nation's economic life; it was willing to leave the competitive process free to exclude competition itself and equated the distribution that the market brought about with the distribution that was socially just; it wanted market forces to take care of economic stability; in short, it considered the market process as an end, when that process should have been considered merely an instrument.

For these reasons "liberalism" was discarded, and the basic principles of the market economy were discarded with it. The place of the market economy was taken by an economy of "dirigism" (Lenkungswirtschaft). But dirigism did not work well even under a dictatorship, for it eliminated the market process and thereby the possibility of consistent economic accounting.

Neither the old-fashioned "liberalism" nor the dirigism of a central administration were acceptable to Müller-Armack. As a synthetical third solution he suggested that the market serve as a supporting framework for the economy but that the market be consciously managed. Such an economy need not be limited to any particular aims. Its aims might for example be the same as those of a welfare state (avoidance of monopolistic exploitation, high employment level, social security). The important thing is that whatever aims are set must be reached by policies that are compatible with the market economy, which work through the market rather than against it. Policies incompatible with the market framework are excluded.

The group of economists who, like Müller-Armack, favor a social market economy call themselves "neo-liberalists," implying that they do not recommend merely a return to a free price system. They reject *laissez faire* and advocate indirect controls in the form of monetary and fiscal policies, together with "rules of the game" for various market parties. The price system is to be freed from those government controls that tend to distort the economic accounting and allocation process, but it is also to be protected against interference from private monopoly.

These ideas are very similar to those that eventually prevailed in other countries once the shortcomings of direct controls became evident. The West German case, however, is interesting for the following reasons:

1. Coupled with the currency reform, the new philosophy made an instantaneous impact. Practically overnight the economic climate changed.

2. The success of the social market economy was achieved under seemingly hopeless conditions. Indeed, the success appeared to be an "economic miracle" to those who had considered the price mechanism obsolete.

3. The neo-liberalists, instead of introducing more and more controls *ad hoc*, established one guiding principle and clung to it however unpleasant the results were in individual cases. They trusted that the market could solve problems better than a great number of bureaucratic controls. While controls were not entirely absent, they became the exception from the rule.

4. The new policy effected a rapidly rising increase in income, a high employment level, and a satisfactory development of West Germany's balance of payments.

The Germans were receptive to this new policy because of their past experience with two inflations, one open and one repressed. By 1948 they were perhaps more immune to inflationist temptations than were most other countries. Furthermore, the Hitler economy of central administration and its final breakdown had created a sense of frustration that strongly favored freedom and a release of pent-up energies. Against the background of dirigism and inflation, the social market economy appeared as the rebirth and vindication of the basic principles on which an unplanned economy could rest.

Several factors that contributed to the success of the social market economy were fortuitous. They were important, since they counterbalanced some of the difficulties which stood in the way of a revival of the German economy. Foreign aid partly offset the cost of occupation and reparation; the partition meant that West Germany could buy food in the world market at better terms of trade; the productive capacity damaged by war was probably less than the capacity constructed during the war; and the world market situation was particularly favorable for German exports, while German import demand proved to be less formidable than might have been expected. The foreign trade situation, however, cannot be ascribed entirely to fortuitous conditions for the volume of exports and imports was greatly influenced by West Germany's domestic economic policy.[3]

The twin birth of the social market economy and the new German currency indicates the paramount importance of monetary stability. Ludwig Erhard,[4] the man most responsible for the success of the social market economy, considered currency stability the mainstay of the new system.

The neo-liberalists argued (1) that the currency had to be stable to avoid a price-wage spiral; (2) that it had to be stable if sufficient private savings were to materialize; (3) that the principles of the market economy excluded the use of price, investment, and exchange controls; (4) that the balance of payments problem could be solved only if the purchasing power of the currency unit remained stable; (5) that the allocation of investment funds had to rest on a rate of interest high enough to equate the demand

---

[3] For an excellent discussion of these points, see Henry C. Wallich, *Mainsprings of the German Revival* (New Haven, Conn.: Yale University Press, 1955).

[4] Ludwig Erhard, *Wohlstand für Alle* (Düsseldorf: Econ-Verlag, 1957), chap. 2.

for loanable funds with their noninflationist supply; and (6) that a "just" distribution of income is possible only under conditions of monetary stability.

Throughout the Western world there is more agreement concerning these propositions today than there was in the years directly following the war. But even now, professed support of these principles goes hand in hand with an expression of regret that perfect monetary stability is not possible. The most common reason cited is the upward pressure on prices that is constantly exerted by powerful groups, and which central banks can block only at the price of unemployment.

How did the social market economy solve this problem during the reconstruction period?

West Germany's economy after 1948 was not a full-employment economy. Such an achievement was inconceivable for a country that had, within a few years, increased its population by 25 percent through the influx of refugees. The social market economy performed astonishingly well in creating employment. Nevertheless, it was difficult for the Adenauer administration to defend a conservative monetary policy in the face of unemployment. The generally accepted recipe for full employment demanded monetary expansion. However, monetary expansion at this time would have endangered monetary stability without appreciably increasing employment. Credit expansion is a proper policy when unemployment is caused by a deficiency in aggregate demand. If, on the other hand, the cause of unemployment is structural, an increasing monetary demand may exhaust itself in price inflation without putting many men back to work. In West Germany, unemployment was structural. Not all the refugees could be drawn into production by mere monetary expansion. Some were unemployable, others lacked the needed industrial skills, while still others could not be moved because of the existing housing shortage. Under these conditions it was much better not to endanger the whole experiment through price inflation. The medicine appropriate for curing the disease of oversaving in the 1930s would not have been proper for an economy that needed more savings to finance an abundance of investment opportunities.

But how could a conservative monetary policy be followed in an economy where labor was permitted to bargain freely for higher wages? The answer is that German labor unions and particularly their top organization, the German Federation of Labor Unions, behaved with great restraint. This restraint in wage demands permitted the continuation of monetary stability, which was in turn the basis for the accumulation of savings needed to finance rapidly increasing investments in a noninflationary way. In addition, relatively low wages made German exports competitive.

Labor's wisdom and restraint can be understood when we contemplate the following facts. All Germans were inflation-conscious. At high cost they had learned that neither open nor repressed inflation is beneficial in the long run. To this we may add that organized labor had a very real interest in the new market economy. First of all, the standard of living improved materially and visibly, demonstrating that the size of the cake may be more important than its distribution. And secondly, labor, too, had had enough of controls. Characteristically, the labor unions had been the first organizations dissolved under Hitler. The labor union is a creature of the market and ceases to exist in a real sense when the market becomes extinct. Therefore labor was willing to support a policy which was determined to prevent inflation, to raise productivity, and to preserve the market.

These reasons were probably more important in explaining labor's contribution to monetary stability than was the pressure which refugees exerted on the labor market.

The neoliberalist attitude toward monopolies is negative. The social market economy, it is argued, should not permit the freedom to exclude competition, though a few exceptions and modifications might be tolerated (such as condition cartels, export cartels, or rationalization cartels).

Obviously, the neoliberalists are unwilling to promise job and income security to any economic group, for such a guarantee would violate the very essence of the market economy. This attitude need not exclude social security for the aged, the ill, and the unemployed. Nevertheless, for two reasons the social market economy will not be eager to develop a comprehensive cradle-to-the-grave social security program. First, when driven too far, such a system will begin to interfere with the proper working of the market mechanism by paralyzing private initiative and by shifting too much responsibility from the individual to the state. Secondly, it may lead to greater collective consumption than is compatible with a high rate of national economic growth.

The neo-liberalists deny that they are less social-minded than the adherents of a system of direct controls. They point out that by emphasizing productivity rather than increasing equality, the social market economy will lead to a higher standard of living for all, even though income differentials will be greater. In addition, they remind us that a stable value of money eliminates the injustices of price inflation, which even price controls might not be able to cure.

GREAT BRITAIN'S POST-WAR SYSTEM OF DIRECT CONTROLS

In none of the developed market economies of the West has nationalization of industry been carried forward to a considerable degree. Socialist economists in England have pointed out that the nationalized sector of the British economy will always remain a minority of the whole,[5]

[5] Francis Williams, *Socialist Britain* (New York: The Viking Press, Inc., 1949), p. 91.

and that it is an error to equate socialism and nationalization.[6] The reason for this reserved attitude toward what at one time seemed to be the most important point in the constitution of the Labor party (1918) can be found in the following circumstances:

1. Probably most decisive was the realization that the state can achieve its main economic purposes by control rather than by public ownership of the means of production. Not all members of the Labor party agree, however, and the majority who do agree are not unanimous in what they mean by control.

2. Since the socialist parties of the West do not advocate revolutionary methods, nationalization implies compensation, a fact that makes it less attractive.

3. Nationalization has created difficult administrative problems. Hugh Gaitskell [7] doubted that "there is any escape from the dilemma that the more independent the boards (of nationalized industries) are allowed to be, the more they will exercise power without responsibility, and the less independent they become, the greater the risk of overcentralization and lack of enterprise."

4. The general economic results of the relatively modest amount of nationalization that was carried through in England (coal, electricity, transport, central banking) were not too favorable. Prices were set below equilibrium levels; costs were not sufficiently considered; capital was invested at artificially low rates of interest and labor employed at artificially high wages; and losses were covered by the state. Investment funds and productive resources were consequently wasted.[8] If the nationalized area of the British economy were to be considerably enlarged, this interference with the price system might grow to major proportions. At the same time a central plan might not be available to see that at least technical consistency is maintained throughout the economy.

5. If the remaining enterprise sector is to perform effectively, private enterprise must feel confident that it will not be nationalized; the sword of Damocles must not be left dangling over it. Commenting on the transition

[6] See W. Arthur Lewis, *The Principles of Economic Planning*, a study prepared for the Fabian Society (London: Dennis Dobson, Ltd., 1949), p. 10; Oliver Franks, *Central Planning and Control in War and Peace* (Cambridge, Mass.: Harvard University Press, 1947), p. 20. German socialists, too, have turned away from nationalization. On November 15, 1959, the Social Democratic party adopted a new program which "makes it absolutely clear that public ownership is but one means to protect the freedom of the individual against the predominance of uncontrolled powerful interests . . . and the new formula therefore reads, 'As much competition as possible—as much planning as necessary.' "—*The Bulletin: A Weekly Survey of German Affairs*, Bonn, November 17, 1959.

[7] Hugh Gaitskell, *Recent Developments in British Socialist Thinking* (London: Co-operative Union, Ltd., 1956), p. 14.

[8] See G. C. Allen, "The British Economy," in *Economic Systems of the West*, vol. 1, p. 75.

from capitalism to socialism, Oskar Lange [9] expresses the belief that if nationalization is contemplated at all, it should be the first rather than the last step. He says:

> The opinion is almost generally accepted that the process of socialization must be as gradual as possible in order to avoid grave economic disturbance. . . . Unfortunately, the economist cannot share this theory of economic gradualism. An economic system based on private enterprise and private property of the means of production can only work as long as the security of private property and of income derived from property and from enterprise is maintained. The very existence of a government bent on introducing socialism is a constant threat to this security. Therefore, the capitalist economy cannot function under a socialist government unless the government is socialist in name only.

6. The reasons advanced for the nationalization of industries are not particularly impressive. The "basic" industries argument fails to define what is basic. The monopoly argument is exposed to the criticism that nationalization intensifies the monopolistic character of an industry and that it is doubtful whether management would be improved in practice. The argument that unified administration can better integrate an industry requires that the gains from better organization are not lost through increasing bureaucratic friction. Finally, the distressed industries argument often wants to keep alive via nationalization industries that are rightly declining in response to changed demand or cost schedules. Other arguments, which urge nationalization as a means of attaining ends like full employment and equalization of income, are poor because the aspired ends can be better achieved by other means.

Since the Labor party has shown little interest in further nationalization, with the possible exception of steel, it can claim only a diluted kind of socialism as its aim. Central planning is not compatible with private enterprise. But we shall have to investigate whether indicative or soft planning can offer some of the advantages of socialist central planning.

More important than nationalization is the role that income equalization plays in British socialism. A more egalitarian income distribution was approached from several sides after the war:

1. Equalization through taxation. This attack on inequality has already gone rather far, considering that the British economy must still rely on private initiative and private saving. We have already seen, furthermore, that excessively progressive taxation can interfere seriously with the proper division of labor.[10]

---

[9] Oskar Lange and Fred M. Taylor, *On the Economic Theory of Socialism* (Minneapolis: University of Minnesota Press, 1938), pp. 122–123. Copyright 1938 by the University of Minnesota.

[10] See Chaps. 5 and 9.

2. Equalization through government spending. Although the measures which fall into this category (free health service, for example) may be controversial when considered separately, or too expensive and inflationary in the aggregate, they are basically compatible with the market economy.

3. Equalization through control of food prices. As an equalitarian and anti-inflation measure this policy is roundabout, wasteful, and clumsy. British food subsidies violated the basic principle of consumers' sovereignty, distorted the price structure, and invited waste. Furthermore, inflation should be attacked by removing its causes rather than by trying to cure its symptoms.

4. Equalization of opportunity. This attack on inequality—which is compatible with the principles of the market economy—goes to the very root of the problem. Freer and better education will increase productivity and the size of the national product that can be distributed.

During the first Labor administration after World War II the British economy enjoyed full employment but maintained it by policies that were inflationary and tended to perpetuate the dollar shortage that had been inherited from the war. Full employment conditions, furthermore, strengthened the bargaining position of the trade unions and made it impossible for the Labor party to resist their pressure for higher wages and shorter hours. Downward adjustments of wages became next to impossible. When this tendency toward higher wages is added to the egalitarian policies of the government, it can be seen that consumers' demand pressed strongly for a larger share of the nation's income at the expense of investment and the ability to export.

Wage negotiations could not have led to constantly increasing wages if they had been conducted within a monetary framework that was not indefinitely expansible. The monetary authorities, however, made available whatever amount of purchasing power was needed for full employment to be maintained in spite of rising wage rates. Insistence on a stable value of money would have created some counter pressure on the labor market, for above a certain point rising wages would have caused unemployment. The full employment policy, however, was sacrosanct.

A policy of monetary stability has to rest on a rate of interest that is high enough to limit credit creation to noninflationary proportions. This rate would have been much higher than the one the administration permitted to prevail. A high rate of interest was not excluded merely to prevent unemployment. An even more direct reason was the unwillingness of the Labor administration to have its investment program restricted. But by following a cheap money policy, the government made "itself responsible for substituting some control in place of the brake that high rates of interest otherwise impose on capital projects." [11]

[11] Roy Harrod, Are These Hardships Necessary? (London: Rupert Hart-Davis, Ltd., 1947), p. 33.

The Labor government wanted to plan investment, that is, "to lay down general strategy in the economic field and to see that the over-all strategical plan is followed without interfering too closely with the tactical decisions of the commanders in the field." [12] However, the aims of the government's investment "plan" were exceedingly vague, and this is not surprising in an economy that did not have an apparatus for central planning, and which was still predominantly a private enterprise economy. Indeed, how can investment priorities be arrived at under these conditions?

> Who is to decide between the relative urgencies of a new bridge in Basutoland, a new hospital in Aberystwyth, a new mousetrap factory in Glasgow, or a new cinema in Oxford? The answer is that nobody can decide, and that therefore conscientious officials, fully knowing that they have not the facts on which to base a judgment, will pass everything that seems on the face of it to be reasonable. The result is always that more licenses are granted than the available resources can fulfill, and that there is an unholy scramble in the course of which many of the most urgent projects are held up because the promoters of the less urgent have been more skilled in the arts of acquiring scarce materials.[13]

These problems could have been avoided if a proper rate of interest had been chosen. But if, for example, a rate of 3 percent was maintained when the rate should have been 10 percent, investment funds tended to be kept from the most urgent needs, such as exports, and spent on such long-term projects as railroad electrification.[14] In addition, cheap interest rates created inflationary pressures that necessitated price controls, just as investment according to priorities required the establishment of a licensing system.

This investment policy shows lack of a thorough understanding of the allocation problem. While vaguely playing with ideas of "planning," the Labor administration gave little thought to the question of how priorities can be established and the proper integration of production processes accomplished short of a full-fledged central plan. The government's development program did not constitute a well-integrated whole. The British economy at that time rested neither on central direction nor on a free market process.

The controls by which the government tried to ensure the cooperation of private industry were to a large extent inherited from the war:

> The doctrinaire belief in the planned economy made the Government reluctant to remove these controls however unsuitable they might be for peace-time purposes. But, in the absence of resolute attempts to deal with inflation directly, these controls had to be retained and even extended.

[12] Williams, p. 92.
[13] Lewis, pp. 56–57.
[14] Harrod, p. 78.

As the maldistribution of resources increased, more and more detailed State intervention seemed to be justified in the day-to-day working of industry. The net output of finished goods from the labor and raw materials available was much lower than it would have been in a free market purged of the inflationary pressure. So that a controlled economy which had been accepted for political reasons now seemed to be essential on grim economic grounds. The vicious circle was complete. Inflation unattended to; controls over the distribution of resources to prevent price rises; maldistribution of resources because of the inherent clumsiness of controls; dwindling production intensifying the inflation; more controls and so on, endlessly.[15]

The Labor government, trying to find its way back to expanding, multilateral world trade, rejected regionalism; but its domestic policies were not always suited to support this attempt. To bridge the postwar dollar gap exports had to be increased in relation to imports. We have already seen, however, that domestic consumption and investment, which tended to re-reduce excessively the volume of goods available for export purposes, led to inflationary pressures that made it difficult to sell abroad.

To meet this problem, too, the Labor government relied on direct instead of indirect monetary controls; again it tried to cure symptoms rather than the cause. To prevent the easy sale of merchandise at home, the government prescribed for each potential export industry the proportion of its output that it had to sell abroad. What the price mechanism would have handled according to the wishes of foreign buyers, the government tried to do by dividing the country's output between the domestic and foreign markets. The mistake was the same as in the government's investment policy: an unnecessary bureaucratic apparatus was created to solve a problem that market forces, unimpaired by inflation, would have solved automatically.

If we consider British consumption, investment, and export policies during the first 5 postwar years as a whole, we see that the basic weakness was that the Labor government tried to do too much. This tendency would have led to price inflation had not the government maintained rather strict and numerous price controls. Price controls, in turn, made it necessary to replace the selective function of the market with direct quantitative controls, and these direct controls were so awkward and uncoordinated that they in turn decreased efficiency, thereby further increasing the inflationary pressure and the disequilibrium in the balance of payments.

It is difficult to understand why the Labor government chose this unsatisfactory way of unpopular "nuisance" controls. At a time when the theory of socialism had come to understand that a price system would have to be artificially created even with government ownership of the material means of production, the Labor government tried to handle its problems

---

[15] John Jewkes, *Ordeal by Planning* (New York: Crowell-Collier and Macmillan, Inc., 1948), p. 77.

without the guidance of prices. It did so in spite of the fact that maintenance of private enterprise would have made the use of the price mechanism easy.

If our diagnosis is correct, if the basic trouble was that the government was trying to do too much with inadequate methods, then the British policy can hardly be referred to as "austerity." The British people voted themselves a higher standard of living than the economy's productivity permitted. In addition, they aggravated the situation by investing too large a part of their resources in time-consuming projects that could have been postponed.

To put our criticism of British reconstruction policies into perspective, two points must be emphasized: first, that many of the social ends of the Labor party were achieved and became, for better or worse, a permanent feature of the system; and, second, that some of the basic difficulties were caused by the fact that Great Britain tried to reach and then to maintain currency convertibility at fixed rates of exchange. This point will be considered in the discussion of a later period when the main inconsistencies, referred to above, had been eliminated. That discussion will include all market economies that try to maintain currency convertibility and fixed exchange rates while simultaneously following full-employment policies.

CHAPTER 25

Exchange Rates, Incomes Policy, and Indicative Planning

THE "MAGIC TRIANGLE"

The market economy rests on price variations. When prices are fixed, automatic adjustments of production to changes in demand and supply are no longer possible and must be replaced by quantitative controls. A policy of price fixing, therefore, must remain a rare exemption in a market economy. Most advocates of a private enterprise system are willing to accept this statement—with one exception, the rate of exchange. The latter enjoys the distinction of being the only price that is kept fixed in terms of gold with the unanimous approval of private business and government authorities. Fixed exchange rates are so often taken for granted that this major violation of the basic principle of the market economy passes nearly unnoticed. The relatively small group of economists who argue for flexible rates must take a defensive position even though the burden of proof ought to rest with the advocates of fixed exchange rates.[1]

[1] See Milton Friedman, "The Case for Flexible Exchange Rates," in *Essays in Positive Economics* (Chicago: University of Chicago Press, 1953), pp. 157–203; Frank D. Graham, *The Cause and Cure of 'Dollar Shortage,'* Essays in International Finance, no. 10 (Princeton, N.J.: Princeton University, 1949); Gottfried Haberler, *Currency*

Foreign currencies and their prices, the rates of exchange, play the same role in international transactions as domestic money plays at home. They are used as means of payment and as units of accounts (or at least as links between the two domestic units that enter any international transaction). Our attitude toward the foreign exchange rates, therefore, follows our attitude toward domestic money. Domestic money is generally accepted because it enjoys unquestionable *price* stability. Economic calculations are carried out on the seemingly firm basis of the monetary unit. The tautology that "a dollar is a dollar" creates the illusion that the price stability of money vouchsafes stability of the purchasing power or *value* of money. As a rule, this illusion is strong enough, even in times of creeping inflation, to maintain the use of money as unit of account, means of payment, and reserve of highest liquidity.

International transactions involve at least two national monetary units whose purchasing powers do not always change in the same degree or even in the same direction. A rate of exchange as a link between two price systems, therefore, should be expected to vary together with the so-called purchasing-power parity, that is, with the ratio of change of the respective domestic purchasing powers of the two national currencies. Nevertheless, there is an almost unanimous desire to make the foreign exchange rate resemble the domestic currency unit by imparting to it absolute price stability in terms of *both* currencies by *fixing* the rate of exchange, for example, by tying both currency units firmly to gold. Furthermore, the general domestic acceptability of money is broadened into free convertibility of one currency into the other at the fixed rate. International transactions can then be calculated and executed on the same firm basis as domestic business.

This predilection for fixed exchange rates rests on the wish to create an international unit of account and a means of payment closely matching the qualities of domestic money.

But the following facts are ignored:

Convertibility (Washington, D.C.: American Enterprise Association, 1954); L. Albert Hahn, "Monetäre Integration—Illusion oder Realität?" in *Internationale Währungs- und Finanzpolitik* (Berlin: Duncker & Humblot, 1961), pp. 99–123; James E. Meade, "The Future of International Trade and Payments," *The Three Banks Review*, no. 50, June 1961; W. M. Scammell, *International Monetary Policy* (London: Macmillan & Co., Ltd., 1961); Egon Sohmen, *Flexible Exchange Rates, Theory, and Controversy* (Chicago: University of Chicago Press, 1961); Charles R. Whittlesey, *International Monetary Issues* (New York: McGraw-Hill, Inc., 1937). For a more complete listing see Fritz Machlup, *Plans for Reform of the International Monetary System*, Special Papers in International Economics no. 3 (Princeton University, 1962), pp. 57–58.

The statements on exchange rates are taken from my article "Fixed or Flexible Exchange Rates?" in *Factors Affecting the United States Balance of Payments*, Joint Economic Committee, 87th Congress, 2d Session (Washington, D.C.: Government Printing Office, 1963), pp. 255–258.

The *price* of the domestic monetary unit is stable by definition and, though the *value* of the unit depends on the long-run effects of domestic monetary policy, this policy is the same for all participants in domestic transactions. The foreign exchange rate, on the other hand, should be a real market price, determined by demand and supply in the foreign exchange market. Demand and supply, in turn, depend on fluctuations in international trade of commodities, services, and securities. Dominant among the factors that cause these fluctuations is the lack of integration of national economic policies. Where two or more nations are involved, a uniform monetary policy becomes mere fiction. Assuming free convertibility at fixed rates of exchange, national monetary authorities must stand ready to equalize disparities in demand and supply in the foreign exchange markets by buying or selling foreign exchange or gold as the occasion demands. But only a surplus position can be maintained indefinitely through the creation of domestic money. *Foreign* money cannot be created *domestically* and cannot be sold indefinitely.

An international payments system with fixed exchange rates must be a compromise composed of the following three elements:

1. The economic policies of the trading countries must reach a reasonable degree of coordination.

2. Foreign exchange or gold reserves must be at the disposal of the trading nations, the amounts of these international reserves depending to a large extent on the degree of coordination of national economic policies.

3. A nation may decide to maintain fixed exchange rates even if it has to give up the *full* convertibility of its currency. The introduction of exchange controls, however, is alien to the basic principles of the market economy. Only relatively mild forms of exchange control can be considered in a compromise that tries to maintain convertibility.

Acceptance of *flexible* rather than *fixed* rates of exchange would be more consistent with the principles of a market economy. If, therefore, inadequate coordination of national economic policies does not permit convertibility at unalterably fixed exchange rates owing to insufficiency of internationally liquid reserves, the presumption is that market economies should give up fixed rates rather than convertibility. If fixed rates of exchange cannot be supported by well-integrated domestic policies and large international reserves, the case is strong for flexible exchange rates.

Coordination of national economic policies must be a joint effort. An individual country can participate in it but cannot achieve it alone. A given country may perform perfectly in maintaining a satisfactory employment level and rate of growth at stable prices, yet its balance-of-payments position may still be disturbed because other countries may follow more inflationary or deflationary policies, or their economies may suffer from recessions. Even the most perfect coordination of national policies would not necessarily establish fixed rates of exchange as equilibrium rates, owing to such influences as changing technologies or crop failures, which are independent of monetary and fiscal policies.[2]

As the price systems of modern market economies become more rigid, and greater emphasis is placed on full employment and economic growth rather than on balance-of-payments equilibrium, the coordination of national economic policies is not as well integrated as it used to be. In the past it was the predominant aim of central banks to defend their gold and foreign exchange reserves in an attempt to maintain free convertibility at unalterably fixed gold parities. Balance of international payments was achieved through the use of gold reserves, short-term capital movements, and adjustments in national price levels. The coordination of national price systems was achieved through appropriate domestic monetary policies whose main instrument was the rate of discount. Changes in short-term rates of interest (in consequence of balance-of-payments disequilibriums) were conscious alterations, superimposed on variations of interest rates owing to domestic demand-and-supply changes in the money markets.

Under the so-called gold mechanism, market economies paid for their *fixed* exchange rates by being forced into *changing* another price of strategic importance, the short-term rate of interest, more than domestic market conditions would have warranted. Through changes in the discount rate the market economies tried to induce just enough equilibrating capital flow and to produce just enough price inflation or deflation to balance international payments in order to maintain both fixed rates of exchange and free convertibility.

In simulating the price stability of the national monetary units in the form of fixed exchange rates, the monetary authorities were forced to change the price of money in the more meaningful sense of the cost of borrowing money. In fact, the gold mechanism violated the "neutrality" of money by exposing the market economy to changes in interest rates that would not have been necessary in a system of flexible exchange rates. Exchange rate fluctuations would have been the automatic and instant results of changing international economic relations. Fixed rates of exchange, on the other hand, forced the market economies to transfer the adjustment function from exchange-rate to interest-rate fluctuations, that is, from natural fluctuations to those induced artificially.

Flexible exchange rates would have affected only international trans-

---

[2] These are the same influences that make it impossible to calculate equilibrium rates of exchange on the basis of purchasing-power parities.

actions, while changes in interest rates had to affect the economy as a whole. The flexible exchange rate would itself have been the equilibrating device, but the discount rate affected international commodity movements only indirectly and belatedly through its pressure on domestic prices and costs.

Before World War I the maintenance of fixed gold parities was not considered a fetter on domestic economic policy. Employment policies were hardly known, and nobody talked about economic growth. Central bank policy was guided by the simple rule that sufficient gold reserves had to be maintained. Domestically, the supply of money was supposed to follow the needs of trade through the discounting and rediscounting of prime commercial paper. One did not see that the so-called "legitimate" demand for credit was itself a function of the rate of interest. Had the central banks been forced to consciously set a rate of interest, the fiction of an automatic monetary policy could not have been maintained and the hollowness of the commercial-loan theory of credit would have become evident. However, since the central banks had the duty to defend their gold reserves through changes in discount rates, the monetary authorities were furnished with a convenient device for the determination of interest rates—without having to follow a conscious domestic monetary policy. Had someone proposed flexible rates of exchange on the grounds that domestic monetary policy should be "neutral," or at least free from outside interference, the central bankers would have been forced to find a substitute for the simple criterion of central bank policy that was the result of the maintenance of fixed rates of exchange. In other words, these fixed rates of exchange were not sought for their own sake alone. They were the kingpin of a system that, while eliminating a conscious national monetary policy, succeeded quite well in coordinating currency circulations internationally.[3]

The combined effects of increasing price rigidities in modern market economies and of growing concern with employment and growth have put an end to automatic monetary policies but, inconsistently, not to the desire to maintain currency convertibility at fixed exchange rates.

Fixed exchange rates are considered necessary because they, sup-

[3] Typical of the desire to have an automatic system is the remark of Governor Strong which J. M. Keynes quotes in "A Treatise on Money" (New York: Harcourt, Brace & World, Inc., 1930), vol. 2, p. 305: "Until we get back to the automatic flow of gold which affects bank reserves and brings into play the automatic flow of gold which affects bank reserves and brings into play the automatic reactions from loss of reserves, I do not believe we are going to have all the satisfaction from the Federal Reserve System that we will have after that time comes * * * I have great confidence that when the time comes to conduct these things as they were in former years, a lot of the need for the type of management which has to be applied in the present situation will be eliminated. It will be more automatic. We won't have to depend so much on judgment, and we can rely more upon the play of natural forces and their reaction on prices * * *."

posedly, provide a firm foundation for international commodity and capital movements, force monetary authorities to integrate their policies with those of other nations, give them greater power to discipline monopolists, and eliminate devaluations or competitive depreciations.

The desire to find a compromise between fixed exchange rates and leeway for domestic monetary and fiscal policies led to the creation of the International Monetary Fund in 1944, which tied the member currencies to gold but permitted parity adjustments when "necessary to correct a fundamental disequilibrium." [4] However, this compromise did not work well. The *fixed* rates of exchange often tended to become *false* rates and the flow of international reserves from deficit to surplus countries advertised impending devaluations and led to disequilibrating speculation.[5] Recently, therefore, the International Monetary Fund and its most important members have moved away from the "adjustable peg" system in favor of permanently fixed rates.

In Chapter 1 we used the combination of fixed exchange rates, currency convertibility, and full-employment (or growth) policies as example for a mixture of incompatible aims or means. Now we shall see that many of the acute balance-of-payments problems faced by the developed market economies are caused by this magic triangle with its incompatible angles. The British economy suffers even more than others from the limits that a fixed exchange rate forces on domestic policies, owing to the British key-currency position, the importance of international trade, and the understandable reluctance to sacrifice domestic social and economic policies to the external equilibrium.

When a country's domestic economic policies lead to inflationary pressures that are worse than other countries', a growing balance-of-payments deficit makes its international liquidity reserves decline. To defend the reserves, the authorities may have to raise interest rates or taxes, with the consequence of growing unemployment. Whatever policy-mix is used, full employment and balance-of-payments equilibrium usually cannot be simultaneously achieved. Similarly, a country at full employment cannot simultaneously cure a balance-of-payments surplus and fight domestic inflation successfully. Inflation can be kept in check by a more restrictive monetary or fiscal policy; but a correction of the balance-of-payments surplus requires credit expansion.[6]

---

[4] *Articles of Agreement: International Monetary Fund*, Art. 4, Sec. 4(f).

[5] It should be noted that this speculation is without risk. If devaluation does take place, those who sold the currency before and repurchased it after the devaluation gain by the amount of the "peg" adjustment. Should the expected devaluation not materialize, the speculators are poorer only by the technical costs of the transfers.

[6] For a description of this dilemma in the West German economy, see *Stabiles Geld—Stetiges Wachstum*, Sachverständigenrat zur Begutachtung der gesamtwirtschaftlichen Entwicklung (Stuttgart und Mainz: Verlag W. Kohlhammer, 1965), chap. 9.

If foreign exchange control is considered alien to the principles of the market economy, the dilemma may be avoided by one of the following policies: adoption of some form of exchange-rate flexibility, very large international reserves that permit painless adjustments, or, finally, a so-called incomes policy which avoids inflation through "moral suasion" rather than inconvenient monetary or fiscal policies.

A consistent advocate of the market economy will argue that exchange-rate flexibility is the only realistic answer to the problem. The exchange rate is a link between two national price systems and should vary roughly with the purchasing power parities of the national currencies.[7] Balance-of-payments equilibrium would be automatic and not, as under fixed rates, the result of a slow and roundabout process by which we try to change domestic costs and prices via policies that interfere with monetary stability, employment, and growth.

Flexible exchange rates are often rejected on the grounds that they lead to competitive exchange depreciation and irresponsible credit expansion in the domestic economy. But undervalued fixed rates are just as dangerous, and a responsible credit policy can be guided just as well or even better by exchange-rate variations than by changes in the liquidity reserves of Central Banks.

Very large international liquidity reserves would permit the postponement of disagreeable choices between domestic and external equilibrium. But they might tempt deficit countries into procrastination and would certainly not help surplus countries that try to combat inflation.

After Britain had returned to currency convertibility and to domestic policies that were more consistent with a market economy, convertibility and fixed gold parities necessitated frequent shifts in monetary and fiscal measures, depending on the international payments situation. This "stop and start" policy has been blamed for the unsatisfactory growth rate of the British economy.[8] Since a repeated shoring-up of Britain's international reserve position through international rescue operations is not a long-run solution, an answer must be found either in exchange-rate flexibility or in an incomes policy. We shall discuss the latter first and then return, once more, to flexible exchange rates as the arrangement that best fits the logic of the market economy.

---

[7] The famous Bullion Report stated as early as 1810: "In the event of the prices of commodities being raised in one country by an augmentation of its circulating medium, while no similar augmentation in the circulating medium of the neighboring country has led to a similar rise in prices, the currencies of the two countries will no longer continue to bear the same relative value to each other as before. The exchange will be computed between these two countries to the disadvantage of the former."

[8] See Thomas Wilson, *Planning and Growth* (New York: St. Martin's Press, Inc., 1964), p. 45.

INCOMES POLICY

It is one of the main arguments against flexible exchange rates that a depreciation of a country's currency will automatically cause a cost-push inflation, since all import prices must rise and wages, supposedly, increase.[9] With fixed exchange rates, on the other hand, inflation must be avoided or reduced to the average level of inflation in all trading countries. Formerly, this would have meant a strict monetary policy to exclude or tone down inflationist pressures caused by demand pull. Today's cost-push inflation has complicated matters. Where industrial monopolies and labor organizations have power to raise prices and wages, the monetary authority's refusal to permit this inflation through credit expansion would lead to unemployment and insufficient growth. At artificially increased prices, a given aggregate demand can purchase only a smaller national product, and the monetary authority is put into the dilemma of having to choose between price stability and full employment. Alternatively, the government of a market economy could try to enforce competition by forbidding monopolistic practices or even collective bargaining. But the democracies of the West are reluctant to imitate methods used by command economies.

In this impasse, the authorities may try to talk the market parties into "reasonable" behavior. In a national emergency and for short periods, this "moral suasion" may succeed. As a long-term policy, however, this so-called "incomes policy" is inconsistent with the basic character of the market economy and is therefore bound to fail, particularly if it tries to be a substitute for the strict monetary and fiscal policies demanded by a combination of fixed exchanges, convertibility, and high employment. Besides, an incomes policy that fails may only be the prelude to price and wage controls that violate the essence of the private enterprise economy.

Sir Roy Harrod defines incomes policy as a campaign of education and propaganda that brings home some basic economic facts to those concerned with wage and price fixing.[10] He forgets that even a full understanding of the underlying dilemma does not furnish precise guidelines for prices and wages in individual sectors of the economy, nor does it prepare an enterprise or labor union for the sacrifice it must make for the benefit of the economy as a whole.

A limiting monetary policy is rejected in the belief that even increasing

---

[9] For this reason Sir Roy Harrod rejects flexible exchange rates, even though "the intellectual case in favor of flexible foreign exchanges is clear." See Roy Harrod, *Reforming the World's Money* (New York: St. Martin's Press, Inc., 1965), p. 34.

[10] Harrod, p. 38.

unemployment will not be able to make the monopolists in industry and labor see reason. How, then, can we assume that the far more gentle instrument of moral suasion will work in the absence of clear guidelines?

Guidelines for correct price and wage setting would have to rest on a very complicated set of criteria, not on simple principles on which everyone could agree. Such guidelines would have to deal with the relationship of wage increases to increases in productivity, both on the average and in individual industries and enterprises; with changes in demand and supply on the different commodity and labor markets; with corporate profits; with capital formation in relation to desired economic growth; and with the balance-of-payments implications of proposed wage and price increases—to mention only a few important points.[11]

It is obvious that such criteria, and guidelines derived from them and from certain policy objectives, could never enable the government to suggest a price and wage pattern that would not lead to endless disputes.[12] Besides, it is uncertain whether a pattern acceptable to the parties involved would lead to the most desirable factor allocation, considering the combined objectives of monetary stability, economic growth, and external equilibrium. We must constantly remind ourselves that the incomes policy is proposed as a substitute for strict monetary and fiscal policies (as well as anti-monopolistic measures). If a high employment level is maintained, labor will find itself in a sellers' market and, in the long run, could not be prevented from making use of its bargaining power whenever general economic conditions would permit.

We have seen that income distribution within the private enterprise economy is unequal and considered unjust by many. It is this persistent feeling that labor is not receiving an adequate share of the national income that makes it most unlikely that labor will follow the exhortations of the government, particularly when high industrial profits indicate that increased productivity has not been fully shared with the consumer through

---

[11] See, for example, the guidelines stated in *The Annual Report of the Council of Economic Advisors 1962* (Washington: U.S. Government Printing Office, 1962), p. 189. These guidelines, however inadequate as practical criteria, are more clearly worded than those of the British White Paper *Incomes Policy, the Next Step* (London: H. M. Stationery Office, 1962, Cmd. 1626). The White Paper, after having admitted that "it is not possible to lay down hard and fast rules," says: "A shortage of labor within a particular industry or firm would not of itself warrant an increase in pay. It is only where the building up of manpower in one industry relatively to others, or the prevention of a threatening decline, is plainly necessary that an increase on these grounds could be justified. Such a need may be either general or related to particular areas or grades." It is difficult to see how this fuzzy statement could convince union leaders to forego wage increases to which they feel their members are entitled. Thomas Wilson is certainly right when he says that "such passages are disheartening and reflect a confusion of thought . . ." (pp. 151–152).

[12] See Gottfried Haberler, *Inflation, Its Causes and Cures* (Washington: American Enterprise Institute, 1966), pp. 12–22.

a sufficient lowering of consumer goods prices. Indeed, incomes policy means a combination of an acceptable "profits policy" with a "wages policy" [13] and, in practice, the request that the government undertake the impossible task of determining in detail what profits, prices, and wages *ought* to be throughout the economy. Furthermore, the administration must win compliance from market parties who are not subject to command.

When the principle of indirect controls is violated through the use of direct quantitative restrictions, the principles of the market economy are disregarded. But they are also disregarded when indirect monetary and fiscal controls are held in abeyance in hopes that the freedom gained will not be misused by the market parties. Incomes policies deprive the market economy of indispensable general controls for fear they might lead to unemployment. The government, trying to break out of the "magic triangle," nevertheless goes ahead with expansionist domestic policies, in the ostrich-like hope that the market parties will be reasonable and will follow guidelines of the administration's design.

LIMITED EXCHANGE RATE FLEXIBILITY [14]

Sir Roy Harrod believes that an incomes policy and a system with flexible exchanges are incompatible because the cost-push of rising import prices would imply price inflation and make it impossible to keep wages down. But if labor is unwilling to have real wages reduced through rising import prices, why should it accept an incomes policy under other circumstances? A policy of exchange-rate flexibility, furthermore, is not proposed as an addition to, but a substitute for an incomes policy. Flexible exchanges are recommended as the natural method to avoid the impasse of the magic triangle in the developed market economies. The artificial fixing of parities is rejected as alien to the logic of the market system, and the maintenance of external equilibrium is entrusted to the price mechanism. The "adjustment process" is the automatic result of price movements and does not have to rest on policies that sacrifice domestic equilibrium. Instead of trying to influence domestic prices and wages, either through monetary or incomes policies, external equilibrium is

[13] See Sir Dennis Robertson, *A Memorandum Submitted to the Canadian Royal Commission on Banking and Finance*, Essays in International Finance no. 42 (Princeton, N.J.: Princeton University, 1962), p. 25.

[14] In connection with the following see George N. Halm, *The "Band" Proposal: The Limits of Permissible Exchange Rate Variations*, Special Papers in International Economics, no. 6 (Princeton, N.J.: Princeton University Press, 1965) of which several passages have been used. See also William Fellner, "On Limited Exchange-rate Flexibility," chap. 5 of *Maintaining and Restoring Balance in International Payments* (Princeton, N.J.: Princeton University Press, 1966).

brought about by continuous parity changes. Domestic policies are, to that extent, relieved of the necessity of following incompatible ends.

Advocates of fixed exchange rates argue that the freedom thus given to national authorities would be an invitation to reckless behavior.[15] While this attitude is exaggerated, the fact remains that complete removal of the disciplinary effects of external disequilibria on domestic policies could have undesirable consequences, by exposing the monetary authorities to even greater pressure for "permissive" credit expansion in the light of monopolistic practices. But *unlimited* flexibility of exchange rates is not needed. Already a *limited* flexibility can release us from an unworkable combination of inconsistent aims and policies.

A widening of the "band" within which exchange rates are permitted to fluctuate would be a constructive compromise between external and internal equilibrium, a compromise that, in contradistinction to an incomes policy, would mean a partial return to the basic principles of the market economy.

The advantages of permitting the exchange rates to vary between predetermined points are the following:

The support points would be a constant reminder that the central bank may be called upon to maintain a perfectly elastic supply of foreign exchange or gold at the upper limit. The domestic policies of the members of the system must be harmonized to the extent that any remaining deviations can be handled through the equilibrating effect of exchange-rate variations on trade, through equilibrating private capital movements, or through the use of official reserves. Thus, monetary discipline will be maintained without excessive hardships. Domestic policies are not "free" of considering external problems, but they are freer than under a system of fixed rates.

Exchange-rate variations within a broadened "band" will induce instant and automatic adjustments in the balance of trade. All domestic prices change instantly for foreign buyers and all foreign prices for domestic buyers since the two price systems are now connected by an elastic link. Therefore we can avoid the difficult, painful, and dangerous attempt to lower (or raise) the whole national price structure by contractionist (or expansionist) monetary policies. Real market forces would take care of trade adjustments, while the support points and variations of the exchanges between the points would provide guidelines for the harmonization of national economics policies. Rigidly fixed parities, by contrast, would prevent the forces of supply and demand from working in the foreign exchange market. For no sufficient reason we deprive ourselves of the services of price changes, the built-in stabilizers which we trust in other markets, and

---

[15] See Robert Triffin, *Gold and the Dollar Crisis* (New Haven, Conn.: Yale University Press, 1961), p. 82 or his even more extreme statement in *Inflation und Währungsordnung* (Erlenbach-Zürich: Eugen Rentsch Verlag, 1963), p. 149.

force ourselves to substitute an artificial change in bank rates for the natural exchange-rate variations that we eliminate when we fix rigid parities. When exchange-rate variations can take care of external equilibrium, bank-rate policy is greatly strengthened and permitted to be predominantly oriented to the achievement of internal equilibrium.

Limited exchange-rate flexibility will also help bring about external equilibrium through its favorable effect on short-term private capital movements. These flows depend on two incentives: interest differentials and exchange-rate variations. We must distinguish between two cases: A *high* interest rate in a *surplus* country that is supposed to dampen an inflationary expansion will tend to attract funds from a *deficit* country that wants to stimulate domestic expansion through a *low* rate. Thus, at fixed exchange rates, the capital movement is disequilibrating. It spoils the stabilizing policy of the surplus country and the full-employment policy of the deficit country by making both surplus and deficit worse. If, on the other hand, the exchange rate is permitted to change, the price of the currency of the surplus country will rise in terms of the monetary unit of the deficit country and, thereby, tone down, prevent, or reverse the disequilibrating flow of short-term funds.

If we reverse our example and let the *surplus* country maintain a *low* rate of interest to combat a domestic recession, the capital flow from the surplus to the deficit country need not be disturbing because the surplus country can afford a reduction in its surplus while the full-employment country will gain needed reserves. In this case interest-rate differentials and exchange-rate variations would pull in the same desirable direction.

Limited exchange flexibility is also recommended as a compromise solution because it can be introduced gradually and need not be applied in all groups of countries to the same extent. However, its most important feature remains its consistency with the principles of the market economy. The same cannot be claimed for fixed rates, exchange controls, or incomes policies.

The recent discussion of the international payments problems [16] has produced many proposals that show little understanding of the importance, first, of the adjustment mechanism that tends to bring about external equilibrium and, second, of a mechanism that will not deprive us of the needed monetary and fiscal controls internally. Either the discussion of the adjustment mechanism gets lost in a debate about the need for liquidity reserves (as if the latter did not depend on the former), or this discussion forgets conveniently the domestic issues, as, for example, the proposals for a return to the semiautomatic gold standard.

What we need is a compromise solution that uses the forces of the

[16] For a fine survey of this discussion see Fritz Machlup, *Plans for Reform of the International Monetary System*, Special Papers in International Economics, no. 3 (Princeton, N.J.: Princeton University, 1962).

market and thereby relieves the responsible authorities of attempts to change, correct, or control market prices—attempts that, in fighting the very system that they are supposed to serve, are bound to lead to disappointing results.

INDICATIVE PLANNING

Several times we have had to come to the conclusion that it is not wise to mix aims or policies indiscriminately, for instance, by substituting government action for market pricing. In a market system the government should support the pricing process where necessary, through indirect monetary or fiscal controls, and not hinder it through price fixing or quantitative restrictions. Perhaps government planning should be excluded a priori, since, as central direction of the economy, it could not play a constructive part in modern private enterprise systems under reasonably normal conditions. However, we deal here with terminological matters. Planning means different things to different people. Since we are speaking of planning in a market economy, Soviet-type planning is clearly not applicable, just as Hitler's dirigism would negate the private enterprise character of an economy.

But these considerations do not entitle us to reject all attempts to use some form of planning for the improvement of a market economy. A mere dislike of the term planning, engendered perhaps by a study of command economies, could lead to the rejection of useful proposals, just as Marxist doctrine has delayed possible improvements in the Soviet economy by its strict exclusion of "capitalist" concepts. Planning, after all, may be interpreted to mean no more than consistent behavior or the attempt to get, via macroeconomics, a bird's eye view, which an individual enterprise could not achieve by its own efforts. The Employment Act of 1946,[17] for example, could well be said to have introduced government planning, since H. D. Dickinson,[18] a liberal socialist, applies "the term planning to schemes of economic control that deal with the broad outlines of economic activity, without regulating details, provided that, so far as they go, they treat the economic system as a whole." Following this very broad definition, most of the policies discussed in Chapter 9 on the role of government in the private enterprise economy could be called planning, provided only that sufficient consistency is maintained. However, not much would be gained by this broad usage of the term, and probably clarity would be lost, since it is always inadvisable to use ambiguous concepts when more

---

[17] See Chap. 9.
[18] H. D. Dickinson, *Economics of Socialism* (New York: Oxford University Press, 1939), p. 15. See also the discussion in the present volume, Chap. 14.

precise terms are available. If planning is to mean something quite different from central planning,[19] adjectives such as "indicative" or "soft" could help avoid confusion.

If we eliminate the striving for consistency in government policies, or the use of national accounts, from the definition of planning, what is left that is new in recent French attempts to let the economy benefit from planning without subjecting it to the disadvantages of overcentralization?

In contrast to the West German return to a social market economy, the French system tries to go beyond mere reliance on private calculations on the basis of given prices. Pierre Massé,[20] General Commissioner of the French Plan for Economic and Social Development, has the opinion that private firms have no reliable basis for calculations since "generalized markets," in which future developments would find an adequate expression, do not exist. While all firms try to plan, none knows for sure how the others will act. The basic idea of indicative planning, therefore, seems simple. It consists in the integration of these individual planning efforts, which, in isolation, are incapable of reaching their aim. Needed is an over-all picture of the economy that shows how all production processes gear into each other. A general input-output picture à la Francois Quesnay or Wassily Leontief will show how any given branch of the economy fits into the productive efforts of the nation. Knowledge of the corresponding growth of all supporting and depending production processes gives individual industries or firms the information that they lack in the unplanned market economy.

Massé's "generalized market" is, of course, no market at all but a rough physical output program that cannot guarantee future prices and profits but is believed to provide a general feeling of security and the foundation for rapid and balanced growth.

"Indicative" planning wants to be more than mere forecasting. When, with the aid of private industry, an overall picture of economic development is gained, industries and enterprises, with the knowledge of what other industries and firms are planning to do, will adjust their own plans until balance is achieved in a process of mutual give and take. Nor is this all. Once this bird's eye view is available, it should become easier to determine the highest growth rate compatible with internal and external equilibrium. Indicative planning supposedly increases productivity because

[19] It is strange that Bertil Ohlin advises against the use of the term planning in connection with command economies, since planning is "a much more general term." See "Die Rolle des öffentlichen Sektors in der Marktwirtschaft" in *Planung in der Marktwirtschaft* (Stuttgart: Deutsche Verlagsgesellschaft, 1964), pp. 159–160.

[20] Pierre Massé, "French Methods of Planning," *Journal of Industrial Economics*, vol. 11, No. 1 (November 1962), pp. 1–17. Reprinted in Morris Bornstein ed., *Comparative Economic Systems* (Homewood, Illinois: Richard D. Irwin, Inc., 1965), pp. 213–228.

each branch of the economy pushes its own contribution to a point that previously would have been considered too dangerous. This, we are told, would be achieved without the necessity of abolishing private enterprise, without command, and without sacrificing any of the advantages of the market economy. French planning, therefore, appears to be the perfect compromise: a system between freedom and planning that enjoys the advantages of both the market and the planned economies while successfully avoiding the disadvantages usually connected with these pure systems.

It should be added that the advocates of indicative planning pride themselves on the fact that, far from being bureaucratic, their system is one of the very few exceptions to Parkinson's law.[21] The *Commissariat au Plan*, with a small staff of about 150 persons, chooses a tentative target rate of growth and makes the necessary estimates for investment and consumption both in the public and private sectors. The major work of seeking balance between the different branches of the economy is done by the so-called *Modernization Commissions*, manned by unpaid specialists. Most of the commissions are "vertical," that is, they deal with the main branches of production (steel, chemicals, transport, and so forth). A smaller number of commissions is "horizontal" in character and deals with problems of finance, manpower, productivity changes, research, and regional development.

The commissions and their working parties transmit their findings to the *Commissariat au Plan*. The latter, finally, establishes on the basis of a chosen growth-rate a composite picture of the development of the economy, a kind of mixture of forecast and program. A mere forecast, of course, could not claim the virtues of a plan. A program, on the other hand, implies some steering by the government, for which instruments are requisite that differ from those indirect controls through monetary and fiscal policies, which, by definition, do not interfere directly with the decisions of private enterprise.

The instruments of French planning are not unlike those used in Yugoslavia: a substantial amount of control by government agencies over the investment funds of the nation (public investments, private investments out of public funds, selective controls over capital issues, selective credit policies in short and medium-term bank lending), selective tax treatment, possible use of price controls, and active encouragement of monopolistic practices in industry. These instruments are used to induce industries and firms to "play the game" or 'follow the rules," in other words, to carry through the program, even though their behavior on the basis of existing market prices and interest rates would be different.

Some of these instruments may be used in efforts to maintain monetary stability. Indeed, it is difficult to disentangle indicative planning and

[21] Massé in Bornstein, p. 215.

stabilization policies. In embarking on a program of maximum growth, the planners have repeatedly neglected the use of stabilizing monetary and fiscal policies and accordingly have been forced to use direct controls even though they interrupted the plan.[22] These repeated inflationary developments (and connected devaluations) are proof that French planning cannot claim to have reached consistency in the economic policies of the government. Indicative planning seems to work only under conditions of price inflation. It must be clearly understood that the stabilization programs were not part of the plans but rather interruptions of the latter, depriving them of the major advantage they were supposed to yield—security concerning future economic development.

It is fascinating to speculate on indicative planning that would be so obviously and firmly tied to inflation that, knowing this fact and acting accordingly, all participants in the economic process would adjust their actions to the prospective rate of inflation with the result of magnifying its harmful effects. If indicative planning wants to foster growth through security via a "generalized market," it must see to it that the "indicators" are free of inflationary distortions, lest these distortions automatically multiply, for example, via reduced savings and increased velocity of circulation of money.

We need not repeat that direct credit and price controls are alien to a system that supposedly maintains freedom for consumers and investors. If the plan rests on an accurate forecast it does not need the stick-and-carrot policies of price and credit controls; if it is a development program that deviates from the course that market forces would have brought about, difficulties must develop because the government, being committed to soft planning, will not follow through in terms of commands. The combination of indicative planning and freedom must lead to inflation again and again, because the clash of two sets of preferences can be avoided, and only temporarily, by credit creation alone. It is doubtful whether high growth rates achieved through inflation are worth the price.

That indicative planning needs only a modest central staff and relatively few commissions and working parties makes it obvious that we deal here with broad targets for the economy as a whole and its major branches, but not with detailed guidelines for individual enterprises. The latter will have to rely on real market prices, or else indicative planning must foster some forms of market sharing. Whether such monopolistic developments would be desirable is doubtful. They may well be an indispensable part of indicative planning, but the economy may lose more through the bad

---

[22] "If the plan commits the government to a policy of trying to reach investment and overall growth rates higher than the level of savings, it will tend to produce reluctance on the part of the authorities to take the necessary anti-inflationary measures in time." Vera Lutz, *French Planning* (Washington, D.C.: American Enterprise Institute, 1965), p. 96.

effects of collusion than it may gain through the increased security of "generalized markets."

The French Plan is supposed to be soft. In the words of Pierre Massé, "every branch of activity is promised the possibility of acquiring its production factors and selling its goods on a balanced market. The promise, however, is only kept if everybody plays the game. The promise acts merely as an incentive. It is not binding on anybody. Firms are not dispensed from working out their valuations and choosing their own attitudes. But they can do so in a better informed manner." [23] The basic weakness of indicative planning could hardly be better stated than in this circuitous praise. What if some important firms do not play the game because existing and developing price relationships show that the program does not coincide with their profit expectations? What if the whole program has to be interrupted by a stabilization program? What if the monopolistic organizations want to use their increased power and do not care for an incomes policy? What if in spite of the promised softness, the government supports its development program through credit controls and tax policies that conflict with the clear indications of the real market?

Considering these and other unanswered questions we must conclude, for the time being at least, that indicative planning has not yet proved to be the perfect compromise between market and plan. The danger exists that it may do more harm than good through inflation, monopolistic policies, and direct controls.

[23] Massé in Bornstein, p. 220.

CHAPTER 26

Plans and Markets
in Developing Countries

INTRODUCTION

In his essay, *The Principles of Economic Planning*, W. Arthur Lewis [1] remarks that "planning is at the same time much more necessary and much more difficult in backward than in advanced countries." The present chapter can be considered a commentary on Lewis' statement. It does not deal with economic development in general, nor is it concerned with *totalitarian* planning in developing countries; it presupposes the absence of a detailed, all-inclusive central plan, but also assumes that a well-functioning market economy does not exist. It tries to determine how economic growth can be fostered in poor countries by a mixed system that seeks to use both the plan and the market.

Understandably, many emerging nations do not want to use an all-inclusive plan because it implies a totalitarian political system and would, most likely, not work well since these countries do not have a bureaucracy that could efficiently operate a Soviet-type system of detailed central commands. On the other hand, market forces have not made a very impressive

[1] W. Arthur Lewis, *The Principles of Economic Planning* (Washington, D.C.: Public Affairs Press, 1951), p. 121.

showing in the past; if they had, the countries with the necessary potential for economic growth would now be more developed than they are. Obviously, the market forces lacked the needed infrastructure to build on and a conducive climate in which to operate. The development of backward countries and areas can only be started by government initiative within a framework of government controls. But it would be wrong to jump to the conclusion that there is a positive correlation between the amount and detail of government planning and the prospective rate of growth. The reverse may be true: the more the government can rely on market forces the better it will be in the long run.

The economic system of the developing countries will be a mixed system that affords the advantages of resolute government action in overcoming existing barriers to economic growth, does not involve an amount of central integration exceeding the capacity of its bureaucracy, and fosters a maximum of cooperation between private business and government.

However, mixed systems are very difficult to operate. They are more complex than either of the pure systems, are in danger of wasting resources when clear directives (either via the market or via a central plan) are lacking, and are likely to lead to inflation when the combined claims of the public and private sector overtax the resources of the economy. What is true for relatively developed countries is even more true for the emerging nations who cannot afford to waste resources or indulge in the amenities of the welfare state.

THE CLOSED CIRCLE OF LIMITING FACTORS

The relatively developed market economies owe their growth to a fortuitous combination of circumstances. When their growth began, they were not overpopulated and a rapid increase in population was accompanied by a rise in per capita income. To these countries Malthus' population law did not apply. Growing markets stimulated private investment. Substantial savings were readily absorbed as an upsurge in technical knowledge (the industrial revolution) helped maintain profitable investment opportunities. An ever growing output could be sold on markets that had an increasing capacity to buy the products of mass production, because rising investment created jobs and higher incomes for a growing population. Although disproportions in the process of growth did occur, nobody found it necessary to talk about "balanced" growth. Each growing industry created markets for other industries. Social services came rather late, since the process of development in this regard was a harsh one, far removed from the welfare-state ideas of today.

Because this process was not centrally or consciously planned, it needed personalities with drive and power to maintain what Joseph Schumpeter [2] called the process of "creative destruction." These persons were the so-called entrepreneurs—business adventurers who dared to break new paths, introduce new techniques, and venture into unknown territory. Whether they did so for profit, power, or other motives, they were the dynamic force in the process of growth. They were sometimes inventors and always innovators. Although they were never very numerous, their pathbreaking work was followed up by other businessmen who took the revolutionary ideas and reduced them to more regular economic behavior in a competitive process. Without these men, economic development would not have materialized. But entrepreneurs and businessmen, in order to thrive, need the right climate—a market economy free from too many restrictions, an adequate infrastructure, a reasonably developed money and credit system, and a sufficient amount of competition.

In this pattern of growth, all contributing factors stimulated one another. Profits meant savings; savings were readily invested; investments created employment; employment created income and expanding markets; expanding markets led to greater profits; and greater profits to higher savings and growing investment.

Looking at today's less developed countries, it is usually easy to see why they did not develop. Often the absence of only one growth factor is enough to paralyze the others. Where natural resources are exceedingly poor, no growth can take place; where poverty all but eliminates net saving, poverty will continue; where entrepreneurship is absent, no use is made of existing potentialities; where weak governments cannot provide essential public services, private investment will not take risks; where monetary incentives cannot move the factors of production, these factors will remain where their productivity is very low or even zero; and where population pressure is strong, any improvement in productivity may be absorbed by population growth.

When we consider these "vicious circles," we can appreciate the enormous task faced by those who are responsible for guiding the development of backward countries. Whichever way they turn, they are met by a closed circle of interdependent limiting factors. How can a breakthrough be achieved?

GUIDELINES FOR DEVELOPMENT POLICY

Let us define economic development as "those changes in the use of productive resources that result in a potentially continuing growth of national income per head in a society with increasing or stable popula-

---

[2] Joseph A. Schumpeter, *Capitalism, Socialism, and Democracy*, 3d ed. (New York: Harper & Row, Publishers, 1950), chap. 7.

tion." [3] How can these changes be accomplished in economies that up to now have not been able to use their resources efficiently?

A clarification of the policies by which economic development can be brought about is urgently needed, because the mixed system does not lend itself to a simple, clear, or even "automatic" program. The following guidelines may be useful.

An economy that is not centrally planned like the Soviet economy must rely to a large extent on the operations of the market. There simply is no alternative. Since the market sector of most backward economies does not work well for some of the reasons indicated above, it must be a main function of the government to help create a climate conducive to the building up of an efficient private sector. In particular, the government should not try to substitute its own activities for activities that can be handled by market forces once the needed preconditions are met.

The government's tasks can be divided into four main parts:

1. The government must outline a consistent development program and determine in detail the investment priorities in the public sector. Public investments concern the whole infrastructure of the economy, including investment in education, training, and health. Considering that these investments have probably all been neglected in the past, and considering the often extremely limited resources in terms of bureaucratic talent and capital, it is obvious that prudent and consistent allocation of available resources in the public sector is of utmost importance. This task may overstrain the administration's capacity so that other tasks, such as a detailed control of the market sector or the premature introduction of an advanced welfare program,[4] may have to be put aside.

2. The government must help create the needed incentives for the operation of the market sector, that is, it must foster "entrepreneurship" and encourage the development of a social pattern in which actions are guided by monetary incentives.

---

[3] Fritz Machlup, "Disputes, Paradoxes, and Dilemmas concerning Economic Development," in *Rivista Internazionale Economiche e Commerciali*, vol. 4, no. 9 (Padova, 1957), p. 9.

[4] "Many backward countries have adopted and are still in the process of imitating the latest policies which it took the advanced industrial countries decades or centuries to develop. The latest most up-to-date legislation on social security, regulations of labor, minimum wages, working conditions, channeling saving through governmental agencies and impounding them for public purpose—all these policies which the developed countries have adopted only in a late stage of their development are often introduced in underdeveloped countries as soon as they are freed from colonial status. Add equalization of income through progressive direct taxation, nationalization of existing enterprises and reservation for the Government of certain industries and you have an economic policy which greatly overtaxes the limited administrative capacities of underdeveloped countries." Gottfried Haberler, "Critical Observations on Some Current Notions in the Theory of Economic Development," in *Scritti in Onore di Giuseppe Ugo Papi* (Milano: Editrice L'industria, 1957), p. 7.

3. Where the danger exists that managerial talent is misdirected into the gaining of quick profits from unproductive activities (investment in real estate, gold, or foreign securities) the government will have to correct the market mechanism so that private investment is channeled into productive endeavors.

4. The government must try to achieve the highest possible level of saving compatible with monetary stability and see to it that private investment funds are properly distributed through the credit system.

Emphasis on the market sector is necessitated not only by the absence of a Soviet-type central plan that makes market operations imperative, but also by the enormity of the government's task compared with its limited resources, both human and financial. This comparison urges the advisability of entrusting to market forces and private incentives every economic activity that can be taken off the government's shoulders. W. Arthur Lewis [5] points out that development planning "requires a strong, competent and incorrupt administration," which is "just what no backward country possesses"; and he suggests that "in the absence of such an administration it is often much better that governments should be laissez-faire than that they should pretend to plan."

It is important to recognize policies that are applicable to developed countries but that do not serve the purposes of developing economies. An example is deficit spending to create employment. Even for the developed economies this policy is valid only under special circumstances. To be guided by it when trying to cure unemployment in poor countries could be very dangerous. Another example is offered by the experiences of the International Bank for Reconstruction and Development. The Bank assumed in the beginning of its operations that profitable investment opportunities abound in underdeveloped countries. But in its *Fourth Annual Report* 1948–1949 the IBRD was ready to admit that "perhaps the most striking single lesson which the Bank has learned in the course of its operations is how limited is the capacity of the underdeveloped countries to absorb capital quickly for really productive purposes." A policy to increase investment, therefore, which may be relatively easy in developed countries, may prove to be extremely involved in poor countries.

These, then, are some guidelines that have to be followed in a mixed economy. But they are not an answer to the question of how the government of a backward country can start a process of sustained growth—how, to use W. W. Rostow's [6] vivid term, a take-off can be accomplished. The government must find some way of removing the roadblocks that stand in the way of development, some policy by which an existing potential can be

[5] Lewis, p. 121.
[6] See W. W. Rostow, *The Stages of Economic Growth* (New York: Cambridge University Press, 1960), chap. 4.

exploited, some "initial ignition" or "pump-priming" scheme on a scale grandiose enough to pull the economy out of a "stagnation" that has lasted, not for years, but for centuries.

All development schemes must be connected with capital formation as an indispensable lever of economic growth. Capital formation, however, poses two problems: means of production must be made available for capital goods production, that is, consumption must be kept below a level that could momentarily be reached if growth did not have to be financed; and available investment funds must be invested in the most productive manner through the cooperation of government and private business. This task of capital formation and allocation is harder for a mixed economy than for a command system of the Soviet type. The government cannot simply force the population into hard work and frugal consumption and must strengthen the private sector before it can assume that capital will be productively invested.

CAPITAL FORMATION

W. Arthur Lewis believes that,

> no nation is so poor that it could not save 12 per cent of its national income if it wanted to: poverty has never prevented nations from launching upon wars, or from wasting their substance in other ways. Least of all can those nations plead poverty as an excuse for not saving, in which 40 per cent or so of the national income is squandered by the top 10 per cent of income receivers, living luxuriously on rents.[7]

If Lewis is right, the governments of poor countries should be able to make a substantial amount of investment funds available, both through taxation and the inducement of private saving. As far as the accumulation of investment funds through taxation is concerned, "there is nothing to prevent collective thrift from being combined with individual enterprise." [8] But it may be extremely difficult for the government of a poor country to abstain from using for public purposes all the funds that it has collected. We have already seen that the demands made on the administration will be enormous when compared with the available means.

As a source of investment funds, private saving fits the logic of a market economy better than taxation does. To some extent private saving

[7] W. Arthur Lewis, *The Theory of Economic Growth* (Homewood, Ill.: Richard D. Irwin, Inc., 1955), p. 236.

[8] Ragnar Nurkse, *Problems of Capital Formation in Underdeveloped Countries* (Oxford: Basil Blackwell & Mott, Ltd., 1953), p. 151.

can be induced by offering higher rates of interest. Much remains to be done in this respect:

> The step that governments of underdeveloped countries usually seem to be least willing to contemplate is the offer of higher rewards to savers. In many underdeveloped countries nominal rates of interest paid on savings deposits, government securities, and similar obligations are lower than rates prevailing in some of the richest countries. Often the maximum rates of interest that banks and other institutions can pay are fixed at low levels by law or regulation. When this situation is combined with a chronic tendency for prices to rise, it is not surprising that much of the community's savings is channeled into gold, foreign exchange, and residential construction.[9]

Discussions of the problem of capital formation in poor countries sometimes refer to "disguised" unemployment. Indeed, labor may be an abundant factor in a backward country, a factor whose marginal productivity may be less than zero, and yet whose surplus units might be used productively if certain conditions were fulfilled. If the unemployed in disguise could be made to produce capital goods, both capital and employment could be created simultaneously!

Economic textbooks used to explain capital formation as a process by which consumer goods are made available to those who produce capital goods. It was considered the essence of saving that men can be employed in the investment goods industry because others are willing to consume less than they are entitled to. Adapted to overpopulated but underdeveloped countries, the same idea suggests that, the high percentage of agricultural labor who have to be fed despite zero productivity should be put to use in the production of capital goods. While this proposal has some merit, it is obvious that major obstacles must be overcome before the absorption of the unemployed in disguise can be achieved: (1) After the release of this labor force, without a reduction in agricultural production, the consumption of those remaining in agriculture must be kept from increasing. (2) The released labor force must be provided with capital goods, however primitive. (3) There must be provision of sufficient monetary inducements for this shift of labor and the laborers must be willing to respond to monetary incentives. (4) Administrative or entrepreneurial initiative is required to organize all these changes.

Disguised unemployment in underdeveloped countries is not to be confused with mass unemployment in developed economies and should not be attacked through deficit spending or big industrial projects of high capital intensity. Increased aggregate spending might do little to move the

[9] Richard B. Goode, "Adding to the Stock of Physical and Human Capital," *American Economic Review*, vol. 49 (May 1959), p. 151.

unemployed from agriculture to industry and, in failing to create productive employment, would create only price inflation. And the choice of capital-intensive investment projects would violate the basic principle of factor allocation. Employment-creating projects in overpopulated poor countries should be as labor-intensive as feasible, though productivity per man employed would be relatively low. What counts is not only the rise in productivity from zero levels but also the number of laborers affected by this rise.

We have seen that the social economy should solve the problem of *how* to produce, not by indiscriminately adopting the newest techniques, but by combining its factors of production according to their relative scarcities. This does not mean that the relative abundance of labor in a given country excludes technological improvements. It is not correct when Benjamin Higgins says that "no technological advance has as yet been discovered which is suited to the factor proportions of the underdeveloped countries." [10] There are many stages of technological development that have been passed by the now developed countries but that might fit the special factor proportions of some poor countries. However, these production methods are not likely to be discovered under the influence of the "demonstration effect," that is, when poor countries try to imitate the rich in a misconceived endeavor to industrialize without proper guidance by factor prices. A relatively poor country cannot afford a nuclear reactor that is mainly to serve as a status symbol.

The scarcity of capital in developing countries ought to be expressed by correspondingly high interest rates. Interest rates that are kept artificially low are not only detrimental to private saving, they are even more dangerous for the other component of capital formation: investment. It is most important that market rates of interest should clearly indicate the scarcity of investment funds, and that the government should refrain from establishing priority schemes that distribute these funds contrary to the allocation that correct rates would have brought about in the private sector of the economy. We have seen that even "rich" countries cannot afford the waste of resources resulting from ill-considered priority schemes. Backward countries can afford this waste even less.

It is true, of course, that heavy investments must be undertaken in the public sector if the development process is to be successfully started and maintained. Where a comparison of interest and profit rates is not possible, priorities must be used. But it is not helpful when the government deceives itself (via low interest rates concerning the relative scarcity of investment funds), invests more than it can afford, overtaxes the productive power of the country, and does not leave sufficient funds for the

[10] Benjamin Higgins, *Economic Development, Problems and Policies* (New York: W. W. Norton & Company, Inc., 1959), p. 258.

private sector. The latter will then suffer both from capital shortage and price inflation. Price inflation is damaging for a country that wants to foster the growth of domestic savings and the influx of foreign capital. In addition, price inflation leads to balance-of-payments difficulties and exchange controls, which, in turn, are another major obstacle to foreign investment.[11]

PRIVATE AND PUBLIC INVESTMENT

If central planning is to be avoided, the government must see that private business and private initiative eventually play a major role in the process of economic growth. Here, as is true of saving, the plight of the backward countries is sometimes overstated. Some business skill is available in all countries. It does not make sense to deny this and at the same time to assume the availability of unlimited governmental administrative skill. Also, not too much entrepreneurship (in the narrower sense) might be needed. Managerial initiative will often be limited to an adaptation of *known* techniques, skills, and methods to the conditions of underdeveloped countries.

It is necessary to make the most of what managerial skills are available and to create a climate in which those possessing such skills find it worthwhile to enter business and to develop initiative. Where "the accepted scale of social prestige places . . . the man of business far down the line," the underdeveloped countries have

> to try to find means of elevating constructive business pursuits to a higher prestige level in the social hierarchy and of diverting the experience and talents of the minority groups from commerce and trade to manufacturing and other more constructive activities. Too often, a by-product of nationalism is covert and overt reaction against such minorities, long before the dominant social groups are ready to supply entrepreneurial talent from their own ranks.[12]

If needed investment funds and business skills cannot be found, the government may be right in embarking on projects outside the public utilities and social overhead area. It must be clear, however, why the private sector of the economy was found wanting. It could be that private capital did not care to invest because the project is out of line with the rest of the economy's growth and therefore not profitable. Private capital cannot

---

[11] On inflation and development see Committee for Economic Development, *How Low Income Countries Can Advance Their Own Growth* (New York: Committee for Economic Development, 1966), pp. 52–55.

[12] William H. Nicholls, "Accommodating Economic Change in Underdeveloped Countries," *American Economic Review*, vol. 49 (May 1959), p. 158.

afford the luxury of showcase industrialization. Because it must follow the guidance of prices and costs, private investment is not likely to lead to unbalanced growth. As Charles P. Kindleberger rightly argues:

> Given uncertainty as to the exact nature of blocks to development, probing along a broad front in reconnaissance strength may make more sense than committing all one's forces to a single salient which may prove unyielding.[13]

Public managers are not always able to apply the type of reasoning that is appropriate to the market sector of the economy. Often they continue to think in terms of priorities rather than cost-price relations. But what is correct and necessary in the public sector is not necessarily conducive to successful private enterprise. For instance, public managers may be tempted to carry the "external economies" argument, from which public enterprise derives its justification, into fields which ought to be reserved for private enterprise if a market economy is to be developed.

Emphasis on external economies is decisive where public investments are not profitable but are nevertheless considered productive. In this category belong public education, public health, and such basic utilities as water, electric power, port installations, and transportation. In all these cases it is assumed that because of these investments the costs of private firms will be reduced. In many instances private investments will not be possible until public investment of this type has taken place. Therefore the latter must play a strategic role in economic development, a role proportionally greater than in developed countries where social overhead expenditures have not been neglected. We already know that private investment cannot be expected to take care of needs whose satisfaction does not permit comparisons between rates of profit and rates of interest.

However, the concept "external economies" has also been more broadly interpreted.[14] It is often applied to the effects which investments by private firms have on the rest of the private sector of the economy. These effects give rise to the argument that economic growth should be balanced to allow a wide range of investment processes to assist each other.

[13] Charles P. Kindleberger, *Economic Development*, 2d ed. (New York: McGraw-Hill, Inc., 1965), p. 128.

[14] "The concept of external economies refers to a situation in which the cost curves of individual firms shift downwards because of the historical development of their environments. For example, an increase in the size of an industry may attract a more efficient labor force and thereby bring benefits to all firms in the industry. Or the growth of transportation facilities in a particular area may lead to a lowering of costs for firms using the services of the transportation industry. The notion of external economies recognizes the interdependence and complementarity of various sectors of the economy. As one part grows, it stimulates other parts not only by increasing demands but also by decreasing costs."—Gerald M. Meier and Robert E. Baldwin, *Economic Development: Theory, History, Policy* (New York: John Wiley & Sons, Inc., 1957), pp. 22–23.

It is understandable, then, that public administrators might want to embark on investments in what would normally be the private sector, even though these investments are not yet profitable. They ascribe to such investment projects important external economies. The lack of profitability seems overcompensated by the projects' beneficial effects on society as a whole. Thus the line between private and public investment areas becomes blurred. There is some danger that large public investments in what normally would be the private sector (for example, steel mills) may, through their very size, violate the principle of balanced growth that underlies the concept of external economies.

Emphasis on "balanced growth" is a sign that investment criteria in underdeveloped countries have lacked consistency and clarity. It should not be necessary to point out that modern mass production of shoes cannot be profitable where the population does not have sufficient purchasing power to buy them; it should likewise be self-evident that it is necessary to consider the effects which innovations in the agricultural sector will have on the industrial sector and vice versa.[15] On the other hand, we must beware lest the request for balanced growth is turned into an argument for autarky. An industry cannot be considered overexpanded if, according to the law of comparative advantage, it can find markets for its products abroad.[16]

INDIAN PLANNING

It is dangerous to make generalizing theoretical remarks about the development of backward countries since these countries differ widely in individual features and none will fit a theoretical model; nor can decisive evidence be gathered from the study of just one country for a relatively short period. Nevertheless, to give at least a little substance to our argument, a glance at Indian planning will be helpful because the structure of the Indian economy comes close to our original assumptions. The Indian economy is not a command economy; it rests to a substantial degree on market forces and must operate its development program, accordingly, as a mixed economy.

Were India already a developed country, its form of planning could be likened to that of France, considering that the Indian *Planning Commission* has as little authority as the French *Commissariat au Plan*, and that the plan itself is the same ambiguous mixture of estimates, forecasts, and targets. The difference is that, up to now, the public sector is rela-

---

[15] Nurkse, p. 7; Lewis, *The Theory of Economic Growth*, pp. 276–277.
[16] Machlup, p. 25. The principles of comparative advantage will be discussed in the following chapter.

tively more important in the Indian plan and the problems facing the Indian economy are far more serious than in France.

If we compare the facts of Indian planning with the guidelines discussed above, we must conclude that the guidelines were not well followed and the results were not auspicious. The first Indian Five Year Plan, which started operation in 1951, tried to strengthen agriculture and improve the infrastructure of the economy. In spite of initial inflation, the results were surprisingly good, with increases in per capita income and food production outstripping the plan estimates. But then the second plan shifted to a totally different course. Quick growth was now to be achieved through increased *public* investment in heavy industry, at the expense of agriculture, private industry, and public services. In addition to rapid industrialization, the plan targets were: a rising living standard, more equal income distribution, and a substantial expansion of employment opportunities. This combination of targets violated by its obvious incompatibility of aims, ways, and means the most basic and implicit rule of planning—that of consistency. Furthermore, the fact that industrialization was undertaken directly by the government did not conform to the rule that a mixed system should rely as much as possible on market operations. The size of the program of quick industrialization, its combination with welfare aims, and its competition with the private sector had to lead to inflation and to a severe external disequilibrium. And all these negative effects were interconnected and self-aggravating.

The government had neither an all-inclusive plan nor a set of consistent market prices by which to determine the size and the details of its industrialization program. Even the fact that investment in heavy industry, with its relatively small labor component, clearly contradicted the avowed aim of creating sufficient employment opportunities did not stop the planners, although it ought to have been obvious that the factor allocation was fundamentally wrong. Had private business been permitted to operate with the aid of an improved infrastructure and on the basis of correct cost calculations, the conflict between investment and employment would have been less pronounced.

The dangerous and costly rejection of market forces, market prices, and private initiative stemmed from reasons as the following: "the profound distrust of the judgment of the individual producers and consumers;" [17] "the intellectual arrogance typical of reformers" that makes them desire to take direct action; [18] "the greater ease of planning in the

---

[17] Haberler, p. 11.
[18] Harry G. Johnson, "Planning and the Market in Economic Development," *Pakistan Economic Journal*, vol. 8, no. 2 (June 1958), pp. 44–55, reprinted in Morris Bornstein, *Comparative Economic Systems: Models and Cases* (Homewood, Ill.: Richard D. Irwin, Inc., 1965), pp. 427–438.

government sphere where activities are directly under control;" [19] the socialist disapproval of the private enterprise economy; and, finally, the fact that "the obscurity of the market's functions makes it easy . . . to confuse opposition to unattractive features of the free enterprise system, which express themselves through the market, such as inequality of income and wealth, with opposition to the market as a mechanism of organization." [20]

In embarking on a rapid industrialization program, the Indian Government's estimates of its financial resources were far too optimistic. Deficit spending led to inflation despite a substantial import surplus. Disregarding these consequences, the third Five Year Plan followed the same basic philosophy as the second and produced, on the whole, the same results. However, the third plan did aim toward the goal of self-sufficiency in agriculture to improve the balance of trade. The fourth plan shows an interesting shift in priorities: agriculture and infrastructure are gaining once more in importance while the steel target has been greatly reduced; and there is a refreshing new emphasis on cooperation between the private and the public sector.

[19] Anne O. Krueger, "Indian Planning Experience," in Theodore Morgan, George W. Betz, N. K. Choudhry editors, *Readings in Development* (Belmont, Cal.: Wadsworth Publishing Company, 1963), p. 414.
[20] Johnson in Bornstein, p. 430.

CHAPTER 27

Economic Systems
and International Trade

INTERNATIONAL TRADE
AND THE PRIVATE ENTERPRISE ECONOMY

The countries of the world are not equally endowed with factors of production. Some enjoy a favorable proportion of skilled labor, capital goods, and natural resources; others abound in unskilled labor but are poor in capital; while still others combine a scarce labor supply with rich natural resources. These various factor endowments lead, in market economies, to different patterns of factor prices, and, accordingly, to diverging commodity prices. If the price structure of country A differs from that of country B, both countries gain from international trade. Each country specializes in the commodities suggested by its relative advantage in factor endowment and benefits when its exports (which pay for its imports) cost less to produce than it would have cost to manufacture the imported goods at home. We have to add those cases where the imported products could not have been produced at all domestically and productions which now can take place because formerly lacking resources can be imported. Furthermore, international trade broadens the market for national industries and thus creates or expands the basis for the economies of scale, that is, the advantages of mass production.

Although the benefits from international trade were stated in the terminology of the market economies, the principles implied are basic and equally true for liberal socialist or centrally planned economies. All types of systems will benefit from international division of labor, though in somewhat different ways.

The residents of a private enterprise economy will import commodities that, in spite of transfer costs, are cheaper than similar home-produced goods; and they will pay for these imports by exports that are competitive in foreign markets. To translate domestic into foreign prices, we need a rate of exchange. Knowing the exchange rate, we can directly compare the prices of two countries. When we know, in addition, the transfer costs (freight, insurance, import duties, and so forth), we can determine which goods will be imported and exported.

Because exports must pay for imports in the long run, international trade between market economies must rest on an adjustment mechanism that establishes external equilibrium. It was shown in Chapter 25 that the adjustment mechanism that fits the basic character of the market economies is offered by a system of flexible exchange rates. In this system, an import surplus of Country A depreciates A's currency unit just enough to lead to external equilibrium. If, on the other hand, the exchange rate is fixed, an import surplus must cause a reduction of the country's foreign exchange or gold reserves. This reduction, in turn, will require a downward adjustment of domestic costs and prices (or a smaller increase than in the export-surplus country).

Obviously, the less productive countries will not be able to trade with the more productive ones on the basis of equal real (or gold) wages. The less efficient a country, the lower its real wages must be to permit exports at competitive prices. This fact does in no way destroy the argument that both the less and the more efficient countries gain from trade as long as it would, in real terms, cost more to produce the imported commodities at home than it costs to produce the exports which pay for the imports.

The classical economists were free-traders; they believed in the international division of labor and considered it foolish to reduce the benefits from trade through creation of artificial trade barriers. Consistently, they could even have argued that free international commodity trade was only a second-best solution, needed because the international movement of factors of production was often impossible.

However, the businessmen who were meeting foreign competition on the home market did not subscribe to the free-trade philosophy of classical economics. On the contrary, they tried to identify their own narrow private interests with those of the nation, arguing that protectionist policies would increase employment, keep money at home, expand domestic markets, keep out the products of cheap labor, and so forth. These arguments always broke off too soon. The protectionists refused to see that relatively inefficient, protected industries would grow at the expense of efficient export industries and that money spent on imports would come back as demand for the products of the country's export industries.

Thus the private enterprise system presented the inconsistent picture of sound theory and often unsound practices in matters of international trade policy. That protectionism often won was mainly due to the fact that special interests demanding protection were far more aggressive as political pressure groups than the unorganized consumers who had to suffer.

However, even classical economics acknowledged a special case where protection might be permissible. An "infant industry" could be allowed to grow to maturity before being exposed to the sharp wind of competition from more advanced countries. While theoretically sound, this argument often led to permanent protection of firms that had been established under the cover of protection but that were never able to achieve a competitive status. The idea, of course, was that an infant-industry tariff should be strictly a temporary measure.

INSULATION AGAINST DEPRESSION

The classical theory of international trade, as indeed classical theory in general, proceeded on the assumption of "full" employment in the trading countries. Admission of the possibility of mass unemployment, however, led to substantial changes in the theory of international trade and commercial policy. It could now be shown that changes in the national income of one country can affect other countries, that fluctuations in economic activity are transmitted from country to country, and that in the process of transmission the balance of payments may be temporarily disturbed.[1]

If it is possible for a country's employment and income level to be adversely affected by another country's depresssion, a case might be made against free trade, because a country's gains through the international division of labor could be lost through unemployment, and therefore protectionist measures might be justifiable in connection with domestic full-employment policies.

This reasoning is certainly wrong when it tries to say that foreign products are to be excluded whenever unemployment occurs in an industry exposed to foreign competition. We must always consider the effect of protection on the country's export industry. Furthermore, such protection-

[1] See Ragnar Nurkse, "Domestic and International Equilibrium," ed. Seymour E. Harris, *The New Economics: Keynes' Influence on Theory and Public Policy* (New York: Alfred A. Knopf, Inc., 1948), pp. 264–292.

ist measures would be beggar-my-neighbor policies; that is, they would create unemployment in other parts of the world.

But how is a country that wants to maintain a high employment level to defend its economy against the contagious effect of depressions in other countries? Let us assume that a falling-off of country A's economic activity causes country B's exports to fall. As investment and employment decline in B's export industries, the whole of B's economy will suffer, for a negative multiplier effect now lowers B's national income in the wake of country A's depression. With falling national income, country B's imports will decline; but because B's imports are not likely to fall as fast as its exports, B will experience a balance-of-payments deficit. If country B, whose exchange rate is fixed, tries to boost its exports and to lower its imports by contractionist monetary policies, it aggravates the process of domestic depression: it can achieve balance-of-payments equilibrium, but only at the cost of a further increase in unemployment. If country B tries to counteract domestically the contraction that was generated by a decline in its exports to country A, that is, if it embarks on expansionist monetary and fiscal policies, its balance-of-payments deficit increases. In this dilemma country B may decide to insulate its economy against contagious foreign depressions through import quotas and exchange controls. Domestic full employment may then be achieved at the price of giving up its currency convertibility and the advantages of multilateral trade. Multilateral trade permits country B to pay for its imports from country A by exports to countries C, D or E, all currencies being freely interchangeable. It maintains the principle of buying and selling in the most favorable markets; that is, it does not reduce international trade to barter in form of bilateral deals.

Multilateral trade implies not only convertibility of currencies but also nondiscrimination. Even where tariff duties are imposed, nondiscrimination can be maintained through unconditional use of the most-favored-nation clause, the mutual promise that the other country will not be treated worse than any third party. Tariffs can be prohibitive, of course; but where they are nonprohibitive and applied in a nondiscriminatory manner, they maintain the principle of international division of labor according to the working of the price mechanisms of the different countries. While imposing, as it were, artificial transportation costs, the tariff still leaves the allocation of productive resources to economic forces. But it is indeed *because* the tariff permits a relatively close interrelation of the trading economies' price systems that the tariff—unless prohibitive—is not considered sufficient when countries try to insulate themselves against foreign depression. More powerful protectionist instruments are employed, instruments that purposely disrupt the interrelation of the price systems of different market economies. In the case of import quotas and exchange controls the government arbitrarily determines what is to be imported, how much, by whom, and from which countries. Imports become largely independent of market forces. This is the very reason why countries that want to insulate their economies turn to these controls. Only direct controls give them sufficient assurance that international economic relations will not hinder their domestic economic policies.

But while quantitative controls provide the desired insulation, it is impossible to handle them in a nondiscriminatory manner.

> Quantitative restrictions make it virtually impossible to prevent discrimination between countries. The most-favored-nation clause is practically inapplicable to quotas and quantitative restrictions in general. For there is no accepted or plausible principle of quota allocation which could be called non-discriminatory and consistent with the most-favored-nation principle. Various systems of quota allocation have been proposed as nondiscriminatory but none is satisfactory. Equal quotas for all countries of supply are clearly inequitable. Allocation in proportion to imports from different countries in some base year is unsatisfactory and unjust in the case of crops which fluctuate from year to year. In the case of industrial products too it is liable to get more and more out of date, as the underlying situation changes.[2]

In case of exchange control the supply of foreign exchange may be allocated uniformly on a percentage basis, but as in the case of quotas, this freezes the pattern of trade that existed in the base period.

We need not assume that all countries that apply direct controls to their international trade have planned economies. They may be market economies that want to defend their employment level and their foreign exchange reserves against the impact of foreign economic fluctuations. But we cannot overlook the fact that these controls are alien to the philosophy of the private enterprise system. Indeed, it is quite possible that a growing use of quotas and exchange controls may, in turn, lead to numerous domestic controls. For this reason the devotee of the private enterprise system cannot argue consistently for the more advanced practices of protectionism without renouncing the basic philosophy on which his economic system is built.[3]

How, then, can a compromise be found between a country's legitimate desire to protect its economy against the contagious effect of foreign depressions and its desire to participate in nondiscriminatory multilateral trade? The problem could be eliminated if the trading countries succeeded in reducing economic fluctuations to manageable proportions without using beggar-my-neighbor policies. Fortunately, domestic monetary and

[2] League of Nations, *Quantitative Trade Controls, Their Causes and Nature* (Geneva: 1943), pp. 25–26.
[3] See Lionel Robbins, *Economic Planning and International Order* (New York: St. Martin's Press, Inc., 1937), pp. 24–26.

fiscal policies aiming at high employment are, as a rule, compatible with multilateral international trade. What maintains a high level of economic activity helps other countries to maintain exports. Furthermore, any aid extended by the depressed country in the form of international lending stimulates its export industry and helps other countries to overcome an acute shortage of foreign exchange.

Balance-of-payments difficulties can result from causes other than depression in foreign countries. For instance, a country can perpetuate an external disequilibrium by maintaining a more inflationary monetary and fiscal policy than its trade partners. If such a country is not willing to live within its means, that is, to adjust its real wages to its productivity, it will be tempted to use quantitative restrictions in international trade, just as it may try to repress inflation at home through price controls. Obviously, nondiscriminatory multilateral trade requires a minimum of adjustment between the national economic policies of the trading countries.

We saw in Chapter 25 that it is not consistent when market economies, whose domestic economic policies are not well integrated, maintain permanently fixed exchange rates, and that the adjustable-peg system has great disadvantages. The logic of the private enterprise system demands flexible exchange rates.

LIBERAL SOCIALISM AND INTERNATIONAL TRADE

Liberal socialist writers admit the advantages of international trade and suggest that fullest use be made of these advantages.[4] It may even be said that those who advocate a planned economy have sometimes shown a clearer conception of the benefits of international trade than have many businessmen in market economies. Furthermore, because the socialist writer assumes full employment, fear of unemployment does not dilute his willingness to have labor employed where it is most productive. Socialist planners look at imports as a valuable addition to the national product and regard exports as the price that must be paid for these imports. In a private enterprise system we are sometimes told that exports are favorable and employment-creating, while imports are unfavorable or unemployment-creating.

How is multilateral, nondiscriminatory trade to take place among liberal socialist economies?

H. D. Dickinson [5] assumes that the supreme economic council would

[4] See, for example, R. L. Hall, *The Economic System in a Socialist State* (New York: St. Martin's Press, Inc., 1937), chap. 12; H. D. Dickinson, *Economics of Socialism* (New York: Oxford University Press, 1939), chap. 7. Both Hall and Dickinson emphasize the classical theory of comparative advantage.

[5] Dickinson, pp. 174, 177.

compute domestic prices, compare them with foreign prices on the basis of a given exchange rate, and determine, accordingly, which commodities should be imported and which exported. Similarly, R. L. Hall [6] suggests that "a list of products may be drawn up in order of advantage, those with the greatest comparative advantage at the top and those with the least at the bottom" and that international trade equilibrium will be established through the rate of exchange at which exports pay for imports.

Dickinson admits that state trading by large national monopolies leads to bilateral monopoly "in which it is probable that there is no determinate stable position of equilibrium, but in which either party has an incentive to get the better of the other by the use of fraud and of force." This remark suggests that the instability of prices could be greater under state trading than under competitive private trading on a broad multilateral basis. But liberal socialist writers point out that the government monopolists would refuse to use their power to the detriment of the consumer or other countries and that "within the 'glass walls' of socialist economy it would be difficult to maintain unreasonable discrimination for long."

But we have to consider the following points. We have already seen that it is not at all obvious that the "glass walls" of the liberal socialist economy will clearly reveal the cost-and-price structures of the nationalized industries.[7] The practical pricing problem of the liberal socialist economy is, as yet, far from satisfactorily solved. Similarly, we had to conclude that the mere existence of socialism will not eliminate the dangers of monopoly.[8] The monopolistic concentration of power is by definition much greater in a socialist than in a private enterprise economy. The liberal socialist argument rests on the rather weak assumption that public managers will play at competition while they are, at the same time, responsible to the central planning board. But even if we assume that the managers will behave as if they were acting competitively, it is not obvious that they would act in a nondiscriminatory fashion in their relations with other countries. It might be assumed, for instance, that they will use state trading to overcome some of the many difficulties that are sure to develop in the execution of the national plan. In addition, there is no reason to take for granted that the wealthier socialist communities will be eager to share their wealth with the poorer. And from this attitude it is a small step to the desire to make full use of the bargaining powers inherent in state trading.

In commercial relations between state trading boards and private commercial firms of nonsocialist countries, the state trading boards are often at an advantage, for many private sellers may be confronted by one buyer, or many private buyers by one seller. To protect the interests of its

[6] Hall, p. 220.
[7] See Chap. 16.
[8] See Chap. 17.

citizens, the government of a private enterprise country may feel compelled to create state trading agencies, thereby violating the basic principles of its own economic system and creating a conflict between its domestic anti-monopolistic and its foreign commercial policies.

SOVIET-TYPE PLANNING AND INTERNATIONAL TRADE

While we do not know how international trade of liberal socialist economies would work *in practice*, we have little difficulty in *imagining* that the price systems of different liberal socialist economies or even of liberal socialist and private enterprise economies could be used to determine imports and exports under a system of flexible exchange rates.

The case of a centrally planned economy of the Soviet type would be different, although it would still be true that, other things remaining equal, international division of labor would prove to be basically beneficial. Also, we can still assume that the Soviet-type economy follows the common-sense attitude of regarding exports as the cost of gaining desired imports, an attitude that is sometimes missing in private enterprise economies. To the benefits from trade can be added one advantage that must count heavily in the government's decision to enter trade, not only with other planned economies but even with private enterprise countries. This is the possibility of giving flexibility to an otherwise very rigid economic structure [9] or, to put it differently, to use imports for the correction of planning errors.[10] Should imports serve to provide strategically important items without which large sections of the planned economy would collapse, these items might be so crucial that their purchase could be worthwhile even at otherwise quite unacceptable terms of trade. In other words, it may be essential for the central planners to import even if these imports are extremely expensive in terms of the exports that have to be given in exchange.

Nevertheless, in spite of these general and special advantages, the basic attitude of Soviet-type planners to international trade is not very enthusiastic for the following reasons given by Franklin D. Holzman: [11]

1. "Planners like to control as many economic variables as possible." Therefore, "it is natural for planners to try to avoid, where possible, the uncertainties of the (oft-times hostile) world market."

[9] See Stanislaw Wellisz, *The Economies of the Soviet Bloc* (New York: McGraw-Hill, Inc., 1964), p. 88.

[10] See Adolf Weber, *Sowjetwirtschaft und Weltwirtschaft* (Berlin: Duncker & Humblot, 1959), p. 231.

[11] Franklyn D. Holzman in Hearings on *Recent Developments in the Soviet Bloc* of the Subcommittee on Europe, House Committee on Foreign Affairs, February 18, 1964.

2. Planners desire "to be as independent as possible of supplies from capitalist nations in case of open hostilities or simply to avoid being put in a position of vulnerability to economic warfare."

3. The Soviet-type economies are to be industrialized "even though this be at the expense of expanded or more profitable foreign trade."

4. "The price systems of the centrally planned economies are sufficiently chaotic and irrational and adapted to the peculiar needs of their domestic economies that it is often difficult for the planners to decide what they should or should not trade." Chaotic prices are also the reason why the currencies of these countries are not held as liquidity reserves by other nations "because of the uncertainty as to what that currency can buy and at what price."

Trade between the Soviet-type economies and western countries takes place on the basis of world market prices since the artificial internal price system of the planned economies would be completely meaningless. It would be quite hopeless to try to find out whether trade moves along the lines of comparative advantage, whether it is non-discriminatory, whether the planned economies engage in dumping, or whether the exchange rates of the bloc currencies correspond to their purchasing power. The price systems of eastern and western economies do not mesh. The partners on both sides will simply have to decide whether they want to trade at world market prices. For the western economies, trade at these prices fits their market system and does not normally add an element of uncertainty, unless the transactions of the Soviet-bloc countries are very erratic. Against this contingency they may be able to protect themselves through trade agreements.

More problematic is the effect of East-West trade on the planned economies. How, for example, will a sudden correction of a planning error which involves the importation of strategically important commodities from the West affect the central plan, or how could a sudden drop in Soviet export earnings, owing, say, to a depression in the West, be prevented from upsetting an otherwise balanced central plan? We saw in Chapter 20 how the Soviet system handles alterations in the state preference schedule that imply changes in factor allocations throughout the economy. Industries with higher priority rating dislodge allocations for low priority areas. In the case of planning mistakes, which are to be corrected through imports of suddenly needed products, exports will have to be stepped up at the expense of the domestic demand that is considered least important. Since domestic prices have no allocative function, the necessary transfers of factors and products to the export sector can be accomplished without consideration of its conceivable absurdity according to comparative costs. Losses through unfavorable terms of trade may be much lower than losses implied in a partial breakdown of the plan. It is not surprising, then, to find cases in which both the Russian import demand and export supply functions are nearly perfectly inelastic: the imports are so critically important that they are bought regardless of price, and exports are sold, however unfavorably.

Normally, of course, Soviet imports and exports will react to changes in world market prices, but these reactions may differ from reactions of private traders in market economies. For example, the state trading agency may find that, owing to increased world market prices for its exports, it need export less than before to earn the foreign exchange needed to pay for its planned imports (a case of a backward sloping supply curve). In this context it is important to remember that Soviet trade is differently motivated than private trade. Not only are exports as such considered a cost item that ought to be reduced, if possible, but also there is no fear of unemployment and the effects of a negative multiplier. Due to these entirely different motivations and the nature of the Soviet price structure, it is impossible to apply the basic principles of western trade to East-West relations. Often it will be completely impossible to tell whether trade proceeds on the principle of comparative advantage and nondiscrimination or whether the exchange rate of the centrally planned economy is, by western standards, a rate which corresponds to the internal purchasing power of the currency.

The Havana Charter for an International Trade Organization,[12] which remains an important document in spite of its withdrawal from legislative consideration, wants to make state trading compatible with nondiscrimination and multilateralism. For this purpose it uses a "commercial considerations" formula. Art. 29 specifies that state trading enterprises shall make purchases and sales "solely in accordance with commercial considerations, including price, quality, availability, marketability, transportation and other conditions of purchase or sale, and shall afford the enterprises of other Member countries adequate opportunity, in accordance with customary business practice, to compete for participation in such purchases or sales." Theoretically speaking, state trading agencies might try to act in this nondiscriminatory fashion to gain the greatest possible advantage from international trade. Practically speaking, however, it must be doubted that state trading agencies will be permitted to behave like unregimented private traders. When state trading is part of a central plan, it is not at all obvious that the aim of the plan will coincide with commercial considerations, which are influenced by world market conditions. In other words, it is improbable that state trading agencies will adhere strictly to commercial behavior if state trading is entrusted, as it undoubtedly will be, with

---

[12] *Havana Charter for an International Trade Organization* (U.S. Department of State, Publication 3206, Commercial Policy Series 114, Washington, D.C., March 24, 1948).

the job of insulating the planned economy against contagious foreign depressions. An "as if" behavior is not a very reliable practical guide:

> It is too much to expect that the right hand of the purchasing agency will completely ignore the left hand of the exporting agency. There will inevitably be a tendency for state-trading enterprises to enter into bilateral arrangements, either explicit or implied, with other state-trading nations or even with countries in which foreign trading is in private hands.[13]

The commercial considerations approach is inadequate even on its own terms, for it implies that the state trading agency will act as though it were buying and selling competitively, while actually the agency has monopolistic and monopsonistic powers. If, however, a monopolist *does* act according to commercial considerations alone, he will often use discrimination as a means of increasing his profit.

The General Agreement on Tariffs and Trade (GATT)[14] follows, in Art. XVII, the exact wording of the commercial considerations formula of the ITO Charter. However, it does not show how this formula can be applied in planned economies.

The perplexity of the question of how nondiscriminatory trade and economic planning can be combined is reflected in the following statement by the chairman of the Contracting Parties of the GATT of June 2, 1959: [15]

> The association of Yugoslavia and Poland's request for accession obviously raise serious problems for the CONTRACTING PARTIES. In the past, the requests for accession which we have received have always been from countries whose economic structure and commercial policy system did not differ greatly from those existing in our own countries. In the case of Yugoslavia, we considered for the first time the possibility of applying the principles of the General Agreement to a country whose economy differs in many important respects from that of our countries. The divergence of economic concepts seems still greater in the case of Poland, and in the near future the CONTRACTING PARTIES will probably have to give serious consideration to the possibility of broadening our philosophy and making our system more flexible so as to enable countries whose economy is based on free enterprise to co-operate fruitfully within this organization with those whose economy is entirely planned. It is too early to predict what solutions we can arrive at in the future and submit to our governments in order to achieve that result, but it is not too early to point out to our governments that this is a problem to which they will have to give careful consideration in coming months.

[13] Raymond F. Mikesell, "Quantitative and Exchange Restrictions under the ITO Charter," *American Economic Review*, vol. 37 (June 1947), p. 366.

[14] General Agreement of Tariffs and Trade, *Basic Instruments and Selected Documents*, vol. 3, *Text of the General Agreement 1958* (Geneva: November 1958).

[15] Information Service, European Office of the United Nations, Geneva, Press Release GATT/454, 2 June 1959.

Obviously, nobody yet knows how a satisfactory compromise can be achieved between the different basic principles that underlie international transactions by market and those that underlie international transactions by centrally planned economies.

INTRABLOC TRADE

Trade between centrally planned economies is subject to difficulties similar to those which beset trade of centrally planned with market economies: international trade creates uncertainties, causes dependence on supplies from other countries, decreases autonomy, and lacks the foundation of consistent pricing. Since the prices in centrally planned economies have no guiding function domestically, they lack the ability to determine what the division of labor among the communist bloc countries ought to be. We cannot be surprised, then, to find that intrabloc trade between Soviet Russia and its satellites is based on world market prices as the only available consistent expression of the relative scarcities of the commodities in question. We must expect, furthermore, that world market prices will not be permitted to influence domestic prices and, via price changes, the allocation of productive resources. Neither are income effects which play an important role in the adjustment process of trade and payments between market economies permitted to affect the plans of the participating countries. "Should exports decline, not only would the Soviets reduce imports, they would also act quickly to reemploy unemployed resources and to shift some of these resources into the production of goods formerly imported." [16]

Actually, the trade relations between Soviet Russia and her satellites are not more than bilateral barter arrangements in which the values of the traded commodities are only *originally* derived from world market prices but, being frozen afterwards, lose this connection more and more as time goes on. Payments are made into reciprocal accounts in the state banks of the trade partners, the exact amounts being established by the rate of exchange.

The disadvantages of these arrangements are plain: the elimination of multilateralism, price rigidity, faulty resource allocation, currency inconvertibility, and the danger of monopolistic or monopsonistic exploitation of given situations by the stronger partner. Obviously, the Soviet Government did make monopolistic use of its bargaining power since, after the Polish and Hungarian riots in 1956, it was officially admitted

[16] Franklyn D. Holzman, "The Operation of Some Traditional Adjustment Mechanisms in the Foreign Trade of Centrally Planned Economies," in Cahiers de l'Isea, Serie *Economie Planifiée*, 1967.

that trade between Russia and its satellites had been full of violations of the principle of equality that should have prevailed. Unfair exchange rates and unfavorable export prices were corrected and a new attempt inaugurated to put intrabloc trade on a more integrated basis.

A Council of Economic Mutual Assistance (CEMA) had existed since 1949, but only in the 1960's was a real attempt made to introduce specialization and the economies of scale into Soviet bloc trade. Ultimate aim was a coordination of the long-term investment plans of all participating countries, that is, supra-national planning, as a result of which intrabloc division of labor could take place. But not even the aims of these new arrangements were clearly stated, obviously for the simple reason that the economic goals of the different bloc members could not be compromised. More regional self-sufficiency was to be combined with increasing intrabloc specialization! Bloc members such as Czechoslovakia and East Germany wanted to find larger market for their industrial products while Rumania and Bulgaria, desiring to build up their own industries, did not want merely to remain the bloc's raw material suppliers.

Though it seems theoretically obvious that bloc trade should be guided by a supranational plan, the difficulties of such planning would be even greater than the obstacles that bar the way to complete coordination of economic policies of different nations in the western world (for instance, in the Common Market). The western economies are already integrated by their interconnected price systems. Yet even western governments insist on monetary and fiscal sovereignty. The desire for a relatively high degree of autonomy is, understandably, much higher in countries that practice total planning and cannot have illusions about the eventual outcome of supranational planning in terms of national sovereignty.

For western observers it may seem as if the advantages of multilateralism could be achieved through multilateral settlements of international accounts on the basis of convertible or transferable rubles, very much like the creation of the European Payments Union (EPU) which managed to extricate Western European countries from the straightjacket of bilateralism after World War II. Indeed, such an attempt is being made through the establishment of an International Bank for Economic Cooperation (IBEC). But the results will not be as favorable as those of the EPU. The reasons are to be found in the planned nature of the economies of the trade partners: the fact that there is no adjustment mechanism that could alleviate the rigidities of planned allocations, the uncertainty as to what transferable rubles could buy, the danger of getting stuck with credit accounts in the IBEC, and the general reluctance to lose economic independence in a supranational arrangement.

SOVIET-BLOC TRADE WITH DEVELOPING COUNTRIES

If Soviet-bloc internal trade is beset with difficulties and, accordingly, relatively small, we cannot be surprised to find that Soviet-bloc trade with developing countries is even less important. In 1964 the total trade of the developing countries as a group with the Soviet bloc was only 5 percent of total trade as against 75 percent accounted for by trade with the developed countries of the Free World. This Soviet-bloc trade, furthermore, was concentrated on a small number of countries reflecting a concentration of aid disbursements by the Soviet bloc.

The structure of Soviet-bloc trade with the developing countries is characterized by bloc imports of raw materials in exchange for the export of machinery and manufactures. This trade pattern helped to alleviate some of the shortcomings in the bloc countries that were the result of the consistently low priority rating of agricultural production.

Admitting that this trade was basically advantageous for both partners, nevertheless, Carole A. Sawyer [17] comes to the following conclusion:

> Trade between the Communist area and the developing countries has been beset with a number of problems, most of which have been associated with the bilateral character of this commerce. In about a half dozen instances, for example, Communist countries have run up debit balances in their clearing accounts with developing countries by rapid importation of raw materials and an inability or unwillingness to provide enough exports of the type required by the developing countries. As a result, the latter have been placed in the incongruous position of extending credits to the Communist countries. This difficulty has been intensified by the fact that the developing countries cannot collect convertible currency for these trade credits and indeed, in most cases cannot even use the credits to make purchases in other Communist countries. . . . Other problems encountered by the developing countries in their trade with the Communist area have included the instability of this trade and re-exports by Communist countries of certain goods imported from the developing countries.

[17] Carole A. Sawyer, *Communist Trade with Developing Countries: 1955–1965* (New York: Frederick A. Praeger, Inc., 1966), p. 85.

CHAPTER 28

Government Agenda in a Private Enterprise Economy

INTRODUCTION

When we omit the Soviet-type economies and the less developed countries, we are left with economies that have in common that they are not centrally planned and are, in the main, based on private enterprise. For this very reason it is imperative that economic policies in the developed countries of the West be compatible with the market mechanism, though acceptance of private property and the market is by no means tantamount to *laissez faire*.

We saw that the private enterprise system needs to be corrected for several reasons. Outstanding among the aims that can only be reached through economic policy measures are greater income equality, social security, maintenance of a sufficient degree of competition, monetary stability, high employment, economic growth, and, finally, external economic equilibrium under conditions of currency convertibility.

Concerning these policy aims, there exist differences of economic philosophy that must be compromised. Fortunately, these are different emphases rather than irreconcilable opposites; or, to put it differently, the policy objectives become competitive only after a high level of employment has been reached. From then on, monetary stability will conflict with a still more ambitious employment level, increasing consumption with growing investment, more equal distribution with the supply of savings, and maintenance of an ambitious growth rate with external equilibrium.

The choices are many and, strictly speaking, they lie outside the field of economics. In a democracy, the citizens should decide how much present consumption they want to sacrifice for economic growth, how far income should be equalized, which collective demand should be satisfied, and what measure of social security ought to be provided. But there need be no difference of opinion as to the desirability of using all the means of production available under conditions of economic freedom.

Differences of opinion can exist with regard to the policies to be employed once the objectives are chosen. There is a potential spectrum of policy mixes from near *laissez faire* to detailed market interference by government agencies. Fortunately the trend seems to be in the direction of a meeting of minds. While market forces alone cannot be expected to produce the desired aims, they are, nevertheless, the *sine qua non* of an economic order without central plan, so that all policies that interfere with the market mechanism must normally be avoided or can only be tolerated in very special cases. The absolutely essential regulation of the market must, as a rule, be limited to indirect controls, that is generally to monetary and fiscal policies.

Clumsy attempts toward regulation by uncoordinated direct controls led to F. A. Hayek's warning that, unless a greater understanding of the market mechanism is achieved, the solution of our problems might have to be sought in totalitarian controls, that is, in controls that at least enjoy the consistency of a central plan. On the other hand, some defenders of the market mechanism were in danger of putting too much trust in it, in the face of political forces that tended to overtax the resilience of the price system. They had to be shown by Lord Keynes and his followers how essential it is for the government to accept responsibility for a high level of employment via fiscal and monetary policies. However, absorbed by the new questions of macroeconomics, the Keynesian group, in turn, tended sometimes to forget the crucial importance of the price mechanism for resource allocation in a system that rests predominantly on private enterprise and not on integration through a central plan.

While a great many questions remain to be answered, there exists little doubt today that a cooperation between an efficient private enterprise sector and a controlling public sector is workable, with many shades of policy mix. To this extent the Keynesian revolution has certainly come to stay, perhaps even in the broader meaning of "Keynes-cum-growth," [1] that

---

[1] See Walter W. Heller, *New Dimensions of Political Economy* (Cambridge, Mass.: Harvard University Press, 1966), pp. 63, 70.

is, as a policy "redirected from a corrective orientation geared to the dynamics of the cycle, to propulsive orientation geared to the dynamics and the promise of growth." But with the ever growing ambition to combine maximum growth with monetary stability and economic freedom, it has become more necessary than ever before that the microcosm of the firms and their intricate interdependence be based on a well working market mechanism. The fuller the use of the available resources, the more difficult it is to keep monopolistic and inflationary forces in check without succumbing to the temptation of using direct controls.

HAYEK AND KEYNES

At the end of World War II discussion about the role of government in the market economies centered around Friedrich A. Hayek's challenging book *The Road to Serfdom*,[2] which contended that the rise of Hitler "was not a reaction against socialist trends of the preceding period but a necessary outcome of those tendencies" (pp. 3–4). Inadequate understanding of the price system and a great many uncoordinated direct controls had supposedly led to a situation in which political dictatorship became unavoidable.

Hayek discusses collectivism, socialism, and central planning. Planning he defines as "a central direction of all economic activity according to a single plan, laying down how the resources of society should be 'consciously directed' to serve particular ends in a definite way" (p. 35). This type of central planning cannot be combined with a market mechanism. Hayek believes that it is dangerously wrong to assume "that it must be possible to find some middle way between 'atomistic' competition and central direction. . . . Although competition can bear some admixture of regulation, it cannot be combined with planning to any extent we like without ceasing to operate as an effective guide to production" (p. 42). Thus, if the government destroys the working of the market through innumerable uncoordinated controls, the economy must eventually become centrally planned to gain an indispensable minimum of integration.

Of course, Hayek does not advocate *laissez faire*. On the contrary, he

[2] F. A. Hayek, *The Road to Serfdom* (Chicago: University of Chicago Press, 1944). For critical appraisals of Hayek's book, see the following: E. F. M. Durbin, *Problems of Economic Planning* (London: George Routledge & Sons, Ltd., and Kegan, Paul, Trench, Trubner & Co., Ltd., 1949), Paper 5; Howard S. Ellis, "Postwar Economic Policies," *Review of Economic Statistics*, vol. 28 (1946); Alvin H. Hansen, *Economic Policy and Full Employment* (New York: McGraw-Hill, Inc., 1947), Appendix A; Carl Landauer, *The Theory of National Economic Planning* (Berkeley and Los Angeles: University of California Press, 1947); Barbara Wootton, *Freedom under Planning* (Chapel Hill, N.C.: University of North Carolina Press, 1945). Page numbers in parentheses in the following paragraphs refer to Hayek's *Road to Serfdom*.

emphasizes that there is "all the difference between deliberately creating a system within which competition will work as beneficially as possible and passively accepting institutions as they are" (p. 17). He admits that there are still "immense possibilities of advancement" available over and above "the crude rules in which the principles of economic policy of the nineteenth century were expressed" (p. 18). Hayek demands that we plan for, rather than against, competition; he is willing to concede a minimum of social security through protection against sickness and accident; and he mentions, at least, "the supremely important problem of combating general economic fluctuations of economic activity and the recurrent waves of large-scale unemployment which accompany them" (p. 121). But he emphasizes that we should not try to guarantee a given standard of life to special persons or groups, arguing that such action would lead to greater insecurity for other people. "If you guarantee to some a fixed part of a variable cake, the share left to the rest is found to fluctuate proportionally more than the size of the whole" (p. 128).

Obviously, Hayek assumes that substantial fluctuations of the national income are unavoidable. This shows that he does not share the optimism of the Keynesians that a combination of monetary and fiscal policies could largely eliminate such fluctuations. At the time of the writing of *Road to Serfdom*, Hayek was hardly thinking of a government policy that would keep permanent watch on aggregate spending. However, several years later, he wrote that "only few will deny that credit expansion can only be useful as long as a condition of *general* unemployment exists, in the sense that unused means of every kind are available." [3] If this statement is interpreted as an approach to Keynesian economics, it should be pointed out that Keynes, on the other hand, did not at all share the dislike that most of his disciples felt for the *Road to Serfdom*. He wrote to Hayek:

> We all have the greatest reason to be grateful to you for saying so well what needs so much to be said. You will not expect me to accept quite all the economic dicta in it. But morally and philosophically I find myself in agreement with virtually the whole of it; and not only in agreement with it, but in a deeply moved agreement. [4]

Though there was and is much disagreement between the followers of Keynes and the Hayekian neoliberalists, we deal here with differences of opinion that are less fundamental than the extremists in both camps led us to believe. Some of Keynes' disciples were so absorbed by problems of macroeconomics and fiscal policy questions that they paid little attention

[3] F. A. Hayek, *Vollbeschäftigung, Inflation und Planwirtschaft* (Erlenbach-Zürich: Eugen Rentsch Verlag, 1951), p. 186.
[4] R. F. Harrod, *The Life of John Maynard Keynes* (New York: Harcourt, Brace & World, Inc., 1951), p. 436.

to monetary policy and the maintenance of a healthy and consistent pricing process. Finally, Keynes had even to remind them that classical economics contained some permanent truths of great significance and that natural forces or even the 'invisible hand' were operating toward equilibrium.[5] Some of Keynes's critics eagerly interpreted this remark as a recantation of his own theories. But only those who never studied the last chapter of the *General Theory* [6] could come to this wrong conclusion. For there he expressly stated that "if our central controls succeed in establishing an aggregate volume of output corresponding to full employment as nearly as is practicable, the classical theory comes into its own from this point onwards" and that "there is no objection to be raised against the classical analysis of the manner in which private self-interest will determine what in particular is produced, in what proportion the factors of production will be combined to produce it, and how the value of the final product will be distributed between them."

Criticism was justified, however, where the aim of full employment was approached with policies that did not fit the market economy, for example, with excessive deficit spending that led to dangerous price inflation, or with direct investment controls that disturbed the allocation process.

Keynes's critics, on the other hand, were guilty of thinking it sufficient to plan for competition. The market economy needs alert regulation to make sure that resources are fully used. The pricing process, furthermore, cannot solve all adjustment problems. Twice Keynes warned against an overburdening of the price mechanism, which exceeded its ability to function properly, and twice he was proved right. When Keynes wrote his essay *The End of Laissez-Faire*[7] in 1926, he had good reason to fear that those who were responsible for England's currency policy had set a task that the market economy could "solve" only with catastrophic consequences. In reintroducing the gold standard, Winston Churchill, as Chancellor of the Exchequer, had chosen the prewar gold parity in spite of the fact that it did not correspond to the purchasing power parity. British prices had risen considerably more than prices in the United States. Return to the prewar dollar-sterling parity meant, under these conditions, that normal trade relations would be possible only if England managed to lower its costs and prices. According to Keynes, this deflationary policy expected too much of the market economy's ability to adjust wages and prices downward. Under the assumption of wage rigidity, he was skeptical about fixed gold parities

[5] John Maynard Keynes, "The Balance of Payments of the United States," *Economic Journal*, vol. 56 (1946), p. 186. See also Chap. 2.

[6] John Maynard Keynes, *The General Theory of Employment, Interest, and Money* (New York: St. Martin's Press, Inc., 1936), pp. 378–379.

[7] John Maynard Keynes, "The End of Laissez-Faire," in *Essays in Persuasion* (New York: Harcourt, Brace & World, Inc., 1932), p. 313.

in general; but a combination of gold standard and overvaluation he considered much worse. The disaster of the coal miners' strike showed that he had been right. Today it is very hard to understand why the British economy was subjected to the ordeal of a perfectly unnecessary deflation.[8] Chapter 25 showed that even today it is generally considered correct that exchange rates should be permanently fixed, although consistent thinking should make it obvious that price fixing in the foreign exchange market violates the principles of the market economy.

Keynes's doubt in the ability of the market economy to solve adjustment problems of an abnormal nature was also justified in the German reparation case. Keynes predicted that the deflation that was to produce the needed German export surplus could be achieved only at the price of severe unemployment.[9] Again he was right. The German deflation led to mass unemployment, which resulted in Hitler's rise to power. We see, incidentally, that National Socialism was not only the result of socialist interference with the economy, as Hayek thinks; it was also caused by an overburdening of the price mechanism at a time when it had already lost much of its resilience.

Doubt in the automatic adjustment processes and the resilience of modern market economies finally produced Keynes's *General Theory*, which showed that equilibrium could be reached under conditions of mass unemployment. The outlines of this theory have already been discussed in Chapter 8.

ECONOMIC GROWTH

Full employment as one of the major aims of economic policy has recently been escalated into the more ambitious goal of maximum economic growth. To some extent, of course, the objectives of full employment and growth overlap in that high employment is a precondition of a satisfactory growth rate. But we have to consider: (1) overfull employment may actually retard growth, (2) full employment can prevail while factors of production are wrongly allocated, and (3) the same employment level will produce different growth rates depending on the division of our productive effort between consumption and investment. Better factor allocation at less than "full" employment may possibly produce a higher GNP than full employment with arbitrary production controls. The fact that economic growth depends on a relative reduction of present consumption

[8] Keynes, "Alternative Aims of Monetary Policy" and "The Economic Consequences of Mr. Churchill," in *Essays in Persuasion*, pp. 186ff, 244ff.

[9] See John Maynard Keynes, "The German Transfer Problem," *Economic Journal*, vol. 39 (March 1929).

in favor of increased investment is too obvious to need elaboration. Continued *expansion* must rest on increased capital goods production. Growth policies, therefore, may easily use measures that will differ from those capable of producing merely full employment of resources.

Today's emphasis on growth is easily explained. Our past successes with full employment policies have stimulated our ambition to reduce the percentage figure of unemployment even further (for example 4 instead of 5 percent of the labor force). And the connected increase in national income offers tempting possibilities for investment *without* reduction in consumption. A political reason is, of course, the "growth-rate competition" that has developed between market-type and Soviet-type economies.[10]

Economic growth seems to be an undisputed aim of economic policy since it would open a cornucopia to satisfy many other aims, both in the private and the public sector of the economy. But we have to remember that growth, when driven too far, can conflict with such other important aims as monetary stability, external equilibrium, *present* consumption, and even long-run growth itself.

For instance, if unemployment can be reduced by one more percent in order to push GNP up by another $20 billion,[11] the inflationary pressures characteristic for a fully employed economy will also be increased. Bertil Ohlin has pointed out [12] that a state of affairs in which labor enjoys the advantages of a sellers' market may not be a pure blessing. It is true that very full employment has the advantage of guaranteeing a relatively high GNP, stimulating automation, and making labor willing to accept labor-saving devices; also, selling costs will be low at a time of high economic activity. But against these beneficial effects Ohlin places the disadvantages of bottlenecks, excessive labor turnover, inflationary pressures, and, if price inflation is repressed by price controls, the adminstrative cost of rationing. To these effects also may be added an adverse balance-of-payments that may necessitate the introduction of foreign exchange controls.

Quite possibly, these disadvantages of overfull employment may outweigh the advantages. It is possible, for example, that an employment level that is less than full may actually be accompanied by a greater production volume. And even if the full-employment output is greater, it may be an

[10] "The comparison of growth rates in different countries is dictated more by an attitude akin to competitive sport than by concern for the next generation. And if some countries have different economic systems, as, e.g., the Soviet Socialist Republics, France, the German Federal Republic and the United States of America, the comparison of growth rates developes into a race in which parts of the public have put their bets on their political pet horse." Fritz Machlup, "Freiheit und Planung in der Marktwirtschaft," in *Protokolle des Wirtschaftstages der CDU/CSU* in Bonn, 1967.

[11] See Walter W. Heller, *New Dimensions of Political Economy*, p. 61.

[12] Bertil Ohlin, *The Problem of Employment Stabilization* (New York: Columbia University Press, 1949), chap. 1.

output of commodities less suited to the wants of the consumers. Means of production may have become unemployed because of changes in consumer demand. If we ignore these changes in consumers' preferences, as a totalitarian regime might, we can maintain full employment by adjusting demand to supply; but this would violate one of the basic individual freedoms which characterize our economic system.

These considerations concerning the frictions, inflationary pressures, and control measures connected with a state of overfull employment suggest that employment policies should seek a compromise between stability and inflation and between freedom and control. The more we insist that direct controls be avoided, the less ambitious we must be in defining the rate of growth we desire. Certainly we must avoid the mistake of considering any form of unemployment as justification for further credit expansion. Disproportions in the economy cannot always be ironed out by raising aggregate expenditure.

A case in point is the policy that advocates low rates of interest for the purpose of carrying investment in plant and equipment "to the full limit of productive capacity."[13] Alvin H. Hansen argues for "a sustained low rate of interest" and even goes so far as to compare the private enterprise system in this respect unfavorably with the Soviet system with its practically unlimited investment outlets. Since Soviet investment "need not stop at the point where the net marginal yield will cover interest cost," investment can "be pushed to the point of full investment." It is not clear what is meant by full investment, how the dividing line between consumption and investment is to be drawn, how loanable funds are to be allocated, and how permanent inflation can be avoided if we aim at "sustained low" rather than at correct or equilibrium rates of interest. Saving would be discouraged and monetary policy would be practically eliminated if we did not permit the rate of interest to play its strategic role as market price.

It is fascinating to notice that Hansen in his argument for maximum growth is willing to artificially lower the rate of interest at the very time when Soviet economists are becoming increasingly aware of the fact that the neglect of the rate of interest in Soviet planning is one of the main shortcomings of their system.[14]

Scepticism about the present emphasis on economic growth per se (that is, without consideration of possibly conflicting aims such as monetary stability or economic freedom) must not lead to the opposite error of relaxing our efforts to achieve the highest growth that is compatible with other aims. As a matter of fact, the better we learn to use our monetary

---

[13] Alvin H. Hansen, *Economic Issues of the 1960s* (New York: McGraw-Hill, Inc., 1960), pp. 52–53.

[14] See Chaps. 20 and 21.

and fiscal policies, the more we refine our tools of instant response to changing conditions, the higher will be the lasting growth that we shall be able to achieve.

Walter W. Heller [15] points out that, in the United States, "the revenue increasing power of the Federal tax system produces a built-in average increase of $7 to $8 billion a year in Federal revenues" and argues that unless it "is offset by such 'fiscal dividends' as tax cuts or expansion of Federal programs, this automatic rise in revenue will become a 'fiscal drag' syphoning too much of the economic substance out of the private economy and thereby choking expansion." Accordingly, he proposes that fiscal strategy should become bolder, it should rely less on automatic stabilizers and more on discretionary action, and "that not only monetary but fiscal policy has to be put on constant, rather than intermittent, alert."

None of these suggestions violates the basic nature of the private enterprise economy. Indeed, Heller is eager to emphasize the importance of the forces of the market.[16]

How the increasing returns from economic growth should be distributed is a question that transcends the competence of the economist but not the competence of a democratic system, which projects the free choice of consumption of the private sector through proper political processes into the public sphere. Excess revenue of the government, owing to economic growth, does not in itself argue for larger expenditures in the public sector since tax reduction could instantly increase private spending. We must admit, however, that excellent arguments (not entirely devoid of economic reasoning) can be made for a public sector that grows perhaps more than proportionally with the over-all expansion of the economy. John Kenneth Galbraith and Alvin H. Hansen's [17] powerful case for better educational facilities and hospitals rather than an endless proliferation of luxury items, which can be sold only through a barrage of costly advertizing, makes good sense, as long as the expansion of the public sector is guided by democratic decisions. Also, there is much to be said for government policies that encourage saving and private investment as the best way of propelling the further growth of a fully employed economy.

It must be remembered that increased satisfaction of collective wants

[15] Heller, *New Dimensions of Political Economy*, pp. 65, 68–69.

[16] "It is often said that the study of economics makes people conservative. In the microeconomic sense, it undoubtedly does. It is hard to study the modern economics of relative prices, resource allocation, and distribution without developing a healthy respect for the market mechanism on three major scores: first, for what Robert Dorfman calls its 'cybernetics,' for the incredible capacity of the price system to receive and generate information and respond to it; second, for its technical efficiency and hard-headedness as a guide to resources and a goad to effort and risk-taking; and third, for its contribution to political democracy by keeping economic decisions free and decentralized." Heller, p. 8.

[17] John Kenneth Galbraith, *The Affluent Society* (Boston: Houghton Mifflin Company, 1958); Alvin H. Hansen, *Economic Issues of the 1960s*.

does not interfere with private production and investment, since most of the commodities and services needed in an expanding public sector are the result of private economic activity. For this reason government action can maintain a high level of employment or help achieve a desired rate of growth without having to change the basic structure of the private enterprise system. For the same reason the nationalization of industry has lost so much of its original appeal.

Our planning for the correct amount of aggregate spending is as important for the best possible performance of the market economy as Hayek's planning for competition. Both types of control can be so designed that the policies involved do not interfere unduly with the pricing process and private initiative. These policies concern "the nature of the environment which the free play of economic forces requires if it is to realize the full potentialities of production;" [18] they erect around the existing market mechanism "so to speak, a system of laws and institutions within which they may be made to work in the right way;" [19] and they create "conditions under which the knowledge and the initiative of individuals are given the best scope so that *they* can plan most successfully." [20]

The designing of these controls is difficult, particularly to achieve a high rate of growth, and it is doubtful that we shall always be able to muster enough restraint. Nevertheless, it should be possible eventually to create a private enterprise system in which the agenda and policies of the government are so carefully designed that each policy is seen as a consistent part of the whole, where direct controls are rare exceptions, and private enterprise, guided by the market, fulfills those microeconomic tasks that command economies manage only clumsily and at the cost of human freedom.

There will always be special cases that violate the basic principle of non-interference through price setting and quantitative controls. Once aware of the chain reaction by which direct controls tend to multiply, we must be much more careful with these bureaucratic devices than with a generously extended satisfaction of collective wants. Where we spend tax money we are aware of the costs; where we dispense benefits to pressure groups through protection, price controls, or even "permissive" credit creation (as in the case of cost-push and administrative price inflation), we often meet no budgetary problems, but the eventual social costs may prove to be very high.

Of course, a system that rests mainly on the market will entail a certain amount of economic insecurity for its members. However, since a high

18 J. M. Keynes, *General Theory*, p. 379.
19 Lionel Robbins, *The Economic Problem in Peace and War* (London: Macmillan & Co. Ltd., 1947), p. 83.
20 F. A. Hayek, *The Road to Serfdom*, p. 35.

level of employment will remove the worst cause of insecurity, this price should not be too high to pay for individualism, whose advantages Keynes set forth so beautifully in the last chapter of his *General Theory* when he wrote:

> But, above all, individualism, if it can be purged of its defects and its abuses, is the best safeguard of personal liberty in the sense that, compared with any other system, it greatly widens the field for the exercise of personal choice. It is also the best safeguard of the variety of life, which emerges precisely from this extended field of personal choice, and the loss of which is the greatest of all the losses of the homogenous or totalitarian state. For this variety preserves the traditions which embody the most secure and successful choices of former generations; it colors the present with the diversification of its fancy; and, being the handmaid of experiment as well as of tradition and of fancy, it is the most powerful instrument to a better future.[21]

ARE MARKET AND PLANNED ECONOMIES CONVERGING?

Recent developments in the private enterprise and the centrally planned economies have been interpreted as signs of a convergence, in the sense that the differences separating the two systems are gradually diminishing. Half a century ago the supporters of capitalism and socialism believed that the struggle between the two systems would end with the complete victory of one system. Orthodox Marxism predicted that capitalism will eventually destroy itself, to be succeeded by a socialist order that has overcome the basic defect of capitalism's "antagonistic conditions of distribution." Defenders of the private enterprise system, on the other hand, doubted the long-run feasibility of a communist order, either because they believed that it would run counter to the most basic instincts of man or because they followed Mises' more sophisticated argument that a system with public ownership of the means of production would lack a genuine market and the possibility of economic calculation. After Soviet Russia proved that a command economy could maintain itself successfully, it seemed to many that not only two but many economic systems could exist simultaneously, characterized by varying mixtures of planning and private initiative.

The convergence idea is the result of changes in the nature of the market and the planned economies that seem to point toward a meeting somewhere in the middle. In the private enterprise economies of the West, the Keynesian revolution, together with a renewed appreciation of the market mechanism, have led to results that, though as yet far from perfect,

[21] Keynes, *General Theory*, p. 380.

have shown conclusively that we can have a private enterprise system that maintains a high level of employment but is, nevertheless, compatible with economic freedom and political democracy. However, prerequisite for this success was the acceptance of government controls in the form of an alert surveillance of aggregate spending and a correction of the level of spending through monetary and fiscal policies. These policies implied that the government had to play a strategic role and, when stated in slovenly terminology, suggested an increasing amount of central planning. Keynes himself was sometimes guilty of choosing unfortunate language, for example, when he proposed "a somewhat comprehensive socialization of investment" [22] as the only means of securing an approximation to full employment. Only the context made it clear that he did not advocate public ownership of private industry but merely a regulation of aggregate expenditure, when necessary, through government deficit spending. Small wonder, then, that Keynesian economics, and public policies derived from it, were interpreted and criticized as a large step in the direction of socialism.

But not only did the private enterprise system seem to tend toward planning and socialism, the Soviet economy, in turn, seemed to move in the opposite direction, favoring decentralization, the use of profit in management of industry, and increasing attention to a price system able to mirror the real scarcity of the factors of production, including capital. Naturally, this development was taken by the western world as sign that the Soviet system was finally developing into a market economy—at the expense of authoritarian central planning.

Since each system seemed to be increasingly influenced by the guiding principle of the other, the layman could indeed get the impression that the systems converged, fortunately, not on a collision course but rather in the sense of a mutual penetration, possibly terminating in the evolution of a new order representing the ideal symbiosis of plan and market. This belief, tempting in its peaceful prospects, has been strengthened by the following circumstances: Since both prototypes must deal with essentially the same basic problems (which were set forth in Chapter 2) it is not surprising that, in the process of trying to solve them, numerous similarities appear. The policies and institutions of the different systems, furthermore, are often referred to by the same terms, though their meaning may change drastically with the social-economic framework in which they are found. It is perfectly normal, for instance, to use the term "planning" in a description of the private enterprise system and quite impossible to avoid reference to prices when discussing the Soviet economy. However, it is obvious that the common use of the same terms in both systems leads to frequent errors of comparison when the analyst, in investigating the

[22] Keynes, p. 378.

other system, cannot free himself from the often totally different connotations that a given term has in his *own* economy.

Unfortunately, the convergence thesis is false and even dangerous. It is the result of poor terminology and unclear thinking; it weakens our ability to discern the essence of the competing systems, and it deprives economic policy of its firm foundation—a clear understanding of the working principles of the economic order to which it is applied. To choose correct economic measures, we must know what fits the system logically and therefore strengthens it, and what is incompatible with its basic principles and therefore harmful in the long run. Once we believe that the systems converge, that they will all be centrally planned and all use the price mechanism, we lose sight of what is essential. The discussions of the present volume had to deal with many policies that were inconsistent in that they violated the principles on which a given system rests and, accordingly, could not lead to the desired results. For the private enterprise economy we had to reject, for example, the following policies: price controls and rationing, permanently fixed exchange rates, excessive income equalization, perfect income security for privileged groups, and so forth; and for the Soviet-type economy: operational freedom for managers combined with fixed output quotas, use of profit rates on the basis of wrong prices, the crude dichotomy of high and low priority sectors in an interdependent production process, and many others.

Once we are fully aware of the basic difference in the structures of the private enterprise and the centrally planned economies, we cannot count on a convergence of the two systems unless we expect a fundamental change in economic philosophy in either East or West. Knowing how extremely difficult it is to integrate the economic policies of the various market economies or to subordinate the different national plans of the Soviet-type economies to a supranational plan for the whole bloc, it seems entirely in vain to hope for a meeting of the two opposed systems somewhere in the middle. For both will have to develop policies that are in harmony with their basic character, and maintaining consistency within two fundamentally different philosophies cannot lead to convergence.

Selected
Bibliography

Four texts on Comparative Systems can be read with advantage in addition to the present volume. William N. Loucks, *Comparative Economic Systems*, 7th ed. (New York: Harper & Row, Publishers, 1965) complements this theoretical analysis through its institutional orientation. Carl Landauer, *Contemporary Economic Systems, A Comparative Analysis* (Philadelphia & New York: J. B. Lippincott Company, 1964) differs, as a liberal socialist treatise, in basic economic philosophy from *Economic Systems*, which emphasizes the advantages of organization through the market. Alfred Oxenfeldt and Vsevolod Holubnychy, *Economic Systems in Action*, 3d ed. (New York: Holt, Rinehart and Winston, Inc., 1965) combines a factual approach with an attitude toward the private enterprise system which is more critical than that of the present volume. Lynn Turgeon, *The Contrasting Economies: A Study of Modern Economic Systems* (Boston: Allyn & Bacon, Inc., 1963) compares the economies of the United States and Soviet Russia problem by problem, using a horizontal rather than a vertical approach.

Three volumes of Readings make it easy for the students of comparative systems to broaden their studies. They are, in the order of their publication: Wayne A. Leeman (ed.), *Capitalism, Market Socialism, and*

Central Planning. Readings in Comparative Economic Systems (Boston: Houghton Mifflin Company, 1963); Marshall I. Goldman, ed., *Comparative Economic Systems. A Reader* (New York: Random House, Inc., 1964); Morris Bornstein, ed., *Comparative Economic Systems. Models and Cases* (Homewood, Ill.: Richard D. Irwin, Inc., 1965). The three volumes can be used simultaneously since there is little overlapping. Two excellent readers are available for those who want to become more intimately acquainted with the problems of the Soviet economy: Franklyn D. Holzman, ed., *Readings on the Soviet Economy* (Chicago: Rand McNally & Company, 1962) and Morris Bornstein and Daniel R. Fusfeld, eds., *The Soviet Economy. A Book of Readings*, rev. ed. (Homewood, Ill.: Richard D. Irwin, Inc., 1966).

The interested student will want to read some of the books and articles mentioned in the numerous footnotes since the passages that have been referred to are closely related to the arguments under discussion.

The literature on comparative economics is enormously large. Any attempt toward a reasonably complete listing would defeat its purpose by leaving the reader exposed to a bewildering *embarras de richesse*.

Index